I0084103

Stanley John Weyman

My Lady Rotha

A Romance

Stanley John Weyman

My Lady Rotha
A Romance

ISBN/EAN: 9783744723794

Printed in Europe, USA, Canada, Australia, Japan

Cover: Foto ©Thomas Meinert / pixelio.de

More available books at **www.hansebooks.com**

𝔄 𝔅omance

BY

STANLEY J. WEYMAN

AUTHOR OF

" A GENTLEMAN OF FRANCE," " UNDER THE RED ROBE,"
" THE HOUSE OF THE WOLF," ETC.

NEW YORK

LONGMANS, GREEN, AND CO.

1895

CONTENTS

LIST OF ILLUSTRATIONS

MY LADY ROTHA.

CHAPTER I.

HERITZBURG.

I NEVER saw anything more remarkable than the change which the death of my lady's uncle, Count Tilly, in the spring of 1632, worked at Heritzburg. Until the day when that news reached us, we went on in our quiet corner as if there were no war. We heard, and some of us believed, that the Palatine Elector, a good Calvinist like ourselves, had made himself King of Bohemia in the Emperor's teeth; and shortly afterwards — which we were much·more ready to believe — that he was footing it among the Dutchmen. We heard that the King of Denmark had taken up his cause, but taken little by the motion; and then that the King of Sweden had made it his own. But these things affected us little : they were like the pattering of the storm to a man hugging himself by the fireside. Through all we lay snug and warm, and kept Christmas and drank the Emperor's health. Even the great sack of Magdeburg, which was such an event as the world, I believe, will never see again, moved us less to fear than to pity; though the city lies something less than fifty leagues north-east of us. The reason of this I am going to tell you.

Our town stands, as all men know, in a nook of the Thuringian Forest, facing south and west towards Hesse, of which my Lady Rotha, Countess of Heritzburg, holds it, though all the land about is Saxon, belonging either to Coburg, or Wei-

1

mar, or Altenburg, or the upper Duchy. On the north and east the forest rises in rolling black ridges, with a grey crag shooting up spire-like here and there; so that from this quarter it was not wonderful that no sound of war reached us. Toward the south and west, where is the mouth of the valley, and whither our people point when they talk of the world, a spur of the mountain runs down on either side to the Werra, which used to be crossed at this point by a wooden bridge. But this bridge was swept away by floods in the winter of 1624, and never repaired as long as the war lasted. Henceforth to come to Heritzburg travellers had to cross in old Joachim's boat, or if the river was very low, tuck up and take the chances. Unless they came by forest paths over the mountains.

Such a position favoured peace. Our friends could not easily trouble us; our allies were under no temptation to quarter troops upon us. For our enemies, we feared them even less. Against them we had a rampart higher than the mountains and wider than the Werra, in the name of Tilly. In those days the name of the great Walloon, victor in thirty fights, was a word to conjure with from the Tyrol to the Elbe. Mothers used it to scare their children, priests to blast their foes. His courage, his cruelty, and his zeal for the Roman Catholic Church combined to make him the terror of the Protestants, while his strange personality and mis-shapen form gave rise to a thousand legends, which men still tell by the fireside.

I think I see him now — as I did see him thrice in his lifetime — a meagre dwarfish man with a long face like a horse's face, and large whiskers. He dressed always in green satin, and wore a small high-peaked hat on his huge wrinkled forehead. A red feather drooped from it, and reached to his waist. At first sight one took him for a natural; for one of those strange monstrosities which princes keep to make them sport; but a single glance from his eyes sent simple men to their prayers, and cowed alike plain burgher and wild Croat. Few loved him, all feared him. I have heard it said that he had no shadow, but I can testify of my own knowledge and not merely for the honour of the family that this was false.

He was brother to my lady's mother, the Countess Juliana. At the time of the match my late lord was thought to have disparaged his blood by mating with a Flemish lady of no more than gentle family. But as Count Tilly rose in the world first to be commander of the Bavarian armies and later to be Generalissimo of the forces of the Empire and a knight of the Golden Fleece, we heard less and less of this. The sneer lost its force until we became glad, Calvinists though we were, to lie secure under his shadow; and even felt a shamed pride in his prowess.

When my lord died, early in the war, leaving the county of Heritzburg to his only child, the protection we derived in this way grew more and more valuable. We of Heritzburg, and we only, lost nothing by the war, except a parcel of idle fellows, of whom more hereafter. Our cows came lowing to their stalls, our corn full weight to the granary. We slept more safely under the distaff than others under the sword; and all because my lady had the right to wear among her sixteen quarterings the coat of Tilly.

Some I know, but only since his death, have cried shame on us for accepting his protection. They profess to think that we should have shut our gates on the Butcher of Magdeburg, and bidden him do his worst. They say that the spirit of the old Protestants is dead within us, and that it is no wonder the cause lies languishing and Swedes alone fight single-eyed. But those who say these things have seldom, I notice, corn or cows: and moreover, as I have hinted, they kept a very still tongue while Tilly lived.

There is our late Burgomaster, Hofman, for instance, he is given to talking after that fashion; and, it is true, he has plenty, though not so much since my lady fined him. But I well remember the last time Tilly visited us. It was after the fall of Magdeburg, and there was a shadow on his grim countenance, which men said never left it again until

the day when the cannon-shot struck him in the ford of the
Lech, and they carried him to Ingolstadt to die. As he
rode under the arch by the Red Hart people looked
strangely at him — for it was difficult to forget what he
had done — as if, but for the Croats in the camp across
the river, they would have torn him from his horse. But
who, I pray you, so polite that day as Master Hofman?
Who but he was first to hold the stirrup and cry, Hail?
It was 'My Lord Count' this, and 'My Lord Count' that,
until the door closed on the crooked little figure and the
great gold spurs. And then it was the same with the
captain of the escort. Faugh! I grow sick when I think
of such men, and know that they were the first to turn
round and make trouble when the time came, and the old
grey wolf was dead. For my part I have always been my
lady's man since I came out of the forest to serve her. It
was enough for me that the Count was her guest and of her
kin. But for flattering him and putting myself forward to
do him honour, I left that to the Hofmans.

However, the gloom we saw on Tilly's face proved truly
to be the shadow of coming misfortune; for three weeks
after he left us, was fought the great battle of Breitenfeld.
Men say that the energy and decision he had shown all his
life forsook him there; that he hesitated and suffered himself to be led by others; and that so it was from the day of
Magdeburg to his death. This may be true, I think, for
he had the blood of women and children on his head; or it
may be that at last he met a foeman worthy of his steel.
But in either case the news of the Swede's victory rang
through North Germany like a trumpet call. It broke
with startling abruptness the spell of victory which had
hitherto — for thirteen long years — graced the Emperor's
flag and the Roman Church. In Hesse, to the west of us,
where the Landgrave William had been the first of all
German Princes to throw in his lot with the Swedes and
defy the Emperor, it awoke such a shout of jubilation and
vengeance as crossed even the Werra; while from the

Saxon lands to the east of us, which this victory saved
from spoliation and punishment, came an answering cry of
thankfulness and joy. Even in Heritzburg it stirred our
blood. It roused new thoughts and new ambitions. We
were Protestants; we were of the north. Those who had
fought and won were our brethren.

And this was right. Nor for a time did I see anything
wrong or any sign of mischief brewing; though tongues in
the town wagged more freely, as the cloud of war rolled
ever southward and away from us. But six months later
the news of Count Tilly's death reached us. Then, or it
might be a fortnight afterwards — so long I think respect
for my lady's loss and the new hatchment restrained the
good-for-naughts — the trouble began. How it arose, and
what shape it took, and how I came athwart it, I am going
to tell you without further preface.

It was about the third Monday in May of that year, 1632.
A broken lock in one of the rooms at the castle had baffled
the skill of our smith, and about nightfall, thinking to take
a cup of beer at the Red Hart on my way back, I went
down to Peter the locksmith's in the town. His forge
stands in the winding lane, which joins the High Street
at the Red Hart, after running half round the town inside
the wall; so that one errand was a fair excuse for the
other. When I had given him his order and come out
again, I found that what with the darkness of the lane and
the blaze of his fire which had got into my eyes, I could
not see a yard before me. A little fine rain was falling
with a chilly east wind, and the town seemed dead. The
pavement felt greasy under foot, and gave out a rank smell.
However, I thought of the cheery kitchen at the Red Hart
and stumbled along as fast as I could, until turning a
corner I came in sight of the lanthorn which hangs over
the entrance to the lane.

I saw it, but short of it, something took and held my eye:
a warm stream of light, which shone across the path, and
fell brightly on the rough surface of the town-wall. It

came from a small window on my left. I had to pass close beside this window, and out of curiosity I looked in. What I saw was so surprising that I stopped to look again.

The room inside was low and small and bare, with an earthen floor and no fireplace. On a ragged pallet in one corner lay an elderly man, to whose wasted face and pallid cheeks a long white moustache, which strayed over the coverlet, gave an air of incongruous fierceness. His bright eyes were fixed on the door as if he listened. A child, three or four years old, sat on the floor beside him, playing with a yellow cat.

It was neither of these figures, however, which held my gaze, but that of a young girl who knelt on the floor near the head of the bed. A little crucifix stood propped against the wall before her, and she had a string of beads in her hands. Her face was turned from me, but I felt that her lips moved. I had never seen a Romanist at prayer before, and I lingered a moment, thinking in the first place that she would have done better had she swung the shutter against the window; and in the next, that with her dark hair hanging about her neck and her head bent devoutly, she looked so weak and fragile that the stoutest Protestant could not have found it in his heart to harm her.

Suddenly a noise, which dully reached me where I stood outside the casement, caused her to start in alarm, and turn her head. At the same moment the cat sprang away affrighted, and the man on the bed stirred and tried to rise. This breaking the spell, I stole quietly away and went round the corner to the door of the inn.

Though I had never considered the girl closely before, I knew who she was. Some eight months earlier, while Tilly, hard pressed by the King of Sweden, still stood at bay, keeping down Saxony with one hand, and Hesse with the other, the man on the pallet, Stephen Wort, a sergeant of jagers, had been wounded in a skirmish beyond the river. Why Tilly, who was used to seeing men die round him like flies in winter, gave a second thought to this man more

than to others, I cannot say. But for some reason, when
he visited us before Breitenfeld, he brought the wounded
sergeant in his train, and when he went left him at the
inn. Some said that the man had saved his life, others
that the two were born on the same day and shared the
same horoscope. More probably Tilly knew nothing of the
man, and the captain of the escort was the active party.
I imagine he had a kindness for Wort, and knowing that
outside our little valley a wounded man of Tilly's army
would find as short shrift as a hamstrung wolf, took occasion to leave him with us.

I thought of all this as I stood fumbling about the door
for the great bell. The times were such that even inns
shut their doors at night, and I had to wait and blow on
my fingers — for no wind is colder than a May wind — until I was admitted. Inside, however, the blazing fire and
cheerful kitchen with its show of gleaming pewter, and its
great polished settles winking solemnly in the heat, made
amends for all. I forgot the wounded man and his daughter and the fog outside. ·There were eight or nine men present, among them Hofman, who was then Burgomaster,
Dietz, the town minister, and Klink our host.

They were people I met every day, and sometimes more
than once a day, and they greeted me with a silent nod.
The lad who waited brought me a cup of beer, and I said
that the night was cold for the time of year. Some one
assented, but the company in general sat silent, sagely sucking their lips, or exchanging glances which seemed to indicate a secret understanding.

I was not slow to see that this had to do with me and
that my entrance had cut short some jest or story. I
waited patiently to learn what it was, and presently I was
enlightened. After a few minutes Klink the host rose from
his seat. First looking from one to another of his neighbours, as if to assure himself of their sympathy, he stole
quietly across the kitchen to a door which stood in one
corner. Here he paused a moment listening, and then on a

sudden struck the door a couple of blows, which made the
pewters ring again.

'Hi! Within there!' he cried in his great voice. 'Are
you packing? Are you packing, wench? Because out
you go to-morrow, pack or no pack! Out you go, do you
hear?'

He stood a moment waiting for an answer, but seemed to
get none; on which he came back to his seat, and chuckling
fatly to himself, looked round on his neighbours for applause. One winked and another rubbed his calves. The
greater number eyed the fire with a sly smile. For my
part I was slow of apprehension. I did not understand but
waited to hear more.

For five minutes we all sat silent, sucking our lips. Then
Klink rose again with a knowing look, and crossed the
kitchen on tiptoe with the same parade of caution as
before. Bang! He struck the door until it rattled on
its hinges.

'Hi! You there!' he thundered. 'Do you hear, you
jade? Are you packing? Are you packing, I say? Because pack or no pack, to-morrow you go! I am a man of
my word.'

He did not wait this time for an answer, but came back
to us with a self-satisfied grin on his face. He drank some
beer — he was a big ponderous man with a red face and
small pig's eyes — and pointed over his shoulders with the
cup. 'Eh?' he said, raising his eye-brows.

'Good!' a man growled who sat opposite to him.

'Quite right!' said a second in the same tone. 'Popish
baggage!'

Hofman said nothing, but nodded, with a sly glance at
me. Dietz the Minister nodded curtly also, and looked
hard at the fire. The rest laughed.

For my part I felt very little like laughing. When I
considered that this clumsy jest was being played at the
expense of the poor girl, whom I had seen at her prayers,
and that likely enough it was being played for the tenth

time — when I reflected that these heavy fellows were sitting at their ease by this great fire watching the logs blaze and the ruddy light flicker up the chimney, while she sat in cold and discomfort, fearing every sound and trembling at every whisper, I could have found it in my heart to get up and say what I thought of it. And my speech would have astonished them. But I remembered, in time, that least said is soonest mended, and that after all words break no bones, and I did no more than sniff and shrug my shoulders.

Klink, however, chose to take offence in his stupid fashion. 'Eh?' he said. 'You are of another mind, Master Schwartz?'

'What is the good of talking like that,' I said, 'when you do not mean it?'

He puffed himself out, and after staring at me for a time, answered slowly: 'But what if I do mean it, Master Steward? What if I do mean it?'

'You don't,' I said. 'The man pays his way.'

I thought to end the matter with that. I soon found that it was not to be shelved so easily. For a moment indeed no one answered me. We are a slow speaking race, and love to have time to think. A minute had not elapsed, however, before one of the men who had spoken earlier took up the cudgels. 'Ay, he pays his way,' he said, thrusting his head forward. 'He pays his way, master; but how? Tell me that.'

I did not answer him.

'Out of the peasant's pocket!' the fellow replied slowly. 'Out of the plunder and booty of Magdeburg. With blood-money, master.'

'I ask no more than to meet one of his kind in the fields,' the man sitting next him, who had also spoken before, chimed in. 'With no one looking on, master. There would be one less wolf in the world then, I will answer for that. He pays his way? Oh, yes, he pays it here.'

I thought a shrug of the shoulders a sufficient answer.

These two belonged to the company my lady had raised in the preceding year to serve with the Landgrave according to her tenure. They had come back to the town a week before this with money to spend ; some people saying that they had deserted, and some that they had returned to raise volunteers. Either way I was not surprised to find them a little bit above themselves; for foreign service spoils the best, and these had never been anything but loiterers and vagrants, whom it angered me to see on a bench cheek by jowl with the Burgomaster. I thought to treat them with silent contempt, but I soon found that they did not stand alone.

The Minister was the first to come to their support. ' You forget that these people are Papists, Master Schwartz. Rank Roman Papists,' he said.

' So was Tilly!' I retorted, stung to anger. 'Yet you managed to do with him.'

' That was different,' he answered sourly; but he winced.

Then Hofman began on me. ' You see, Master Steward,' he said slowly, ' we are a Protestant town — we are a Protestant town. And it ill beseems us — it ill beseems us to harbour Papists. I have thought over that a long while. And now I think it is time to rid ourselves of them — to abate the nuisance in fact. You see we are a Protestant town, Master Schwartz. You forget that.'

' Then were we not a Protestant town,' I cried, jumping up in a rage, and forgetting all my discretion, ' when we entertained Count Tilly ? When you held his stirrup, Burgomaster ? and you, Master Dietz, uncovered to him ? Were not these people Papists when they came here, and when you received them ? But I will tell you what it is,' I continued, looking round scornfully, and giving my anger vent, for such meanness disgusted me. ' When there was a Bavarian army across the river, and you could get anything out of Tilly, you were ready to oblige him, and clean his boots. You could take in Romanists then, but now that he is dead and your side is uppermost, you grow scrupulous.

Pah! I am ashamed of you! You are only fit to bully children and girls, and such like!' and I turned away to take up my iron-shod staff.

They were all very red in the face by this time, and the two soldiers were on their feet. But the Burgomaster restrained them. 'Fine words!' he said, puffing out his cheeks — 'fine words! Dare say the girl can hear him. But let him be, let him be — let him have his say!'

'There is some else will have a say in the matter, Master Hofman!' I retorted warmly, as I turned to the door, 'and that is my lady. I would advise you to think twice before you act. That is all!'

'Hoop-de-doo-dem-doo!' cried one in derision, and others echoed it. But I did not stay to hear; I turned a deaf ear to the uproar, wherein all seemed to be crying after me at once, and shrugging my shoulders I opened the door and went out.

The sudden change from the warm noisy kitchen to the cold night air sobered me in a moment. As I climbed the dark slippery street which rises to the foot of the castle steps, I began to wish that I had let the matter be. After all, what call had I to interfere, and make bad blood between myself and my neighbours? It was no business of mine. The three were Romanists. Doubtless the man had robbed and hectored in his time, and while his hand was strong; and now he suffered as others had suffered.

It was ten chances to one the Burgomaster would carry the matter to my lady in some shape or other, and the minister would back him up, and I should be reprimanded; or if the Countess saw with my eyes, and sent them off with a flea in their ears, then we should have all the rabble of the town who were at Klink's beck and call, going up and down making mischief, and crying, 'No Popery!' Either way I foresaw trouble, and wished that I had let the matter be, or better still had kept away that night from the Red Hart.

But then on a sudden there rose before me, as plainly as

if I had still been looking through the window, a vision of
the half-lit room looking on the lane, with the sick man on
the pallet, and the slender figure kneeling beside the bed.
I saw the cat leap, saw again the girl's frightened gesture
as she turned towards the door, and I grew almost as hot as
I had been in the kitchen. 'The cowards!' I muttered —
'the cowards! But I will be beforehand with them. I will
go to my lady early and tell her all.'

You see I had my misgivings, but I little thought what
that evening was really to bring forth, or that I had done
that in the Red Hart kitchen which would alter all my life,
and all my lady's life; and spreading still, as a little crack
in ice will spread from bank to bank, would leave scarce a
man in Heritzburg unchanged, and scarce a woman's fate
untouched.

CHAPTER II.

THE COUNTESS ROTHA.

MY LADY ROTHA, Countess of Heritzburg in her own right,
was at this time twenty-five years old and unmarried. Her
maiden state, which seems to call for explanation, I attri-
bute to two things. Partly to the influence of her friend
and companion Fraulein Anna Max of Utrecht, who was
reputed in the castle to know seven languages, and to
consider marriage a sacrifice; and partly to the Countess's
own disposition, which led her to set a high value on the
power and possessions that had descended to her from her
father. Count Tilly's protection, which had exempted
Heritzburg from the evils of the war, had rendered the
support of a husband less necessary; and so she had been
left to follow her own will in the matter, and was now
little likely to surrender her independence unless her
heart went with the gift.

Not that suitors were lacking, for my lady, besides her

wealth, was possessed of the handsomest figure in the world, with beautiful features, and the most gracious and winning address ever known. I remember as if it were yesterday Prince Albert of Rammingen, a great match but an old man. He came in his chariot with a numerous retinue, and stayed long, taking it very hardly that my lady was not to be won; but after a while he went. His place was taken by Count Frederick, a brother of the Margrave of Anspach, a young gentleman who had received his education in France, and was full of airs and graces, going sober to bed every night, and speaking German with a French accent. Him my lady soon sent about his business. The next was a more famous man, Count Thurn of Bohemia, he who began the war by throwing Slawata and Martinitz out of window in Prague, in '19, and paid for it by fifteen years of exile. He wore such an air of mystery, and had such tales to tell of flight and battle and hairbreadth escapes, that he was scarcely less an object of curiosity in the town than Tilly himself; but he knelt in vain. And in fine so it was with them all. My lady would have none of them, but kept her maiden state and governed Heritzburg and saw the years go by, content to all appearance with Fraulein Anna and her talk, which was all of Voetius and Beza and scores of other learned men, whose names I could never remember from one hour to another.

It was my duty to wait upon her every day after morning service, and receive her orders, and inform her of anything which I thought she ought to know. At that hour she was to be found in her parlour, a long room on the first floor of the castle, lighted by three deeply-recessed windows and hung with old tapestry worked by her great-grandmother in the dark days of the Emperor Charles, when the Count of Heritzburg shared the imprisonment of the good Landgrave of Hesse. A screen stood a little way within the door, and behind this it was my business to wait, until I was called.

On this morning, however, I had no patience to wait, and I made myself so objectionable by my constant coughing that at last she cried, with a cheerful laugh, 'What is it, Martin? Come and tell me. Has there been a fire in the forest? But it is not the right time of year for that.'

'No, my lady,' I said, going forward. Then out of shyness or sheer contradictoriness I found myself giving her the usual report of this and that and the other, but never a word of what was in my mind. She sat, according to her custom in summer, in the recess of the farthest window, while Fraulein Anna occupied a stool placed before a reading-desk. Behind the two the great window gave upon the valley. By merely turning the head either of them could look over the red roofs of Heritzburg to the green plain, which here was tolerably wide, and beyond that again to the dark line of forest, which in spring and autumn showed as blue to the eye as thick wood smoke.

While I spoke my lady toyed with a book she had been reading, and Fraulein Anna turned over the pages on the desk with an impatient hand, sometimes looking at my lady and sometimes tapping with her foot on the floor. She was plump and fair and short, dressing plainly, and always looking into the distance; whether because she thought much and on deep matters, or because, as the Countess's woman once told me, she could see nothing beyond the length of her arm, I cannot say. When I had finished my report, and paused, she looked up at my lady and said, 'Now, Rotha, are you ready?'

'Not quite, Anna,' my lady answered, smiling. 'Martin has not done yet.'

'He tells in ten minutes what another would in five,' Fraulein said crossly. 'But to finish?'

'Yes, Martin, what is it?' my lady assented. 'We have eaten all the pastry. The meat I am sure is yet to come.'

I saw that there was nothing else for it, and after all it

was what I had come to do. 'Your excellency knows the
Bavarian soldier and his daughter, who have been lodging
these six months past at the Red Hart?' I said.

'To be sure.'

'Klink talks of turning them out,' I continued, feeling
my face grow red I scarcely knew why.

'Is their money at an end?' the Countess asked shrewdly.
She was a great woman of business.

'No,' I answered, 'but I dare say it is low.'

'Then what is the matter?' my lady continued, looking
at me somewhat curiously.

'He says that they are Papists,' I answered. 'And it is
true, as your excellency knows, but it is not for him to say
it. The man will not be safe for an hour outside the walls,
nor the girl much longer. And there is a small child
besides. And they have no where else to go.'

My lady's face grew grave while I spoke. When I
stopped she rose and stood fronting me, tapping on the
reading-desk with her fingers. 'This must not be allowed,
Martin,' she said firmly. 'You were right to tell me.'

'Master Hofman and the Minister——'

'Yes,' she interposed, nodding quickly. 'Go to them.
They will see Klink, and——'

''They are just pushing him on,' I said, with a groan.

'What!' she cried; and I remember to this day how her
grey eyes flashed and how she threw back her head in
generous amazement. 'Do you mean to say that this is
being done in spite, Martin? That after escaping all the
perils of this wretched war these men are so thankless as
to turn on the first scape-goat that falls into their hands?
It is not possible!'

'It looks like it, my lady,' I muttered, wondering whether
I had not perhaps carried the matter too far.

'No, no,' she said, shaking her head, 'you must have
made a mistake; but go to Klink. Go to Klink and tell
him from me to keep the man for a week at least. I will
be answerable for the cost, and we can consider in the

meantime what to do. My cousin the Waldgrave Rupert visits me in a day or two, and I will consult him.'

Still I did not like to go without giving her a hint that she might meet with opposition, and I hesitated, considering how I might warn her without causing needless alarm or seeming to presume. Fraulein Anna, who had listened throughout with the greatest impatience, took advantage of the pause to interfere. 'Come, Rotha,' she said. 'Enough trifling. Let us go back to Voetius and our day's work.'

'My dear,' the Countess answered somewhat coldly, 'this is my day's work. I am trying to do it.'

'Your work is to improve and store your mind,' Fraulein Anna retorted with peevishness.

'True,' my lady said quietly; 'but for a purpose.'

'There can be no purpose higher than the acquirement of philosophy — and religion,' Fraulein Anna said. Her last words sounded like an afterthought.

My lady shook her head. 'The duty of a Princess is to govern,' she said.

'How can she govern unless she has prepared her mind by study and thought ? ' Fraulein Anna asked triumphantly.

'I agree within limits,' my lady answered. 'But —— '

'There is no *but !* Nor are there any limits that I see !' the other rejoined eagerly. 'Let me read to you out of Voetius himself. In his maxims —— '

'Not this minute,' the Countess answered firmly. And thereby she interrupted not Fraulein Anna alone but a calculation on which, without any light from Voetius, I was engaged ; namely, how long it would take a man to mow an acre of ground if he spent all his time in sharpening his scythe ! Low matters of that kind however have nothing in common with philosophy I suppose ; and my lady's voice soon brought me back to the point. 'What is it you want to say, Martin ? ' she asked. 'I see that you have something still on your mind.'

'I wish your excellency to be aware that there may be a good deal of feeling in the town on this matter,' I said.

'You mean that I may make myself unpopular,' she answered.

That was what I did mean — that at the least. And I bowed.

My lady shook her head with a grave smile. 'I might give you an answer from Voetius, Martin,' she said; 'that they who govern are created to protect the weak against the strong. And if not, *cui bono?* But that, you may not understand. Shall I say then instead that I, and not Hofman or Dietz, am Countess of Heritzburg.'

'My lady,' I cried — and I could have knelt before her — 'that is answer enough for me!'

'Then go,' she said, her face bright, 'and do as I told you.'

She turned away, and I made my reverence and went out and down the stairs and through the great court with my head high and my heart high also. I might not understand Voetius; but I understood that my lady was one, who in face of all and in spite of all, come Hofman or Dietz, come peace or war, would not blench, but stand by the right! And it did me good. He is a bad horse that will not jump when his rider's heart is right, and a bad servant that will not follow when his master goes before! I hummed a tune, I rattled my staff on the stones. I said to myself it was a thousand pities so gallant a spirit should be wasted on a woman : and then again I fancied that I could not have served a man as I knew I could and would serve her should time and the call ever put me to the test.

The castle at Heritzburg, rising abruptly above the roofs of the houses, is accessible from the town by a flight of steps cut in the rock. On the other three sides the knob on which it stands is separated from the wooded hills to which it belongs by a narrow ravine, crossed in one place by a light horse-bridge made in modern days. This forms the chief entrance to the castle, but the road which leads to it from the town goes so far round that it is seldom used, the flight of steps I have mentioned leading at once and more conveniently from the end of the High Street. Half

way down the High Street on the right hand side is the
Market-place, a small paved square, shaded by tall wooden
houses, and having a carved stone pump in the middle. A
hundred paces beyond this on the same side is the Red
Hart, standing just within the West Gate.

From one end of the town to the other is scarcely a step,
and I was at the inn before the Countess's voice had ceased
to sound in my ears. The door stood open, and I went in,
expecting to find the kitchen empty or nearly so at that
hour of the day. To my surprise, I found at least a dozen
people in it, with as much noise and excitement going
forward as if the yearly fair had been in progress. For a
moment I was not observed. I had time to see who were
present — Klink, the two soldiers who had put themselves
forward the evening before, and half a score of idlers.
Then the landlord's eye fell on me and he passed the word.
A sudden silence followed and a dozen faces turned my
way; so that the room, which was low in the roof with
wide beetle-browed windows, seemed to lighten.

'Just in time, Master Schwartz!' cried one fellow. 'You
can write, and we are about a petition! Perhaps you will
draw it up for us.'

'A petition,' I said shortly, eyeing the fellow with contempt. 'What petition?'

'Against Papists!' he answered boldly.

'And favourers, aiders, and abettors!' exclaimed another
in the background.

'Master Klink, Master Klink,' I said, trying to frown
down the crowd, 'you would do well to have a care. These
ragamuffins —— '

'Have a care yourself, Master Jackanapes!' the same
voice cried. 'This is a town meeting.'

'Town meeting!' I said, looking round contemptuously.
'Gaol-meeting, you mean, and likely to be a gaol-filling.
But I do not speak to you; I leave that to the constable.
For Master Klink, if he will take a word of advice, I will
speak with him alone.'

They cried out to him not to speak to me. But Klink
had still sense enough to know that he might be going too
fast, and though they hooted and laughed at him — being
for the most part people who had nothing to lose — he
came out of the house with me and crossed the street that
we might talk unheard. As civilly as I could I delivered
my message; and as exactly, for I saw that the issue
might be serious.

I was not surprised when he groaned, and in a kind of
a tremor shook his hands. 'I am not my own master,
Schwartz,' he said. 'And that is the truth.'

'You were your own master last night,' I retorted.

'These fellows are all for " No Popery." '

'Ay, and who gave them the cue?' I said sharply. 'It
is not the first time that the fat burgher has raised the
lean kine and been eaten by them. Nor will it be the last.
It serves you right.'

'I am willing enough to do what my lady wishes,' he
whimpered; 'but ——'

'But you are not master of your own house, do you
mean?' I exclaimed. 'Then fetch the constable. That is
simple. Or the Burgomaster.'

'Hush!' he said, 'he is hotter than any one.'

'Then,' I answered flatly, 'he had better cool, and you
too. That is all I have to say. And mark me, Klink,' I
continued sternly, 'see that no harm happens to that girl
or her father. They are in your house, and you have
heard what my lady says. Let those ruffians interfere
with them and you will be held to answer for it.'

'That is easy talking,' he muttered peevishly; 'but if I
cannot help it?'

'You will have to help it!' I rejoined, losing my temper
a little. 'You were fool enough, or I am much mistaken,
to set a light to this stack, and now you will have to
smother the flame, or pay for it. That is all, my friend.
You have had fair warning. The rest is in your own
hands.'

And with that I left him. He was a stupid man but a sly one too, and I doubted his sincerity, or I might have taken another way with him. In the end, doubtless, it would have been the same.

As I turned on my heel to go, the troop round the door raised a kind of hoot; and this pursued me as I went up the street, bringing the blood to my cheeks and almost provoking me to return. I checked the impulse however, and strode on as if I did not hear; and by the time I reached the market-place the cry had ceased. Here however it began afresh; a number of loose fellows and lads who were loafing about the stalls crying 'No Popery!' and 'Popish Schwartz!' as I passed, in a way which showed that the thing was premeditated and that they had been lying in wait for me. I stopped and scowled at them, and for a moment they ceased. But the instant my back was turned the hooting began again — with an ugly savage note in it — and I had not got quite clear of the place when some one flung a bundle of carrots, which hit me sharply on the back. I swung round in a rage at that, and dashed hot foot into the middle of the stalls in the hope of catching the fellow. But I was too late; an old woman over whom I fell was the only sufferer. The rascals had fled down an alley, and, contenting myself with crying after them that they were a set of cowards, I set the old lady on her legs, and went on my way.

But I had my thoughts. Such an insult had not been offered to me since I first came to the town to serve my lady, and it filled me with indignation. It seemed, besides, not a thing to be sneezed at. I took it for a sign of change, of bad times coming. Moreover — and this troubled me as much as anything — I had recognised among the fellows in the square two more of the fifty men my lady had sent to serve with Hesse. There seemed ground for fearing that they had deserted in a body and come back and were in hiding. If this were so, and the Burgomaster, instead of repressing them, encouraged their excesses, they were likely to prove a source of trouble and danger — real danger.

I paused on the steps leading up to the castle, in two minds whether I should not go to the Burgomaster and tell him plainly what I thought; for I felt the responsibility. My lady had no male protector, no higher servant than myself, and we had not a dozen capable men in the castle. The Landgrave of Hesse, our over-lord, was away with the King of Sweden, and we could expect no immediate support from him. In the event of a riot in the town therefore — and I knew that, in the great Peasants' War of a century before, our town had been rebellious enough — we should be practically helpless. An hour and a little ill-fortune might place my lady in the hands of her mutinous subjects; and though the Landgrave would be certain sooner or later to chastise them, many things might happen in the interval.

In the end I went on up the steps, thinking that I had better leave Hofman alone, since I could not trust him, and should only by applying to him disclose our weakness. There was a way indeed which occurred to me as I reached the head of the stairs, but I had not taken two steps across the terrace, as we call that part of the court which overlooks the town, before it was immediately driven out again. Fraulein Max was walking up and down with a book, sunning herself. I think that she had been watching for me, for the moment I appeared she called to me.

I went up to her reluctantly. I was anxious, and in no mood to listen to one of those learned disquisitions with which she would sometimes favour us, without any thought whether we understood her or no. But this I soon found was not what I had to fear. Her face wore a frown and her tone was peevish; but she closed her book, keeping her place in it with her finger.

'Master Martin,' she said, peering at me with her short-sighted eyes, 'you are a very foolish man, I think.'

'Fraulein!' I muttered in surprise. What did she mean ?

'A very foolish one!' she repeated. 'Why are you disturbing your lady ? Why do you not leave her to her studies and her peace instead of distracting her mind with these stories of a man and a girl ? A man and a girl, and Papists! Piff! What are they to us ? Don't you understand that your lady has higher work and something else to do ? Go you and look after your man and girl.'

'But my lady's subjects, Fraulein —— '

'Her subjects ?' she replied, almost violently. 'Papists are no subjects. Or to what purpose the *Cujus Regio?* But what do you know of government ? You have heard and you repeat.'

'But, Fraulein,' I said humbly, for her way of talking made me seem altogether in the wrong, and a monster of indiscretion, 'if my lady does not interfere, the man and the girl you speak of will suffer. That is clear.'

She snapped her fingers.

'Piff!' she cried, screwing up her eyes still more. 'What has that to do with us ? Is there not suffering going on from one end of Germany to the other? Do not scores die every day, every hour? Can we prevent it? No. Then why trouble us for this one little, little matter? It is theirs to suffer, and ours to think and read, and learn and write. We were at peace to do all this, and then you come with your man and girl, and the peace is gone !'

'But, Fraulein —— '

'You do no good by saying Fraulein, Fraulein!' she replied. 'Look at things in the light of reason. Trouble us no more. That is what you have to do. What are this man and girl to you that you should endanger your mistress for their sakes?'

'They are nothing to me,' I answered.

'Then let them go!' she replied with suppressed passion. 'And undo your folly the best way you can, and the sooner the better! Chut! That when the mind is set on higher things it should be distracted by such mean and miserable objects! If they are nothing to you, why in heaven's name obtrude them on us?'

After that she would not hear another word, but dismissed me with a wave of her hand as if the thing were fully settled and over; burying herself in her book and turning away, while I went into the house with my tail between my legs and all my doubts and misgivings increased a hundredfold. For this which she had put into words was the very thought, the very way out of it, which had occurred to me! I had only to let the matter drop, I had only to leave these people to their fate, and the danger and difficulty were at once at an end. For a time my lady's authority might suffer perhaps; but at the proper season, when the Landgrave was at home and could help us, we might cheaply assert and confirm it.

All that day I went about in doubt what I should do; and night came without resolving my perplexities. At one moment I thought of my duty to my lady, and the calamities in which I might involve her. At another I pictured the girl I had seen praying by her father's bed — pictured her alone and defenceless, hourly insulted by Klink, and with terror and uncertainty looming each day larger before her eyes; or, worse still, abandoned to all the dangers which awaited her, in the event of the town refusing to give her shelter. Considering that I had seen her once only — to notice her — it was wonderful how clearly I remembered her.

CHAPTER III.

THE BURGOMASTER'S DEMAND.

As it turned out, the other party took the burden of decision from my shoulders. When I came out of chapel next morning, I found Hofman on the terrace waiting for me, and with him Master Dietz wearing his Geneva gown and a sour face. They wished to see my lady. I said it was early yet, and tried to hold them in talk if only that I might learn what they would be at. But they repulsed my advances, said that they knew her excellency always transacted her business at this hour — which was perfectly true — and at last sent me to the parlour whether I would or no.

Under such circumstances I did not linger behind the screen, but advanced at once, and interrupting Fraulein Max, who had just begun to read aloud, while my lady worked, said that the Burgomaster desired the honour of an interview with the Countess.

The latter passed her needle once through the stuff, and then looked up. 'Do you know what he wants, Martin?' she said in a quiet tone.

I said I did not.

She bent her head and worked for a moment in silence. Then she sighed gently, and without looking up, nodded to me. 'Very well, I will see him here,' she said. 'But first send Grissel and Gretchen to wait on me. Let Franz bring two stools and place them, and bid him and Ernst keep the door. My footstool also. And let the two Jacobs wait in the hall.'

I gave the orders and took on myself to place two extra lackeys in the hall that we might not seem to be short of men. Then I went to the Burgomaster, and attended him and Master Dietz to the parlour.

They bowed three times according to custom as they advanced, and my lady, taking one step forward, gave her hand to the Burgomaster to kiss. Then she stepped back and sat down, looking with a pleasant face at the Minister. 'I would fain apologise for troubling your excellency,' the Mayor began slowly and heavily. 'But the times are trying.'

'Your presence needs no apology, Master Hofman,' my lady answered, smiling frankly. 'It is your right to see me on behalf of the town at all times. It would grieve me much, if you did not sometimes exercise the privilege. And for Master Dietz, who may be able to assist us, I am glad to see him also.'

The Minister bowed low. The Burgomaster only puffed out his cheeks. Doubtless he felt that courage at the Red Hart and courage in my lady's parlour were two different things. But it was too late to retreat, for the Minister was there to report what passed; and after a glance at Dietz's face he proceeded. 'I am not here in a private capacity, if it please your excellency,' he said. 'And I beg your excellency to bear this in mind. I am here as Burgomaster, having on my mind the peace of the town; which at present is endangered — very greatly endangered,' he repeated pompously.

'I am sorry to hear that,' my lady answered.

'Nevertheless it is so,' he replied with a kind of obstinacy. 'Endangered by the presence of certain persons in the town, whose manners are not conformable. These persons are Papists, and the town, your excellency remembers, is a Protestant town.'

'Certainly I remember that,' my lady said gravely.

'Hence of this combination, your excellency will understand, comes a likelihood of evil,' he continued. 'On which, hearing you took an interest in these persons, however little deserved, it seemed to be my duty to lay the matter before you.'

'You have done very rightly,' the Countess answered

quietly. 'Do I understand then, Master Hofman, that the
Papists you complain of are conspiring to break the peace
of the town?'

The Burgomaster gasped. He was too obtuse to see at
once that my lady was playing with him. He only wondered how he had managed to convey so strange a notion
to her mind. He hastened to set her right. 'No — oh,
no,' he said. 'There is no fear of that. There are but
three of them.'

'Are they presuming to perform their rites in public
then?' my lady rejoined. 'If so, of course it cannot be
permitted. It is against the law of the town.'

'No,' he answered, more slowly and more reluctantly as
the drift of her questions began to dawn upon him. 'I
do not know that that is so. I have not heard that it is
so. But they are Papists.'

'Well, but with their consciences we have nothing to
do!' she said more sharply. 'I confess, I fail as yet to
see, Master Hofman, how they threaten the peace of the
town.'

The Burgomaster stared. 'I do not know that they
threaten it themselves,' he said slowly. 'But their presence stirs up the people, if your excellency understands;
and may lead, if the matter goes on, to a riot or worse.'

'Ha! Now I comprehend!' my lady cried in a hearty
tone. 'You fear your constables may fail to cope with
the rabble?'

He admitted that that was so.

'And you desire such assistance as I can offer towards
maintaining the law and protecting these persons; who
have of course a right to protection?'

Master Hofman began to see whither he had been led,
and glared at the Countess with his mouth wide open.
But for the moment he could not find a word to say.
Never did I see a man look more at a loss.

'Well, I must consider,' my lady resumed, her finger to
her cheek. 'Rest assured, you shall be supported. Martin,'

she continued, turning to me, 'let word be sent to the four foresters at Gatz to come down to the castle this evening. And send also to the charcoal-burners' camp. How many men should there be in it?'

'Some half-score, my lady,' I answered, adding two-thirds to the truth.

'Ah? And let the huntsman come down and bring a couple of feeders. Doubtless with our own men, we shall be able to place a score or thirty at your disposal, Master Hofman, and stout fellows. These, with your constables and such of the peaceful burghers as you see fit to call to your assistance, should be sufficient to quell the disorderly.'

I could have laughed aloud, Master Hofman looked so confounded. Never man had an air of being more completely taken aback. By offering her help to put down any mob, the Countess had deprived him of the plea he had come to prefer; that he was afraid he could not answer for the safety of the Papists, and that therefore they must withdraw or be expelled. This he could no longer put forward, and consequently he was driven either to adopt my lady's line, or side openly with the party of disorder. I saw his heavy face turn a deep red, and his jaw fall, as he grasped the situation. His wits worked slowly; and had he been left to himself, I do not doubt that he would have allowed things to remain as they were, and taken the part assigned to him.

But Master Dietz, who had listened with a lengthening face, at this moment interposed. 'Will your excellency permit me to say a few words?' he said.

'I think the Burgomaster has made the matter clear,' my lady answered.

'Not in one respect,' the Minister rejoined. 'He has not informed your excellency that in the opinion of the majority of the burghers and inhabitants of this town the presence of these people is an offence and an eyesore.'

'It is legal,' my lady answered icily. 'I do not know what opinion has to do with it.'

'The opinion of the majority.'

'Sir!' my lady said, speaking abruptly and with height-
ened colour, 'in Heritzburg I am the majority, by your
leave.'

He frowned and set his face hard, but his eyes sank
before hers. 'Nevertheless your excellency will allow,'
he said in a lower tone, 'that the opinion of grave and
orderly men deserves consideration?'

'When it is on the side of law, every consideration,' the
Countess answered, her eyes sparkling. 'But when it is
ranged against three defenceless people in violation of the
law, none. And more, Master Dietz,' she continued, her
voice ringing with indignation, 'it is to check such opinion,
and defend against it those who otherwise would have no -
defence, that I conceive I sit here. And by my faith I
will do it!'

She uttered the last words with so much fire and with
her beautiful face so full of feeling, that I started forward
where I stood; and for a farthing would have flung Dietz
through the window. The little Minister was of a stern
and hard nature, however. The nobility of my lady's position was lost upon him. He feared her less than he would
have feared a man under the same circumstances; and
though he stood cowed, and silenced for the moment, he
presently returned to the attack.

'Your excellency perhaps forgets,' he said with a dry
cough, 'that the times are full of bloodshed and strife,
though we at Heritzburg have hitherto enjoyed peace. I
suggest with respect therefore, is it prudent to run the
risk of bringing these evils into the town for the sake of
one or two Papists, whom it is only proposed to send elsewhere?'

My lady rose suddenly from her chair, and pointed with
a finger, which trembled slightly, to the great window
beside her. 'Step up here!' she said curtly.

Master Dietz, wondering greatly, stepped on to the daïs.
Thence the red roofs of the town, some new and smart, and

some stained and grey with lichens, and all the green valley
stretching away to the dark line of wood, were visible,
bathed in sunshine. The day was fine, the air clear, the
smoke from the chimneys rose straight upward.

'Do you see?' she said.

The Minister bowed.

'Then take this for answer,' she replied. 'All that you
see is mine to rule. It came to me by inheritance, and
I prize the possession of it, though I am a woman, more
highly than my life; for it came to me from Heaven and
my fathers. But were it a hundred times as large, Master
Dietz — were there a house for every brick that now stands
there, and an acre for every furrow, and sheep as many
as birds in the air, even then I would risk all, and double
and treble all, rather than desert those whom my law de-
fends, be they three, or thirty, or three hundred! Let that
be your answer! And for the peace you speak of,' she
continued, turning on a sudden and confronting us, her face
aglow with anger, 'the peace, I mean, which you have
hitherto enjoyed, it should shame you to hear it mentioned! Have the Papists harried you? Have you suffered in life or limb, or property? No. And why?
Because of my honoured uncle, a Papist! For shame! —
for shame, I say! As it has been dealt out to you, go
and do to others!'

But for the respect which held me in her presence, I
could have cried 'Huzza!' to her speech; and I can tell you,
it made Master Minister look as small as a mouse. He
stepped down from the daïs with his face dark and his
head trembling; and after that I never doubted that he
was at the bottom of the movement against the Worts,
though the ruffianly deserters I have mentioned supplied
him with the tools, wanting which he might not have
taken up the work. He stood a moment on the floor
looking very black and grim, and with not a word to say,
but I doubted he was not beaten. What line he would
have taken, however, I cannot tell, for he had scarcely

descended — my lady had not resumed her seat — when
there rose from the court below a sudden babel of noise,
the trampling of hoofs and feet on the pavement, and a
confused murmur of voices. For a moment I looked at my
lady and she at me. It struck me that that at which the
Burgomaster had hinted was come to pass: that some of
the town ragamuffins had dared to invade the castle. The
same idea doubtless occurred to her, for she stepped, though
without any appearance of alarm, to the window, which
commanded a side view of the terrace. She looked out.

I, a little to her right, saw her smile; then in a moment
she turned. 'This could not be better,' she said, resuming
in an instant her ordinary manner. I think she was a little
ashamed, as people of quality are wont to be, of the feeling she had betrayed. 'I see some one below who will
advise me, and who, if I am doing wrong, as you seem to
fear, Master Burgomaster, will tell me of it. My cousin,
the Waldgrave Rupert, whom I expected to-morrow, has
arrived to-day. Be good enough to wait while I receive
him, and I will then return to you.'

Bidding me have the two served with some refreshment,
she stepped down from the daïs, and withdrew with Fraulein Max and her women, leaving the townsmen to discuss
the new arrival with what appetite they might.

They liked it little, I fancy. In a moment their importance was gone, their consequence at an end. The name of
the Waldgrave Rupert made them feel how small they
were, despite their boasting, beside the youngest member
of the family. The very swish of my lady's robe as she
swept through the doorway flouted them, her departure
was an offence; and this, following on the scolding they
had received, produced a soreness and irritation in their
minds, which ill-prepared them, I think, for the sequel.

I have sometimes thought that had I remained with
them, and paid them some attentions, the end might have
been different; but my duties called me elsewhere. The
house was in a ferment; I was wanted here and there,

both to give orders and to see them carried out. It was
some time before I was at liberty even to go to the hall
whither my lady had descended to receive her guest, and
where I found the two standing together on the hearth,
under the great Red Hart which is the cognizance of the
family.

I had not seen the Waldgrave Rupert — a cadet of the
noble house of Weimar and my lady's cousin once removed
— since his boyhood. I found him grown into a splendid
man, as tall and almost as wide as myself; who used to be
called in the old forest days before I entered my lady's service 'the strong man of Pippel.' As he stood on the
hearth, fair-haired and ruddy-faced, with a noble carriage
and a frank boyish smile, I had seldom looked on a hand-
somer youth. He fell short of my lady's age by two years;
but as I looked from one to the other, they seemed so
fitting a pair, the disparity went for nothing. He was
young and strong, full of spirit and energy and fire.
Surely, I thought, the right man has come at last!

In this belief I was more than confirmed when he came
forward and greeted me pleasantly, vowing that he remembered me well. His voice and laugh seemed to fill the
room; the very ring of his spurs on the stones gave assurance of power. I saw my lady look at him with an air of
affectionate pride — she had seen him more lately than I
had — as if his youth, and strength, and beauty already
belonged to her. As for his smile, it was infectious. We
grew in a moment brighter, younger, and more cheerful. The
house which yesterday had seemed quiet and lonesome —
we were a small family for so great a dwelling — took on a
new air. The servants went about their tasks more quickly,
the maids laughed behind doors. The place seemed in an
hour transformed, as I have seen a valley in the mountains
changed on a sudden by the rising of the sun.

As a fact, when I had been in his presence five minutes,
the Burgomaster and the Minister upstairs seemed as
common and mean and insignificant a pair of fellows as

any in Germany. I wondered that I could ever have feared them. The Countess had told him the story, and he asked me one or two questions about them, his tone high, and his head in the air. I answered him, and was for accompanying him upstairs, when he went to see them, with my lady by his side, and his whip slapping his great thigh boots until the staircase rang again. But my lady had an errand and sent me on it, and so I was not present at the end of this interview which I had myself brought about.

But I suppose that the scolding my lady had given them was no more than a flea-bite beside the rating the young Waldgrave inflicted! It was notorious for a score of leagues round, and he told them so in good round terms, that the Heritzburg land had been spared by friend and foe for Count Tilly's sake; for his sake and his alone — a Papist. How, then, he asked them, had they the face to do this dirty trick, and threaten my lady besides? With much more of the same kind, and hard words, not to say menaces; sparing neither Mayor nor Minister, so that they went off at last like whipped dogs or thieves that have seen the gallows.

Afterwards something was said; but at the time no one missed them. Except by myself, scarce a thought was given to them after they went out of the door. The house was all agog about the new-comer; the still-room full of work and the chimneys smoking. The young lord was everywhere, and the maids were mad about him. I had my hands full, and every one in the house seemed to be in the same case. No one had time to look abroad.

Except Fraulein Anna Max, my lady's companion. I found her about four o'clock in the afternoon sitting alone in the hall. She had a book before her as usual, but on my entrance she pushed it away from her, and looked up at me, screwing up her eyes in the odd way peculiar to her.

'Well, Master Steward,' she said — and her voice sounded ill-natured, 'so the fire has been lit — but not by you.'

'The fire?' I answered, utterly at a loss for the moment.

'Ay,' she rejoined, with a bitter smile, 'the fire. Don't you hear it burning?'

'I hear nothing,' I said coldly.

'Go to the terrace, and perhaps you will!' she answered. Her words filled me with a vague uneasiness, but I was too proud to go then or seem to heed them. An hour or two later, however, when the sun was half down, and the shadows of the chimneys lay far over the roofs, and the eastern woods were aglow, I went to the wall which bounds the terrace and looked down. The hum of the town came up to my ears as it has come up to that wall any time these hundred years. But was I mistaken, or did there mingle with it this evening a harsher note than usual, a rancorous murmur, as of angry voices; and something sterner, lower, and more menacing, the clamour of a great crowd?

CHAPTER IV.

THE FIRE ALIGHT.

I LAUGHED at my own fears when the morning came, and showed no change except that cheerful one, which our guest's presence had worked inside the castle. Below, to-day was as yesterday. The sun shone as brightly on the roofs, the smoke of the chimneys rose as peacefully in the air; the swallows circling round the eaves swung this way and that as swiftly and noiselessly as of old. The common sounds of everyday life, the clank of the pump in the market-place as the old crones drew water, and the cry of the wood-cutter hawking his stuff, alone broke the stillness. I sniffed the air, and smiling at Fraulein Anna's warning, went back into the house, where any fears which yet lingered in my mind took instant flight at sound of the Waldgrave's voice, so cheerful was it, so full of life and strength and confidence.

3

I do not know what it was in him, but something there was which carried us all the way he wished us to go. Did he laugh at the thought of danger; straightway we laughed too, and this though I knew Heritzburg and he did not. Did he speak scornfully of the burghers; forthwith they seemed to us a petty lot. When he strode up and down the terrace, showing us how a single gun placed here or there, or in the corner, would in an hour reduce the town; on the instant we deemed him a Tilly. When he dubbed Hofman and Dietz, 'Old Fat and Lean,' the groom-boys, who could not be kept from his heels, sniggered, and had to be whipped back to the stables. In a word, he won us all. His youth, his gaiety, his confidence, were irresistible.

He dared even to scold my lady, saying that she had cosseted the townsfolk and brought this trouble on herself by pleasuring them; and she, who seemed to us the proudest of the proud, took it meekly, laughing in his face. It required no conjuror to perceive that he admired her, and would fain shine in her presence. That was to be expected. But about my mistress I was less certain, until after breakfast nothing would suit her but an immediate excursion to the White Maiden — the great grey spire which stands on the summit of the Oberwald. Then I knew that she had it in her mind to make the best figure she could; for though she talked of showing him game in that direction, and there was a grand parade of taking dogs, all the world knows that the other side of the valley is the better hunting-ground. I was left to guess that the White Maiden was chosen because all the wide Heritzburg land can be seen from its foot, and not corn and woodland, pasture and meadow only, but the gem of all — the town nestling babelike in the lap of the valley, with the grey towers rising like the face of some harsh nurse above it.

My lord jumped at the plan. Doubtless he liked the prospect of a ride through the forest by her side. When she raised some little demur, stepping in the way of her own proposal, as I have noticed women will, and said some-

thing about the safety of the castle, if so many left it, he
cried out eagerly that she need not fear.

'I will leave my people,' he said. 'Then you will feel
quite sure that the place is safe. I will answer for them
that they will hold your castle against Wallenstein himself.'

'But how many are with you?' my lady asked curiously; a little in mischief too, perhaps, for I think she
knew.

His handsome face reddened and he looked rather foolish
for a moment. 'Well, only four, as a fact,' he said. 'But
they are perfect paladins, and as good as forty. In your
defence, cousin, I would pit them against a score of the
hardiest Swedes that ever followed the King.'

My lady laughed gaily.

'Well, for this day, I will trust them,' she said.
'Martin, order the grooms to saddle Pushka for me. And
you, cousin, shall have the honour of mounting me. It is
an age since I have had a frolic.'

Sometimes I doubt if my lady ever had such a frolic
again. Happier days she saw, I think, and many and many
of them, I hope; but such a day of careless sunny gaiety,
spent in the May greenwood, with joy and youth riding by
her, with old servants at her heels, and all the beauties of
her inheritance spread before her in light and shadow, she
never again enjoyed. We went by forest paths, which
winding round the valley, passed through woodlands,
where the horses sank fetlock-deep in moss, and the laughing voices of the riders died away among the distant trunks.
Here were fairy rings deep-plunged in bracken, and chalky
bottoms whence springs rose bright as crystal, and dim
aisles of beeches narrowing into darkness, where last year's
leaves rustled ghostlike under foot, and the shadow of a
squirrel startled the boldest. Once, emerging on the open
down where the sun lay hot and bright, my lady gave her
horse the rein, and for a mile or more we sped across the
turf, with hoofs thundering on either hand, and bits jingling, and horses pulling, only to fall into a walk again with

flushed cheeks and brighter eyes, on the edge of the farther wood. Thence another mile, athwart the steep hillside through dwarf oaks and huge blackthorn trees, brought us to the foot of the Maiden, and we drew rein and dismounted, and stood looking down on the vale of Heritzburg, while the grooms unpacked the dinner.

There is a niche in the great pillar, a man's height from the ground, in which one person may conveniently sit. The young Waldgrave spied it.

'Up to the throne, cousin!' he cried, and he helped her to it, sitting himself on the ledge at her feet, with his legs dangling. 'Why, there is the Werra!' he continued.

A large quantity of rain had fallen that spring, and the river which commonly runs low between its banks, was plainly visible, a silver streak crossing the distant mouth of the valley.

'Yes,' my lady answered. 'That is the Werra, and beyond it is, I suppose, the world.'

'Whither I must go back this day week,' he said, between sighing and smiling. 'Then, hey for the south and Nuremberg, the good cause and the great King.'

'You have seen him?'

'Once only.'

'And is he so great a fighter?' my lady asked curiously.

'How can he fail to be when he and his men fight and pray alternately,' the Waldgrave answered; 'when there is no license in the camp, and a Swede thinks death the same as victory?'

'Where is he now?'

'At Munich, in Bavaria.'

'How it would have grieved my uncle,' my lady said, with a sigh.

'He died as he would have wished to die,' the Waldgrave answered gently. 'He believed in his cause, as the King of Sweden believes in his; and he died for it. What more can a man ask? But here is Franz with all sorts of good things. And I am afraid a feast of beauty, however perfect, does not prevent a man getting hungry.'

'That is a very pretty compliment to Heritzburg,' my lady said, laughing.

'Or its chatelaine!' I heard him murmur, with a tender look. But my lady only laughed again and called to me to come and name the hills, and tell my lord what land went with each of the three hamlets between which the lower valley is divided.

Doubtless that was but one of a hundred gallant things he said to her, and whereat she laughed, during the pleasant hour they whiled away at the foot of the pillar, basking in the warm sunshine, and telling the valley farm by farm. For the day was perfect, the season spring. I lay on my side and dreamed my own dream under the trees, with the hum of insects in my ears. No one was in a hurry to rise, or set a term to such a time.

Still we had plenty of daylight before us when my lady mounted and turned her face homewards, thinking to reach the castle a little after five. But a hare got up as we crossed the open down, and showing good sport, as these long-legged mountain hares will, led us far out of our way, and caused us to spend nearly an hour in the chase. Then my lady spied a rare flower on the cliffside; and the young Waldgrave must needs get it for her. And so it wanted little of sunset when we came at last in sight of the bridge which spans the ravine at the back of the castle. I saw in the distance a lad seated on the parapet, apparently looking out for us, but I thought nothing of it. The descent was steep and we rode down slowly, my lady and the Waldgrave laughing and talking, and the rest of us sitting at our ease. Nor did the least thought of ill occur to my mind until I saw that the lad had jumped down from the wall and was running towards us waving his cap.

My lady, too, saw him.

'What is it, Martin?' she said, turning her head to speak to me.

I told her I would see, and trotted forward along the side of the path until I came within call. Then I cried sharply to the lad to know what it was. I saw something in his face which frightened me; and being frightened and blaming myself, I was ready to fall on the first I met.

'The town!' he answered, panting up to my stirrup. 'There is fighting going on, Master Martin. They are pulling down Klink's house.'

'So, so,' I answered, for at the first sight of his face I had feared worse. 'Have you closed the gate at the head of the steps?'

'Yes,' he said, 'and my lord's men are guarding it.'

'Right!' I answered. And then my lady came up, and I had to break the news to her. Of course the young Waldgrave heard also, and I saw his eyes sparkle with pleasure.

'Ha! the rascals!' he cried. 'Now we will trounce them! Trust me, cousin, we will teach these boors such a lesson as they shall long remember. But what is it?' he continued, turning to my lady who had not spoken. 'The Queen of Heritzburg is not afraid of her rebellious subjects?'

My lady's eyes flashed. 'No, I am not afraid,' she said, with contempt. 'But Klink's house? Do you mean the Red Hart, Martin?'

I said I did.

She plucked her horse by the head, and stopped short under the arch of the gateway. I think I see her now bending from her saddle with the light on the woods behind her, and her face in shadow. 'Then those people are in danger!' she said, her voice quivering with excitement. 'Martin, take what men you have and go down into the town. Bring them off at all risks! See to it yourself. If harm come to them, I shall not forgive you easily.'   .

The Waldgrave sprang from his horse, and cried out that he would go. But my lady called to him to stay with her.

'Martin knows the streets, and you do not,' she said,

sliding unassisted to the ground. 'But he shall take your men, if you do not object.'

We dismounted, in a confused medley of men and horses, in the stable court, which is small, and being surrounded by high buildings, was almost dark. The grooms left at home had gone to the front of the house to see the sight, and there was no one to receive us. I bade the five men who had ridden with us get their arms, and leaving the horses loose to be caught and cared for by the lad who had met us, I hastened after my lady and the Waldgrave, who had already disappeared under the arch which leads to the Terrace Court.

To pass through this was to pass from night to day, so startling was the change. From one end to the other the terrace was aglow with red light. The last level beams of the sun shone straight in our eyes as we emerged, and so blinded us, that I advanced, seeing nothing before me but a row of dark figures leaning over the parapet. If we could not see, however, we could hear. A hoarse murmur, unlike anything I had heard before, came up from the town, and rising and falling in waves of sound, now a mere whisper, and now a dull savage roar, caused the boldest to tremble. I heard my lady cry, 'Those poor people! Those poor people!' and saw her clench her hands in impotent anger; and that sight, or the sound — which seemed the more weirdly menacing as the town lay in twilight below us, and we could make out no more than a few knots of women standing in the market-place — or it may be some memory of the helpless girl I had seen at Klink's, so worked upon me that I had got the gate unbarred and was standing at the head of the steps outside before I knew that I had stirred or given an order.

Some one thrust a half pike into my hand, and mechanically I counted out the men — four of the Waldgrave's and five, six, seven of our own. A strange voice — but it may have been my own — cried, 'Not by the High Street. Through the lane by the wall!' and the next moment we

were down out of the sunlight and taking the rough steps
three at a time. The High Street reached, we swung round
in a body to the right, and plunging into Shoe Wynd, came
to the locksmith's, and thence went on by the way I had
gone that other evening.

The noise was less down in the streets. The houses
intervened and deadened it. At some of the doors women
were standing, listening and looking out with grey faces,
but one and all fled in at our approach, which seemed to
be the signal, wherever we, came, for barring doors and
shooting bolts; once a man took to his heels before us,
and again near the locksmith's we encountered a woman
bare-headed and carrying something in her arms. She
almost ran into the midst of us, and at the last moment
only avoided us by darting up the side-alley by the forge.
Whether these people knew us for what we were, and so
fled from us, or took us for a party of the rioters, it was
impossible to say. The narrow lanes were growing dark,
night was falling on the town; only the over-hanging eaves
showed clear and black against a pale sky. The way we
had to go was short, but it seemed long to me; for a dozen
times between the castle steps and Klink's house I thought
of the poor girl at her prayers, and pictured what might be
happening.

Yet we could not have been more than five minutes going
from the steps to the corner beyond the forge, whence we
could see Klink's side window. A red glare shone through
it, and cleaving the dark mist which filled the alley fell
ruddily on the town wall. It seemed to say that we were
too late; and my heart sank at the sight. Nor at the sight
only, for as we turned the corner, the hoarse murmur we
had heard on the Terrace, and which even there had
sounded ominous, swelled to an angry roar, made up of
cries and cursing, with bursts of reckless cheering, and
now and again a yell of pain. The street away before us,
where the lane ran into it, was full of smoky light and
upturned faces; but I took no heed of it, my business was

with the window. I cried to the men behind me and hurried on till I stood before it, and clutching the bars — the glass was broken long ago — looked in.

The room was full of men. For a moment I could see nothing but heads and shoulders and grim faces, all crowded together, and all alike distorted by the lurid light shed by a couple of torches held close to the ceiling. Some of the men standing in such groups as the constant jostling permitted, were talking, or rather shouting to one another. Others were savagely forcing back their fellows who wished to enter; while a full third were gathered with their faces all one way round the corner where I had seen the sick man. Here the light was strongest, and in this direction I gazed most anxiously. But the crowded figures intercepted all view; neither there nor anywhere else could I detect any sign of the girl or child. The men in that corner seemed to be gazing at something low down on the floor, something I could not see. A few were silent, more were shouting and gesticulating. .

I stretched my hands through the bars, and grasping a man by the shoulders, dragged him to me. 'What is it?' I cried in his ear, heedless whether he knew me, or took me for one of the ruffians who were everywhere battling to get into the house — at the window we had anticipated some by a second only. 'What is it?' I repeated fiercely, resisting all his efforts to get free.

'Nothing!' he answered, glaring at me. 'The man is dead; cannot you see?'

'I can see nothing!' I retorted. 'Dead is he?'

'Ay, dead, and a good job too!' the rascal answered, making a fresh attempt to get away. 'Dead when we came in.'

'And the girl?'

'Gone, the Papist witch, on a broomstick!' he answered. 'Through the wall or the ceiling or the keyhole, or through this window; but only on a broomstick. The bars would skin a cat!'

I let him go and looked at the bars. They were an inch

thick, and a very few inches apart. It seemed impossible
that a child, much more a grown woman, could pass between them. As the fellow said, there was barely room for
a cat to pass.

Yet my mind clung to the bars. Klink might have
hidden the girl, for without doubt he had neither foreseen
nor meant anything like this. But something told me that
she had gone by the window, and I turned from it with
renewed hope.

It was time I did turn. The crowd had got wind of our
presence and resented it. All who could not get into the
house to slake their curiosity or anger, had pressed into
the narrow alley where we stood, while the air rang with
cries of 'No Popery! Down with the Papists!' When I
turned I found my fellows hard put to it to keep their
position. To retreat, close pressed as we were, seemed as
difficult as to stand; but by making a resolute movement
all together, we charged to the front for a moment, and
then taking advantage of the interval, fell back as quickly
as we could, facing round whenever it seemed that our
followers were coming on too boldly for safety.

In this way, the knaves with me being stout and some of
them used to the work, we retreated in good order and
without hurt as far as the end of Shoe Wynd. Then I discovered to my dismay that a portion of the mob had made
along the High Street and were waiting for us on the steep
ascent where the wynd runs into the street.

Hitherto no harm had been done on either side, but we
now found ourselves beset front and back, and to add to the
confusion of the scene night had set in. The narrow wynd
was as dark as pitch, save where the light of a chance torch
showed crowded forms and snarling faces, while the din and
tumult were enough to daunt the boldest.

That moment, I confess, was one of the worst I have
known. I felt my men waver; a little more and they
might break and the mob deal with us as it would. On
the other hand, I knew that to plunge, exposed to attack

as we were from behind, into the mass of men who blocked the way to the steps, would be madness. We should be surrounded and trodden down. There were not perhaps fifty really dangerous fellows in the town; but a mob I have noticed is a strange thing. Men who join it, intending merely to look on, are carried away by excitement, and soon find themselves cursing and fighting, burning and raiding with the foremost.

A brief pause and I gave the word to face about again. As I expected, the gang in the alley gave way before us, and the pursued became the pursuers. My men's blood was up now, their patience exhausted; and for a few moments pike and staff played a merry tune. But quickly the mob behind closed up on our heels. Stones began to be thrown, and presently one, dropped I think from a window, struck a man beside me and felled him to the ground.

That was our first loss. Drunken Steve, a great gross fellow, always in trouble, but a giant in strength, picked him up — we could not leave the man to be murdered — and plunged on with us bearing him under his arm.

'Good man!' I cried between my teeth. And I swore it should save the drunkard from many a scrape. But the next moment another was down, and him I had to pick up myself. Then I saw that we were as good as doomed. Against the stones we had no shield.

The men saw it too, and cried out, beside themselves with rage. We were as rats, set in a pit to be worried — in the dark with a hundred foes tearing at us. And the town seemed to have gone mad — mad! Above the screams and wicked laughter, and all the din about us, I heard the great church bell begin to ring, and hurling its notes, now sharp, now dull, down upon the seething streets, swell and swell the tumult until the very sky seemed one in the league against us!

Blind with fury — for what had we done? — we turned on the mob which followed us and hurled it back — back almost to the High Street. But that way was no exit for us; the crowd stood so close that they could not even fly. Round we whirled again, wild and desperate now, and charged down the alley towards the West Gate, thinking possibly to win through and out by that way. We had almost reached the locksmith's — then another man fell. He was of the Waldgrave's following, and his comrade stooped to raise him; but only to fall over him, wounded in his turn.

What happened after that I only knew in part, for from that moment all was a medley of random blows and strug-glings in the dark. The crowd seeing half of us down, and the rest entangled, took heart of grace to finish us. I remember a man dashing a torch in my face, and the blow blinding me. Nevertheless I staggered forward to close with him. Then something tripped me up, something or some one struck me from behind as I fell. I went down like an ox, and for me the fight was over.

Drunken Steve and two of the Waldgrave's men fought across me, I am told, for a minute or more. Then Steve fell and an odd thing happened. The mob took fright at nothing — took fright at their own work, and coming suddenly to their senses, poured pell-mell out of the alley faster than they had come into it. The two strangers, knowing nothing of the way or the town, knocked at the nearest door and were taken in, and sheltered till morning.

CHAPTER V.

MARIE WORT.

THERE never was one of my forefathers could read, or knew so much as a horn-book when he saw it; and there-fore I, though a clerk, have a brain pan that will stand as much as any scholar's and more than many a simple man's.

Otherwise the blow. I got that night must have done me some great mischief, instead of merely throwing me into a swoon, in which I lay until the morning was well advanced.

When I came to myself with an aching head and a dry mouth, I was hard put to it for a time to think what had happened to me. The place in which I lay was dark, with spots of red lights like flaming eyes here and there. An odour of fire and leather and iron filled my nostrils. A hoarse soughing as of a winded horse came and went regularly, with a dull rumbling and creaking that seemed to shake the place. Dizzy as I was, I rose on my elbow with an effort, and looked round. But my eyes swam, I could see nothing which enlightened me, and with a groan I fell back. Then I found that I was lying on a straw-bed, with bandages round my head, and gradually the events of the night came back to me. My mind grew clearer. Yet it still failed to tell me where I was, or whence came the hoarse choking sound, like the sighing of some giant of the Harz, which I heard.

At last, while I lay wondering and fearing, a door opened and let into the dark place a flood of ruddy light. Framed in this light a young girl appeared, standing on the threshold. She held a tray in her hand, and paused to close the door behind her. The bright glow which shone round her, gave her a strange unearthly air, picking out gold in her black locks and warming her pale cheeks; but for all that I recognised her, and never was I more astonished. She was no other than the daughter of the Papist Wort — the girl to rescue whom we had gone down to the Red Hart.

I could not restrain an exclamation of surprise, and the girl started and stopped, peering into the corner in which I lay.

'Master Martin,' she said in a low tone, 'was that you?'

I had never heard her speak before, and I found, perhaps by reason of my low state, and a softness which pain in-

duces in the roughest, a peculiar sweetness in her voice. I
would not answer for a moment. I made her speak again.

'Master Martin,' she said, advancing timidly, 'are you
yourself again?'

'I don't know,' I muttered. In very fact I was so much
puzzled that this was nearly the truth. 'If you will tell
me where I am, I may be able to say,' I added, turning my
head with an effort.

'You are in the kitchen behind the locksmith's forge,'
she answered plainly. 'He is a good man, and you are in
no danger. The window is shuttered to keep the light
from your eyes.'

'And the noise I hear is the bellows at work?'

'Yes,' she answered, coming near. 'It is almost noon.
If you will drink this broth you will get your strength
again.'

I seized the bowl and drank greedily. When I set it
down, my eyes seemed clearer and my mind stronger.

'You escaped?' I said. The more I grew able to think,
the more remarkable it seemed to me that the girl should
be here — here in the same house in which I lay.

'Through the window,' she answered, in a faint voice.

As she spoke she turned from me, and I knew that she
was thinking of her father and would fain hide her face.

'But the bars?' I said.

'I am very small,' she answered in the same low tone.

I do not know why, but perhaps because of the weakness
and softness I have mentioned, I found something very
pitiful in the answer. It stirred a sudden rush of anger in
my heart. I pictured this helpless girl chased through the
streets by the howling pack of cravens we had encountered,
and for a few seconds, bruised and battered as I was, I felt
the fighting spirit again. I half rose, then turned giddy,
and sank back again. It was a minute or more before I
could ask another question. At last I murmured —

'You have not told me how you came here?'

'I was coming up the alley,' she answered, shuddering,

'when at the corner by this house I met men coming to meet me. I fled into the passage to escape them, and finding no outlet, and seeing a light here, I knocked. I thought that some woman might pity me and take me in.'

'And Peter did?'

'Yes,' she answered simply. 'May Our Lady reward him.'

'We were the men you met,' I said drowsily. 'I remember now. You were carrying your brother.'

'My brother?'

'Yes, the child.'

'Oh, yes,' she answered, in rather a strange fashion; but I was too dull to do more than notice it. 'The child of course.'

I could ask no more, for my head was already splitting with pain. I lay back, and I suppose went off into a swoon again, sleeping all that day and until the morning of the next was far advanced.

Then I awoke to find the place in which I lay changed from a cave of mystery to a low-roofed dingy room; the shutter of the window standing half-open, admitted a ray of sunshine and a breath of pure air. A small fire burned on the hearth, a black pot bubbled beside it. For the room itself, a litter of old iron stood in every corner; bunches of keys and rows of rusty locks — padlocks, fetter-locks, and door-locks — hung on all the walls. One or two chests, worm-eaten and rickety, but prized by their present possessor for the antiquity of their fastenings, stood here and there; with a great open press full of gun-locks, match-locks, wheel-locks, spring-locks and the like. Half a dozen arquebuses and pistols decorated the mantel-piece, giving the room something of the air of an armoury.

In the midst of all this litter sat old Peter himself, working away, with a pair of horn glasses on his forehead, at a small lock; which seemed to be giving him a vast amount of trouble. A dozen times at least I watched him fit a number of tiny parts together, only to scatter them again in his leather apron, and begin to pare one or other of them with a little file. At length he laid the work down, as if he were tired, and looking up found my eyes fixed upon him.

He nodded cheerfully. 'Good,' he said. 'Now you look yourself, Martin. No more need of febrifuges. Another night's sleep, and you may go abroad.'

'What day is it?' I said, striving to collect my thoughts.

'Friday,' he answered, looking at me with his shrewd, pleasant eyes. He was an old man, over sixty, a widower with two young children, and clever at his trade. I never knew a better man. 'Wednesday night you came here,' he continued, showing in his countenance the pleasure it gave him to see me recovering.

'I must go to the castle,' I exclaimed, rising abruptly and sitting up. 'Do you hear? I must go.'

'I do not see the necessity,' he answered, looking at me coolly, and without budging an inch.

'My lady will need me.'

'Not at all,' he answered, in the same quiet tone. 'You may make your mind easy about that. The Countess is safe and well. She is in the castle, and the gates are shut.'

'But she has not——' Then I stopped. I was going to say too much.

'She has not half a dozen men with her, you would say,' he replied. 'Well, no. But one is a man, it seems. The young lord has turned a couple of cannon on the town, and all our valiant scoundrels are shaking in their shoes.'

'A couple of cannon! But there are no cannon in the castle!'

'You are mistaken,' Peter answered drily. He had a very dry way with him at times. 'I have seen the muzzles of them, myself, and you can see them, if you please, from the attic window. One is trained on the market-place, and one to fire down the High Street. To-morrow morning our

Burgomaster and the Minister are to go up and make their
peace. And I can tell you some of our brisk boys feel the
rope already round their necks.'

'Is this true ? ' I said, hardly able to believe the tale.

' As true as you please,' he answered. 'If you will take
my advice you will lie quietly here until to-morrow morning, and then go up to the castle. No one will molest you.
The townsfolk will be only too glad to find you alive, and
that they have so much the less to pay for. I should not
wonder if you saved half a dozen necks,' Peter added
regretfully. 'For I hear the Countess is finely mad about
you.'

At this mention of my lady's regard my eyes filled so
that I had much ado to hide my feelings. Affecting to find
the light too strong I turned my back on Peter, and then for
the first time became aware that I had a companion in misfortune. On a heap of straw behind me lay another man,
so bandaged about the head that I could see nothing of his
features.

'Hallo !' I exclaimed, raising myself that I might have
a better view of him. ' Who is this ? '

'Your man Steve,' Peter said briefly. 'But for him and
another, Master Martin, I do not think that you would be
here.'

' You do well to remind me,' I answered, feeling shame
that I had not yet thanked him, or asked how I came to
be in safety. ' How was it ? '

' Well,' he said, ' it began with the girl. The doings on
Wednesday night were not much to my mind, as you may
suppose, and I shut up early and kept myself close. About
seven, when the racket had not yet risen to its height, there
came a knocking at my door. For a while I took no notice
of it, but presently, as it continued, I went to listen, and
heard such a sobbing on the step as the heart of man could
not resist. So I opened and found the Papist girl there
with a child. I do not know,' Peter continued, pushing
forward his greasy old cap and rubbing his head, 'that I

4

should have opened it if I had been sure who it was. But
as the door was open, the girl had to come in.'
'I do not think you will repent it!' I said.
'I don't know that I shall,' he answered thoughtfully.
' However, she had not been long inside and the bolts shot
on us, when there began a most tremendous skirmish in the
lane, which lasted off and on for half an hour. Then followed a sudden silence. I had given the girl some food,
and told her she might sleep with the children upstairs, and
we were sitting before the fire while she cried a bit — she
was all over of a shake, you understand — when on a sudden she stood up, and listened.
' " What is it ? " I said.
' She did not answer for a while, but still stood listening,
looking now at me and now towards the forge in a queer
eager kind of way. I told her to sit down, but she did not
seem to hear, and presently she cried, " There is some one
there ! "
' " Well," said I, " they will stop there then. I don't
open that door again to-night."
' She looked at me pitifully, but sat down for all the
world as if I had struck her. Not for long, however. In a
minute she was up again, and began to go to and fro between the kitchen and the forge door like nothing else but
a cat looking for her kittens. " Sit down, wench," I said.
But this time she took no heed, and at last the sight of her
going up and down like a dumb creature in pain was too
much for me, and I got up and undid the door. She was
out in a minute, seeming not a bit afraid for herself, and
sure enough, there were you and Steve lying one on the
top of the other on the step, and so still that I thought
you gone. Heaven only knows how she heard you.'
' Peter,' I said abruptly, ' have you any water handy ? '
' To be sure,' he replied, starting up. ' Are you thirsty ? '
I nodded, and he went to get it, blaming himself for his
thoughtlessness. He need not have reproached himself,
however. I was not thirsty; but I could not bear that he

should sit and look at me at that moment. The story he
had told had touched me — and I was still weak; and I
could not answer for it, I should not burst into tears like
a woman. The thought of this girl's persistence, who in
everything else was so weak, of her boldness who in her
own defence was a hare, of her strange instinct on our behalf who seemed made only to be herself protected — the
thought of these things touched me to the heart and filled
me with an odd mixture of pity and gratitude! I had gone
to save her, and she had saved me! I had gone to shield
her from harm, and heaven had led me to her door, not in
strength but in weakness. She had fled from me who came
to help her; that when I needed help, she might be at hand
to give it!

'Where is she?' I muttered, when he came back and I
had drunk.

'Who? Marie?' he asked.

'Yes, if that is her name,' I said, drinking again.

'She is lying down upstairs,' he answered. 'She is worn
out, poor child. Not that in one sense, Master Martin,' he
continued, dropping his voice and nodding with a mysterious air, 'she *is* poor. Though you might think it.'

'How do you mean?' I said, raising my head and meeting his eyes. He nodded.

'It is between ourselves,' he said; 'but I am afraid there
is a good deal in what our rascals here say. I am afraid,
to be plain, Master Martin, that the father was like all
his kind: plundered many an honest citizen, and roasted
many a poor farmer before his own fire. It is the way of
soldiers in that army; and God help the country they march
in, be it friend's or foe's!'

'Well?' I said impatiently; 'but what of that now?'
The mention of these things fretted me. I wanted to hear
nothing about the father. 'The man is dead,' I said.

'Ay, he is,' Peter answered slowly and impressively.
'But the daughter? She has got a necklace round her neck
now, worth — worth I dare say two hundred men at arms.'

'What, ducats?'

'Ay, ducats! Gold ducats. It is worth all that.'

'How do you know?' I said, staring at him. 'I have never seen such a thing on her. And I have seen the girl two or three times.'

'Well, I will tell you,' he answered, glancing first at the window and then at Steve to be sure that we were not overheard. 'I'll tell you. When we had carried you into the house the other night she took off her kerchief, to tear a piece from it to bind up your head. That uncovered the necklace. She was quick to cover it up, when she remembered herself, but not quick enough.'

'Is it of gold?' I asked.

He nodded. 'Fifteen or sixteen links I should say, and each as big as a small walnut. Carved and shaped like a walnut too.'

'It may be silver-gilt.'

He laughed. 'I am a smith, though only a locksmith,' he said. 'Trust me for knowing gold. I doubt it came from Magdeburg; I doubt it did. Magdeburg, or Halle, which my Lord Tilly ravaged about that time. And if so there is blood upon it. It will bring the girl no luck, depend upon it.'

'If we talk about it, I'll be sworn it will not!' I answered savagely. 'There are plenty here who would twist her neck for so much as a link of it.'

'You are right, Master Martin,' he answered meekly. 'Perhaps I should not have mentioned it; but I know that you are safe. And after all the girl has done nothing.'

That was true, but it did not content me. I wished he had not seen what he had, or that he had not told me the tale. A minute before I had been able to think of the girl with pure satisfaction; to picture with a pleasant warmth about my heart her gentleness, her courage, her dark mild beauty that belonged as much to childhood as womanhood, the thought for others that made her flight a perpetual saving. But this spoiled all. The mere possession of this

. she came presently to me with a bowl of broth in her
hands and a timid smile on her lips .   .   .

necklace, much more the use of it, seemed to sully her in
my eyes, to taint her freshness, to steal the perfume from
her youth.

For I am peasant born, of those on whom the free-com-
panions have battened from the beginning; and spoil won
in such a way seemed to me to be accursed. Whether I
would or no, horrid tales of the storming of Magdeburg
came into my mind: tales of streets awash with blood, of
churches blocked with slain, of women lying dead with living babes in their arms. And I shuddered. I felt the
necklace a blot on all. I shrank from one, who, with the
face of a saint, wore under her kerchief gold dyed in such
a fashion!

That was while I lay alone, tossing from side to side,
and troubling myself unreasonably about the matter; since
the girl was nothing to me, and a Papist. But when she
came presently to me with a bowl of broth in her hands and
a timid smile on her lips — a smile which gave the lie to
the sadness of her eyes and the red rims that surrounded
them — I forgot all, necklace and creed. I took the bowl
silently, as she gave it. I gave it back with only one
'Thank you,' which sounded hoarse and rustic in my
ears; but I suppose my eyes were more eloquent, for she
blushed and trembled. And in the evening she did not
come. Instead one of the children brought my supper, and
sitting down on the straw beside me, twittered of Marie
and 'Go' and other things.

'Who is Go?' I said.

'Go is Marie's brother,' the child answered, open-eyed at
my ignorance. 'You not know Go?'

'It is a strange name,' I said, striving to excuse myself.

'*He* is a strange man,' the little one retorted, pointing to
Steve. 'He does not speak. Now you speak. Marie says —'

'What does Marie say?' I asked.

'Marie says you saved his life.'

'Well, you can tell her it was the other way,' I exclaimed
roughly.

Twice that night when I awoke I heard a light footstep, and turned to see the girl, moving to and fro among the rusty locks and ancient chests in attendance on Steve. He mended but slowly. She did not come near me at these times, and after a glance I pretended to fall asleep that I might listen unnoticed to her movements, and she be more free to do her will. But whenever I heard her and opened my eyes to see her slender figure moving in that dingy place, I felt the warmth about my heart again. I forgot the gold necklace; I thought no more of the rosary, only of the girl. For what is there which so well becomes a woman as tending the sick; an office which in a lover's eyes should set off his mistress beyond velvet and Flanders lace.

CHAPTER VI.

RUPERT THE GREAT.

I HAVE known a man very strong and very confident, whom the muzzle of a loaded pistol, set fairly against his head, has reduced to reason marvellously. So it fared with Heritzburg on this occasion. My lady's cannon, which I went up to the roof at daybreak to see — and did see, to my great astonishment, trained one on the Market Square, and one down the High Street — formed the pistol, under the cooling influence of which the town had so far come to its senses, that the game was now in my lady's hands. Peter assured me that the place was in a panic, that the Countess could hardly ask any amends that would not be made, and that as a preliminary the Burgomaster and Minister were to go to the castle before noon to sue for pardon. He suggested that I and the girl should accompany them.

'But does Hofman know that we are here?' I asked.

'Since yesterday morning,' the locksmith answered, with a grin. 'And no one more pleased to hear it! If he had

not you to present as a peace-offering, I doubt he would
have fled the town before he would have gone up. As it is,
they had fine work with him at the town-council yesterday.'

'He is in a panic ? Serve him right !' I said.

'I am told that his cheeks shake like jelly,' Peter
answered.

'Two of the Waldgrave's men are dead, you know, and
some say that the Countess will hang him out of hand.
But you will go up with him ? '

'Yes,' I said. 'I see no objection.'

Some one else objected, however. When the plan was
broached to the girl, she looked troubled. For a moment
she did not speak, but stood before us silent and confused.
Then she pointed to Steve.

'When is he going, if you please ? ' she asked, in a
troubled voice.

' He must go in a litter by the road,' I answered. ' Peter
here will see to it this morning.'

' Could I not go with him ? ' she said.

I looked at Peter, and he at me. He nodded.

' I see no reason why you should not, if you prefer it,' I
said. 'Either way you will be safe.'

'I should prefer it,' she muttered, in a low tone. And
then she went out to get something for Steve, and we saw
her no more.

'Drunken Steve is in luck,' Peter said, looking after her
with a smile. ' She is wonderfully taken with him. She is
a — she is a good girl, Papist or no Papist,' he added
thoughtfully.

I am not sure that he would have indorsed that later in
the day. At the last moment, when I was about to leave
the house to go up to the castle my way, and Steve and his
party were on the point of starting by the West Gate and
the road, something happened which gave both of us a kind
of shock, though neither said a word to the other. Marie
had brought down the little boy, a brave-eyed, fair-haired
child about three years old, and she was standing with us in

the forge waiting with the child clinging to her skirt, when on a sudden she turned to Peter and began to thank him. A word and she broke down.

'Pooh, child!' Peter said kindly, patting her on the shoulder. 'It was little enough, and I am glad I did it. No thanks.'

She answered between her sobs that it was beyond thanks, and called on Heaven to reward him.

'If I had anything,' she continued, looking at him timidly, 'if I had anything I could give you to prove my gratitude, I would so gladly give it. But I am alone, and I have nothing worth your acceptance. I have nothing in the world, unless,' she added with an effort, 'you would like my rosary.'

'No,' Peter said almost roughly. I noticed that he avoided my eye. 'I do not want it. It is not a thing I use.'

She said she had nothing; and we knew she had that chain! Yet Heaven knows her face as she said it was fair enough to convert a Beza! She said she had nothing; we knew she had. Yet if ever genuine gratitude and thankfulness seemed to shine out of wet human eyes, they shone out of hers then.

What I could not stomach was the ingratitude. The fraud was too gross, too gratuitous, since she need have offered nothing. I turned away and went out of the forge without waiting for her to recover herself. I dreaded lest she should thank me in the same way.

I knew Peter, and knew he could have no motive for traducing her. He was old enough to be her grandfather, and a quiet good man. Therefore I was sure that she had the chain, three or four links of which should be worth his shop of old iron.

But besides I had the evidence of my own eyes. There was a crinkle, a crease in her kerchief, for which the presence of the necklace would account; it was such a crease as a necklace of that size would cause. I had marked it when she brought the child into the room in her arms. The boy's right arm had been round her neck, and I had seen him relax his hold of her hair and steady himself by placing his little palm on that wrinkle, as on a sure and certain and familiar stay. So I knew that she had the necklace, and that she had lied about it.

But after all it was nothing to me. The girl was a Papist, a Bavarian, the daughter of a roistering freebooting rider, versed in camp life. If with a fair outside she proved to be at heart what every reasonable man would expect to find her, what then? I had no need to trouble my head. I had affairs enough of my own on my hands.

Yet the affair did trouble me. The false innocence of the child's face haunted and perplexed me, and would not leave me, though I tried to think of other things and had other things to think of. I was to meet the Burgomaster in the market-place, and go thence with him, and I had promised myself that I would make good use of my opportunities; that I would lose no point of the town's behaviour, that not a lowering face should escape me, nor a quarter whence danger might arise in the future. But the girl's eyes made havoc of all my resolutions, and I had fairly reached the market-place before I remembered what I was doing.

There indeed a sight, which in a moment swept the cobwebs from my brain, awaited me. The square was full of people, not closely packed, but standing in loose groups, and all talking in voices so low as to produce a dull sullen sound more striking than silence. The Mayor and four or five Councillors occupied the steps of the market-house. Raised a head and shoulders above the throng, and glancing at it askance from time to time with scarcely disguised apprehension, they wore an air of irresolution it was impossible to mistake. Hofman in particular looked like a man with the rope already round his neck. His face was pale, his fat cheeks hung pendulous, his eyes never rested on anything for more than a second. They presently lit on

me, and then if farther proof of the state of his mind was
needed, I found it in the relief with which he hailed my
appearance; relief, not the less genuine because he hastened to veil it from the jealous eyes that from every part
of the square watched his proceedings.

The crowd made way for me silently.   One in every two,
perhaps, greeted me, and some who did not greet me, smiled
at me fatuously.   On the other hand, 1 was struck by the
air of gloomy expectation which prevailed.   I discerned
that a very little would turn it into desperation, and saw,
or thought I saw, that cannon, or no cannon, this was a
case for delicate and skilful handling.   The town was panic-
stricken, partly at the thought of what it had done, partly
at the sight of the danger which threatened it.   But panic is
a double-edged weapon.   It takes little to turn it into fury.

I made for the opening into the High Street, and the
Burgomaster, coming down the steps, passed through the
crowd and met me there.

'This is a bad business, Master Martin,' he said, facing
me with an odd mixture of shamefacedness and bravado.
'We must do our best to patch it up.'

'You had your warning,' I answered coldly, turning with
him up the street, every window and doorway in which had
its occupant.   Dietz and two or three Councillors followed
us, the Minister's face looking flushed and angry, and as
spiteful as a cat's.   'Two lives have been lost,' I continued, 'and some one must pay for them.'

Hofman mopped his face.   'Surely,' he said, 'the three
dead on our side, Master Martin——'

'I do not see what they have to do with it,' I answered,
maintaining a cold and uninterested air, which was torture
to him.   'It is your affair, however, not mine.'

'But, my dear friend — Martin,' he stammered, plucking
my sleeve, 'you are not revengeful.   You will not make it
worse?   You won't do that?'

'Worse?' I retorted.   'It is bad enough already.   And
I am afraid you will find it so.'

He winced and looked at me askance, his eyes rolling in a fever of apprehension. For a moment I really thought that he would turn and go back. But the crowd was behind; he was on the horns of a dilemma, and with a groan of misery he moved on, looking from time to time at the terrace above us. 'Those cursed cannon,' I heard him mutter, as he wiped his brow.

'Ay,' I said, sharply, 'if it had not been for the cannon you would have seen our throats cut before you would have moved. I quite understand that. But you see it is our turn now.'

We were on the steps and he did not answer. I looked up, expecting to see the wall by the wicket-gate well-manned; but I was mistaken. No row of faces looked down from it. All was silent. A single man, on guard at the wicket, alone appeared. He bade us stand, and passed the word to another. He in his turn disappeared and presently old Jacob, with a half-pike on his shoulder, and a couple of men at his back, came stiffly out to receive us with all the formality and discipline of a garrison in time of war. He acknowledged my presence by a wink, but saluted my companions in the coldest manner possible, proceeding at once to march us without a word spoken to the door of the house, where we were again bidden to stand.

All this filled me with satisfaction. I knew what effect it would have on Hofman, and how it would send his soul into his shoes. At the same time my satisfaction was not unmixed. I felt a degree of strangeness myself. The place seemed changed, the men, moving stiffly, had an unfamiliar air. I missed the respect I had enjoyed in the house. For the moment I was nobody; a prisoner, an alien person admitted grudgingly, and on sufferance.

I comforted myself with the reflection that all would be well when I reached the presence. But I was mistaken. I saw indeed my lady's colour come and go when I entered, and her eyes fell. But she kept her seat, she looked no more at me than at my companions, she uttered no greeting

or word of acknowledgment. It was the Waldgrave who
spoke — the Waldgrave who acted. In a second there
came over me a bitter feeling that all was changed; that
the old state of things at Heritzburg was past, and a rule to
which I was a stranger set in its place.

Three or four of my lady's women were grouped behind
her, while Franz and Ernst stood like statues at the farther
door. Fraulein Anna sat on a stool in the window-bay,
and my lady's own presence was, as at all times, marked
by a stateliness and dignity which seemed to render
it impossible that she should pass for second in any company. But for all that the Waldgrave, standing up straight
and tall behind her, with his comeliness, his youth, and his
manhood and the red light from the coat of arms in the
stained window just touching his fair hair, did seem to me
to efface her. It was he who stood there to pardon or
punish, praise or blame, and not my lady. And I resented
it.

Not that his first words to me were not words of
kindness.

'Ha, Martin,' he cried, his face lighting up, 'I hear you
fought like an ancient Trojan, and broke as many heads as
Hector. And that your own proved too hard for them !
Welcome back. In a moment I may want a word with
you ; but you must wait.'

I stood aside, obeying his gesture ; and he apologised,
but with a very stern aspect, to Hofman and his companions for addressing me first.

'The Countess Rotha, however, Master Burgomaster,' he
continued, with grim suavity, 'much as she desires to treat
your office with respect, cannot but discern between the
innocent and the guilty.'

'The guilty, my lord?' Hofman cried, in such a hurry
and trepidation, I could have laughed. 'I trust that there
are none here.'

'At any rate you represent them,' the Waldgrave
retorted,

'I, my lord?' The Mayor's hair almost stood on end at the thought.

'Ay, you; or why are you here?' the Waldgrave answered. 'I understood that you came to offer such amends as the town can make, and your lady accept.'

Poor Hofman's jaw fell at this statement of his position, and he stood the picture of dismay and misery. The Waldgrave's peremptory manner, which shook him out of the rut of his slow wits, and upset his balanced periods, left him prostrate without a word to say. He gasped and remained silent. He was one of those people whose dull self-importance is always thrusting them into positions which they are not intended to fill.

'Well?' the Waldgrave said, after a pause, 'as you seem to have nothing to say, and judgment must ultimately come from your lady, I will proceed at once to declare it. And firstly, it is her will, Master Burgomaster, that within forty-eight hours you present to her on behalf of the town a humble petition and apology, acknowledging your fault; and that the same be entered on the town records.'

'It shall be done,' Master Hofman cried. His eagerness to assent was laughable.

'Secondly, that you pay a fine of a hundred gold ducats for the benefit of the children of the men wantonly killed in the riot.'

'It shall be done,' Master Hofman said, — but this time not so readily.

'And lastly,' the Waldgrave continued in a very clear voice, 'that you deliver up for execution two in the market-place, one at the foot of the castle steps, and one at the West Gate, for a warning to all who may be disposed to offend again — four of the principal offenders in the late riot.'

'My lord!' the Mayor cried, aghast.

'My lord, if you please,' the Waldgrave answered coldly. 'But do you consent?'

Hofman looked blanker than ever. 'Four?' he stammered.

'Precisely ; four,' the young lord answered.

'But who ? I do not know them,' the Mayor faltered.

The Waldgrave shook his head gently. 'That is your concern, Burgomaster,' he said, with a smile. 'In forty-eight hours much may be done.'

Hofman's hair stood fairly on end. Craven as he was, the thought of the crowd in the market-place, the thought of the reception he would have, if he assented to such terms, gave him courage.

'I will consult with my colleagues,' he said with a great gulp.

'I am afraid that you will not have the opportunity,' the Waldgrave rejoined, in a peculiarly suave tone. 'Until the four are given up to us, we prefer to take care of you and the learned Minister. I see that you have brought two or three friends with you ; they will serve to convey what has passed to the town. And I doubt not that within a few hours we shall be able to release you.'

Master Hofman fell a trembling.

'My lord,' he cried, between tears and rage, 'my privileges !'

'Master Mayor,' the Waldgrave answered, with a sudden snap and snarl, which showed his strong white teeth, '*my dead servants.*'

After that there was no more to be said. The Burgomaster shrank back with a white face, and though Dietz, with rage burning in his sallow cheeks, cried 'woe to him' who separated the shepherd from the sheep, and would have added half-a-dozen like texts, old Jacob cut him short by dropping his halberd on his toes and promptly removed him and the quavering Burgomaster to strong quarters in the tower. Meanwhile the other members of the party were marched nothing loth to the steps, and despatched through the gate with the same formality which had surprised us on our arrival.

Then for a few moments I was happy, in spite of doubts and forebodings ; for the moment the room was cleared of servants, my lady came down from her place, and with tears in her eyes, laid her hand on my rough shoulder, and thanked me, saying such things to me, and so sweetly, that though many a silken fool has laughed at me, as a clown knowing no knee service, I knelt there and then before her, and rose tenfold more her servant than before. For of this I am sure, that if the great knew their power, we should hear no more of peasants' wars and Rainbow banners. A smile buys for them what gold will not for another. A word from their lips stands guerdon for a life, and a look for the service of the heart.

However, few die of happiness, and almost before I was off my knees I found a little bitter in the cup.

'Well, well,' the Waldgrave said, with a comical laugh, and I saw my lady blush, 'these are fine doings. But next time you go to battle, Martin, remember, more haste less speed. Where would you have been now, I should like to know, without my cannon?'

'Perhaps still in Peter's forge,' I answered bluntly. 'But that puzzles me less, my lord,' I continued, 'than where you found your cannon.'

He laughed in high good humour. 'So you are bit, are you?' he said. 'I warrant you thought we could do nothing without you. But the cannon, where do you think we did find them? You should know your own house.'

'I know of none here,' I answered slowly, 'except the old cracked pieces the Landgrave Philip left.'

'Well?' he retorted, smiling. 'And what if these be they?'

'But they are cracked and foundered!' I cried warmly. 'You could no more fire powder in them, my lord, than in the Countess's comfit-box!'

'But if you do not want to burn powder?' he replied. 'If the sight of the muzzles be enough? What then, Master Wiseacre?'

'Why, then, my lord,' I answered, drily, after a pause of astonishment, 'I think that the game is a risky one.'

'Chut, you are jealous!' he said, laughing.

'And should be played very moderately.'

'Chut,' he said again, 'you are jealous! Is he not, Rotha? He is jealous.'

My lady looked at me laughing.

'I think he is a little,' she said. 'You must acknowl-edge, Martin,' she continued, pleasantly, 'that the Wald-grave has managed very well?'

I must have assented, however loth; but he saved me the trouble. He did not want to hear my opinion.

'Very well?' he exclaimed, with a laugh of pleasure; 'I should think I have. Why, I have so brightened up your old serving-men that they make quite a tolerable garrison — mount guard, relieve, give the word and all, like so many Swedes. Oh, I can tell you a little briskness and a few new fashions do no harm. But now,' he continued, com-placently, 'since you are so clever, my friend, where is the risk?'

'If it becomes known in the town,' I said, 'that the can-non are dummies ——'

'It is not known,' he answered peremptorily.

'Still, under the circumstances,' I persisted, 'I should with submission have imposed terms less stringent. Espe-cially I should not have detained Master Hofman, my lord, who is a timid man, making for peace. He has influence. Shut up here he cannot use it.'

'But our terms will show that we are not afraid,' the Waldgrave answered. 'And that is everything.'

I shrugged my shoulders.

'Chut!' he said, half in annoyance and half in good humour. 'Depend upon it, there is nothing like putting a bold face on things. That is my policy. But the truth is you are jealous, my friend — jealous of my excellent generalship; but for which I verily believe you would be decorating a gallows in the market-place at this moment. Come, fair cousin,' he added, gleefully, turning from me and snatching up my lady's gloves and handing them to her, 'let us out. Let us go and look down at our conquest, and leave this green-eyed fellow to rub his bruises.'

My lady looked at me kindly and laughed. Still she assented, and my chance was gone. It was my place now to hold the door with lowered head, not to argue. And I did so. After all I had been well treated; I had spoken boldly and been heard.

For a time after the sound of their voices had died away on the stairs, I stood still. The room was quiet and I felt blank and purposeless. In the first moments of return every-day duties had an air of dulness and staleness. I thought of one after another, but had not yet brought myself to the point of moving, when a hand, raising the latch of one of the inner doors, effectually roused me. I turned and saw Fraulein Anna gliding in. She did not speak at once, but came towards me as she had a way of coming — close up before she spoke. It had more than once disturbed me. It did so now.

'Well, Master Martin,' she said at last, in her mild spiteful tone, 'I hope you are satisfied with your work; I hope my lord's service may suit you as well as my lady's.'

CHAPTER VII.

THE PRIDE OF YOUTH.

BUT I am not going to relate the talk we had on that, Fraulein Anna and I. I learned one thing, and one only, and that I can put very shortly. I saw my face as it were in a glass, and I was not pleased with the reflection. Listening to Fraulein Anna's biting hints and sidelong speeches — she did not spare them — I recognized that I was jealous; that the ascendency the young lord had gained with my lady and in the castle did not please me; and that if I would not make a fool of myself and step out of my place, I must take myself roundly to task. Much might be forgiven to Fraulein Anna, who saw the quiet realm wherein she reigned invaded, and the friend she had gained won from her in an hour. But her case differed from mine. I was a servant, and woe to me if I forgot my place!

Perhaps, also, it gave me pleasure to find my uneasiness shared. At any rate, I felt better afterwards, and a message from my lady, bidding me rest my head and do nothing for the day, comforted me still further. I went out, and finding the terrace quiet, and deserted by all except the sentry at the wicket, I sat down on one of the stone seats which overlook the town and there began to think. The sun was behind a cloud and the air was fresh and cool, and I presently fell asleep with my head on my arms.

While I slept my lady and the Waldgrave came and began to walk up and down the terrace, and gradually little bits of their talk slid into my dreams, until I found myself listening to them between sleeping and waking. The Waldgrave was doing most of the speaking, in the boyish, confident tone which became him so well. Presently I heard him say —

'The whole art of war is changed, fair cousin. I had it from one who knows, Bernard of Weimar. The heavy battalions, the great masses, the slow movements, the system invented by the great Captain of Cordova are gone. Breitenfeld was their death-blow.'

'Yet my uncle was a great commander,' my lady said, with a little touch of impatience in her tone.

'Of the old school.'

I heard her laugh. 'You speak as if you had been a soldier for a score of years, Rupert,' she said.

'Age is not experience,' he answered hardily. 'That is the mistake. How old was Alexander when he conquered Egypt? Twenty-three, cousin, and I am twenty-three. How old was the Emperor Augustus when he became Consul of Rome? Nineteen. How old was Henry of

England when he conquered France? Twenty-seven.
And Charles the Fifth at Pavia? Twenty-five.'
'Sceptres are easy leading-staves,' my lady answered
deftly. 'All these were kings, or the like.'
'Then take Don John at Lepanto. He, too, was twenty-
five.'
'A king's son,' my lady replied quickly.
'Then I will give you one to whom you can make no
objection,' he answered in a tone of triumph: 'Gaston de
Foix, the Thunderbolt of Italy. He who conquered at
Como, at Milan, at Ravenna. How old was he when he
died, leaving a name never to be forgotten in arms?
Twenty-three, fair cousin. And I am twenty-three.'
'But then you are not Gaston de Foix,' my lady retorted,
laughter bubbling to her lips; 'nor a king's nephew.'
'But I may be.'
'What? A king's nephew?' the Countess answered,
laughing outright. 'Pray where is the king's niece?'
'King's niece?' he exclaimed reproachfully — and I
doubt not with a kind look at her, and a movement as if
he would have paid her for her sauciness. 'You know I
want no king's niece. There is no king's niece in the
world so sweet to my taste, so fair, or so gracious as
the cousin I have been fortunate enough to serve during
. the last few days; and that I will maintain against the
world.'
'So here is my glove!' my lady answered gaily, finish-
ing the speech for him. 'Very prettily said, Rupert. I
make you a thousand curtsies. But a truce to compliments.
Tell me more.'
He needed no second bidding; though I think that she
would have listened without displeasure to another pretty
speech, and an older man would certainly have made one.
But he was full of the future and fame — and himself. He
had never had such a listener before, and he poured forth
his hopes and aspirations, as he strode up and down, so
gallant of figure and frank of face that it was impossible

not to feel with him. He was going to do this; he was
going to do that. He would make the name of Rupert of
Weimar stand with that of Bernard. Never was such a
time for enterprise. Gustavus Adolphus, with Sweden and
North Germany at his back, was at Munich; Bavaria,
Franconia, and the Rhine Bishoprics were at his feet.
The hereditary dominions of the Empire, Austria, Silesia,
Moravia, with Bohemia, Hungary, and the Tyrol, must
soon be his; their conquest was certain. Then would
come the division of the spoil. The House of Weimar,
which had suffered more in the Protestant cause than any
other princely house of Germany, which had resigned for
its sake the Electoral throne and the rights of primogeni-
ture, must stand foremost for reward.

'And which kingdom shall you choose?' my lady asked,
with a twinkle in her eye which belied her gravity.
'Bohemia or Hungary? or Bavaria? Munich I am told is
a pleasant capital.'

'You are laughing at me!' he said, a little hurt.

'Forgive me,' she said, changing her tone so prettily that
he was appeased on the instant. 'But, speaking soberly,
are you not curing the skin before the bear is dead? The
great Wallenstein is said to be collecting an army in
Bohemia, and if the latest rumour is to be believed, he has
already driven out the Saxons and retaken Prague. The
tide of conquest seems already to be turning.'

'We shall see,' the Waldgrave answered.

'Very well,' my lady replied. 'But, besides, is there
not a proverb about the lion's share? Will the Lion of the
North forego his?'

'We shall make him,' the young lord answered. 'He
goes as far as we wish and no farther. Without German
allies he could not maintain his footing for a month.'

'Germany should blush to need his help,' my lady said
warmly.

'Never mind. Better times are coming,' he answered.
'And soon, I hope.'

With that they moved out of hearing, crossing to the other side of the court and beginning to walk up and down there; and I heard no more. But I had heard enough to enable me to arrive at two or three conclusions. For one thing, I felt jealous no longer. My lady's tone when she spoke to the Waldgrave convinced me that whatever the future might bring forth, she regarded him in the present with liking, and some pride perhaps, but with no love worthy of the name. A woman, she took pleasure in his handsome looks and gallant bearing; she was fond of listening to his aspirations. But the former pleased her eye without touching her heart, and the latter never for a moment carried her away.

I was glad to be sure of this, because I discerned something lacking on his side also. It was 'Rotha,' 'sweet cousin,' 'fair cousin,' too soon with him. He felt no reverence, suffered no pangs, trembled under no misgivings, sank under no sense of unworthiness. He thought that all was to be had for pleasant words and the asking. Heritzburg seemed a rustic place to him, and my lady's life so dull and uneventful, my lady herself so little of a goddess, that he deemed himself above all risk of refusal. A little difficulty, a little doubt, the appearance of a rival, might awaken real love. But it was not in him now. He felt only a passing fancy, the light offspring of propinquity and youth.

But how, it may be asked, was I so wise that, from a few sentences heard between sleeping and waking, I could gather all this, and draw as many inferences from a laugh as Fraulein Anna Max from a page of crabbed Latin? The question put to me then, as I sat day-dreaming over Heritzburg, might have posed me. I am clear enough about it now. I could answer it if I chose. But a nod is as good as a wink to a blind horse, and a horse with eyes needs neither one nor the other.

Presently I saw Fraulein Anna come out and go sliding along one side of the court to gain another door. She had a great book under her arm and blinked like an owl in the

sunshine, and would have run against my lady if the Waldgrave had not called out good-humouredly. She shot away
at that with a show of excessive haste, and was in the act
of disappearing like a near-sighted rabbit, when my lady
called to her pleasantly to come back.

She came slowly, hugging the great book, and with her
lips pursed tightly. I fancy she had been sitting at a
window watching my lady and her companion, and that
every laugh which rose to her ears, every merry word,
nay the very sunshine in which they walked, while she sat
in the dull room with her unread book before her, wounded
her.

'What have you been doing, Anna?' my lady asked
kindly.

'I have been reading the "Praise of Folly,"' Fraulein
Max answered primly. 'I am going to my Voetius now.'

'It is such a fine day,' my lady pleaded.

'I never miss my Voetius,' Fraulein answered.

The Waldgrave looked at her quizzically, with scarcely
veiled contempt. 'Voetius?' he said. 'What is that?
You excite my curiosity.'

Perhaps it was the contrast between them, between his
strength and comeliness and her weak figure and pale
frowning face, that moved me; but I know that as he said
that, I felt a sudden pity for her. And she, I think, for
herself. She reddened and looked down and seemed to go
smaller. Scholarship is a fine thing; I have heard Fraulein Anna herself say that knowledge is power. But I
never yet saw a bookworm that did not pale his fires before
a soldier of fortune, nor a scholar that did not follow the
courtier and the ruffler with eyes of envy.

Perhaps my lady felt as I did, for she came to the
rescue. 'You are too bad,' she said. 'Anna is my friend,
and I will not have her teased. As for Voetius, he is a
writer of learning, and you would know more about many
things, if you could read his works, sir.'

'Do you read them?' he asked.

'I do!' she answered.

'Good heavens!' he exclaimed, staring at her freely and affecting to be astonished. 'Well, all I can say is that you do not look like it!'

My lady fired up at that. I think she felt for her friend. 'I do not thank you,' she said sharply. 'A truce to such compliments, if you please. Anna,' she continued, 'have you been to see this poor girl from the town?'

'No,' Fraulein Max answered.

'She has come, has she not?'

'And gone — to the stables!' And Fraulein Anna laughed spitefully. 'She is used to camp life, I suppose, and prefers them.'

'But that is not right,' my lady said, with a look of annoyance. She turned and called to me. 'Martin,' she said, 'come here. This girl — the papist from the town — why has she not been brought to the women's quarters in the house?'

I answered that I did not know; that she should have been.

'We will go and see,' my lady answered, nodding her head in a way that promised trouble should any one be found in fault. And without a moment's hesitation she led the way to the inner court, the Waldgrave walking beside her, and Fraulein Anna following a pace or two behind. The latter still hugged her book, and her face wore a look of secret anticipation. I took on myself to go too, and followed at a respectful distance, my mind in a ferment.

The stable court at Heritzburg is small. The rays of the sun even at noon scarcely warm it, and a shadow seemed to fall on our party as we entered. Two grooms, not on guard, were going about their ordinary duties. They started on seeing my lady, who seldom entered that part without notice; and hastened to do reverence to her.

'Where is the girl who was brought here from the town?' she said, in a peremptory tone.

The men looked at one another, scared by her presence, yet not knowing what was amiss. Then one said, 'Please your excellency, she is in the room over the granary.'

'She should be in the house, not here,' my lady answered harshly. 'Take me to her.'

The man stared, and the Waldgrave, seeing his look of astonishment, interposed, murmuring that perhaps the place was scarcely fit.

'For me?' my lady said, cutting him short, with a high look which reminded me of her uncle, Count Tilly. 'You forget, sir cousin, that I am not a woman only, but mistress here. Ignorance, which may be seemly in a woman, does not become me. Lead on, my man.'

The fellow led the way up a flight of outside steps which gave access to the upper granary floor; and my lady followed, rejecting the Waldgrave's hand and gazing with an unmoved eye at the unfenced edge on her left; for the stairs had no rail. At the top the groom opened the door and squeezed himself aside, and my lady entered. The Waldgrave had given place to Fraulein Anna — whom desire to see what would happen had blinded to the risks of the stairs — and she was not slow to follow. The young lord and I pressed in a pace behind.

'This is not a fit place for a maiden!' I heard my lady say severely; and then she stopped. That was before I could see inside, the sudden pause coming as I entered. The loft was dark, the unglazed windows being shuttered; but my eyes are good, and I knew the place, and saw at once — what my lady had seen, I think, at a second glance only — that the man beside whom the girl was kneeling — or had been kneeling, for as I entered she rose to her feet with a word of alarm — was bandaged from his chin to his crown, was helpless and maundering, talking strange nonsense, and rolling his head restlessly from side to side.

'Why, you are a child!' my lady said; and this time her voice was soft and low and full of surprise. 'Who is this?'

she continued, pointing to the man; who never ceased to babble and move.

'It is Steve, my lady,' I said. 'He was hurt below, in the town, and the girl has been nursing him. I suppose she — I think no one told her to go elsewhere,' I added by way of apology for her.

'Where could she be better?' my lady said in a low voice. 'Child,' she continued gently, 'come here. Do not be afraid.'

The girl had shrunk back at the sound of my lady's first words, or at sight of so large a company, and had taken her stand on the farther side of Steve, where she crouched trembling and looking at us with a terrified face. Hearing herself summoned, she came slowly and timidly forward, the little boy who had run to her holding her hand, and hiding his face in her skirts.

'I am the countess,' my lady said, looking at her closely, but with kindness, 'and I have come to see how you fare.'

It was a hard moment for the girl, but she did the very best thing she could have done, and one that commended her to my lady's heart for ever. For, bursting into tears — I doubt not the sound of a woman's voice speaking mildly to her touched her heart — she dropped on her knees before the countess and kissed her hand, sobbing piteous words of thankfulness and appeal.

'Chut! chut!' my lady said, a little tremor in her own voice. 'You are safe now. Be comforted. You shall be protected here, whatever betide. But you have lost your father? Yes, I remember, child. Well, it is over now. You are quite safe. See, this gentleman shall be your champion. And Martin there. He is a match for any two. Tell me your name.'

'Marie — Marie Wort.' The girl answered suppressing her tears with an effort.

'How old are you?'

'Seventeen, please your excellency.'

'And where were you born, Marie?'

'At Munich, in Bavaria.'

'You are a Romanist, I hear?'

'If it please your excellency.'

'It does not please me at all,' my lady answered promptly; but she said it with so much mildness that Marie's eyes filled again. 'I warn you, we shall try to convert you — by kindness. So you are nursing this poor fellow?' And my lady went up to Steve, and touched his hand and spoke to him. But he did not know her, and she stepped back, looking grave.

'The fever is on him now,' Marie said timidly. 'He is at his worst; but he will be better by-and-by, if your excellency pleases.'

'He is fortunate in his nurse,' my lady answered, gazing searchingly at the other's pale face. 'Will you stay with him, child, or would you rather come into the house, where my women could take care of you, and you would be more comfortable?'

A look of distress flickered in the girl's eyes. She hesitated and looked down, colouring painfully. I dare say that with feminine tact she knew that my lady even now thought it scarcely proper for her to be there — in a house where only the men about the stable lived. But she found her answer.

'He was hurt trying to protect me,' she murmured, in a low voice.

My lady nodded. 'Very well,' she said; and I saw that she was not displeased. 'You shall stay with him. I will see that you are taken care of. Come, Rupert, I think we have seen enough.'

She signed to us to go before her, and we all went out, and she closed the door. At the head of the steps, when the Waldgrave offered her his hand, she waved it away, and stood.

'Bring me a hammer and a nail,' she cried.

Three or four men, nearly half our garrison, had collected below, hearing where we were. One of these ran

. . . with her own hands she drove the nail. . . Then
she turned . . .

and fetched what she called for; while we all waited and wondered what she meant. I took the hammer and nail from the man and went up again with them.

'Give me my glove,' she said, turning abruptly to the Waldgrave.

He had possessed himself of one in the course of the conversation I have partly detailed; and no doubt he did not give it up very willingly. But there was no refusing her under the circumstances.

'Hold it against the door!' she said.

He obeyed, and with her own hands she drove the nail through the glove, pinning it to the middle of the door. Then she turned with a little colour in her face.

'That is my room!' she said, with a ring of menace in her tone. 'Let no one presume to enter it. And have a care, men! Whatever is wanted inside, place at the threshold and begone.'

Then she came down, followed by the Waldgrave, and walked through the middle of us and went back to the terrace, with Fraulein Anna at her heels. The Waldgrave lingered a moment to look at a sick horse, and I to give an order. When we reached the terrace court a few minutes later, we found my lady walking up and down alone in the sunshine.

'Why, where is the learned Anna?' the Waldgrave said.

'She is gone to amuse·herself,' my lady answered, laughing. 'Voetius is put aside for the moment in favour of Master Dietz!'

'No?' the young lord exclaimed, in a tone of surprise. 'That yellow-faced atomy? She is not in love with him?'

'No, sir, certainly not.'

'Then what is it?'

'Well, I think she is a little jealous,' my lady answered with a smile. 'We have been so long colloguing with a papist, Anna thinks some amends are due to the Church. And she is gone to make them. At any rate, she asked me a few minutes ago if she might pay a visit to Dietz. "For

what purpose ? " I said. " 'To discuss a point with him,"
she answered. So I told her to go, if she liked, and by this
time I don't doubt that they are hard at it.'
' Over Voetius ? '
' No, sir,' my lady answered gaily. ' Beza more probably,
or Calvin. You know little of either, I expect. I do not
wonder that Anna is driven to seek more improving
company.'

CHAPTER VIII.

A CATASTROPHE.

ALL that day the town remained quiet, and all day the
Waldgrave and my lady walked to and fro in the sunshine;
or my lady sat working on one of the stone seats, while he
built castles in the air, which she knocked down with a sly
word or a merry glance. Fraulein Anna, always with the
big book, flitted from door to door, like an unquiet spirit.
The sentries dozed at their posts, old Jacob in his chair in
the guard-room, the cannons under their breech-clouts. If
this could be said to be a state of siege, it was the most
gentle and joyous one paladin ever shared or mistress
imagined.

But no message reached us from the town, and that disturbed me. Half a dozen times I went to the wall and,
leaning over it, listened. Each time I came away satisfied.
All seemed quiet; the market-place rather fuller perhaps
than on common days, the hum of life more steady and
persistent; but neither to any great extent. Despite this I
could not shake off a feeling of uneasiness. I remembered
certain faces I had seen in the town, grim faces lurking in
corners, seen over men's shoulders or through half-open
doors ; and a dog barking startled me, the shadow of a crow
flying over the court made me jump a yard.

Night only added to my nervousness. I doubled all the
guards, stationing two men at the town-wicket and two at
the stable-gate, which leads to the bridge. And not content with these precautions, though the Waldgrave laughed
at them and me, I got out of bed three times in the night,
and went the round to assure myself that the men were at
their posts.

When morning came without mishap, but also without
bringing any overture from the town, the Waldgrave
laughed still more loudly. But my lady looked grave. I
did not dare to interfere or give advice — having been once
admitted to say my say — but I felt that it would be a
serious thing if the forty-eight hours elapsed and the town
refused to make amends. My lady felt this too, I think;
and by-and-by she held a council with the Waldgrave; and
about midday my lord came to me, and with a somewhat
wry face bade me have the prisoners conducted to the
parlour.

He sent me at the same time on an errand to another
part of the castle, and so I cannot say what passed. I
believe my lady dealt with the two very firmly; reiterat-
ing her judgment of the day before, and only adding that
in clemency she had thought better of imprisoning them,
and would now suffer them to go to their homes, in the
hope that they would use their influence to save the town
from worse trouble.

I met the two crossing the terrace on their way to the
gate and was struck by something peculiar in their aspect.
Master Hofman was all of a tremble with excitement and
eagerness to be gone. His fat, half-moon of a face shone
with anxiety. He stuttered when he tried to give me good
day as I passed; and he seemed to have eyes only for the
gate, dragging his smaller companion along by the arm,
and more than once whispering in his ear as if to adjure
him not to waste a moment.

The little Minister, on the other hand, hung back and
marched slowly, his face wearing a look of triumph which

showed very plainly — or so I construed it — that he regarded his release in the light of a victory. His sallow
cheeks were flushed, and his eyes gleamed spitefully as he
looked from side to side. He held himself bolt upright,
with a square Bible clasped to his breast, and as he passed
me he could not refrain from a characteristic outbreak.
Doubtless to bridle himself before my lady had almost
choked him. He laughed in my face. 'Dry bones!' he
cackled. ' And mouths that speak not!'

'Speak plainly yourself, Master Dietz,' I answered, for I
have never thought ministers more than other men. 'Then
perhaps I shall be able to understand you.'

'Sounding brass and a tinkling cymbal!' he replied,
cracking his fingers in my face and laughing triumphantly.

He would have said more, I imagine; but at that moment
the Burgomaster fell bodily upon him, and drove him by
main force through the gate which had been opened. Outside even, he made some attempts to return and defy us,
crying out 'Whited sepulchres!' and the like. But the
steps were narrow and steep, and Hofman stood like a
feather bed in the way, and presently he desisted. The
two stumbled down together and we saw no more of
them.

The men about me laughed; but I had reason for thinking it far from a laughing matter, and I hastened into the
house that I might tell my lady. When I entered the
parlour, however, where I found her with the Waldgrave
and Fraulein Anna, she held up her hand to check me.
She and the Waldgrave were laughing, and Fraulein Anna,
half shy and half sullen, was leaning against the table
looking at the floor, with her cheeks red.

'Come,' my lady was saying, 'you were with him half
an hour, Anna. You can surely tell us what you talked
about. Don't be afraid of Martin. He knows all our
secrets.'

'Or perhaps we are indiscreet,' the Waldgrave said
gravely, but with a twinkle in his eye. ' When a young

lady visits a gentleman in captivity, the conversation
should be of a tender nature.'
'Which shows, sir, that you know little about it,' Frau-
lein Anna answered indignantly. 'We talked of Voetius.'
'Dear me!' my lord said. 'Then Master Dietz knows
Voetius?'
'He does not. He said he considered such pagan learning
useless,' Fraulein Anna answered, warming with her subject.
'That it tended to pride, and puffed up instead of giving
grace. I said that he only saw one side of the matter.'
'In that resembling me,' my lord murmured.
My lady repressed him with a look. 'Yes,' she said
pleasantly. 'And what then, Anna?'
'And that he might be wrong in this, as in other matters.
He asked me what other matters,' Fraulein Max continued,
growing voluble, and almost confident, as she reviewed the
scene. 'I said, the inferiority of women to men. He said,
yes, he maintained that, following Peter Martyr. Well, I
said he was wrong, and so was Peter Martyr. "But you do
not convince me," he answered. "You say that I am wrong
on this as on other points. Cite a point, then, on which I
am wrong." "You know no Greek, you know no Oriental
tongue, you know no Hebrew!" I retorted. "All pagan
learning," he said. "Cite a point on which I am wrong.
I am not often wrong. Cite a point on which I am con-
fessedly wrong." So' — Fraulein Anna laughed a little,
excited laugh of pleasure — 'I thought I would take him
at his word, and I said, "Will you abide by that? If I
show you that you have been wrong, that you have been
deceived only to-day, will you acknowledge that Peter
Martyr was wrong?" He said, oh yes, he would, if I
could convince him. I said, "Exemplum! You came
here because you were afraid of our cannon. Granted?
Yes. Well, our cannon are cracked. They are *brutum
fulmen* — an empty threat. We could not fire them, if we
would. So there, you see, you were wrong." Well, on
that ——'

But what Master Dietz said on that, and what she
answered, we never knew, for the Waldgrave, bounding
from the table, with a crash which shook the room, swore
a very pagan oath.

'Himmel!' he cried in a voice of passion. 'The woman
has ruined us! Do you understand, Countess? She has
told them! And they have taken the news to the town!'

'I do understand,' my lady said softly, but with a paling
face. 'By this time it is known.'

'Known! Yes; and our shutting up that poisonous
little snake will only make him the more bitter!' my lord
answered, striking the table a great blow in his wrath.
'We are undone! Oh, you idiot, you idiot!' and breaking
off suddenly he turned to Fraulein Max, who stood weeping and trembling by the table. 'Why did you do it?'

'Hush!' my lady said nobly; and she put her arm round
Fraulein Anna. 'She is so absent. It was my fault. I
should not have let her see them. Besides, she did not
know that they were going to be released. And it is done
now, and cannot be undone. The question is, what ought
we to do?'

'Yes, what?' my lord cried bitterly, with a glance at the
culprit, which showed that he was very far from forgiving
her. 'I am sure I do not know, any more than the dog
there!'

My lady looked at me anxiously.

'Well, Martin,' she said, 'what do you say?'

But I had nothing to say, I felt myself at a loss. I
knew, better than any of them, the Minister's sour nature,
and I had seen with my own eyes the state of resentment
and rage in which he had left us. His news would fall
like a spark dropped on powder. The town, brooding in
gloom, foreboding, and terror, would in a moment blaze
into fierce wrath. Every ruffian who had felt his neck
endangered by the Countess's sentence, every family that
had lost a member in the late riot, every one who had an
old grievance to avenge, or a new object to gain, would in

an hour be in arms; while those whose advantage lay commonly on the side of order might stand aloof now — some
at the instance of Dietz, and others through timidity and
that fear of a mob which exists in the mind of every
burgher. What, then, had we to expect? My lady must
look to have her authority flouted — that for certain; but
would the matter end with that? Would the disorder stop
at the foot of the steps?

'I think we are safe enough here, if your excellency asks
me,' I said, after a moment's thought. 'A dozen men could
hold the wicket-gate against a thousand.'

'Safe!' my lady cried in a tone of surprise. 'Yes,
Martin, safe! But what of those who look to me for protection? Am I to stand by and see the law defied? Am
I to——' She paused. 'What is that?' she said in a
different tone, raising her hand for silence.

She listened, and we listened, looking at one another
with meaning eyes; and in a moment she had her answer.
Through the open windows, with the air and sunshine, came
a sound which rose and fell at intervals. It was the noise
of distant cheering. Full and deep, leaping up again and
again, in insolent mockery and defiance, it reached us where
we stood in the quiet room, and told us that all was known.
While we still listened, another sound, nearer at hand,
broke the inner stillness of the house — the tramp of a
hurrying foot on the stairs. Old Jacob thrust in his head
and looked at me.

'You can speak,' I said.

'There is something wrong below,' he muttered, abashed
at finding himself in the presence.

'We know it, Jacob,' my lady said bravely. 'We are
considering how to right it. In the mean time, do you go
to the gates, my friend, and see that they are well
guarded.'

'We could send to Hesse-Cassel,' the Waldgrave suggested, when we were again alone.

'It would be useless,' my lady answered. 'The Land-

6

grave is at Munich with the King of Sweden; so is
Leuchtenstein.'

'If Leuchtenstein were only at home ——'

'Ah!' the Countess answered with a touch of impatience;
'but then he is not. If he were — well, even he could
scarcely make troops where there are none.'

'There are generally some to be hired,' the Waldgrave
answered. 'What if we send to Halle, or Weimar, and
inquire? A couple of hundred pikes would settle the
matter.'

'God forbid!' my lady answered with a shudder. 'I
have heard enough of the doings of such soldiers. The
town has not deserved that.'

The Waldgrave looked at me, and slightly shrugged his
shoulders; as much as to say that my lady was impracti-
cable. But I, agreeing with every word she said, only
loved her the more, and could make him no answer, even if
my duty had permitted it. I hastened to suggest that, the
castle being safe, the better plan was to wait, keeping on
our guard, and see what happened; which, indeed, seemed
also to be the only course open to us.

My lady saw this and agreed; I withdrew, to spend the
rest of the day in a feverish march between the one gate
and the other. We could muster no more than twelve
effective men, including the Waldgrave; and though these
might suffice for the bare defence of the place, which had
only two assailable points, the paucity of our numbers kept
me in perpetual fear. I knew my lady's proud nature so
well that I dreaded humiliation for her as I might have
feared death for another; with a terror which made the
possibility of her capture by the malcontents a misery to
me, a nightmare which would neither let me rest nor
sleep.

My lord soon recovered his spirits. In an hour or two
he was as buoyant and cheerful as before, dividing the
blame of the *contretemps* between Fraulein Anna and myself, and hinting that if he had been left to manage the

matter, the guilty would have suffered, and Dietz not gone
scot-free. But I trembled. I did not see how we could be
surprised ; I thought it improbable that the townsfolk
would try to effect anything against us ; impossible that
they should succeed. Yet, when the stern swell of one of
Luther's hymns rose from the town at sunset, and I remembered how easily men's hearts were inflamed by those
strains ; and again, when a huge bonfire in the market-place
dispelled the night, and for hours kept the town restless
and waking, I shuddered, fearing I knew not what. I will
answer for it, my lady, who never ceased to wear a cheerful countenance, did not sleep that night one half so ill
as I.

And yet I was caught napping. A little before daybreak,
when all was quiet, I went to take an hour's rest. I had
lain down, and, as far as I could judge later, had just fallen
into a doze, when a tremendous shock, which made the very
walls round me tremble, drew me to my feet as if a
giant hand had plucked me from the bed. A crashing
sound, mingled with the shiver of falling glass, filled
the air. For a few seconds I stood trembling and bewildered in the middle of the room — in the state of disorder
natural to a man rudely awakened. I could not on the
instant collect myself or comprehend what had happened.
Then, in a flash, the fears of the day returned to my mind,
and springing to the door, half-dressed as I was, I ran down
to the courtyard.

Some of the servants were already there, a white-
cheeked, panic-stricken group of men and women inter-
mixed ; but, for a moment, I could get no answer to my
questions. All spoke at once, none knew. Then — it was
just growing light — from the direction of the stable-gate a
man came running out of the dusk with a half-pike on his
shoulder.

'Quick !' he cried. 'This way, give me a musket.'

'What is it ? ' I answered, seizing him by the arm.

'They have blown up the bridge — the bridge over the

ravine !' he replied, panting. 'Quick, a gun ! A part is
left, and they are hacking it down !'

In a moment I saw all. 'To your posts !' I shouted.
'And the women into the house! See to the wicket-gate,
Jacob, and do not leave it !' Then I sprang into the guard-
house and snatched down a carbine, three or four of which
hung loaded in the loops. The sentry who had brought
the news seized another, and we ran together through the
stable court and to the gate, four or five of the servants following us.

Elsewhere it was growing light. Here a thick cloud of
smoke and dust still hung in the air, with a stifling reek of
powder. But looking through one of the loopholes in the
gate, I was able to discern that the farther end of the
bridge which spanned the ravine was gone — or gone in
part. The right-hand wall, with three or four feet of the
roadway, still hung in air, but half a dozen men, whose
figures loomed indistinctly through a haze of dust and
gloom, were working at it furiously, demolishing it with
bars and pickaxes.

At that sight I fell into a rage. I saw in a flash what
would happen if the bridge sank and we were cut off from
all exit except through the town-gate. The dastardly nature
of the surprise, too, and the fiendish energy of the men combined to madden me. I gave no warning and cried out no
word, but thrusting my weapon through the loophole aimed
at the nearest worker, and fired.

The man dropped his tool and threw up his arms, staggered forward a couple of paces, and fell sheer over the
broken edge into the gulf. His fellows stood a moment in
terror, looking after him, but the sentry who had warned
me fired through the other loophole, and that started them.
They flung down their tools and bolted like so many rab-
bits. The smoke of the carbine was scarce out of the
muzzle, before the bridge, or what remained of it, was
clear.

I turned round and found the Waldgrave at my elbow.

'Well done!' he said heartily. 'That will teach the rascals a lesson!'

I was trembling in every limb with excitement, but
before I answered him, I handed my gun to one of the men
who had followed me. 'Load,' I said, 'and if a man comes
near the bridge, shoot him down. Keep your eye on the
bridge, and do nothing else until I come back.'

Then I walked away through the stable-court with the
Waldgrave; who looked at me curiously. 'You were only
just in time,' he said.

'Only just,' I muttered.

'There is enough left for a horse to cross.'

'Yes,' I answered, 'to-day.'

'Why to-day?' he asked, still looking at me. I think
he was surprised to see me so much moved.

'Because the rest will be blown up to-night,' I answered
bluntly. 'Or may be. How can we guard it in the dark?
It is fifty paces from the gate. We cannot risk men there
— with our numbers.'

'Still it may not be,' he said. 'We must keep a sharp
look-out.'

'But if it *is*?' I answered, halting suddenly, and looking
him full in the face. 'If it is, my lord?' I continued.
'We are provisioned for a week only. It is not autumn,
you see. Then the pickle tubs would be full, the larder
stocked, the rafters groaning, the still-room supplied. But
it is May, and there is little left. The last three days we
have been thinking of other things than provisions; and we
have thirty mouths to feed.'

The Waldgrave's face fell. 'I had not thought of that,'
he said. 'The bridge gone, they may starve us, you
mean?'

'Into submission to whatever terms they please,' I
answered. 'We are too few to cut our way through the
town, and there would be no other way of escape.'

'What do you advise, then?' he asked, drawing me aside
with a flustered air. 'Flight?'

'A horse might cross the bridge to-day,' I said.

'But any terms would be better than that!' he replied with vehemence.

'What if they demand the expulsion of the Catholic girl, my lord, whom the Countess has taken under her protection?'

'They will not!' he said.

'They may,' I persisted.

'Then we will not give her up.'

'But the alternative — starvation?'

'Pooh! It will not come to that!' he answered lightly. 'You leap before you reach the stile.'

'Because, my lord, there will be no leaping if we do reach it.'

'Nonsense!' he cried masterfully. 'Something must be risked. To give up a strong place like this to a parcel of clodhoppers — it is absurd! At the worst we could parley.'

'I do not think my lady would consent to parley.'

'I shall say nothing to her about it,' he answered. 'She is no judge of such things.'

I had been thinking all the while that he had that in his mind, and on the spot I answered him squarely that I would not consent. 'My lady must know all,' I said, 'and decide for herself.'

He started, looking at me with his face very red. 'Why, man,' he said, 'would you browbeat me?'

'No, my lord,' I said firmly, 'but my lady must know.'

'You are insolent!' he cried, in a passion. 'You forget yourself, man, and that your mistress has placed me in command here!'

'I forget nothing, my lord,' I answered, waxing firmer. 'What I remember is that she is my mistress.'

He glared at me a moment, his face dark with anger, and then with a contemptuous gesture he left me and walked twice or thrice across the court. Doubtless the air did him good, for presently he came back to me. 'You are an ill-

bred meddler !' he said with his head high, 'and I shall remember it. But for the present have your way. I will
tell the Countess and take her opinion.'

He went into the house to do it, and I waited patiently in
the courtyard, watching the sun rise and all the roofs grow
red; listening to the twittering of the birds, and wondering what the answer would be. I had not set myself
against him without misgiving, for in a little while all
might be in his hands. But fear for my mistress out-
weighed fears on my own account; and in the thought of
her shame, should she awake some morning and find herself
trapped, I lost thought of my own interest and advancement.
I have heard it said that he builds best for himself who
builds for another. It was so on this occasion.

He came back presently, looking thoughtful, as if my
lady had talked to him very freely, and shown him a side
of her character that had escaped him. The anger was
clean gone from his face, and he spoke to me without
embarrassment; in apparent forgetfulness that there had
been any difference between us. Nor did I ever find him
bear malice long.

'The Countess decides to go,' he said, 'either to Cassel
or Frankfort, according to the state of the roads. She will
take with her Fraulein Max, her two women, and the
Catholic girl, and as many men as you can horse. She
thinks she may safely leave the castle in charge of old
Jacob and Franz, with a letter directed to the Burgomaster
and council, throwing the responsibility for its custody on
them. When do you think we should start?'

'Soon after dark this evening,' I answered, 'if my lady
pleases.'

' Then that decides it,' he replied carelessly, the dawn of
a new plan and new prospects lighting up his handsome
face. 'See to it, will you?'

CHAPTER IX.

WALNUTS OF GOLD.

NIGHT is like a lady's riding-mask, which gives to the
most familiar features a strange and uncanny aspect.
When to night are added silence and alarm, and that worst
burden of all, responsibility — responsibility where a broken
twig may mean a shot, and a rolling stone capture, where
in a moment the evil is done — then you have a scene and
a time to try the stoutest.

To walk boldly into a wall of darkness, relying on daylight knowledge, which says there is no wall; to step over
the precipice on the faith of its depth being shadow — this
demands nerve in those who are not used to the vagaries of
night. But when the darkness may at any instant belch
forth a sheet of flame; when every bush may hide a
cowardly foe and every turn a pitfall, and there are women
in company and helpless children, then a man had need to
be an old soldier or forest-born, if he would keep his head
cool, and tell one horse from another by the sound of its
hoofs.

We started about eight, and started well. The Waldgrave and half a dozen men crossed first on foot, and took
post to protect the farther end of the bridge. Then I led
over the horses, beginning with the four sumpter beasts.
Satisfied after this that the arch remained uninjured, and
that there was room and to spare, I told my lady, and she
rode over by herself on Pushka. Marie Wort tripped after
her with the child in her arms. Fraulein Max I carried.
My lady's women crossed hand in hand. Then the rest.
So like a troop of ghosts or shadows, with hardly a word
spoken or an order given, we flitted into the darkness, and
met under the trees, where those who had not yet mounted

got to horse. Led by young Jacob, who knew every path in
the valley and could find his way blindfold, we struck away
from the road without delay, and taking lanes and tracks
which ran beside it, presently hit it again a league or more
beyond the town and far on the way.
' That was a ride not to be forgotten. The night was
dark. At a distance the dim lights of the town did not
show. The valley in which we rode, and which grows
straighter as it approaches the mouth and the river, seemed
like a black box without a lid. The wind, laden with
mysterious rustlings and the thousand sad noises of the
night, blew in our faces. Now and then an owl hooted, or
a branch creaked, or a horse stumbled and its rider railed
at it. But for the most part we rode in silence, the women
trembling and crossing themselves — as most of our people
do to this day, when they are frightened — and the men
riding warily, with straining eyes and ears on the stretch.

Before we reached the ford, which lies nearly eight miles
from the castle, the Waldgrave, who had his place beside
my lady, began to talk ; and then, if not before, I knew that
his love for her was a poor thing. For, being in high
spirits at the success of our plan — which he had come to
consider *his* plan — and delighted to find himself again in
the saddle with an adventure before him, he forgot that the
matter must wear a different aspect in her eyes. She was
leaving her home — the old rooms, the old books, and
presses and stores, the duties, stately or simple, in which her
life had been passed. And leaving them, not in the daylight, and with a safe and assured future before her, but by
stealth and under cover of night, with a mind full of
anxious questionings !

To my lord it seemed a fine thing to have the world
before him ; to know that all Germany beyond the
Werra was convulsed by war, and a theatre wherein a
bold man might look to play his part. But to a woman,
however high-spirited, the knowledge was not reassuring.
To one who was exchanging her own demesne and peace

and plenty for a wandering life and dependence on the protection of men, it was the reverse.

So, while my lord talked gaily, my lady, I think, wept; doing that under cover of darkness and her mask, which she would never have done in the light. He talked on, planning and proposing; and where a true lover would have been quick to divine the woman's weakness, he felt no misgiving, thrilled with no sympathy. Then I knew that he lacked the subtle instinct which real love creates; which teaches the strong what it is the feeble dread, and gives a woman the daring of a man.

As we drew near the ford, I·dropped back to see that all crossed safely. Pushka, I knew, would carry my lady over, but some of the others were worse mounted. This brought me abreast of the Catholic girl, though the darkness was such that I recognized her only by the dark mass before her, which I knew to be the child. We had had some difficulty in separating her from Steve, and persuading her that the man ran no risk where he lay; otherwise she had behaved admirably. I did not speak to her, but when I saw the gleam of water before us, and heard the horses of the leaders begin to splash through the shallows, I leant over and took hold of the boy.

'You had better give him to me,' I said gruffly. 'You will have both hands free then. Keep your feet high, and hold by the pommel. If your horse begins to swim leave its head loose.'

I expected her to make a to-do about giving up the child; but she did not, and I lifted it to the withers of my horse. She muttered something in a tone which sounded grateful, and then we splashed on in silence, the horses putting one foot gingerly before the other; some sniffing the air with loud snorts and outstretched necks, and some stopping outright.

I rode on the upstream side of the girl, to break the force of the water. Not that the ford is dangerous in the daytime (it has been bridged these five years), but at night, and with so many horses, it was possible one or another might stray from the track; for the ford is not straight, but slants across the stream. However, we all passed safely; and yet the crossing remains in my memory.

As I held the child before me — it was a gallant little thing, and clung to me without cry or word — I felt something rough round its neck. At the moment I was deep in the water, and I had no hand to spare. But by-and-by, as we rode out and began to clamber up the farther bank, I laid my hand on its neck, suspecting already what I should find.

I was not mistaken. Under my fingers lay the very necklace which Peter had described to me with so much care! I could trace the shape and roughness of the walnuts. I could almost count them. Even of the length of the chain I could fairly judge. It was long enough to go twice round the child's neck.

As soon as I had made certain, I let it be, lest the child should cry out; and I rode on, thinking hard. What, I wondered, had induced the girl to put the chain round its neck at that juncture? She had hidden it so carefully hitherto, that no eye but Peter's, so far as I could judge, had seen it. Why this carelessness now, then? Certainly it was dark, and, as far as eyes went, the chain was safe. But round her own neck, under her kerchief, where it had lain before, it was still safer. Why had she removed it?

We had topped the farther bank by this time, and were riding slowly along the right-hand side of the river; but I was still turning this over in my mind, when I heard her on a sudden give a little gasp. I knew in a moment what it was. She had bethought her where the necklace was. I was not a whit surprised when she asked me in a tremulous tone to give her back the child.

'It is very well here,' I said, to try her.

'It will trouble you,' she muttered faintly.

'I will say when it does,' I answered.

She did not answer anything to that, but I heard her

breathing hard, and knew that she was racking her brains for some excuse to get the child from me. For what if daylight came and I still rode with it, the necklace in full view? Or what if we stopped at some house and lights were brought? Or what, again, if I perceived the necklac and took possession of it!

This last idea so charmed me — I was in a grim humour — that my hand was on the necklace, and almost before I knew what I was doing, I was feeling for the clasp which fastened it. Some fiend brought the thing under my fingers in a twinkling. The necklace seemed to fall loose of its own accord. In a moment it was swinging and swaying in my hand. In another I had gathered it up and slid it into my pouch.

The trick was done so easily and so quickly that I think some devil must have helped me; the child neither moving nor crying out, though it was old enough to take notice, and could even speak, as children of that age can speak — intelligibly to those who know them, gibberish to strangers.

I need not say that I never meant to steal a link of the thing. The temptation which moved me was the temptation to tease the girl. I thought this a good way of punishing her. I thought, first to torment her by making her think the necklace gone; and then to shame her by producing it, and giving it back to her with a dry word that should show her I understood her deceit.

So, even when the thing was done, and the chain snug in my pocket, I did not for a while repent, but hugged myself on the jest and smiled under cover of the darkness. I carried the child a mile farther, and then handed it down to Marie, with an appearance of unconsciousness which it was not very hard to assume, since she could not see my face. But doubtless every yard of that mile had been a torture to her. I heard her sigh with relief as her arms closed round the boy. Then, the next moment I knew that she had discovered her loss. She uttered a sobbing cry, and I heard her passing her hands through the child's clothing, while her breath came and went in gasps.

She plucked at her bridle so suddenly that those who rode behind ran into us. I made way for them to pass. 'What is it?' I said roughly. 'What is the matter?'

She muttered under her breath, with her hands still searching the child, that she had lost something.

'If you have, it is gone,' I said bluntly. 'You would hardly find a hayrick to-night. You must have dropped it coming through the ford?'

She did not answer, but I heard her begin to sob, and then for the first time I felt uncomfortable. I repented of what I had done, and wished with all my heart that the chain was round the child's neck again. 'Come, come,' I said awkwardly, 'it was not of much value, I suppose. At any rate, it is no good crying over it.'

She did not answer; she was still searching. I could hear what she was doing, though I could not see; there were trees overhead, and it was as much as I could do to make out her figure. At last I grew angry, partly with myself, partly with her. 'Come,' I said roughly, 'we cannot stay here all night. We must be moving.'

She assented meekly, and we rode on. But still I heard her crying; and she seemed to be hugging the child to her, as if, now the necklace was gone, she had nothing but the boy left. I tried to see the humour in the joke as I had seen it a few minutes before, but the sparkle had gone out of it, I felt that I had been a brute. I began to reflect that this girl, a stranger and helpless, in a strange land, had nothing upon which she could depend but these few links of gold. What wonder, then, if she valued them; if, like all other women, she hid them away and fibbed about them; if she wept over them now they were gone?

Of course it was in my power in a moment to bring them back again; and nothing had seemed easier, a few minutes before, than to hand them back — with a little speech which should cover her with confusion and leave me unmoved.

Now, though I wished them round her neck again with all
the good-will in life, and though to effect my wish I had
only to do what I had planned — only to stretch out my
hand with that word or two — I sat in my saddle hot and
tongue-tied, my fingers sticking to the chain.

Her grief had somehow put a new face on the matter.
I could not bear to confess that I had caused it wantonly
and for a jest. The right words would not come, while
every moment which prolonged the silence between us
made the attempt seem more hopeless, the task more difficult; till, like the short-sighted craven I was, I thrust
back the chain into my pocket, and, determining to take
some secret way of restoring it, put off the crisis.

In a degree I was hurried to this decision by our arrival
at the place where we were to rest. This was an outlying
farm belonging to Heritzburg and long used by the family,
when journeying to Cassel. Alas! when we came to it,
cold, shivering, and hungry, we found it ruined and tenant-
less, with war's grim brand so deeply stamped upon the
face of everything that even the darkness of night failed to
hide the scars. I had not expected this, and for a while I
forgot the necklace in anxiety for my lady's comfort. I
had to get lights and see fires kindled, to order the disposal
of the horses, to unpack the food; for we found no scrap,
even of fodder for the beasts, in the grimy, smoke-stained
barn, which I had known so well stored. Nor was the
house in better case. Bed and board were gone, and half
the roof. The door lay shattered on the threshold, the
window-frames, smashed in wanton fury, covered the floor.
The wind moaned through the empty rooms; here and there
water stood in puddles. Round the hearth lay broken
flasks, and rotting *débris*, and pewter plates bent double —
the relics of the ravager's debauch.

We walked about, with lights held above our heads, and
looked at all this miserably enough. It was our first
glimpse of war, and it silenced even the Waldgrave. As
for my mistress, I well remember the look her face wore.

when I left her standing with her women, who were already in tears, in the middle of the small chamber assigned
to her. I had known her long enough to be able to read
the look, and to be sure that she was wondering whether
it would always be so now. Had she exchanged Heritzburg, its peace and comfort, for such nights as these,
divided between secret flittings and lodgings fit only for
the homeless and wretched ?

But neither by word nor sign did she betray her fears;
and in the morning she showed a face that vied with the
Waldgrave's in cheerfulness. Our horses had had little
exercise of late and were in poor condition for travelling.
We gave them, therefore, until noon to rest, and a little
after that hour got away; one and all, I think — with the
exception perhaps of Marie Wort — in better spirits. The
sun was high, the weather fine, the country on either side
of us woodland, with fine wild prospects. Hence we saw
few signs of the ravages which were sure to thrust themselves on the attention wherever man's hand appeared.
We could forget for the moment war, and even our own
troubles.

We proposed to reach the little village of Erbe by sunset,
but darkness overtook us on the road. The track, over-
grown and narrowed by spring shoots, was hard to follow
in daylight; to attempt to pursue it after nightfall seemed
hopeless. We had halted, therefore, and the Waldgrave
and my lady were considering whether we should camp
where we were, or pick our way to a more sheltered spot,
when young Jacob, who was leading, cried out that he saw
the glimmer of a camp-fire some way off among the trees.
The news threw our party into the greatest doubt. My
lady was for stopping where we were, the Waldgrave for
going on. In the end the latter had his way, and it was
agreed that we should join the company before us, or at
any rate parley with them and learn their intentions.
Accordingly we shook up our tired horses and moved
cautiously forward.

The distant gleam which had first caught Jacob's eye soon widened into a warm and ruddy glow, in which the polished beech-trunks stood up like the pillars of some great building. Still drawing nearer, we saw that there were two fires built a score of paces apart, in a slight hollow. Round the one a number of men were moving, whose black figures sometimes intervened between us and the blaze. Two or three dogs sprang up and barked at us, and a horse neighed out of the darkness beyond. The other fire seemed at first sight to be deserted; but as the dogs ran towards us, still barking, first one man, then another, rose beside it, and stood looking at us. The arrival of a second party in such a spot was no doubt unexpected.

Judging that these two were the leaders of the party, I went forward to announce my lady's rank. One of the men, the shorter and younger, a man of middle height and middle age and dark, stern complexion, came a few paces to meet me.

·'Who are you?' he said bluntly, looking beyond me at those who followed.

'The Countess Rotha of Heritzburg, travelling this way to Cassel,' I answered; 'and with her, her excellency's kinsman, the noble Rupert, Waldgrave of Weimar.'

The stranger's face lightened strangely, and he laughed. 'Take me to her,' he said.

Properly I should have first asked him his name and condition; but he had the air, beyond all things, of a man not to be trifled with, and I turned with him.

My lady had halted with her company a score of paces from the fire. I led him to her bridle.

'This,' I said, wondering much who he was, 'is her excellency the Countess of Heritzburg.'

My lady looked at him. He had uncovered and stood before her, a smile that was almost a laugh in his eyes. 'And I,' he said, 'have the honour to be her excellency's humble and distant cousin, General John Tzerclas, sometimes called, of Tilly.'

CHAPTER X.

THE CAMP IN THE FOREST.

As the stranger made his announcement, I chanced to turn my eyes on the Waldgrave's face; and if there was one thing more noteworthy at the moment than the speaker's air of perfect and assured composure, it was my lord's look of chagrin. I could imagine that this sudden and unexpected discovery of a kinsman was little to his mind; while the stranger's manner was as little calculated to reconcile him to it. But there was something more than this. I fancy that from the moment he heard Tzerclas' name he scented a rival.

My lady, on the other hand, did not disguise her satisfaction. 'I am pleased to make your acquaintance,' she exclaimed, looking at the stranger with frank surprise. ' Your name, General Tzerclas, has long been known to me. But I was under the impression that you were at present in command of a body of Saxon troops in Bohemia.'

'My troops, such as they are, lie a little nearer,' he answered, smiling; 'so near that they and their leader are equally at your service, Countess.'

'For the present I shall be content to claim your hospitality only,' my lady answered lightly. 'This is my cousin, the Waldgrave Rupert.'

'Of Weimar?' the general said, bowing.

'Of Weimar, sir,' the young lord answered.

The stranger said no more, but saluting him with a kind of careless punctilio, took hold of my lady's rein and led her horse forward into the firelight.

While he assisted her to dismount I had time to glance round; and the cheerful glow of the fire, which disclosed arms and accoutrements and camp equipments flung here and there in splendid profusion, did not blind me to other

7

appearances less pleasant. Indeed, that very profusion
did something to open my eyes to those appearances, and
thereby to the nature of the men amongst whom we had
come. The glittering hilts and battered plate, the gaudy
cloaks and velvet housings which I saw lying about the
roots of the trees, seemed to smack less of a travellers'
camp than a robbers' bivouac; while the fierce, swarthy
faces which clustered round the farther fire, reminded me
of nothing so much as of the swash-buckling escort which
had more than once accompanied Count Tilly to Heritzburg.
Then, indeed, under the old tiger's paw Tilly's riders had
been as lambs. But we were not now at Heritzburg, nor
was Count Tilly here. And whether these knaves would
be as amenable in the greenwood, whether the Waldgrave
had not done us all an ill service when he voted for moving
on, were questions I had a difficulty in answering to my
satisfaction; the more as, even before we were off our
horses, the rude stare the men fixed on my lady raised my
choler.

On the other hand their leader's bearing left nothing to
be desired. He welcomed my mistress to the camp with
perfect good breeding, the Waldgrave with civility. He
hastened the preparation of supper, and in every way
seemed bent on making us comfortable ; sending his knaves
to and fro with a hearty good-will, which showed that whoever stood in awe of them, he did not.

Meanwhile, I had a third fire kindled a score of paces
away, where a small thicket held out the hope of privacy,
and here I placed our women, bidding three or four of
the steadier men remain with them. The injunction was
scarcely needed however. Our servants were simple fellows born in Heritzburg. They eyed with shyness and
awe the swaggering airs and warlike demeanour of Tzerclas'
followers, and would not for a year's wages have intruded
on their circle without invitation.

The moment I had seen to this I returned to my lady,
and then for the first time I had an opportunity of examin-

ing our host. A man of middle height, sinewy and well-
formed, with an upright carriage, he looked from head to
foot the model of a soldier of fortune, and moved with a
careless grace, which spoke of years of manly exercise.
His face was handsome, cold, dark, stern ; the nose promi-
nent, the forehead high and narrow. Trimly pointed moustachios and a small pointed beard, both perfectly black,
gave him a peculiar and somewhat cynical aspect; and
nothing I ever witnessed of his dealings with his troops
led me to suppose that this belied the man. He could be,
as he was now, courteous, polished, almost genial. I judged
that he ˜could be also the reverse. He was richly, even
splendidly, dressed, and seemed to be about forty years
of age.

My lady sent me for Fraulein Max, who had been overlooked, and was found cowering beside the newly kindled
fire in company with Marie Wort and the women. Though
I think she had only herself to thank for her effacement,
she was inclined to be offended. But I had no time to
waste on words, and disregarding her ill temper I brought
her, feebly sniffing, to my lady, who introduced her to her
new-found kinsman.

' Pardon me,' he said, looking negligently round him.
' That reminds me. I, too, have a presentation to make.
Where is — oh yes, here is friend Von Werder. I thought,
my friend,' he continued, addressing the other and older
man whom we had seen by his fire, 'that you had disappeared as mysteriously as you came. Herr von Werder,
Countess, was my first chance guest to-night. You are
the second.'

He spoke in a tone of easy patronage, with his back half
turned to the person he mentioned. I looked at the man.
He seemed to be over fifty years old, tall, strong, and grey-
moustachioed. And that was almost all I could see, for, as
if acknowledging an inferiority, and admitting that the
terms on which he had been with his host were now
altered, he had withdrawn himself a pace from the fire.

Sitting on the opposite side of it near the outer edge of light and wearing a heavy cloak, he disclosed little of his appearance, even when he rose in acknowledgment of my lady's salute.

'Herr von Werder is not travelling with you, then?' my lady said; chiefly, I think, for the sake of saying something that should include the man.

'No, he is not of my persuasion,' the general answered in the same tone of good-natured contempt. 'Whither are you bound, my friend?' he continued, glancing over his shoulder and throwing a note of command into his voice. 'I did not ask you, and you did not tell me.'

'I am going north,' the stranger answered in a husky tone. 'It may be as far as Magdeburg, general.'

'And you come from?'

'Last, sir? Frankfort.'

'Well, as you say last, whence before that?'

'The Rhine Bishoprics.'

'Ah! Then you have seen something of the war? If you were there before it swept into Bavaria, that is. But a truce to this,' he continued. 'Here is supper. I beg you not to judge of my hospitality by this night's performance, Countess. I hope to entertain you more fittingly before we part.'

Though he made this apology, the supper needed none. Indeed, it was such as made me stare — there in the forest — and was served in a style and with accompaniments I little expected to find in a soldiers' camp. Silver dishes and chased and curious flagons, flasks of old Rhenish and Burgundy, glass from Nuremberg, a dozen things which made my lady's road equipage seem poor and trifling, appeared on the board. And the cooking was equal to the serving. The wine had not gone round many times before the Waldgrave lost his air of reserve. He complimented our host, expressed his surprise at the excellence of the entertainment, asked with a laugh how it was done, and completely resumed his usual manner. Perhaps he talked a little too freely, a little too fast, and viewed by the other's side, he grew younger.

What my lady saw or thought as she sat between the two men it was impossible to say, but she seemed in high spirits. She too talked gaily and laughed often; and doubtless the novelty of the scene, the great fires, the dark background, the burnished trunks of the beeches, the bizarre splendour of the feast, the laughter and snatches of song which came from the other fire, were well calculated to excite and amuse her.

'These are not all your troops ?' I heard her ask.

'Not quite,' the general answered drily. 'My men lie six hours south of us. I hope that you will do me the honour of reviewing them to-morrow.'

'You are marching south, then ? '

'Yes. Everything and every one goes south this year.'

'To join the King of Sweden ? '

'Yes,' the general answered, holding out his silver cup to be filled, and for that reason perhaps speaking very deliberately, 'to join the King of Sweden — at Nuremberg. But you have not yet told me, countess,' he continued, 'why you are afield. This part is not in a very settled state, and I should have thought that the present time was ——'

'A bad one for travelling?' my lady answered. 'Yes. But, I regret to say, Heritzburg is not in a very settled state either.' And thereon, without dwelling much on the cause of her troubles, she told him the main facts which had led to her departure.

I saw his lip curl and his eyes flicker with scorn. 'But had you no gunpowder ?' he said, turning to the Waldgrave.

'We had, but no cannon,' he answered confidently.

'What of that ?' the general retorted icily. 'I would have made a bomb, no matter of what, and fired it out of a leather boot hooped with cask-irons! I would have had half a dozen of their houses burning about their ears before they knew where they were, the insolents ! '

The Waldgrave looked ashamed of himself. 'I did not

think of that,' he said; and he hastened to hide his
confusion in his glass.

'Well, it is not too late,' General Tzerclas rejoined,
showing his teeth in a smile. 'If the Countess pleases, we
will soon teach her subjects a lesson. I am not pushed for
time. I will detach four troops of horse and return with
you to-morrow, and settle the matter in a trice.'

But my lady said that she would not have that, and persisted so firmly in her refusal that though he pressed the
offer upon her, and I could see was keenly interested in its
acceptance, he had to give way. The reasons she put forward were the loss of his time and the injury to his cause ;
the real one consisted, I knew, in her merciful reluctance
to give over the town to his troops, a reluctance for which
I honoured her. To appease him, however, for he seemed
inclined to take her refusal in bad part, she consented to go
out of her way to visit his camp.

At this point my lady sent me on an errand to her
women, which caused me to be away some minutes. When
I came back I found that a change had taken place. The
Waldgrave was speaking, and, from his heated face and the
tone of his voice, it was evident that the old wine which
had begun by opening his heart had ended by rousing his
pugnacity.

'Pooh! I protest *in toto!*' he said as I came up. 'I
deny it altogether. You will tell me next that the
Germans are worse soldiers than the Swedes!'

'Pardon me, I did not say so,' General Tzerclas answered.
The wine had taken no effect on him, or perhaps he had
drunk less. He was as suave and cold as ever.

'But you meant it!' the younger man retorted.

'No, I did not mean it,' the general answered, still
unmoved. 'What I said was that Germany had produced
no great commander in this war, which has now lasted
thirteen years.'

'Prince Bernard of Weimar, my kinsman!' the Waldgrave cried.

'Pardon me,' Tzerclas replied politely. 'Pardon me again if I say that I do not think he has earned that title. He is a soldier of merit. No more.'

'Wallenstein, then?'

'You forget. He is a Bohemian.'

'Count Tilly, then?'

'A Walloon,' the general answered with a shrug. 'The King of Sweden? A Swede, of course.'

'A German by the mother's side,' my lady said with a smile.

'As you, Countess, are a Walloon,' Tzerclas answered with a low bow. 'Yet doubtless you count yourself a German?'

'Yes,' she said, blushing. 'I am proud to do so.'

What courteous answer he would have made to this I do not know. She had scarcely spoken before a deep voice on the farther side of the fire was heard to ask 'What of Count Pappenheim?'

The speaker was Von Werder, who had long sat so modestly silent that I had forgotten his presence. He seemed scarcely to belong to the party; though Fraulein Max, who sat on the Waldgrave's left hand, formed a sort of link stretched out towards him. Tzerclas had forgotten him too, I think, for he started at the sound of his voice and gave him but a curt answer.

'He is no general,' he said sharply. 'A great leader of horse he is ; great at fighting, great at burning, greatest at plundering. No more.'

'It seems that you allow no merit in a German!' the Waldgrave cried with a sneer. He had drunk too much.

But Tzerclas was not to be moved. There was some-thing fine in the toleration he extended to the younger man. 'Not at all,' he said quietly. 'Yet I am of opinion that, even apart from arms, Germany has shown since the beginning of this war few men of merit.'

'The Duke of Bavaria,' the same deep voice beyond the fire suggested.

'Maximilian?' Tzerclas answered. This time he did
not seem to resent the stranger's interference. 'Yes, he is
something of a statesman. You are right, my friend. He
and Leuchtenstein, the Landgrave's minister — he too is a
man. I will give you those two. But even they play
second parts. The fate of Germany lies in no German
hands. It lies in the hands of Gustavus Adolphus and
Oxenstierna, Swedes; of Wallenstein, a Bohemian; of —
I know not who will be the next foreigner.'

'That is all very well; but you are a foreigner yourself,'
the Waldgrave cried.

'Yes, I am a Walloon,' Tzerclas said, still quietly,
though this time I saw his eyes flicker. 'It is true ; why
should I deny it ? You represent the native, and I the
foreign element. The Countess stands between us, repre-
senting both.'

The Waldgrave rose with an oath and a flushed face, and
for a moment I thought that we were going to have trouble.
But he remembered himself in time, and sitting down again
in silence, gazed sulkily at the fire.

The movement, however, was enough for my lady. She
rose to her feet to break up the party; and turning her
shoulder to the offender, began to thank General Tzerclas
for his entertainment. This made the Waldgrave, who was
compelled to stand by and listen, look more sulky than
ever ; but she continued to take no notice of him, and
though he remained awkwardly regarding her and waiting
for a word, as long as she stood, she went away without
once turning her eyes on him. The general snatched a
torch from me and lighted her with his own hand to our
part of the camp, where he took a respectful leave of her ;
adding, as he withdrew, that he would march at any hour
in the morning that might suit her, and that in all things
she might command his servants and himself.

He had sent over for her use a small tent, provided
originally, no doubt, for his own sleeping quarters; and we
found that in a hundred other ways he had shown himself

thoughtful for her comfort. She stood a moment looking about her with satisfaction; and when she turned to dismiss me, there was, or I was mistaken, a gleam of amusement in her eye. After all, she was a woman.

CHAPTER XI.

STOLEN!

THE night was still young, and when I had seen my mistress and her women comfortably settled, I sauntered back towards the middle of the camp. The three fires stood here, and there, and there, among the trees, like the feet of a three-legged stool; while between them lay a middle space which partook of the light of all, and yet remained shadowy and ill-defined. A single beech which stood in this space, and served in some degree to screen our fire from observation, added to the darkness of the borderland. At times the flames blazed up, disclosing trunk and branches; again they waned, and only a shadowy mass filled the middle space.

I went and stood under this tree and looked about me. The Waldgrave had disappeared, probably to his couch. So had Von Werder. Only General Tzerclas remained beside the fire at which we had supped, and he no longer sat erect. Covered with a great cloak he lay at his ease on a pile of furs, reading by the light of the fire in a small fat book, which even at that distance I could see was thumbed and dog's-eared. Such an employment in such a man — in huge contrast with the noisy brawling and laughter of his following — struck me as remarkable. I felt a great curiosity to know what he was studying, and in particular whether it was the Bible. But the distance between us was too great and the light too uncertain; and after straining my eyes awhile I gave up the attempt, consoling myself with the thought that had I been nearer I had perhaps been no wiser.

I was about to withdraw, tolerably satisfied, to seek my own rest, when a stick snapped sharply behind me. Unwilling to be caught spying, I turned quickly and found myself face to face with a tall figure, which had come up noiselessly behind me. The unknown was so close to me, I recoiled in alarm; but the next moment he lowered his cloak from his face, and I saw that it was Von Werder.

'Hush, man!' he said, raising his hand to enforce caution. 'A word with you. Come this way.'

He gave me no time to demur or ask questions, but taking obedience for granted, turned and led the way down a narrow path, proceeding steadily onwards until the glare of the fire sank into a distant gleam behind us. Then he stopped suddenly and faced me, but the darkness in which we stood among the tree-trunks still prevented me seeing his features, and gave to the whole interview an air of mystery.

'You are the Countess of Heritzburg's steward?' he said abruptly.

'I am,' I answered, wondering at the change in his tone, which, deep before, had become on a sudden imperative. By the fire and in Tzerclas' company he had spoken with a kind of diffidence, an air of acknowledged inferiority. Not a trace of that remained.

'The Waldgrave Rupert,' he continued — 'he is a new acquaintance?'

'He is not an old friend,' I replied. I could not think what he would be at with his questions. All my instincts were on the side of refusing to answer them. But his manner imposed upon me, though his figure and face were hidden; and though I wondered, I answered.

'He is young,' he said, as if to himself.

'Yes, he is young,' I answered dryly. 'He will grow older.'

He remained silent a moment, apparently in thought.

Then he spoke suddenly and bluntly. 'You are an honest man, I believe,' he said. 'I watched you at supper, and I think I can trust you. I will be plain with you. Your mistress had better have stayed at Heritzburg, steward.'

'It is possible,' I said. I was more than half inclined to think so myself.

'She has come abroad, however. That being so, the sooner she is in Cassel, the better.'

'We are going thither,' I answered.

'You were!' he replied; and the meaning in his voice gave me a start. 'You were, I say?' he continued strenuously. 'Whither you are going now will depend, unless you exert yourself and are careful, on General John Tzerclas of the Saxon service. You visit his camp to-morrow. Take a hint. Get your mistress out of it and inside the walls of Cassel as soon as you can.'

'Why?' I said stubbornly. 'Why?' For it seemed to me that I was being asked all and told nothing. The man's vague warnings chimed in with my own fears, and yet I resented them coming from a stranger. I tried to pierce the darkness, to read his face, to solve the mystery of his altered tone. But the night baffled me; I could see nothing save a tall, dark form, and I fell back upon words and obstruction. 'Why?' I asked jealously. 'He is my lady's cousin.'

'After a fashion,' the stranger rejoined coldly and slowly, and not at all as if he meant to argue with me. 'I should be better content, man, if he were her uncle. However, I have said enough. Do you bear it in mind, and as you are faithful, be wary. So much for that. And now,' he continued, in a different tone, a tone in which a note of anxiety lurked whether he would or no, 'I have a question to ask on my own account, friend. Have you heard at any time within the last twelve months of a lost child being picked up to the north of this, in Heritzburg or the neighbourhood?'

'A lost child?' I repeated in astonishment.

'Yes!' he retorted impatiently. And I felt, though I

could not see, that he was peering at me as I had lately peered at him. 'Isn't that plain German? A lost child, man? There is nothing hard to understand in it. Such a thing has been heard of before — and found, I suppose. A little boy, two years old.'

'No,' I said, 'I have heard nothing of one. A child two years old? Why, it could not go alone; it could not walk!'

In the darkness, which is a wonderful sharpener of ears, I heard the man move hastily. 'No,' he said with a stern note in his voice, 'I suppose not; I suppose it could not. At any rate, you have not heard of it?'

'No,' I said, 'certainly not.'

'If it had been found Heritzburg way,' he continued jealously, 'you would have, I suppose?'

'I should have — if any one,' I answered.

'Thank you,' he said curtly. 'That is all now. Good night.'

And suddenly, with that only, and no warning or further farewell, he turned and strode off. I heard him go plunging through the last year's leaves, and the noise told me that he trod them sternly and heavily, with the foot of a man disappointed, and not for the first time.

'It must be his child,' I thought, looking after him.

I waited until the last sound of his retreat had died away, and then I made my own way back to the camp. As chance would have it, I hit it close to the servants' fire, and before I could turn was espied by some of those who sat at it. One, a stout, swarthy fellow, with bright black eyes, and a small feather in his cap, sprang up and came towards me.

'Why so shy, comrade?' he cried, with a hiccough in his voice. 'Himmel! There are a pair of us!' And he raised his hand and laid it on my head — with an effort, for I am six feet and two inches. 'Peace!' and he touched me on the breast. 'War!' and he touched himself. 'And a good broad piece you are, and a big piece, and a heavy piece, I'll warrant!' he continued.

'I might say the same for you!' I retorted, suffering him to lead me to the fire.

'Oh, I?' he cried with a drunken swagger. 'I am a double gold ducat, true metal, stamped with the Emperor's man-at-arms! Melted in the Low Countries under Spinola — that is, these thirteen years back — minted by Wallenstein, tried by the noble general!

> "Clink! Clink! Clink!
> Sword and stirrup and spur.
> Ride! Ride! Ride!
> Fast as feather or fur!"

That is my sort! But come, welcome! Will you drink? Will you play? Will you 'list? Come, the night is young,

> " For the night-sky is red,
> And the burgher's abed,
> And bold Pappenheim's raiding the lea!"

Which shall it be, friend?'

'I will drink with you or play with you, captain,' I answered, seeing nothing else for it, 'so far as a poor man may; but as for enlisting, I am satisfied with my present service.'

'Ha! ha! I can quite understand that!' he answered, winking tipsily. 'Woman, lovely woman! Here's to her! Here's to her! Here's to her, lads of the free company!

> " Drink, lads, drink!
> Firkin and flagon and flask.
> Hands, lads, hands!
> A round to the maid in the mask!"

Why, man, you look like a death's head! You are too sober! Shame on you, and you a German!'

'An Italian were as good a toper!' one of the men beside him growled.

'Or a whey-fed Switzer!'

'Perhaps you are better with the dice!' the captain, in-

tendant, or what he was, continued. 'You will throw a-
main? Come, for the honour of your mistress!'

I had nearly a score of ducats of my own in my pouch,
and so far I could pay if I lost. I thought that I might
get some clue to Tzerclas' nature and plans by humouring
the man, and I assented.

'The dice, lads, the dice!' he cried. Ludwig, the others
called him.

'" Ho, the roof shall be red
    O'er the heretic's head,
For bold Pappenheim's raiding the lea!"'

The dice, the dice!'

'Your guest looks scared,' one said, looking at me grimly.
'Perhaps he is a heretic!'

'Chut! we are all heretics for the present!' Ludwig
answered recklessly. 'A fig for a credo and a fig for a
psalm! Give me a good horse and a good sword and fat
farmhouses. I ask no more. Shall it be a short life and a
merry one? The highest to have it?'

'Content,' I said, trying to fall into his humour.

'A ducat a throw?' he asked, posing the caster. A man,
as he spoke, placed a saddle between us, while half a dozen
others pressed round to watch us. The flame leaping up
shone on their dark, lean faces and gleaming eyes, or picked
out here and there the haft of a knife or the butt of a
pistol. Some wore steel caps, some caps of fur, some
gaudy handkerchiefs twisted round their heads. There were
Spaniards, Bohemians, Walloons among them; a Croat or
two; a few Saxons. 'Come,' cried the captain, rattling the
dice-box. 'A ducat a throw, Master Peace? Between
gentlemen?'

'Content,' I said, though my heart beat fast. I had never
even seen men play so high.

'So!' growled a German who crouched beside me — a
one-eyed man, fat and fair, the one fair-faced man in the
company; ''tis a cock of a fine hackle!'

'See me strip him!' Captain Ludwig rejoined gleefully.
And he threw and I threw, and I won; while the flame,
leaping and sinking, flung its ruddy light on the walls of
our huge, leafy chamber. Then he won. Then I won. I
won again, again, again!

'He has the fiend's own luck!' a Pole cried with a curse.

'Steady, Ludwig!' quoth another. 'Will you be beaten
by a clod-pate?'

'Fill his cup!' my opponent cried hardily. 'He has the
knack of it! But I will strip him! Beat up the fire there!
I can't see the spots. That is nine ducats you have won,
good broad-piece! Throw away!'

I threw, and at it we went again, but now luck began to
run against me, though slowly. The hollow rattle of the
dice, the voices calling the numbers, the oath and the cry of
triumph went on monotonously: went on — and I think the
spirit of play had fairly got hold of me — when a stern voice
suddenly broke in on our game.

'Put up, there, you rascals!' Tzerclas cried from his
fire. 'Have done, do you hear, or it will be the worse for
you! Kennel, I say!'

Captain Ludwig swore under his breath. 'Ugh!' he
muttered, 'just as I was getting my hand in! What is the
score? Seven ducats to me; and little enough for the
trouble. Hand over, comrade. You know the proverb.'

In haste to be gone after the warning we had received, I
plunged my hand into my pouch, and drew out in a hurry,
not a fistful of ducats as I intended, but a score of links of
gold chain, which for a moment glittered in the firelight.
As quickly as I could I thrust the chain — it was Marie
Wort's, of course — back into my pocket, but not before the
German sitting beside me had seen it. I looked at him
guiltily while I fumbled for the money, and he tried to look
as if he had seen nothing. But his one eye sparkled evilly,
and I saw his lips tremble with greed. He made no
remark, however, and in a moment I found the money and
paid my debt.

Most of the men had already laid themselves down and were snoring, with their feet to the fire. I muttered good night, and seizing my cap went off. To gain my quarters, I had to walk across the open under the beech-tree. I had just reached this tree, and was passing through the shadow under the branches, when the sound of a light footstep at my heels startled me, and turning in my tracks I surprised the one-eyed German.

'Well,' I said wrathfully — I was not in the best of tempers at losing — 'what do you want?'

The action and the challenge took him aback. 'Want?' he grumbled, recoiling a step. 'Nothing. Is this your private property?'

He had *thief* written all over his fat, pale face, and I knew very well what private property he wanted. If I ever saw a sneaking, hang-dog visage it was his! The more I looked at him the more I loathed him.

'Go!' I said; 'get home, you cur! or I will break every bone in your body.'

He glared at me with a curse in his one eye, but he saw that I was too big for him. Besides, General Tzerclas lay reading by his fire thirty paces away. Baffled and furious, the rascal slunk off with a muttered word, and went back the way he had come.

I found Ernst on guard, and after seeing to the fire and hearing that all was well, I lay down beside him in my cloak. But I found it less easy to sleep. The firelight, playing among the leaves and branches overhead, formed likenesses of the men I had left, now grotesque masks, and now scowling faces, fierce-eyed and grim. Von Werder's warning, too, recurred to me with added weight and would not leave me at peace. I wondered what he meant; I wondered what he suspected, still more, what he knew.

And yet had I need to wonder, or do more than look round and use my wits? What was our position? How were we situate? In the camp and in the hands of a soldier of fortune; a man cold and polite, probably cruel and pos-

sibly brutal, lacking enthusiasm, lacking, or I was mistaken, religion, without any check save such as his ambition
or fears imposed upon him. And for his power, I saw him
surrounded by desperadoes, soldiers in name, banditti in
fact, savage, reckless, and unscrupulous; the men, or the
twin-brothers of the men, who under another banner had
sacked Magdeburg and ravaged Halle.

What was to prevent such a man making his advantage
out of us? What was to prevent him marching back to
Heritzburg and seizing town and castle under cover of my
lady's name, or detaining us as long as he saw fit, or as
suited his purpose? The Landgrave and his Minister were
far away, plunged in the turmoil of a great war. The
Emperor's authority was at an end. The Saxon circle to
which we belonged was disorganized. All law, all order,
all administration outside the walls of the cities were in
abeyance. In his own camp and as far beyond it as his
sword could reach the soldier of fortune was lord, absolute
and uncontrolled.

This trouble kept me turning and tossing for a good hour.
At one moment, I made up my mind to rouse my lady
before it was light and be gone with the dawn, if I could
persuade her; at another, I judged it better to wait until
the camp was struck and the horses were saddled, and then
to bid Tzerclas, while our numbers were something like
equal, go his way and let us go ours — to Frankfort or
Cassel, or wherever strong walls and honest citizens, with
wives and daughters of their own, held out a prospect of
safety.

The mind once roused to activity works, whether a man
will or no. When I had thought that matter threadbare,
I fell, in my own despite and to my great torment, on
another; the gold necklace. Through the day, and pend-
ing some opportunity of restoring the chain by stealth, I
had shunned its owner. Her dejection, her silence, the
way in which she drooped in the saddle, all had reproached
me. To avoid that reproach, still more to avoid the meek-

ness of her eyes, I had ridden at a distance from her, some-times at the head of our company, sometimes at the tail, but never where she rode. And all day I had had a dozen things to consider.

Yet, in spite of this care and preoccupation, I had not succeeded in keeping her out of my mind. At fords and broken bits of the road, or at steep places where the track wound above the Werra, the thought, 'How will she cross this?' had occurred to me, so that I had found it hard to hold off from her at such places. And, then, there was the necklace. It burned in my pocket. It made me feel, whenever my hand lighted on it, like a thief, and as mean as the meanest. For a time, it is true, after our meet-ing with Tzerclas, I had managed to forget it ; but now, in the watches of the night, I was consumed with longing to be rid of the thing, to see it back in her possession, to close the matter before some inconceivable trick of spiteful for-tune put it out of my power to do so. For, what if an accident happened to me and the chain were found in my pocket ? What would she think of me then ? Or if the last accident of all befell me, and she never got her own ?

These imaginations, working in a mind already fevered, spurred me so painfully that I felt I could hardly wait till morning. Two or three times in the night I rose on my elbow and looked round the sleeping camp, and wished that I could return the chain to her then and there.

I could not. And at last, not long before daybreak, I fell asleep. But even then the chain did not leave me at peace. It haunted my dreams. It slid through my fingers and fell away into unfathomable depths. Or a man with his face hidden dangled it before my eyes, and went away, away, away, while I stood unable to move hand or foot. Or I was digging in a pit for it, digging with nails and bleeding fingers, believing it to be another inch, always another inch below, yet never able to reach it however hard I worked.

I awoke at last, bathed in perspiration and unrefreshed,

to find the sun an hour up and the camp beginning to stir itself. Here and there a man was renewing the fires, while his fellows sat up yawning, or, crouching chin and knees together, looked on drowsily. The chill morning air, the curling smoke, the song of the lark as it soared into the blue heaven, the snort and neigh of the tethered horses, the sounds of waking life and reality seemed to bless me. I thanked Heaven it was a dream.

Young Jacob was tending our fire, and I sat awhile, watching him sleepily. 'It will be a fine day,' I said at last, preparing to get to my feet.

'For certain,' he answered. Then he looked at me shyly. 'You were in the wars, last night, Master Martin?' he said.

'In the wars?' I exclaimed. 'What do you mean?' And I stared at him ; waiting, with one knee and one foot on the ground for his answer.

He pointed to my cloak. I looked down, and saw to my surprise a great slit in it — a clean cut in the stuff, a foot long. For a moment I looked at the slit, wondering stupidly and trying to remember how I could have done it. Then a sudden flash of intelligence entered my mind, and with a dreadful pang of terror, I thrust my hand into my pouch. The chain was gone !

I sprang to my feet. I tore off the pouch and peered into it. I shook my clothes like one possessed. I stooped and searched the ground where I had lain. But all fruitlessly. The chain was gone !

As soon as I knew this for certain, I turned on Jacob, and seizing him by the throat, shook him to and fro. 'Wretch !' I said. 'You have slept ! You have slept and let us be robbed ! You have ruined me ! '

He gurgled out a startled denial, and the others came round us and got him from me. But my outcry had roused all our part of the camp; even my lady put her head out of the tent and asked what was the matter. Some one told her.

'That is bad,' she said kindly. 'What is it you have lost, Martin ?'

Over her shoulder I saw a pale face peer out — Marie Wort's; and on the instant I felt my rage die down into a miserable chill, the chill of despair.

'Seven ducats,' I said sullenly, looking down at the ground, for the truth, at sight of her, crushed me. I was a thief ! This had made me one. Who was I to cry out that I was robbed ?

'It must be one of the strangers,' my lady said in a low voice and with an air of disturbance. 'Do you ——'

I sprang away without waiting to hear more — they must have thought me mad. I tore to the spot where I had diced the night before. Three or four men sat round the fire, swearing and grumbling, as is the manner of their kind in the morning; but the man I wanted was not among them.

'Where is Ludwig ?' I panted. 'Where is he ?'

A form, wrapped head and all in a cloak, struggled for a moment with its coverings, and freeing itself at last, rose to a sitting posture. It was Captain Ludwig.

'Who wants me ?' he muttered sleepily.

'I !' I cried, stooping and seizing him by the shoulder. I was trembling with excitement. 'I have been robbed ! Do you hear, man ? I have been robbed ! In the night !'

He shook me off impatiently. 'Well, what is that to me ?' he grunted. And he turned to warm himself.

'Where is the Saxon who sat by me last night ?' I demanded, almost beside myself with fury.

'How do I know ?' he answered, shrugging his shoulders peevishly. 'Robbed ? Well, you are not the first person that has been robbed. You need not make such an outcry about it. There is more than one thief about, eh, Taddeo ?' And he winked cunningly at his comrade.

The man's indifference maddened me. I could scarcely keep my hands off him. Fortunately, Taddeo's answer put an end to my doubts.

. . Ludwig, all his indifference cast to the winds, continued
to stamp and scream . . .

'There is one less, at any rate, captain,' he said carelessly, stooping forward to stir the embers. 'The Saxon
is gone.'

'Himmel! He has, has he? Without leave?' Ludwig
answered. 'The worse for him if we catch him, that
is all!'

'He went off with the German and his servants an hour
before sunrise,' Taddeo said with a yawn.

'He had better not let our noble general overtake him!'
Ludwig answered grimly, while I stood still, stricken
dumb by the news. 'But enough of that. Where is my
cap?'

Taddeo pushed it towards him with his foot, and he took
it up and put it on. He had no sooner done so, however,
than a thought seemed to strike him. He snatched the cap
off again, and, plunging his hand into it, groped in the
lining. The next instant he sprang to his feet with a howl
of rage.

Taddeo looked at him in astonishment. 'What is it?'
he asked.

For answer, Ludwig ran at him and dealt him a tremendous kick. 'There, pig, that is for you!' he cried venge-
fully, his eyes almost starting from his head. 'You will
not ask what it is next time! That Saxon hound has
robbed me — that is what it is. But he shall pay for it.
He shall hang before night! Every ducat I had he has
taken, pig, dog, vermin that he is! But I'll be even with
him. I'll lash ——'

And Master Ludwig, all his indifference cast to the winds,
continued to stamp and scream so loudly that in the end
Tzerclas overheard him, and appeared.

'What is this?' the general said harshly. 'Is that man
mad?'

Ludwig grew a little calmer at sight of him. 'The
Saxon, Heller,' he answered, scowling. 'He has deserted with fifty ducats of mine, general; good honest
money!'

'The worse for you,' Tzerclas answered cynically. 'And
the worse for him, if I catch him. He will hang.'
    ' He has taken a gold chain of mine also,' I said, thrust-
ing myself forward.
    The general looked hard at me.   'Umph!' he said.
'Which way has he gone? '
    ' He left with the German gentleman and his two
servants at daybreak,' Taddeo answered, rubbing himself.
'I thought that he had orders to go with them.'
    ' He has gone north, then ? '
    'North they started,' Taddeo whimpered.
    The general turned to Ludwig. 'Take two men,' he said
curtly, ' and follow him. But, whether you catch him or
not, see that you are back two hours before noon. And let
me have no more noise.'
    Ludwig saluted hastily, and, it will be believed, lost no
time in obeying his orders. In two minutes he was in the
saddle, and dashed out of camp, followed by two of his
men and one of my lady's, whom I took leave to add to the
party for the better care of my property, should it be
recovered.   I looked after them with longing eyes, and
listened to the last beat of the hoofs as they passed through
the forest.   And then for three hours I had to wait in a
dreadful state of suspense and inaction.   At the end of that
time the party rode in again, the horses bloody with
spurring, the riders gloomy and chapfallen.   They had
galloped four leagues without coming on the slightest trace
of the fugitive or his companions.
    ' The German never went north,' Ludwig said, looking
darkly at his chief.
    Tzerclas smoothed his chin with his thumb and fore-
finger. 'Are you sure of that ? ' he asked.
    ' Quite, general.   They have all gone south together,'
Ludwig answered, 'and are far enough away by this
time.'
    ' Umph! Well, we start in an hour.'
    And that was all! I wandered away and stood staring

at the ground. I remembered that Peter the locksmith had valued the chain at two hundred ducats, a sum exceeding any I could pay. But that was not the worst. What was I to say to the girl? How was I to explain a piece of folly, mischief, call it what you will, that had turned out so badly? If I told her the truth, would she believe me?

At that thought I started. Why tell her the truth at all? Why not leave her in ignorance? She would be none the worse, for the chain was gone. And I, who had never meant to steal it, should be the better, seeing that I should escape the humiliation of confessing what I had done. Confession could do no good to her. And in what a position it would place me!

Leaning against a tree and driving my heel moodily into the soil, I was still battling with this temptation — for a temptation I knew it was, even then — when a light touch fell on my sleeve. I turned, and there was the girl herself, waiting to speak to me!

CHAPTER XII.

NEAR THE EDGE.

'WILL you give me back my — my chain, if you please?' she said timidly.

And she stood with clasped hands and blushing cheeks, as if she were the culprit. Her eyes looked anywhere to avoid mine. Her voice trembled, and she seemed ready to sink into the earth with shame. She was small, weak, helpless. But her words! Had they come from the judge sitting on his bench, with axe and branding-iron by his side, they could not have cowed me more completely, or deprived me more quickly of wit and courage.

'Your chain?' I stammered, stricken almost voiceless. 'What do you mean?'

'If you please,' she whispered, her face flushing more
and more, her eyes filling. ' My chain.'

'But how — what makes you think that I have got it ? '
I muttered hoarsely. ' What makes you come to me ? '

To confess, of my own motive and unsuspected, had been
bad enough and shameful enough ; but to be accused, unmasked, convicted — and by her ! This was too much.
My face burned, my eyes were hot as fire.

She twisted the fingers of one hand tightly round the
other, but she did not look up. ' You took it from the
child's neck as we passed through the ford,' she said in a
low voice, 'that night I lost it.'

' I did !' I exclaimed. ' I did, girl ? '

She nodded firmly, her lip trembling. But she never
looked up ; nor into my face !

Yet her insistence angered me. How did she know, how
could she know ? I put the question into words. ' How
do you know ? ' I said harshly. ' Who told you so ? Who
told you this — this lie, woman ? '

'The child,' she answered, shivering under my words.

I opened my mouth and drew in my breath. I had
never thought of that. I had never thought, save once
for a brief moment, of the child talking, and, on the
instant, I stood speechless ; convicted and confounded !
Then I found my voice again.

'The child told you !' I muttered incredulously. ' The
child ? Why, it cannot talk ! '

' It can,' she said, her voice breaking. ' It can talk to
me, and I can understand it. Oh, I am so sorry !' And with
that she broke down. She turned away and, covering her
face with her hands, began to sob bitterly. Her shoulders
heaved, and her slender frame shook with the storm.

A thief, and a liar ! That was what I had made myself.
I stood glaring at her, my breast full of sullen passion. I
hated her and her necklace. I wished that it had been
buried a thousand fathoms deep in the sea ! That moment
in the ford, one moment only, a moment of folly, had

wrecked me. I raged against her and against myself. I
could have struck her. If she had only left me alone, if
she had not come to question me and accuse me, I should
not have lied; and then, perhaps, I might have recovered
the necklace, somehow and some day, and, giving it back
to her, told her the story and kept my honesty. Now I had
lied, and she knew it. And I hated her. I hated her,
sobbing and shaking and shivering before me.

And then a ray of sunlight, passing through the branches,
fell on her bowed head. A hundred paces away, little
more, they were striking the camp. The men's voices,
their harsh jests and rude laughter, reached us. I heard
one man called, and another, and orders given, and the
jingle of the bits and bridles. All was unchanged, everything was proceeding in its usual course. One thing only
in the world was altered — Martin Schwartz, the steward.

. I found no words to lie to her farther, to deny or protest;
and when we had stood thus for a short time, she turned.
She began to move slowly away from me, though the passion of her tears seemed to increase rather than slacken
as she went, and shook her frame with such vehemence
that she could scarcely walk.

For a time I stood looking after her in sullen shame,
doing and saying nothing to stay her. Then, suddenly,
a change came over me. She looked so friendless, so frail,
and gentle and helpless, that, in the middle of my selfish
shame, my heart smote me. I felt a sudden welling up of
pity and repentance, which worked so quickly and wonderfully in me, that before she had gone a score of paces from
me, my hand was on her shoulder.

'Stop! Stay a moment!' I muttered hoarsely. 'I have
been lying to you. I took the necklace — from the child's
neck. It is all true.'

She ceased crying, but she did not turn or look at me.
She seemed to be struggling for composure, and presently,
with her face still averted, she murmured —

'Why did you take it? Will you please to tell me?'

As well as I could, I did tell her; how and why I had taken it, what I had done with it, and how I had lost it. She listened, but she made no sign, she said nothing; and her silence hurt me at last so keenly that I added with bitterness —

'I lied before, and you need not believe what I say now. Still, it is true.'

She turned her face quickly to me, and I saw that her cheeks were hot and her eyes shining. 'I believe it — every word,' she said.

'I will not lie to you again.'

'You never did,' she answered. And she stole a glance at me, a faint smile flickering about her lips. 'Your face never did, Master Martin.'

'Yet you wept sore enough for your chain,' I said.

She looked at me for a moment with something like anger in her gentle eyes, so that for that instant she seemed transformed. And she drew away from me.

'Did you think that I wept for that?' she said in a tone of offence. 'I did not.'

'Then for what?' I asked clumsily.

She looked two or three ways before she answered, and in the distance some one called me.

'There! you are wanted,' she said hurriedly.

'But you have not answered my question,' I said.

She took a step from me and paused, with her head half turned. 'I wept — I wept because I thought that I had lost a friend,' she said in a low voice. 'And I have few, Master Martin.'

She was gone, before I could answer, through the trees and back to the camp. And I had to follow. Half a dozen voices in half a dozen places were calling my name. The general's trumpet was sounding. I slipped aside and joined the camp from another quarter, and in a moment was in the middle of the hubbub, beset by restive horses and swaying poles, clanging kettles and swearing riders, and all the hurry and confusion of the start. My lady called to me

sharply to know where I had been, and why I was late.
The Waldgrave wanted this, Fraulein Max that. The
general frowned at me from afar. It would have been no
great wonder if I had lost my temper.

But I did not; I was in no risk of doing so. I had gone
near the edge and had been plucked back. Late, and when
all seemed over, I had been given a place for repentance;
and gratitude and relief so filled my breast that I had a
smile for every one. The sun seemed to shine more
brightly, the wind to blow more softly — the wind which
blew from Marie Wort to me. Thank God!

As I fell in behind my lady — the general riding alone
some way in the rear — the Waldgrave came up and
took his place at her side; greeting her with an awkward
air which seemed to prove that this was his first appearance in her neighbourhood. He made a show of hiding
his uneasiness under a face of careless gaiety, such as was
his natural wear; and for awhile he rattled on gallantly.
But my lady's cool tone and short answers soon stripped
him, and left him with no other resource but to take
offence. He took it, and for a mile or so rode on in gloomy
silence, brooding over his wrongs. Then, anger giving
way to self-reproach, he grew tired of this.

With a sudden gesture he leaned over and laid his hand
on the withers of my lady's horse. 'Tell me, what is the
matter, fair cousin?' he said in a softened tone. 'What
have I done?'

'You should know,' she answered, giving him one keen
glance, but speaking more gently than before.

'I know?' he replied hardily. 'I am sure I don't.'

My lady shook her head. 'I think you do,' she said.

'I suppose you are angry with me for — for standing up
for Germany last night?' he muttered, withdrawing his
hand and speaking coldly in his turn.

'No, not for that,' my lady rejoined. 'Certainly not for
that. But for being too German in one of your habits,
Rupert. Which do you think made the better figure last

night — you who were flushed with wine, or General Tzerclas who kept his head cool? You who bragged like a
boy, or General Tzerclas who said less than he meant?
You who were rude to your host; or he who made every
allowance for his guest?'

'Allowance!' my lord cried, firing up at the word. And
I could see that he reddened to the nape of his neck with
anger. 'There was no need!'

'Yes, allowance,' my lady answered firmly. 'There was
every need.'

'You would have me drink nothing, I suppose?' he said
fretting and fuming.

'I would rather you drank nothing than too much,' she
replied. 'Because a German and a drunkard have come to
mean the same thing, is that a reason for deepening the
reproach? For shame, Rupert!'

'You treat me like a boy!' he cried bitterly. And I
thought that she was hard on him.

'Well, you have only yourself to thank,' she retorted
cruelly, 'if I do. You behave like a boy. And I do not
like to have to blush for my friends.'

That cut him deeply. He uttered a half-stifled cry of
anger and reined in his horse. 'You have said enough,'
he said, speaking thickly. 'You shall have no farther
cause to blush in my case. I will relieve you.' And on
the instant, with a low bow, he turned his horse's head and
rode down the column towards the rear, leaving my lady to
go on alone.

I confess I thought that she had been hard on him;
perhaps she thought so too, now he was gone. And here
were the beginnings of a pretty quarrel. But I did not
guess the direction it was likely to take, until a horseman
spurred quickly by me, and in a moment General Tzerclas,
his velvet cloak hanging at his shoulder, had taken the
Waldgrave's place, and with his head bent low over his
horse's neck was talking to my lady. I saw him indicate
this and that quarter with his gauntleted hand. I could

fancy that this was Cassel, and that Frankfort, and another
his camp, and that he was proposing plans and routes.
But what he said I could not hear. He had a low, quiet
way of talking, very characteristic of him, which flattered
those to whom he addressed himself and baffled others.
And this, I suppose, it was that made me suspicious.
For the longer I rode behind him and the more I considered him, the less I liked both him and the prospect.
He was in the prime of his age and strength, inferior to
the Waldgrave in height and the air of youth, but superior
in that which the other lacked — the bearing of a man of
the world, tried by good and evil fortune, and versed in
many perils. Cool and resolute, handsome in a hard-bitten
fashion, gifted, as I guessed, with infinite address, he possessed much to take the fancy of a woman; particularly of
such a one as my lady, long used to comfort, and now learning in ill-fortune the value of a strong arm.

The possibility of such an alliance, thus suddenly thrust
on my notice, chilled me. Anything, I said, rather than
that. The Waldgrave had not left his post five minutes
before I began to think of him with longing, before I began
to invest him with all manner of virtues. At least, he was
a German, of a great and noble family, tied to the soil,
and fettered in his dealings by a hundred traditions;
while this man riding before me possessed not one of
these qualities!

Von Werder's warning, which the loss of Marie Wort's
necklace had driven from my mind for a time, recurred
with double force now, and did not tend to reassure me.
I listened with all my might, trying to learn whether my
lady was pledging herself to any course, for I knew that if
she once promised I should find it hard to move her. But
I could not catch a syllable, and presently there came an
interruption which diverted my thoughts.

One of the two men who rode in front, and served for
the advanced guard of our party, came galloping back with
his hand raised and a grin on his dark face. He pulled up

his horse a few paces short of General Tzerclas and my
lady, and reported that he had found the Saxon.
'What! Heller?' the general exclaimed. 'Here, Ludwig! Where are you?'

Ludwig, and I, and two or three more, spurred forward,
and passing by my lady, who reined in her horse, came a
hundred paces farther on upon the other trooper. He had
dismounted and was stooping over a man's body, which lay
under a great tree that stood a few yards from the track.

'So, so? He is dead, is he?' the captain cried, leaping
from his saddle.

'Ay, this hour or more,' the trooper answered with a
grunt. 'And robbed!'

'Robbed?' Ludwig shrieked. 'Then you have done it,
you scoundrel.'

'Not I!' the fellow said coolly. 'Who ever it was
killed him, robbed him. You can see for yourself that
he has been dead an hour or more.'

The sudden hope which had dawned in my breast sank
again. The man lay on his back, with his one eye staring,
and his mean, livid face turned up to the tree and the sunshine. His cap had fallen off, and a shock of hay-coloured
hair added to the horror of his appearance. I tried in vain
to hide a qualm as I watched the soldiers passing their
practised hands over his clothes; but I was alone in this.
No one else seemed to feel any emotion. The dead man
lay and his comrades searched him, and I heard a hundred
ribald and loose things said, but not one that smacked of
pity or regret. So the man had lived, without love or
mercy, and so he died.

Ludwig stood up at last. 'He has not the worth of his
boots upon him!' he said, with a savage snarl. And he
kicked the body.

'Look in his cap!' I said.

A man took it up, but only to hold it out to me. Some
one had already ripped it up with a knife.

'His boots!' I suggested desperately.

In a moment they were drawn off, turned up, and shaken. But nothing fell out. The dead man had been stripped clean. There was not so much as a silver piece upon him.

We got to horse gloomily, one man the richer by his belt, another by his boots. His arms were gone already. And so we left him lying under the tree for the next traveller to bury, if he pleased. I know it has an ill sound now, but we were in an evil mood, and the times were rough. 'The dog is dead, let the dog lie!' one growled. And that was his epitaph.

With him disappeared, as it seemed to me, my last chance of recovering the necklace. Whoever had robbed him, that was gone. A week might see it pass through a score of hands, a day might see it broken up, and spent, a link here and a link there. It was gone, and I had to face the fact and make up my mind to its consequences.

I am bound to say that the reflection gave me less pain than I could have believed possible a few hours before. Then it would almost have maddened me. Now it troubled me, but not beyond endurance, leading me to go over with a jealous eye all the particulars of my interview with Marie, but renewing none of the shame which had attended the first discovery of my loss. By turning my head I could see the girl plodding patiently on, a little behind me in the ranks; and I turned often. It no longer pained me to meet her eyes.

An hour before sunset we crossed the brow of a low, furze-covered hill, and saw before us a shallow green valley or basin, through which the river wound in a hundred zigzags. The hovels of a small village, with one or two houses of a better size, stood dotted about the banks of the stream. Over the largest of the buildings a banner hung idly on a pole, and from this as from the centre of a circle ran out long rows of wattled huts, which in the distance looked like bee-hives. Endless ranks of horses stood hobbled in another place, with a forest of carts and sledges, and here a drove of oxen, and there a monstrous flock of sheep. One of the men with us blew a few notes on a trumpet; and the sound, being taken up at once and repeated, in a moment filled the mimic streets with a hurrying, buzzing crowd, that lent the scene all the animation possible.

'So, this is your camp?' my lady exclaimed, her eyes sparkling.

'This is my camp,' General Tzerclas answered quietly. 'And it and I are equally at your service. Presently we will bid you welcome after a more fitting fashion, Countess.'

'And how many men have you here?' she asked quickly.

'Two thousand,' he answered, with a faint smile.

CHAPTER XIII.

OUR QUARTERS.

AT this time I had never seen a camp, nor viewed any large number of armed men together, and my curiosity, as we dropped gently down the hill, while the sun set and the shadows of evening fell upon the busy scene, was mingled with some uneasiness. The babble of voices, of traders crying their wares, of men quarrelling at play, of women screaming and scolding, rose up continually, as from a fair; and the nearer we approached the more like a fair, the less like my anticipations, seemed the place we were entering. I looked to see something gay and splendid, the glitter of weapons and the gleam of flags, some reflection of the rich surroundings the general allowed himself. I saw nothing of the kind; no show of ordered lines, no battalia drilling, no picquets, outposts, or sentinels. On the contrary, all before us seemed squalid, noisy, turbulent; so that as I descended into the midst of it, and left the quiet uplands and the evening behind us, I felt my gorge rise, and shivered as with cold.

A furlong short of the camp a troop of officers on horse-back came to meet us, and saluting their general — some with hiccoughs — fell in tumultuously behind us; and their feathered hats and haphazard armour took the eye finely. But the next to meet us were of a different kind — beggars; troops of whom, men, women, and children, assailed us with loud cries, and, wailing and imploring aid, ran beside our horses, until Tzerclas' men rode out at them and beat them off. To these succeeded a second horde, this time of gaudy, slatternly women, who hung about the entrance to the camp, with hucksters, peddlers, thieves, and the like, without number; so that our way seemed to lie through the lowest haunts of a great city. Not one in four of all I saw had the air of a soldier or counted himself one.

And this was the case inside the camp as well as outside. Everywhere booths and stalls stood among the huts, and sutlers plied their trade. Everywhere men wrangled, and women screamed, and naked children scuttered up and down. While we passed, the general's presence procured momen-tary respect and silence. The moment we were gone, the stream of ribaldry poured across our path, and the tide of riot set in. I saw plenty of bearded ruffians, dark men with scowling faces, chaffering, gaming or sleeping; but little that was soldierly, little that was orderly, nothing to proclaim that this was the lager of a military force, until we had left the camp itself behind us and entered the village.

Here in a few scattered houses were the quarters of the principal officers; and here a degree of quiet and decency and some show met the eye. A watch was set in the street, which was ankle-deep in filth. A few pennons fluttered from the eaves, or before the doors. In front of the largest house a dozen cannon, the wheels locked together with chains, were drawn up, and behind the buildings were groups of tethered horses. Two trumpeters, who seemed to be waiting for us, blew a blast as we appeared, and a dozen officers on foot, some with pikes and some with par-

tisans, came up to greet the general. But even here ugly
looks and insolent faces were plentiful. The splendour was
faded, the rich garments were set on awry. Hard by the
cannon, in the shadow of the house, a corpse hung and
dangled from the branch of an oak. The man had kicked
off his shoes before he died, or some one had taken them,
and the naked feet, shining in the dusk, brushed the
shoulders of the passers-by.

Some might have taken it for an evil omen; I found it a
good one, yet wished more than ever that we had not met
General Tzerclas. But my lady, riding beside him and
listening to his low-voiced talk, seemed not a whit disappointed by what she saw, by the lack of discipline, or the
sordid crowd. Either she had known better than I what to
expect in a camp, or she had eyes only for such brightness
as existed. Possibly Von Werder's warning had so coloured
my vision that I saw everything in sombre tints.

We found quarters prepared for us, not in the general's
house, the large one by the cannon, but in a house of four
rooms, a little farther down the street. It was convenient,
it had been cleaned for us, and we found a meal awaiting
us; and so far I was bound to confess that we had no
ground for complaint. The general accompanied my lady
to the door, and there left her with many bows, requesting
permission to wait on her next day, and begging her in the
mean time to send to him for anything that was lacking to
her comfort.

When he was gone, and my lady had surveyed the place,
she let her satisfaction be seen. The main room had been
made habitable enough. She stood in her redingote, tapping the table with her whip.

'Well, Martin, this is better than the forest,' she said.

'Yes, your excellency,' I answered reluctantly.

'I think we have done very well,' she continued; and she
smiled to herself.

'We are safe from the rain, at any rate,' I said bluntly.
My tongue itched to tell her Von Werder's warning, but

Fraulein Anna and Marie Wort were in the room, and I did not think it safe to speak.

I could not stay and not tell, however, and I jumped at the first excuse for retiring. There was a kind of wooden platform in front of the houses, and running their whole length ; a walk, raised out of the mud of the street and sheltered overhead by the low, wide eaves. A woman and some children had climbed on to it, and begging with their palms through the windows almost deafened us. I ran out and drove them off, and set a man in front to keep the place free. But the wretched creatures' entreaties haunted me, and when I returned I was in a worse temper than before.

The Waldgrave met me at the door, and to my surprise laid his hand on my shoulder. 'This way, Martin,' he said in a low voice. 'I want a word with you.'

I went with him across the road, and leaned against the fallen trunk of a tree, which was just visible in the dark ness. Through the unglazed windows of the house we could see the lighted rooms, the Countess and her attendants moving about, Fraulein Anna sitting with her feet tucked up in a corner, the servants bringing in the meal. All in a frame of blackness, with the hoarse sounds of the camp in our ears, and the pitiful wailing of the beggars dying away in the distance. It was a dark night, and still.

The Waldgrave laughed. 'Dilly, dilly, dilly! Come and be killed,' he muttered. 'Two thousand soldiers? Two thousand cut-throats, Martin. Pappenheim's black riders were gentlemen beside these fellows!'

'Things may look more cheerful by daylight,' I said.

'Or worse!' he answered.

I told him frankly that I thought the sooner we were out of the camp the better.

'If we can get out! Of course, it is better for the mouse when it is out of the trap!' he answered with a sneer. 'But there is the rub.'

'He would not dare to detain us,' I said. I did not believe my words, however.

'He will dare one of two things,' the Waldgrave answered firmly, 'you may be sure of that: either he will march your lady back to Heritzburg, and take possession in her name, with this tail at his heels — in which case, Heaven help her and the town. Or he will keep her here.'

I tried to think that he was prejudiced in the matter, and that his jealousy of General Tzerclas led him to see evil where none was meant. But his fears agreed so exactly with my own, that I found it difficult to treat his suggestions lightly. What the camp was, I had seen; how helpless we were in the midst of it, I knew; what advantage might be taken of us, I could imagine.

Presently I found an argument. 'You forget one thing, my lord,' I said. 'General Tzerclas is on his way to the south. In a week we shall be with the main army at Nuremberg, and able to appeal to the King of Sweden or the Landgrave or a hundred friends, ready and willing to help us.'

The Waldgrave laid his hand on my arm. 'He does not intend to go south,' he said.

I could not believe that; and I was about to state my objections when the noisy march of a body of men approaching along the road disturbed us. The Waldgrave raised his hand and listened.

'Another time!' he muttered — already we began to fear and be secret — 'Go now!'

In a trice he disappeared in the darkness, while I went more slowly into the house, where I found my lady inquiring anxiously after him. I thought that the young lord would follow me in, and I said I had seen him. But he did not come, and presently wild strains of music, rising on the air outside, took us all by surprise and effectually diverted my lady's thoughts.

The players proved to be the general's band, sent to serenade us. As the weird, strange sweetness of the air, with its southern turns and melancholy cadences, stole into the room and held the women entranced — while moths flut-

tered round the lights and the servants pressed to the door
to listen, and now and then a harsh scream or a distant
oath betrayed the surrounding savagery — I felt my eyes
drawn to my lady's face. She sat listening with a rapt
expression. Her eyes were downcast, her lashes drooped
and veiled them; but some pleasant thought, some playful
remembrance curved her full lips and dimpled her chin.
What was the thought, I wondered? was it gratification,
pleasure, complacency, or only amusement? I longed to
know.

On one point I was resolved. My lady should not sleep
that night until she had heard the warning I had received
from Von Werder. To that end I did all I could to catch
her alone, but in the result I had to content myself with an
occasion when only Fraulein Anna was with her. Time
pressed, and perhaps the Dutch girl's presence confused
me, or the delicacy of the position occurred to me *in mediis
rebus*, as I think the Fraulein called it. At any rate, I
blurted out the story a little too roughly, and found myself
called sharply to order.

'Stay!' my lady said, and I saw too late that her colour
was high. 'Not so fast, man! I think, Martin, that since
we left Heritzburg you have lost some of your manners!
See to it, you recover them. Who told you this tale?'

'Herr von Werder,' I answered with humility; and I was
going on with my story. But she raised her hand.

'Herr von Werder!' she said haughtily. 'Who is he?'

'The gentleman who supped with us last night,' I reminded her.

She stamped the floor impatiently. 'Fool!' she cried, 'I
know that! But who is he? Who is he? He should be
some great man to prate of my affairs so lightly.'

I stuttered and stammered, and felt my cheek redden
with shame. *I did not know.* And the man was not here,
and I could not reproduce for her the air of authority, the
tone and look which had imposed on me : which had given
weight to words I might otherwise have slighted, and im-

portance to a warning that I now remembered was a stranger's. I stood, looking foolish.

My lady saw her advantage. 'Well,' she said harshly, 'who is he? Out with it, man! Do not keep us waiting.'

I muttered that I knew no more of him than his name.

'Perhaps not that,' she retorted scornfully.

I admitted that it might be so.

My lady's eyes sparkled and her cheeks flamed. 'Before Heaven, you are a fool!' she cried. 'How dare you come to me with such a story? How dare you traduce a man without proof or warranty! And my cousin! Why, it passes belief. On the word of a nameless wanderer admitted to our table on sufferance you accuse an honourable gentleman, our kinsman and our host, of — Heaven knows of what, I don't! I tell you, you shame me!' she continued vehemently. 'You abuse my kindness. You abuse the shelter given to us. You must be mad, stark mad, to think such things. Or —— '

She stopped on a sudden and looked down frowning. When she looked up again her face was changed. 'Tell me,' she said in a constrained voice, 'did any one — did the Waldgrave Rupert suggest this to you?'

'God forbid!' I said.

The answer seemed to embarrass her. 'Where is he?' she asked, looking at me suspiciously.

I told her that I did not know.

'Why did he not come to supper?' she persisted.

Again I said I did not know.

'You are a fool!' she replied sharply. But I saw that her anger had died down, and I was not surprised when she continued in a changed tone, 'Tell me; what has General Tzerclas done to you that you dislike him so? What is your grudge against him, Martin?'

'I have no grudge against him, your excellency,' I answered.

'You dislike him?'

I looked down and kept silence.

'I see you do,' my lady continued. 'Why? Tell me why, Martin.'

But I felt so certain that every word I said against him would in her present mood only set him higher in her favour that I was resolved not to answer. At last, being pressed, I told her that I distrusted him as a soldier of fortune — a class the country folk everywhere hold in ab-horrence; and that nothing I had seen in his camp had tended to lessen the feeling.

'A soldier of fortune!' she replied, with a slight tinge of wonder and scorn. 'What of that? My uncle was one. Lord Craven, the Englishman, the truest knight-errant that ever followed banished queen — if all I hear be true — he is one; and his comrade, the Lord Horace Vere. And Count Leslie, the Scotchman, who commands in Stralsund for the Swede, I never heard aught but good of him. And Count Thurn of Bohemia — him I know. He is a brave man and honourable. A soldier of fortune!' she continued thoughtfully, tapping the table with her fingers. 'And why not? Why not?'

My choler rose at her words. 'He has the sweepings of Germany in his train,' I muttered. 'Look at his camp, my lady.'

She shrugged her shoulders. 'A camp is not a nunnery,' she said. 'And at any rate, he is on the right side.'

'His own!' I exclaimed.

I could have bitten my tongue the next moment, but it was too late. My lady looked at me sternly. 'You grow too quick-witted,' she said. 'I have talked too much to you, I see. I am no longer in Heritzburg, but I will be respected, Martin. Go! go at once, and to-morrow be more careful.'

Result — that I had offended her and done no good. I wondered what the Waldgrave would say, and I went to bed with a heart full of fancies and forebodings, that, bat-tening on themselves, grew stronger and more formidable the longer I lay awake. The night was well advanced and the immediate neighbourhood of our quarters was quiet. The sentry's footsteps echoed monotonously as he tramped up and down the wooden platform before them. I could almost hear the breathing of the sleepers in the other rooms, the creak of the floor as one rose or another turned. There was nothing to keep me from sleep.

But my thoughts would not be confined to the four walls or the neighbourhood; my ears lent themselves to every sound that came from the encircling camp, the coarse song chanted by drunken revellers, the oath of anger, the shrill taunt, the cry of surprise. And once, a little before midnight, I heard something more than these: a sudden roar of voices that swelled up and up, louder and fiercer, and then died in a moment into silence — to be followed an instant later by fierce screams of pain — shriek upon shriek of such mortal agony and writhing that I sat up on my pallet, trembling all over and bathed in perspiration; and even the sleepers turned and moaned in their dreams. The cries grew fainter. Then, thank Heaven! silence.

But the incident left me in no better mood for sleep, and with every nerve on the stretch I was turning on the other side for the twentieth time when I fancied I heard whispering outside; a faint muttering as of some one talking to the sentinel. The sentry's step still kept time, however, and I was beginning to think that my imagination had played me a trick, when the creak of a door in the house, followed by a rustling sound, confirmed my suspicions. I rose to my feet. The next instant a low scream and the harsh voice of the watchman told me that something had happened.

I passed out of the house, without alarming any one, and was not surprised to find Jacob pinning a captive against the wall with one hand, while he threatened him with his pike. There was just light enough to see this, and no more, the wide eaves casting a black shadow on the prisoner's face.

'What is it, Jacob?' I said, going to his assistance. 'Whom have you got?'

'I do not know,' he answered sturdily, 'but I'll keep him. He was trying to get in or out. Steady now,' he added gruffly to his captive, 'or I will spoil your beauty for you!'

'In or out?' I said.

'Ay, I think he was coming out.'

There was a fire burning in the road a score of paces away. I ran to it and fetched a brand, and blowing the smouldering wood into a blaze, threw the light on the fellow's face. Jacob dropped his hand with a cry of surprise, and I recoiled. His prisoner was a woman — Marie Wort.

She hung down her head, trembling violently. Jacob had thrust back the hood from her face, and her loosened hair covered her shoulders.

'What does it mean?' I cried, struggling with my bewilderment. 'Why are you here, girl?'

Instead of answering she cowered nearer the wall, and I saw that she was trying to hide something behind her under cover of her cloak.

'What have you got there?' I said quickly, laying my hand on her wrist.

She flashed a look at me, her small teeth showing, a mutinous glare on her little pale face. 'Not my chain!' she snapped.

I dropped her arm and recoiled as if she had struck me; though the words did not so much hurt as surprise me. And I was quick to recover myself. 'What is it, then?' I said, returning to the attack. 'I must know, Marie, and what you are doing here at this time of night.'

As she did not answer I put her cloak aside, and discovered, to my great astonishment, that she was holding a platter full of food. It shook in her hand. She began to cry.

'Heavens, girl!' I exclaimed in my wonder, 'have you not had enough to eat?'

She lifted her head and looked at me through her tears,

her eyes sparkling with indignation. 'I have!' she said almost fiercely. 'But what of these?' — and she flung her disengaged hand abroad, with a gesture I did not at once comprehend. 'Can you sleep in their beds, and lie in their houses, and eat from their meal-tubs, and think of them starving, and *not* get up and help them? Can you hear them whining for food like dogs, and starve them as you would not starve a dog? I cannot. I cannot!' she repeated wildly. 'But you, you others, you of the north, you have no hearts! You lie soft and care nothing!'

'But what — who are starving?' I said in amazement. Her words outran my wits. 'And where is the man in whose bed I am lying?'

'Under the sky! In the ditch!' she answered passionately. 'Are you blind?' she continued, speaking more quietly and drawing nearer. 'Do you think your general built this village? If not, where are the people who lived in it a month ago? Whining for a crust at the camp gate. Living on offal, or starving. Fighting with the dogs for bones. I heard a man outside this house cry that it was all his, and that he was starving. You drove him off. I heard his wife and babes wailing outside a while ago, and I came out. I could not bear it.'

I looked at Jacob. He nodded gravely. 'There was a woman here, with a child,' he said.

'Heaven forgive us!' I cried. Then — 'Go in, girl,' I continued. 'I will see the food put where they will get it; but do you go to bed.'

She obeyed meekly, leaving me wondering at the strange mixture of courage and fearfulness which makes up some women, and those the best; who fly from a rat, yet face every extremity of pain without flinching. A Romanist? And what of that? It seemed to me a small thing, as I watched her gliding in. If she knew little and that awry, she loved much.

I looked at Jacob and he at me. 'Is it true, do you think?' I said.

'I doubt it is,' he answered stolidly, dropping the smouldering brand on the ground and treading it out with his
heel. 'I have seen soldiers and sutlers and women since
I came into camp ; and beggars. But peasants not one.
I doubt we have eaten them out, Master Martin. But
soldiers must live.'

The little heap of red embers glowed dully in the road
and gave no light. The darkness shut us in on every side,
even as the camp shut us in. I looked out into it and
shuddered. It seemed to my eyes peopled with horrors :
with gaping mouths that cursed us as they set in death,
with lean hands that threatened us, and tortured faces of
maids and children ; with the despair of the poor. Ghosts
of starving men and women glared at us out of spectral
eyes. And the night seemed full of omens.

CHAPTER XIV.

THE OPENING OF A DUEL.

I NEVER knew where the Waldgrave spent that night, but
I think it must have been with the fairies. For when he
showed himself early next morning, before my lady appeared, I noticed at once a change in him ; and though at
first I was at a loss to explain it, I presently saw that that
had happened whioh might have been expected. The
appearance of a rival had laid the spark to his heart, and
while the love-light was in his eyes, a new gravity, a new
gentleness added grace to his bearing. The temper and
pettiness of yesterday were gone. Other things, too, I
saw — that his face flushed when my lady's voice was
heard at the door, that his eyes shone when she entered.
He had a nosegay of flowers for her — wild flowers ho
had gathered in the early morning, with tho dew upon
them — which he offered her with a little touch of
humility.

Doubtless the fret and passion of yesterday had not been
thrown away on him. He had learned in the night both
that he loved, and the lowliness that comes of love. It
wanted but that, it seemed to me, to make him perfect in
a woman's eyes; and I saw my lady's dwell very kindly
on him as he turned away. A little, I think, she wondered; his tone was so different, his desire to please so
transparent, his avoidance of everything that might offend
so ready. But such service wins its way; and my lady's
own kindness and gaiety disposing her to meet his advances, she seemed in a few moments to have forgotten
whatever cause of complaint he had given her.

The general's band came early, to play while she ate, but
I noticed with satisfaction that the music moved her little
this morning, either because she was taken up with talking
to her companion, or because the romantic circumstances
of the evening, darkness and vague surroundings, and the
lassitude of fatigue, were lacking. With the sunshine and
fresh air pouring in through the open windows, the strains
which yesterday awoke a hundred associations and stirred
mysterious impulses fell almost flat.

The Waldgrave made no attempt to resume the conversation he had held with me by the fallen tree. Either love,
or respect for his mistress, made him reticent, or he was
practising self-control. And I said nothing. But I understood, and set myself keenly to watch this duel between
the two men. If I read the general's intentions aright, the
young lord's influence with the Countess could scarcely
grow except at the general's expense; his suit, if successful, must oust that which the elder man, I was sure, medi-
tated. And this being so, all my wishes were on one side.
My fear of the general had so grown in the night, that I
suspected him of a hundred things; and could only think
of him as an antagonist to be defeated — a foe from
whom we must expect the worst that force or fraud could
effect.

He came soon after breakfast to pay his respects to my

lady, and alighted at the door with great attendance and endless jingling of bits and spurs. He brought with him several of his officers, and these he presented to the Countess with so much respect and politeness that even I could find no fault with the action. One or two of the men, rough Silesians, were uncouth enough; but he covered their mistakes so cleverly that they served only to set off his own good breeding.

He had not been in the room five minutes, however, before I saw that he remarked the change which had come over the Waldgrave, and perhaps some corresponding change in my lady's manner; and I saw that it chafed him. He did not lose his air of composure, but he grew less talkative and more watchful. Presently he let drop something aimed at the young man; a light word, inoffensive, yet likely to draw the other into a debate. But the Waldgrave refrained, and the general soon afterwards rose to take leave.

He had come, it seemed, to invite my lady's presence at a shooting-match which was to take place outside the camp at noon. He spoke of the match as a thing arranged before our arrival, but I have no doubt that the plan had its origin in a desire to please my lady and fill the day. He spoke, besides, of a hunting-party to take place next morning, with a banquet at his quarters to follow; of a review fixed for the day after that; and, in the still remoter distance, of races and a trip to a neighboring waterfall, with other diversions.

I heard the arrangements made, and my lady's frank acceptance, with a sinking heart; for under the perfect courtesy of his manner, behind the frank desire to give her pleasure which he professed, I felt his power. While he spoke, though I could find no fault with him, I felt the steel hand inside the silk glove. And these plans? Even my lady, though her eyes sparkled with anticipation — she loved pleasure with a healthy, honest love — looked a little startled.

'But I thought that you were marching southwards, General Tzerclas,' she said. 'At once I mean?'

'I am,' he answered, bowing easily — he had already risen. 'But an army, Countess, marches more slowly than a travelling party. And I am expecting despatches which may vary my route.'

'From the King of Sweden?'

'Yes,' he answered. 'The King has arrived at Nurem-berg, and expects shortly to be attacked by Wallenstein, who is on the march from Egra.'

'But shall you be in time for the battle?' she asked, her eyes shining.

'I hope so,' he replied, smiling. 'Or my part may be less glorious — to cut off the enemy's convoys.'

'I should not like that!' she exclaimed.

'Nevertheless, it is a very necessary function,' he said. 'As the Waldgrave Rupert will tell your excellency.'

The young lord agreed, and a moment later the general with his jingling attendants took his leave and clattered out and mounted before the door. My lady went to the window and waved adieu to him, and he lowered his great plumed hat to his stirrup.

'At noon?' he cried, making his horse curvet in the roadway.

'Without fail!' my lady answered gaily, and she stood at the window looking out until the last gleam of steel sank in a cloud of dust and the beggars closed in before the door.

The Waldgrave leaned against the wall behind her with his lips set and a grave face. But he said nothing, and when she turned he had a smile for her. It seemed to me that these two had changed places; the Waldgrave had grown older and my lady younger.

A few minutes before noon, Captain Ludwig and a sub-officer of the same rank, a Pole with long hair, came to conduct my lady to the scene of the match. They were arrayed in all their finery, and made a show of such eti-

quette as they knew. For our part we did not keep them
waiting; five minutes saw us mounted and riding through
the camp. This wore, to-day, a more martial and less disorderly appearance. The part we traversed was clear of
women and gamesters, while sentries stationed at the gate,
and a guard of honour which fell in behind us at the same
spot, proved that the eye of the master could even here
turn chaos into order. I do not know that the change
pleased me much, for if it lessened my dread of the cut-
throats by whom we were surrounded, it increased the awe
in which I held their chief.

The shooting was fixed to take place in a narrow valley
diverging from the river, a mile or more from the camp.
It was a green, gently-sloping place, such as sheep love;
but the sheep had long ago been driven into quarters, and
the shepherd to the listing-sergeant or the pike. A few
ruined huts told the tale ; the hills which rose on either
side were silent and untrodden.

Not so the valley itself, which lay bathed in sunshine. It
roared with the babel of a great multitude. A straight
course, two hundred yards in length, had been roped off
for the shooting, and round this the crowd thronged and
pushed, or, breaking here or there into fragments, wandered up and down outside the lines, talking and gesticulating, so that the place seemed to swarm with life and
movement and colour.

I had seen such a spectacle and as large a crowd at
Heritzburg — once a year, it may be. But there the gath-
ering had not the wild and savage elements which here
caught the eye ; the hairy, swarthy faces and black, gleaming eyes, the wild garb, and brandished weapons and fierce
gestures, that made this crowd at once curious and formidable. The babel of unknown tongues rose on every side.
Poland and Lithuania, Scotland and the Rhine, equally
with Hungary, Italy, and Bohemia, had their representa-
tives in this strange army.

General Tzerclas and his staff occupied a mound near the

lower end of the valley. On seeing our party approach, he
rode down to meet us, followed by thirty or forty officers,
whose dress and equipments, even more than those of their
men, fixed the attention; for while some wore steel caps
and clumsy cuirasses, with silk sashes and greasy trunk-
hose, others, better acquainted with the mode, affected
huge flapped hats and velvet doublets, with falling collars
of lace, and untanned boots reaching to the middle of the
thigh. One or two wore almost complete armour; others,
gay silks, stained with wine and weather. Their horses,
too, were of all sizes, from tall Flemings to small, wiry
Hungarians, and their arms were as various. One huge fat
man, whose flesh swayed as he moved, carried a steel mace
at his saddle-bow. Another swept along with a lance, rak-
ing the sky behind him. Great horse-pistols were common, and swords with blades so long that they ploughed
the ground.

Varying in everything else, in one thing these warlike
gentry agreed. As they came prancing towards us, I did
not see a face among them that did not repel me, nor one
that I could look at with respect or liking. Where dissipa-
tion had not set its seal so plainly as to oust all others, or
some old wound did not disfigure, cruelty, greed, and recklessness were written large. The glare of the bully shone
alike under flapped hat and iron cap. One might show a
swollen visage, flushed with excess, and another a thin,
white, cruel face; but that was all the odds.

The sight of such a crew should have opened my lady's
eyes and enlightened her as to the position in which we
stood. But women see differently from men. Too often
they take swagger for courage, and recklessness for manhood. And, besides, the very defects of these men, their
swashbuckling manners and banditti guise, only set off
the more the perfect dress and quiet bearing of their
leader, who, riding in their midst, seemed, with his cold,
calm face and air of pride, like nothing so much as the
fairy prince among the swine.

He wore a suit of black velvet, with a falling collar of Utrecht lace, and a white sash. A feather adorned his hat, and his furniture and sword-hilt were of steel. This, I afterwards learned, was a favourite costume with him. At odd times he relapsed into finery, but commonly he affected a simplicity which suited his air and features, and lost nothing by comparison with the tawdriness of his attendants.

He sprang from his horse at the foot of the slope, and, resigning it to a groom, took my lady's rein and, bareheaded, led her to the summit of the mound. The Waldgrave with Fraulein Anna followed, and the rest of us as closely as we could. The officers crowded thick upon us and would have edged us out, but I had primed my men, and though they quailed before the others' scowls and curses, they kept together, so that we not only had the advantage of watching the sport from a position immediately behind the Countess, but heard all that passed.

At the end of the open space I have mentioned stood three targets in a line. These were peculiar, for they consisted of dummies cased in leather, shaped so exactly to the form of men, that, at a distance of two hundred yards, it was only by the face I could tell that they were not men. Where the features should have been was a whitened circle, and on the breast of each a heart in chalk. They were so life-like that they gave an air of savagery to the sport, and made me shudder. When I had scanned them, I turned and found Captain Ludwig at my elbow.

'What is it?' he said, grinning. 'Our targets? Fine practice, comrade. They are the general's own invention, and I have known them put to good use.'

'How?' I asked. He spoke under his breath. I adopted the same tone.

'You will know by and by,' he answered, with a wink. 'Sometimes we find a traitor in the camp; or we catch a spy. Then — but you need not fear. Drawing-room practice to-day. There is no one in them.'

10

'In them ?' I muttered, unable to take my eyes from his face.

He nodded. 'Ay, in them,' he answered, smiling at my look of consternation. 'Time has been I have known one in each, and cross-bow practice. That makes them squeal! With powder and a flint-lock — pouf! It is all over. Unless you put the butter-fingers first; then there is sport, perhaps.'

Little wonder that after that I paid no attention to the shooting, which had begun; nor to the brawling and disagreement which from the first accompanied it, and which it needed all the general's authority to quell. I thought only of our position among these wretches. If I had felt any doubt of General Tzerclas' character before, the doubt troubled me no more.

But it did occur to me that Ludwig might be practising on me, and I turned to him sharply. 'I see!' I said, pre-tending that I had found him out. 'A good joke, captain!'

He grinned again. 'You would not call it one,' he said dryly, 'if you were once in the leather. But have it your own way. Come, there is a good shot, now. He is a Swiss, that fellow.'

But I could take no interest in the shooting, with that ghastly tale in my head. I felt for the moment the veriest coward. We were ten in the midst of two thousand — ten men and four helpless women! Our own strength could not avail us, and we had nothing else under heaven to de-pend upon, except the scruples, or interest, or fears of a mercenary captain; a man whose hardness the thin veil of politeness barely hid, who might be scrupulous, gentle, merciful — might be, in a word, all that was honourable. But whence, then, this story? Why this tale of cruelty, passing the bounds of discipline?

It so disheartened me that for some time I scarcely noticed what was passing before me; and I might have continued longer in this dull state if the Waldgrave's voice, civilly declining some proposition, had not caught my ear.

I gathered then what the offer was. Among the matches was one for officers, and in this the general was politely inviting his guest to compete. But the Waldgrave continued firm. 'You are very good,' he answered with perfect frankness and good temper. 'But I think I will not expose myself. I shoot badly with a strange gun.'

It was so unlike him to miss a chance of distinction, or underrate his merits, that I stared. He was changed, indeed, to-day; or he thought the position very critical, the need of caution very great.

The general continued to urge him; and so strongly that I began to think that our host had his own interests to serve.

'Oh, come,' he said, in a light, gibing tone which just stopped short of the offensive. 'You must not decline. There are five competitors — two Bohemians, a Scot, a Pole, and a Walloon; but no German. You cannot refuse to shoot for Germany, Waldgrave?'

The Waldgrave shook his head, however. 'I should do Germany small honour, I am afraid,' he said.

The general smiled unpleasantly. 'You are too modest,' he said.

'It is not a national failing,' the Waldgrave answered, smiling also.

'I fancy it must be,' the general retorted. 'And that is the reason we see so little of Germans in the war!'

The words were almost an insult, though a dull man, deceived by the civility of the speaker's tone, might have overlooked it. The Waldgrave understood, however. I saw him redden and his brow grow dark. But he restrained himself, and even found a good answer.

'Germany will find her champions,' he said, 'when she seriously needs them.'

'Abroad!' the general replied, speaking in a flash, as it were. The instant the word was said, I saw that he repented it. He had gone farther than he intended, and changed his tone. 'Well, if you will not, you will not,' he continued smoothly. 'Unless our fair cousin can succeed where I have failed, and persuade you.'

'I ?' my lady said — she had not been attending very closely. 'I will do what I can. Why will you not enter, Rupert? You are a good shot.'

'You wish me to shoot ?' the Waldgrave said slowly.

'Of course !' she answered. 'I think it is a shame General Tzerclas has so few German officers. If I could shoot, I would shoot for the honour of Germany myself.'

The Waldgrave bowed. 'I will shoot,' he said coldly.

'Good !' General Tzerclas answered, with a show of *bon-homie*. 'That is excellent. Will you descend with me ? Each competitor is to fire two shots at the figure at eighty paces. Those who lodge both shots in the target, to fire one shot at the head only.'

The young lord bowed and prepared to follow him.

'Comrade,' Ludwig said in my ear, as I watched them go, 'your master had better have stood by his first word.'

'Why ?'

'He will do no good.'

'Why not?' I asked.

'The Bohemian yonder — the fat man — will shoot round him. His little pig's eyes see farther than others. Besides, the devil has blessed his gun. He cannot miss.'

'What ! That tun of flesh ?' I cried, for he was pointing to the gross, unwieldy man, at whose saddle-bow I had marked the iron mace. 'Is he a Bohemian ?'

Ludwig nodded. 'Count Waska, they call him. There is no man in the camp can shoot with him or drink with him.'

'We shall see,' I said grimly.

I had little hope, however. The Waldgrave was a good shot; but a man was not likely to have a reputation for shooting in such a camp as this, where every one handled pistol or petronel, unless his aim was something out of the common. And listening to the talk round me, I found that Count Waska's comrades took his victory for granted.

Their confidence explained General Tzerclas' anxiety to

trap the Waldgrave into shooting. The jealous feeling
which had been all on the Waldgrave's side yesterday,
had spread to him to-day. He wished to see his rival
beaten in my lady's presence.

I longed to disappoint him; I felt sore besides for
the honour of Germany. I could not leave my lady, or
I would have gone down to see that the Waldgrave had
fair play, and a clean pan, and silence when he fired. But
I watched with as much excitement as any in the field, all
that passed; I doubt if I ever took part in a match myself
with greater keenness and interest than I felt as a spectator of this one.

From our elevated position we could see everything, and
the sight was a curious one. The rabble of spectators —
soldiers and women, sutlers and horse-boys — stretched
away in two dark lines, ten deep, being kept off the range
by a dozen men armed with whips. The clamour of their
hoarse shouting went up continuously, and sometimes almost
deafened us. Immediately below us, at the foot of the
mound, the champions and their friends were gathered,
settling rests, keying up the wheels of their locks, and
trying the flints. Owing to the Waldgrave's presence,
which somewhat imposed upon the other officers both by
reason of his rank and strangeness, the contest seemed
likely to be conducted more decently than those which had
preceded it. He was invited to shoot first, and when he
excused himself on the ground that he was not yet familiar
with his gun, Count Waska good-humouredly consented to
open the match.

His weapon, I remarked — and I treasured up the knowledge and have since made use of it — was smaller in the
bore than the others. He came forward and fired very carelessly, scarcely stooping to the rest; but he hit the figure
fairly in the breast with both bullets and retired, a stolid
smile on his large countenance.

The Waldgrave was the next to advance, and if he felt
one half of the anxiety I felt myself, it was a wonder he

let off his gun at all. General Tzerclas had returned to the Countess's side, and was speaking to her; but he paused at the critical moment, and both stood gazing, my lady with her lips parted and her eyes bright. The desire to see the stranger shoot was so general that something like silence prevailed while he aimed. I had time to conjure up half a dozen miseries — the gun might not be true, the powder weak; and then, bang! I saw the figure rock. He had hit it fairly in the breast, and I breathed again.

My lady cried, 'Vivat! good shot!' and he looked up at her before he primed his pan for a second trial. This time I felt less fear, the crowd less interest. The babel began afresh. His second bullet struck somewhat lower, but struck; and he stood back, his face flushed with pleasure. Honour, at any rate, was safe.

The Scot hit with both balls, the Pole with one only. Last of all the Walloon, a grim dark officer in a stained buff coat, who seemed to be unpopular with the soldiery, fired in the midst of such a storm of gibes and hisses that I wondered he could aim at all. He did, however, and hit with his second bullet. Even so he and the Pole stood out, leaving the Waldgrave, Count Waska, and the Scot to fire at the head.

Huge was the clamour which followed on this, half the company bellowing out offers to stake all that they had on the Count — money, chains, armour. Meanwhile I looked at the general to see how he took it. He had fallen silent, and my lady also. They stood gazing down on the com-petitors and their preparations, as if they were aware that more hung on the issue than a simple match at arms.

Count Waska advanced for the final shot, and this time he made ample use of the rest, aiming long and carefully over it. He fired, and I looked eagerly at the target. A roar of applause greeted the shot. The bullet had pierced the whitened face a little to the left, high up.

It was the Waldgrave's turn now. He came forward, with an air of quiet confidence, and set his weapon on the crutch. This time two or three voices were raised, gibing him; the crowd was growing jealous of its champion's reputation. I longed to be down among them, and I saw my lady's eyes flash and her colour rise. She looked indignantly at Tzerclas. But the general's face was set. He did not seem to hear.

Flash! Plop! In a moment I was shouting with the rest, shouting lustily for the honour of the house! The Waldgrave had lodged his ball in the upper part of the face towards the right-hand side. If Waska had put in the one eye, he had put in the other.

We shouted. But the camp hung silent, gloomily wondering whether this were luck or skill. And the general stood silent too. It was not until my lady had cried, 'Vivat! Vivat Weimar!' in her frank, brave voice, that he spoke and echoed the compliment.

When he had spoken, sullen silence fell upon the crowd again. I saw men look at us — not pleasantly; until the Scot by taking his place at the crutch diverted their attention. It seemed to me that he was an hour arranging the rest and his weapon, scraping his priming this way and that, and putting in a fresh flint at the last moment. At length he fired. A roar of laughter followed. He had missed the target altogether.

How it was arranged I do not know, but we saw at once that Waska and the Waldgrave were about to take another shot. The Bohemian, as he levelled his weapon with care, looked up at us.

'We have put in his eyes,' he said in his guttural tones. 'I propose to put in his nose. If his excellency can better that, I give him the bone.'

He aimed very diligently, amid such a silence you could have heard a feather drop, and fired. He did as he had promised. His ball pierced the very middle of the face, a little below and between the two shots.

A wild roar of applause greeted the achievement. Even we who felt our honour at stake shouted with the rest and

threw up our caps; while my lady took off in her admiration a slender gold chain which she wore round her neck
and flung it to the champion, crying 'Vivat Bohemia!
Vivat Waska!'

He bowed with grotesque gallantry, and one of the
bystanders picked up the chain and gave it to him. We
smiled; for, too fat to kneel or stoop, he could no more
have recovered the gift himself than he could have taken
wings and flown. Fraulein Anna muttered something about
Tantalus and water, but I did not understand her, and in a
moment the Waldgrave gave me something else to think
about.

He stepped forward when the noise and cheering had
somewhat subsided, and like his antagonist he looked up
also.

'I do not see what there is left for me to do,' he said,
with a gallant air. 'I could give him a mouth, but I fear
I may set it on awry.'

Thrice he took aim, and, dissatisfied, forbore to fire.
The crowd, silent at first, and confident of their champion's
victory, began to jeer. At length he pulled. Plop! The
smoke cleared away. An inch below Waska's last shot
appeared another orifice. The Waldgrave had put in the
mouth.

We waved our caps and shouted until we were hoarse;
and the crowd shouted. But it soon became evident, amid
the universal clamour and uproar, that there were two
parties: one acclaiming the Waldgrave's success, and another and larger one crying fiercely that he was beaten —
that he was beaten! that his shot was not so near the
centre of the target as Count Waska's. The Waldgrave's
promise to make the mouth had been heard by a few only,
mainly his friends; and while these, headed by the Bohemian, who showed that his clumsy carcase still contained
some sparks of chivalry, tried to explain the matter to
others, the camp with one voice bellowed against him, the
more excited brandishing fists and weapons in the air,

while the less moved kept up a stubborn and monotonous chant of 'Waska! Waska! Waska!'

The only person unaffected by the tumult appeared to be the Waldgrave himself; who stood looking up at us in silence, a smile on his face. Presently, the noise still continuing, I saw him clap Count Waska on the shoulder, and the two shook hands. The Count seemed by his gestures — for the uproar and tumult were so great that all was done in dumb show — to be deprecating his retreat. But the younger man persisted, and by-and-by, after saluting the other competitors, he turned away, and began to force his way up the mound. It was time he did; the crowd had burst its bounds and flooded the range. The scene below was now a sea of wild confusion.

Such an ending seemed stupid in the extreme; in any place where ordinary discipline prevailed, it would have been easy to procure silence and restore order. And my lady, her face flushed with indignation, turned impatiently to the general, to see if he would not interfere. But he was, or he affected to be, powerless. He shrugged his shoulders with an indulgent smile, and a moment later, seeing the Waldgrave on his way to join us and the crowd still persistent, he gave the word to retire. The officers, who in the last hour had pressed on us inconveniently, fell back, and waiting only for the Waldgrave to reach his horse, we rode down the mound, and turned our faces towards the camp.

For a space, and while the uproar still rang in my ears, I could scarcely speak for indignation. Then came a reaction. I saw my lady's face as she rode alongside the Waldgrave and talked to him. And my spirits rose. General Tzerclas had the place on her other hand, but she had not a word for him. It was not so much that the young lord had distinguished himself and done well, but that in an awkward position he had borne himself with dignity and self-control. That pleased her.

I saw her eyes shine as she looked at him, and her mouth

grow tender; and I told myself with exultation that the Waldgrave had done something more than rival Waska — he had scored the first hit in the fight, and that no light one. The general would be wise, if he looked to his guard; fortunate, if he did not look too late.

CHAPTER XV.

THE DUEL CONTINUED.

I FELL to wondering, as we rode home, whether we should find all safe; for we had left Marie Wort and my lady's woman to keep house with two only of the men. From that, again, I strayed into thoughts of the chain, and of Marie herself, so that the very head of what happened when we reached the house escaped me. The first I knew of it, Fraulein Anna's horse backed suddenly into mine, and brought us all up short with a deal of jostling and plunging. When I looked forward to learn what was amiss, I saw a man lying on his face under my lady's horse, and so near it that the beast's feet were touching his head. The man was crying out something in a pitiful tone, and two or three of the general's officers who were riding abreast of me were swearing roundly, and there was great confusion.

General Tzerclas said something, but my lady overbore him. 'What is it?' I heard her cry. 'Get up, man, and speak. Don't lie there. What is it?'

The man rose to his knees, and cried out, 'Justice, justice, lady!' in a wild sort of way, adding something — which I could not understand, for he spoke in a vile *patois* — about a house. He was in a miserable plight, and looked scarcely human. His face was sallow, his eyes shone with famine, his shrunken limbs peered through mud-stained rags that only half covered him.

'Which is your house?' my lady asked gently. And when one of the officers who had ridden up abreast of her

would have intervened, she raised her hand with a gesture there was no mistaking. 'Which is your house?' she
repeated.

The man pointed to the one in which we had our
quarters.

'What! That one?' my lady cried incredulously. 'Then
what has brought you to this?' For the creature looked
the veriest scarecrow that ever hung about a church-porch.
His head and feet had no covering, his hair was foully
matted. He was filthy, hideous, famine-stricken.

And desperate. For, half-cringing, half-defiant, he pointed
his accusing finger at the general. 'He has! He and his
army!' he cried. 'That house was mine. Those fields
were mine. I had cattle, they have eaten them. I had
wood, they have burned it. I had meat, they have taken
it. I was rich, and I am *this!* I had, and I have not —
only a wife and babes, and they are dying in a ditch. May
the curse of God —— '

'Hush!' my lady cried, in an unsteady voice. And, without adding a word, she turned to General Tzerclas and
looked at him; as if this were Heritzburg, and she the
judge, he the criminal.

Doubtless the position was an awkward one. But he
showed himself equal to it. 'There has been foul play
here,' he said firmly. 'I think I remember the man's face.'
Then he turned and raised his hand. 'Let all stand back,'
he said in a stern, curt tone.

We fell back out of hearing, leaving him and my lady
with the man. For some time the general seemed to be
putting questions to the fellow, speaking to my mistress
between whiles. Presently he called sharply for Ludwig.
The captain went forward to them, and then it was very
plain what was going on, for the general raised his voice,
and made the rating he administered to his subaltern audible even by us. Back Ludwig came by-and-by, with a dark
sneer on his face, and we saw the general hand money to
the man.

'Teufel!' one of the fellows who rode beside me muttered, surprise in his voice. 'When the general gives,
look to your necks. It will cost some one dear, this!
I would not be in that clod's shoes for his booty ten times
told!'

Possibly. But I was not so much interested on the
clown's account as on my lady's; and one needed only half
an eye to see what the general's liberality had effected with
her. She was all smiles again, speaking to him with the
utmost animation, leaning towards him as she rode. She
forgot the Waldgrave, who had fallen back with the rest of
us; she forgot all but the general. He went with her to
the door of the house, gave his hand to help her to dismount, lingered talking to her on the threshold. And my
heart sank. I could have gnashed my teeth with anger as
I stood aside uncovered, waiting for him to go.

For how could we combat the man? Such an episode as
this, which should have opened my lady's eyes to his true
character, served only to restore him to favour and blind
her more effectually. It had undone all the good of the
afternoon; it had effaced alike the Waldgrave's success and
the general's remissness; it had given Tzerclas, who all
day had been losing slowly, the upper hand once more. I
felt the disappointment keenly.

I suppose it was that which made me think of consulting
Fraulein Anna, and begging her to use her influence with
my lady to get out of the camp. At any rate, the idea
occurred to me. I could not catch her then; but later in
the evening, when some acrobats, whom the general had
sent for the Countess's diversion, were performing outside,
and my lady had gone out to the fallen tree to see them the
better, I found the Fraulein alone in the outer room. She
looked up at my entrance.

'Who is it?' she said sharply, peering at me with her
white, short-sighted face. 'Oh, it is you, Mr. Thickhead,
is it? I know whom you have sneaked in to see!' she
added spitefully.

' That is well,' I answered civilly. ' For I came in to see you, Fraulein.'

'Oh!' she retorted, nodding her head in a very unpleasant manner. 'Then you want something. I can guess what it is. But go on.'

' If I want something,' I answered, 'and I do, it is in your own behalf, Fraulein. You heard what I said to my lady last night? I did not persuade her. Can you persuade her — to leave the camp and its commander?'

Fraulein Max shook her head. 'Why should I?' she said, smoothing out her skirt with her hands, and looking at me with a cunning smile. 'What have I to gain by persuading her, Master Schwartz?'

'Safety,' I said.

'Oh!' she cried ironically. 'Then let me remind you of something. When we were all safe and comfortable at Heritzburg — safe, mind you — who was it disturbed us? Who was it stirred up my lady to make trouble — *more improbi anseris* — and though I warned him what would come of it, persisted in it until we had all to flee at night like so many vagrants? Ay, and have never had a quiet night since! Who was that, Master Martin?'

' Fraulein,' I answered patiently, forbearing to remind her how much she had been herself in fault, ' I may have been wrong then. It does not alter the situation now.'

'Does it not?' she replied. 'But I think it does. You had your way at Heritzburg, and what came of it? Trouble and misery. You want your way now, but I shall not help you to it. I have had enough of your way, and I do not like it.'

She laughed triumphantly, seeing me silenced; and I stood looking at her, wondering what argument I could use. Doubtless she had had a comfortless time on the journey from Heritzburg, jogging through fords and over ruts, and along steep places, wet, tired, and scared, deprived of her books and all her home pleasures. She had had time and to spare to lay up many a grudge against me. Now it was her turn, and I read in her face her determination to make the most of it.

I might frighten her; and that seemed my only chance. 'Well, Fraulein,' I said after a pause, 'you may have been right then, and you may be right now. But I hope you have counted the cost. If my lady shows herself determined to leave, to-morrow and perhaps the next day the power of going will remain in her hands. Later it will have passed from her. Familiarity breeds contempt, and even the Countess of Heritzburg cannot stay long in such a camp as this, where nothing is respected, without losing that respect which for the moment protects her. In a day or two, in a few days, the hedge will fall. And then, Fraulein, we may all look to ourselves.'

But Fraulein Anna laughed shrilly. '*O tu anser!*' she cried contemptuously. 'Open your eyes! Cannot you see that the general is knee-deep in love with her? In a week he will be head over ears, and her slave!'

I stared at her. Doubtless she knew; she was a woman. I drew a deep breath. 'Well,' I said, 'and what of that?'

She looked at me spitefully. 'Ask my lady!' she said. 'How should I know?'

I returned her gaze, and thought awhile. Then I said coldly, 'I think it is you who are the fool, Fraulein. Take it for granted that what you tell me is true. Have you considered what will happen should my lady repulse him? What will happen to her and to us?'

'She will not,' Fraulein Max answered.

But I saw that the shaft had gone home. She fidgeted on her seat. And I persisted. 'Still, if she does?' I said. 'What then?'

'She will not!' she answered. 'She must not!'

'By Heaven!' I cried, 'you are on his side!'

She blinked at me with her short-sighted eyes. 'And why not?' she said slowly. 'On whose side should I be? My Lord Waldgrave's? He never gives me a word, and seldom recognises my existence. On yours? If you want help, go to the black-eyed puling girl you have brought in, who is always creeping and crawling round us, and would oust me if she and you could manage it and she had the breeding. Chut! don't talk to me,' she continued maliciously, the colour rising to her pale cheeks. 'I wonder that you dare to come to me with such proposals! Is my lady to be ruled by her servants? Has she no judgment of her own? Why, you fool, I have but to tell her, and you are disgraced!'

'As you please, Fraulein,' I said sullenly, stung to anger by one part of her harangue. 'But as to Marie Wort——'

'Marie Wort?' she cried, catching me up and mocking my tone. 'Who said anything about her, I should like to know? Though for my part, had I my way, the popish chit should be whipped!'

'Fraulein!' I cried.

She laughed bitterly. 'Oh, you are fools, you men!' she said. 'But I have made you angry, and that is enough. Go! Yes, go. I have supped on folly. Go, before your mistress comes in; or I must out with all, and lose a power over you.'

I went sullenly. While we had been talking the room had been growing dark. Then it had grown light again with a smoky, dancing glare that played fantastically on the walls and seemed to rise and sink with the murmur of applause outside. They had brought torches made of pine-knots that my lady might see the longer, and in the yellow circle of light which these shed, the mountebanks, monstrously dressed and casting weird shadows, were wrestling and leaping and writhing. The light reached, but fitfully and by flashes, the log on which my lady sat enthroned, with General Tzerclas and the Waldgrave at her side. Still farther away the crowd surged and laughed and gibed in the darkness.

I looked at my lady and found one look enough. I read the utter hopelessness of the attempt I had just made. She was enjoying herself. Fear was not natural to her,

and she saw nothing to fear either in the man beside her or
the crowd beyond. Suspicion was no part of her character,
and she saw nothing to suspect. Had I won Fraulein Max
over to my side, as I felt sure that the general had bought
her to his, I should equally have had my trouble for my
pains, and no more.

My only hope lay in the Waldgrave. He alone, could he
once warm into flower the love that hung trembling in the
bud, might move her as I would have her moved. But,
then, the time ? Every hour we remained where we were,
every day that rose and found us in the camp, rendered
retreat more difficult, the general's plans more definite.
He might not yet have made up his mind; he might not
yet have hardened his heart to the point of employing
force; *his* passion might be still in the bud, his ambition
unshaped. But how long dared I give him?

Assured that here lay the stress, I watched the young
lord's progress with an anxiety scarcely less than his own.
And the longer I watched the higher rose my hopes. It
seemed to me that he went steadily forward in favour,
while the general stood still. More than once during the
next two days the latter showed himself irritable or capri-
cious. The iron hand began to push through the silken
glove. And though, on every one of these occasions, Tzerclas covered his mistake with the dexterity of a man of the
world, and my lady's eyes could scarcely be said to be
opened, a little coolness resulted, of which the Waldgrave
had the benefit.

He, on his part, seemed imperturbable. Love had to all
appearance changed his nature. A dozen times in the two
days the impulse to fly at his rival's throat must have been
strong upon him, yet through all he remained calm, pleasant, and courteous, and carried an old head on young
shoulders.

I wondered at last why he did not speak, for I marked
the cloud on the general's brow growing darker and darker,
and I found the forced inaction and suspense intolerable.

Then I gathered, I cannot say why, that the Waldgrave would not speak until after the great banquet to which the general had bidden my lady. It had been deferred a day or two, but on the third day after the shooting-match it took place.

CHAPTER XVI.

THE GENERAL'S BANQUET.

I SUPPOSE it was not love only that enabled the Waldgrave to carry himself so prudently at this time ; but with it a sense of the peril in which we all stood. He was so far from betraying this, however, that no one could have worn an air more gallant or seemed in every way more free from care. General Tzerclas had supplied us with a couple of tailors, and there were rich stuffs to be bought in the camp ; and the young lord did not neglect these opportunities. When he came on the morning of the great day to attend my lady to the banquet, he wore a suit of dark-blue velvet with a falling collar of white lace, and sash and points of lighter blue — the latter setting off his fair complexion to advantage. His hair, which had grown somewhat, flowed from under a broad-leafed hat decked with an ostrich feather, and he wore golden spurs, and high boots with the tops turned down. As he caracoled up and down before the house, with the sun shining on his fair head, he looked to my eyes as beautiful as Apollo. What the women thought of him I do not know, but I saw my lady gazing at him from a window when his back was turned, and then, again, when he looked towards the house, she was gone. And I thought I knew what that meant.

She wore, herself, a grey riding-coat with a little silver braid about it, and a silver belt; and we all made what show we could ; so that when we started to the general's quarters we were something to look at. The camp itself nothing could cleanse, but the village had been swept and

11

the street watered. Pennons and cornets waved here and there in the sunshine, and green boughs garnished the fronts of the houses. Two tall poles, painted after the Venetian fashion and hung with streamers, stood before the general's quarters, the windows of which were almost hidden by a large trophy formed of glittering pikes and flags of many colours. The road here was strewn with green rushes, and opposite the house were ranked twelve trumpeters, who proclaimed my lady's arrival with a blare which shook the village.

On either side of the door a guard of honour was drawn up. I was not disposed to admire anything much, but it must be confessed that the sun shining on pike and corselet and steel cap, and on all the gay and gaudy colours and green leaves, produced a lively and striking effect. The moment my lady's horse stopped, four officers stepped from the doorway and stood at attention; after whom the general himself appeared bare-headed, and held my lady's stirrup while she dismounted. The Waldgrave performed a like service for Fraulein Anna, and I and Jacob for Marie Wort and the women.

Our host first conducted my lady into a withdrawing-room, where were only Count Waska and three colonels. This room, which was small, was fitted with a rich carpet and chairs covered with Spanish leather, as good as any my lady had in the castle at Heritzburg; and the walls were hidden behind Cordovan hangings. Here among other things were a large cage of larks and a strange, misshapen dwarf that stood hardly as high as my waist-belt, but was rumoured to be forty years old. He said several witty things to my lady, and one or two that I fancy the general had taught him, for they brought the blood to her cheeks. On a table stood another very rare and curious thing — a gold or silver-gilt fountain that threw up distilled waters, and continually cooled and sweetened the air. There were besides, gold cups and plates and jewelled arms and Venice glass, which fairly dazzled me; so that as I stood at the

door with Jacob and the two maids I wondered at the rich-
ness and splendour of everything, and yet could not get
out of my head the squalor of the hot, seething camp outside, and the poverty of the country round, which the army
had eaten as bare as my hand.

After a short interval spent in listening to the dwarf's
quips and cranks, General Tzerclas conducted my lady with
much ceremony to the next room, where the banquet was
laid. The floor of this larger room was strewn with scented
rushes, the walls being adorned with trophies of arms and
heads of deer and wolves, peering from ambushes of green
leaves. At the upper end, where was the private door of
entrance, was a dais table laid for eight persons; below
were tables for forty or more. On the dais the general
sat in the middle, having my lady on the right, and next to
her Count Waska; on his left he had the Waldgrave, and
beyond him Fraulein Anna. The two women stood behind
my lady, holding her fan and vinaigrette. At the lower
end of the room the general's band, placed in a kind of
cage, played soft airs, while between the courses a gipsy
girl danced very prettily, and a juggler diverted the company with his tricks.

·As for the diversity of meats and fishes, and especially of
birds, which was set on, it surprised me beyond measure;
nor can I understand whence, in the wasted condition of
the country, it was procured. For wines, Burgundy,
Frontignac, and Tokay were served at the high table, and
Rhine wines below. The courses continued to succeed one
another for nearly three hours, but such was the skill of the
musicians that the time seemed short. One man in particular won my lady's approbation. He played on a new
instrument, shaped somewhat like a viol, but smaller and
more roundly framed. Though it had three strings only
and was a trifle shrill, it had a wonderful power of touching
the heart, arousing the memory and producing a sweet
melancholy. The general would have had my lady accept
it, and said that he could easily procure another from the

Milanese ; but she declined gracefully, on the ground that without the player it would be a dumb boon.

There was so much gaiety in all this — and decent observance too, for the general's presence kept good order — that I did not wonder that my lady's eyes sparkled and betrayed the gratification she felt. All was for her, all in her honour. Even I, who looked at the scene through green glasses and could not hear a word the general said without striving to place some ill construction on it — even I felt myself somewhat carried away, when the first toast, that of the Emperor, was given in the midst of cheering, partly serious, partly ironical. It was followed by that of the Elector of Saxony. The King of Sweden came next, and was received in an equally equivocal manner. Not so, however, the fourth, which was given by General Tzerclas standing, with his plumed hat in his hand.

' All in Tokay ! ' he cried in his deep voice. ' The most noble and high-born, the Countess Rotha of Heritzburg, who honours us with her presence ! Hoch ! Hoch ! Hoch ! '

And draining his goblet, which was of green Nuremberg glass, and of no mean value, he dashed it to the floor, an example which was immediately followed by all present, so that the crash of glass and clang of sword-hilts filled the room with high-pitched sounds that seemed to intoxicate the ear.

My lady rose and bowed thrice, with her cheek crimson and her eyes soft. Then she turned to retire, while all remained standing. The general accompanied her as far as the door of the withdrawing-room, the Waldgrave following with Fraulein Anna ; while the dwarf marched side by side with me, keeping step with an absurd gravity which filled the room with laughter. On the threshold the general and his companions left us with low bows ; but in a trice Tzerclas came back to say a word in my ear.

' See to the other door,' he muttered, flashing a grim look at me. ' There may be deep drinking. If any offer so much as a word of rudeness here, he shall hang, drunk or sober. Have a care, therefore, that no one has the chance.'

Then my heart sank, for I knew, hearing his tone and seeing his face, as he said that, that Fraulein Anna was right. He loved my mistress. He loved her! I went away to my place by the door, feeling as if he had struck me in the face. For if she loved him in return that were bad enough; and if she did not, what then, seeing that we were in his power?

Certainly he had omitted nothing on this occasion that might charm her. I thought the feast over; but in the withdrawing-room a fresh collation of dainty sweets and syrups awaited my lady, with a great gold bowl of rose-water. The man, too, who had played on the Italian viol brought it in, that she might see and examine it more closely. From my post at the door, I saw Fraulein Anna flitting about, bringing her short-sighted eyes down to everything, thrusting her face into the rose-water, and peering at the weapons and stuffs as if she would eat them. All the while, too, I could hear her prattling ceaseless praise of everything — the general's taste, the general's wealth, his generosity, his skill in Latin, his love for Cæsar — the fat book I had seen him studying by the fire — above all, his appreciation of Voetius, of whom I shrewdly believe he had never heard before.

My lady sat almost silent under the steady shower of words, listening and thinking, and now and then touching the strings of the viol which lay forgotten on her lap. Perhaps she was dreaming of her two admirers, perhaps only giving ear to the growing tumult in the room we had left, where the revellers were still at their wine. By-and-by we heard them break into song, and then in thunder the chorus came rolling out —

'Hoch! Who rides with old Pappenheim knee to knee
The sword is his title, the world is his fee!
He knows nor Monarch, nor Sire, nor clime
Who follows the banner of bold Pappenheim!'

My lady's lip curled. 'Is there no one on our side they can sing ?' she muttered, tapping the viol impatiently with her fingers. 'Have we no heroes ? Has Count Bernard never headed a charge or won a fight ? Pappenheim ? I am tired of the man.'

The note jarred on her, as it had on me when I first heard these men, paid by the north, singing the praises of the great southern raider. But a moment later she turned her head to hear better, and her face grew thoughtful. A great shout of 'Waska ! Waska !' rang above the jingling of glasses and snatches of song; and then, 'The Waldgrave ! The Waldgrave !' This time the cry was less boisterous, the voices were fewer.

My lady turned to me. 'What is it ?' she said, a note of anxiety in her voice.

I was unable to tell her and I listened. By-and-by a roar of laughter made itself heard, and was followed by a cry of 'Waska !' as before. And then, 'The Thuringian Code ! The Thuringian Code ! It is his turn !'

'They are drinking, your excellency,' I said reluctantly. 'It is a drinking match, I think !'

She rose with a grand gesture, and set the little viol back on the table. 'I am going,' she said, almost fiercely. 'Let the horses be called.'

Fraulein Max looked scared, but my lady's face forbade argument or reply ; and for my part I was not a whit unwilling. I turned and gave the order to Jacob. While he was away the Countess remained standing, tapping the floor with her foot.

'On this day — on this day they might have abstained !' she muttered wrathfully, as the chorus of riot and laughter grew each moment louder and wilder.

I thought so too, and was glad besides of anything which might work a breach between her and the general. But I little knew what was going to happen. It came upon us while we waited, with no more warning than I have described. The door by which we had left the banqueting

chamber flew suddenly open, and three men, borne in on a
wave of cheering and uproar, staggered in upon us, the
leader reeling under the blows which his applauding
followers rained upon his shoulders.

'There! Said I not so?' he cried thickly, lurching
to one side to escape them, and almost falling. 'Where
ish your Waska. Your Waska now I'd like to know!
Waska is great, but I am — greater — greater, you see. I
can shoot, drink, fight, and make love better than any
man here! Eh! Who shays I can't? Eh? Itsh the
Countesh! My cousin the Countesh! Ah!'

Alas, it was the Waldgrave! And yet not the Waldgrave.
This man's face was pale and swollen and covered with
perspiration. His eyes were heavy and sodden, and his
hair strayed over them. His collar and his coat were open
at the neck, and his sash and the front of his dress were
stained and reeking with wine. His hands trembled, his
legs reeled, his tongue was too large for his mouth. He
smiled fatuously at us. Yet it *was* the Waldgrave —
drunk!

My lady's face froze as she looked at him. She raised
her hand, and the men behind him fell back abashed and
left him standing there, propping himself uncertainly
against the wall.

'Well, your excellenshy,' he stuttered with a hiccough —
the sudden silence surprised him — 'you don't congratu-
latsh me! Waska is under table. Under table, I shay!'

My lady looked at him, her eyes blazing with scorn.
But she said nothing; only her fingers opened and closed
convulsively. I turned to see if Jacob had come back
He entered at that moment and General Tzerclas with him.

'Your excellency's horses are coming,' the general said
in his usual tone. Then he saw the Waldgrave and the
open door, and he started with surprise. 'What is this?'
he said. His face was flushed and his eyes were bright.
But he was sober.

The drunken man tried to straighten himself. 'Ashk

Waska!' he said. Alas! his good looks were gone. I regarded him with horror, I knew what he had done.

'The horses?' the general muttered.

My lady drew a deep breath, as a person recovering consciousness does, and turned slowly towards him. 'Yes,'
she said, shuddering from head to foot, 'if you please. I
wish to go.'

The young lord heard the horses come to the door, and
staggered forward. 'Yesh, letsh go. I'll go too,' he stuttered with a foolish laugh. 'Letsh all go. Except Waska!
He is under the table. Letsh all go, I say! Eh? Whatsh
thish?'

I pushed him back and held him against the wall while
the general led my lady out. But, oh the pity of it, the
wrath, the disappointment that filled my breast as I did so!
This was the end of my duel! This was the stay to which
I had trusted! The Waldgrave's influence with my lady?
It was gone — gone as if it had never been. A spider's
web, a rope of sand, a straw were after this a stronger
thing to depend upon, a more sure safeguard, a stouter
holdfast for a man in peril!

*   *   *   *   *   *

He came to my lady next morning about two hours after
sunrise, when the dew was still on the grass and the birds
— such as had lost their first broods or were mating late —
were in full song. The camp was sleeping off its debauch,
and the village street was bright and empty, with a dog
here and there gnawing a bone, or sneaking round the
corner of a building. My lady had gone out early to the
fallen tree with her psalm book; and was sitting there in
the freshness of the morning, with her back to the house
and the street, when his shadow fell across the page and
she looked up and saw him.

She said 'good morning' very coldly, and he for a
moment said nothing, but stood, sullenly making a hole in
the dust with his toe and looking down at it. His face
was pale, where it was not red with shame, and his eyes

were heavy and dull; but otherwise the wine he had taken had left no mark on his vigorous youth.

My lady after speaking looked down at her book again, and he continued to stand before her like a whipped school-boy, stealing every now and then a furtive look at her. At length she looked up again.

'Do you want anything?' she said.

This time he returned her gaze, with his face on fire, trying to melt her. And I think that there were not many more unhappy men at that moment than he. His fancy, liking, love were centred in the woman before him; in a mad freak he had outraged, insulted, estranged her. He did not know what to do, how to begin, what plea to put forward. He could for the moment only look, with shame and misery in his face.

It was a plea that would have melted many, but my lady only grew harder. 'Did you hear me?' she said proudly. 'Do you want anything?'

'You know!' he cried impetuously, and his voice broke out fiercely and seemed to beat against her impassiveness as a bird against the bars of its cage. 'I was a beast last night. But, oh, Rotha, forgive me.'

'I think that we had better not talk about it,' my lady answered him stonily. 'It is past, and we need not quarrel over it. I shall be wiser next time,' she added. 'That is all.'

'Wiser?' he muttered.

'Yes; wiser than to trust myself to your protection,' she replied ruthlessly.

He shrank back as if she had struck him, and for a moment pain and rage brought the blood surging to his cheeks. He even took a step as if to leave her; but when love and pride struggle in a young man, love commonly has it, and he turned again and stood hesitating, the picture of misery.

'Is that all you will say to me?' he muttered, his voice unsteady.

My lady moved her feet uneasily. Then she shut her
book, and looked round as if she would have willingly
escaped. But she was not stone ; and when at length she
turned to him, her face was changed.

' What do you want me to say ? ' she asked gently.

' That some day you will forgive me.'

' I forgive you now,' she rejoined firmly. ' But I cannot
forget. I do not think I ever can,' she went on. ' Last
night I was in your charge among strangers. If danger
had arisen, whose arm was to shield me, if not yours ? If
any had insulted me, to whom was I to look, if not to you ?
Yes, you may well hide your face,' my lady continued, waxing bitter, despite herself. ' I am not at Heritzburg now,
and you should have remembered that. I am here with
scanty protection, with few means to exact respect, a refu-
gee, if you like, a mark for scandal, and your kinswoman.
And you ? for shame, Rupert ! '

He fell on his knees and seized her hand. ' You are
killing me ! ' he cried in a choking voice, his face pale, his
breath coming quickly. ' For I love you, Rotha, I love
you ! And every word of reproach you utter is death to
me.'

' Hush, Rupert ! ' she said quickly. And she tried to
withdraw her hand. He had taken her by surprise.

But he was not to be silenced ; he kept her hand, though
he rose to his feet. ' It is true,' he answered. ' I have
waited long enough. I must speak now, or it may be too
late. I tell you, I love you ! '

The Countess's face was crimson, her brow dark with
vexation. ' Hush ! ' she said again, and more imperatively.
' I have heard enough. It is useless.'

' You have not heard me ! ' he answered. ' Don't say so
until you have heard me.' And he sat down suddenly on
the tree beside her, and looked into her face with pleading ·
eyes. ' You are letting last night weigh against me,' he
went on. ' If that be all, I will never drink more than
three cups of wine at a time as long as I live. I swear it.'

She shook her head rather sadly. 'That is not all, Rupert,' she said.

'Then what will you have?' he answered eagerly. He saw the change in her, and his eyes began to burn with hope as he looked. Her milder tone, her downcast head, her altered aspect, all encouraged him. 'I love you, Rotha!' he cried, raising her hand to his lips. 'What more will you have? Tell me. All I have, and all I ever shall have — and I am young and may do great things — are yours. I have been riding behind you day by day, until I know every turn of your head, and every note of your voice. I know your step when you walk, and the rustle of your skirt among a hundred! And there is no other woman in the world for me! What if I am the youngest cadet of my house?' he continued, leaning towards her; 'this war will last many a year yet, and I will carve you a second county with my sword. Wallenstein did. Who was he? A simple gentleman. Now he is Duke of Friedland. And that Englishman who married a king's sister? They succeeded, why should not I? Only give me your love, Rotha! Trust me; trust me once more and always, and I will not fail you.'

He tried to draw her nearer to him, but the Countess shook her head, and looked at him with tears in her eyes. 'Poor boy,' she said slowly. 'Poor boy! I am sorry, but it cannot be. It can never be.'

'Why?' he cried, starting as if she had stung him.

'Because I do not love you,' she said.

He dropped her hand and sat glaring at her. 'You are thinking of last night!' he muttered.

She shook her head. 'I am not,' she said simply. 'I suppose that if I loved you, that and worse would go for nothing. But I do not.'

Her calmness, her even tone went to his heart and chilled it. He winced, and uttering a low cry turned from her and hid his face in his hands.

'Why not?' he said thickly, after an interval. 'Why can you not love me?'

'Why does the swallow nest here and not there?' the Countess answered gently. 'I do not know. Why did my father love a foreigner and not one of his own people? I do not know. Neither do I know why I do not love you. Unless,' she added, with rising colour, 'it is that you are young, younger than I am; and a woman turns naturally to one older than herself.'

Her words seemed to point so surely to General Tzerclas that the young man ground his teeth together. But he had not spirit to turn and reproach her then; and after remaining silent for some minutes, he rose.

'Good-bye,' he said in a broken voice. And he lifted her hand to his lips and kissed it.

The Countess started. The words, the action impressed her disagreeably. 'You are not going — away I mean?' she said.

'No,' he answered slowly. 'But things are — changed. When we meet again it will be as ——'

'Friends!' she cried, her voice tender almost to yearning. 'Say it shall be so. Let it be so always. You will not leave me alone here?'

'No,' he said simply, and with dignity. 'I shall not.'

Then he went away, quite quietly; and if the beginning of the interview had shown him to small advantage, the same could not be said of the end. He went down the street and through the camp with his head on his breast and a mist before his eyes. The light was gone out of the sunshine, the greenness from the trees. The day was grey and dreary and miserable. The blight was on all he saw. So it is with men. When they cannot have that which seems to them the best and fairest and most desirable thing in the world, nothing is good or pleasant or to be desired any longer.

CHAPTER XVII.

STALHANSKE'S FINNS.

It was my ill luck, on that day which began so inaus-
piciously, to see two shadows: one on a man's face, the
Waldgrave's, and of that I need say no more; the other,
the shadow of a man's body, an odd, sinister outline,
crooked and strange and tremulous, that I came upon in
a remote corner of the camp, to which I had wandered in
my perplexity; a place where a few stunted trees ran down
a steep bank to the river. I had never been to this place
before, and, after a glance which showed me that it was the
common sink and rubbish-bed of the camp, I was turning
moodily away, when first this shadow and then the body
which cast it caught my eye. The latter hung from the
branch of an old gnarled thorn, the feet a few inches from
the ground. A shuddering kind of curiosity led me to go
up and look at the dead man's face, which was doubled up on
his breast; and then the desire to test the nerves, which is
common to most men, induced me to stand staring at him.

The time was two hours after noon, and there were few
persons moving. The camp was half asleep. Heat, and
flies, and dust were everywhere — and this gruesome thing.
The body was stripped, and the features were swollen and
disfigured; but, after a moment's thought, I recognized
them, and saw that I had before me the poor wretch who
had appealed to my lady's compassion after the shooting-
match, and to whom the general had opened his hand so
freely. The grim remarks I had then heard recurred now,
and set me shuddering. If any doubt still remained in my
mind, it was dissipated a moment later by a placard which
had once hung round the dead man's neck, but now lay in
the dust at his feet. I turned it over. Chalked on it in
large letters were the words 'Beggars, beware!'

I felt at first, on making the discovery, only horror and indignation, and a violent loathing of the camp. But these feelings soon passed, and left me free to consider how the deed touched us. Could I prove it? Could I bring it home to the general to my lady's satisfaction, beyond denial or escape, and so open her eyes? And if I could, would it be wise, by doing so, to rouse his anger while she remained in the camp and in General Tzerclas' power? I might only hasten the catastrophe.

I found this a hard nut to crack, and was still puzzling over it, with my eyes on the senseless form which was already so far out of my thoughts, when a heavy hand fell on my shoulder and a harsh voice grated on my ear.

'Well, Master Steward, a penny for your thoughts! They should be worth having, to judge by the way you rub your chin.'

I started and looked round. The speaker was Captain Ludwig, who, with two of his fellows, had come up behind me while I mused. Something in his tone rather than his words — a note of menace — warned me to be careful; while the glum looks of his companions, as they glanced from me to the dead man, added point to the hint, and filled my mind with a sudden sense of danger. I had learned more than I had been intended to learn; I had found out something I had not been intended to find out. The very quietness and sunshine and the solitude of the place added horror to the moment. It was all I could do to hide my discomfiture and face them without flinching.

'My thoughts?' I said, forcing a grin. 'They were not very difficult to guess. A sharp shrift, and a short rope? What else should a man think here?'

'Ay?' Ludwig said, watching me closely with his eyes half closed and his lips parted.

He would say no more, and I was forced to go on. 'It is not the first time I have seen a man dancing on nothing!' I said recklessly; 'but it gave me a turn.'

He kicked the placard. 'You are a scholar,' he said. 'What is this?'

My face grew hot. I dared not deny my learning, for I did not know how much he knew; but, for the nonce, I wished heartily that I had never been taught to read.

'That?' I said, affecting a jovial tone to cover my momentary hesitation. 'A seasonable warning. They are as thick here as nuts in autumn. We could spare a few more, for the matter of that.'

'Ay, but this one?' he retorted, coolly tapping the dead man with a little stick he carried, and then turning to look me in the face. 'You have seen him before.'

I made a great show of staring at the body, but I suppose I played my part ill, for before I could speak Ludwig broke in with a brutal laugh.

'Chut, man!' he said, with a sneer of contempt; 'you know him; I see you do. And knew him all along. Well, if fools will poke their noses into things that do not concern them, it is not my affair. I must trouble you for your company awhile.'

'Whither?' I said, setting my teeth together and frowning at him.

'To my master,' he replied, with a curt nod. 'Don't say you won't,' he continued with meaning, 'for he is not one to be denied.'

I looked from one to another of the three men, and for a moment the desperate clinging to liberty, which makes even the craven bold, set my hands tingling and sent the blood surging to my head. But reason spoke in time. I saw that the contest was too unequal, the advantage of a few minutes' freedom too trivial, since the general must sooner or later lay his hand on me; and I crushed down the impulse to resist.

'What scares you, comrades?' I said, laughing savagely. They had recoiled a foot. 'Do you see a ghost or a Swede, that you look so pale? Your general wants me? Then let him have me. Lead on! I won't run away, I warrant you.'

Ludwig nodded as he placed himself by my side. 'That is the right way to take it,' he said. 'I thought that you might be going to be a fool, comrade.'

'Like our friend there,' I said dryly, pointing to the senseless form we were leaving. 'He made a fuss, I suppose?'

Ludwig shrugged his shoulders. 'No,' he answered, not he so much; but his wife. Donner! I think I hear her screams now. And she cursed us! Ah!'

I shuddered, and after that was silent. But more than once before we reached the general's quarters the frantic desire to escape seized me, and had to be repressed. I felt that this was the beginning of the end, the first proof of the strong grasp which held us all helpless. I thought of my lady, I thought of Marie Wort, and I could have shrieked like a woman; for I was powerless like a woman — gripped in a hand I could not resist.

The camp grilling and festering in the sunshine — how I hated it! It seemed an age I had lived in its dusty brightness, an age of vague fears and anxieties. I passed through it now in a feverish dream, until an exclamation, uttered by my companion as we turned into the street, aroused me. The street was full of loiterers, all standing in groups, and all staring at a little band of horsemen who sat motionless in their saddles in front of the general's quarters. For a moment I took these to be the general's staff. Then I saw that they were dressed all alike, that their broad, ruddy faces were alike, that they held themselves with the same unbending precision, and seemed, in a word, to be ten copies of one stalwart man. Near them a servant on foot was leading two horses up and down, and they and he had the air of being on show.

Captain Ludwig, holding me fast by the arm, stopped at the first group of starers we came to. 'Who are these?' he asked gruffly.

The man he addressed turned round, eager to impart his knowledge. 'Finns!' he said; 'from head-quarters — Stalhanske's Finns. No less, captain.'

My companion whistled. 'What are they doing here?' he asked.

The other shook his head. 'I don't know,' he said. 'Their leader is with the general. What do you think of them, Master Ludwig?'

But Ludwig only grunted, looking with disparaging eyes at the motionless riders, whose air betrayed a certain consciousness of their fame and the notice which they were exciting. From steel cap to spurred boot, they showed all metal and leather. Nothing gay, nothing gaudy; not a chain or a sash differenced one from another. Grim, stern, and silent, they stared before them. Had no one named the King of Sweden's great regiment, I had known that I was looking no longer on brigands, but on soldiers — on part of the iron line that at Breitenfeld broke the long repute of years, and swept Pappenheim from the hillside like chaff before the storm.

After hesitating a moment, Ludwig went forward a few paces, as if to enter the house, taking me with him. Then he paused. At the same instant the man who was leading the two horses turned. His eye lit on me, and I saw an extraordinary change come over the fellow's face. He stopped short and, pulling up his horses, stared at me. It seemed to me, too, that I had seen him before, and I returned his look; but while I was trying to remember where, the door of the general's quarters opened. Two or three men who were loitering before it, stepped quickly aside, and a tall, stalwart man came out, followed by General Tzerclas himself.

I looked at the foremost, and in a twinkling recognized him. It was Von Werder. But an extraordinary change had come over the traveller. He was still plainly dressed, in a buff coat, with untanned boots, a leather sword-belt, and a grey hat with a red feather; and in all of these there was nothing to catch the eye. But his air and manner as he spoke to his companion were no longer those of an inferior, while his stern eye, as it travelled over the crowd in the street, expressed cold and steady contempt.

As the servant brought up his horse, he spoke to his

12

companion. 'You are sure that you can do it — with
these?' he said, flicking his riding-whip towards the silent
throng.

'You may consider it done,' the general answered rather
grimly.

'Good! I am glad. Well, man, what is it?'

He spoke the last words to his servant. The man
pointed to me and said something. Von Werder looked
at me. In a moment every one looked at me. Then
Von Werder swung himself into his saddle, and turned
to General Tzerclas.

'That is the man, I am told,' he said, pointing suddenly
to me with his whip.

'He is at your service,' the general answered with a
shrug of indifference.

In an instant Von Werder's horse was at my side. 'A
word with you, my man,' he said sharply. 'Come with
me.'

Ludwig had hold of my arm still. He had not loosed
me, and at this he interposed. 'My lord,' he cried to the
general, 'this man — I have something to ——'

'Silence, fool!' Tzerclas growled. 'And stand aside, if
you value your skin!'

Ludwig let me go; immediately, as if an angel had
descended to speak for me, the crowd parted, and I was
free — free and walking away down the street by the side
of the stranger, who continued to look at me from time to
time, but still kept silence. When we had gone in this
fashion a couple of hundred paces or more, and were clear
of the crowd, he seemed no longer able to control himself,
though he looked like a man apt at self-command. He
waved his escort back and reined in his horse.

'You are the man to whom I talked the other night,' he
said, fixing me with his eyes — 'the Countess of Heritzburg's steward?'

I replied that I was. His face as he looked down at me,
with his back to his following, betrayed so much agitation

that I wondered more and more. Was he going to save us ?
Could he save us ? Who was he ? What did it all mean ?
Then his next question scattered all these thoughts and
doubled my surprise.

'You had a chain stolen from you,' he said harshly,
'the night I lay in your camp?'

I stared at him with my mouth open. 'A chain?' I
stammered.

'Ay, fool, a chain!' he replied, his eyes glaring, his
cheeks swelling with impatience. 'A gold chain — with
links like walnuts.'

'It is true,' I said stupidly. 'I had. But——'

'Where did you get it?'

I looked away. To answer was easy; to refrain from
answering, with his eye upon me, hard. But I thought of
Marie Wort. I did not know how the chain had come into
her hands, and I asked him a question in return.

'Have you the chain?' I said.

'I have!' he snarled. And then in a sudden outburst of
wrath he cried, 'Listen, fool! And then perhaps you will
answer me more quickly. I am Hugo of Leuchtenstein,
Governor of Cassel and Marburg, and President of the
Landgrave's Council. The chain was mine and came back
to me. The rogue who stole it from you, and joined himself to my company, blabbed of it, and where he got it.
He let my men see it. He would not give it up, and they
killed him. Will that satisfy you?' he continued, his face
on fire with impatience. 'Then tell me all — all, man, or it
will be the worse for you! My time is precious, and I
cannot stay!'

I uncovered myself. 'Your excellency,' I stammered,
'the chain was entrusted to me by a — a woman.'

'A woman?' he exclaimed, his eyes lightening. 'Man,
you are wringing my heart. A woman with a child?'

I nodded.

'A child three years old?'

'About that, your excellency.' On which, to my aston-

ishment, he covered his face with both his hands, and I saw
the strong man's frame heave with ill-suppressed emotion.
'My God, I thank thee!' I heard him whisper; and if ever
words came from the heart, those did. It was a minute or
more before he dared to uncover his face, and then his eyes
were moist and his features worked with emotion.

'You shall be rewarded!' he said unsteadily. 'Do not
fear. And now take me to him — to her.'

I was in a maze of astonishment, but I had sense enough
to understand the order. We had halted scarcely more
than a hundred yards from my lady's quarters, and I led
the way thither, comprehending little more than that something advantageous had happened to us. At the door he
sprang from his horse, and taking me by the arm, as if he
were afraid to suffer me out of his reach, he entered,
pushing me before him.

The principal room was empty, and I judged my lady was
out. I cried 'Marie! Marie!' softly; and then he and I
stood listening. The sunshine poured in through the windows; the house was still with the stillness of afternoon.
A bird in a cage in the corner pecked at the bars. Outside
the bits jingled, and a horse pawed the road impatiently.

'Marie!' I cried. 'Marie!'

She came in at last through a door which led to the back
of the house, and I stepped forward to speak to her. But
the moment I saw her clearly, the words died on my lips.
The pallor of her face, the disorder of her hair struck me
dumb. I forgot our business, my companion, all. 'What
is it?' was all I could say. 'What is the matter?'

'The child!' she cried, her dark eyes wild with anxiety.
'The child! It is lost! It is lost and gone. I cannot find
it!'

''The child? Gone?' I answered, my voice rising almost
to a shout, in my surprise. 'It is missing? Now?'

'I cannot find it,' she answered monotonously. 'I left
it for a moment at the back there. It was playing on the
grass. Now it is gone.'

I looked at Count Leuchtenstein. He was staring at the
girl, listening and watching, his brow contracted, his face
pale. But I suppose that this sudden alarm, this momen-
tary disappearance did not affect him, from whom the child
had been so long absent, as it affected us; for his first words
referred to the past.

"This child, woman?" he said in his deep voice, which
shook despite all his efforts. "When you found it, it had
a chain round its neck?"

But Marie was so wrapped up in her sudden loss that
she answered him without thought, listening the while.
"Yes," she said mechanically, "it had."

"Where did you find it, then — the child?" he asked
eagerly.

"In the forest by Vach," she replied, in the same indifferent tone.

"Was it alone?"

"It was with a dead woman," she answered. She was
listening still, with a strained face — listening for the pattering of the little feet, the shrill music of the piping voice.
Only half of her mind was with us. Her hands opened
and closed continually with anxiety; she held her head on
one side, her ear to the door. When the Count went to put
another question, she turned upon him so fiercely, I hardly
knew her. "Hush!" she said, "will you? They are here,
but they have not found him. They have not found him!"

And she was right; though I, whose ears were not sharpened by love, did not discern this until two men, who had
been left at home with her, and who had been out to search,
came in empty-handed and with scared looks. They had
hunted on all sides and found no trace of the child, and,
certain that it could not have strayed far itself, pronounced
positively that it had been kidnapped.

Marie at that burst into weeping so pitiful, that I was
glad to send the men out, bidding them make a larger circuit and inquire in the camp. When they were gone, I
turned to Count Leuchtenstein to see how he took it. I

found him leaning against the wall, his·face grave, dark,
and thoughtful.

'There seems a fatality in it!' he muttered, meeting my
eyes, but speaking to himself. 'That it should be lost
again — at this moment! Yet, God's will be done. He
who sent the chain to my hands can still take care of the
child.'

He paused a moment in deep thought, and then, advancing to Marie Wort, who had thrown herself into a chair and
was sobbing passionately with her face on the table, he
touched her on the shoulder.

'Good girl!' he said kindly. 'Good girl! But doubtless
the child is safe. Before night it will be found.'

She sprang up and faced him, her cheeks flaming with
anger. I suppose the questions he had put to her had made
no distinct impression on her mind.

'Oh,' she cried, in the voice of a shrew, 'how you prate!
By night it will be found, will it? How do you know?
But the child is nothing to you — nothing!'

'Girl,' he said solemnly, yet gently, 'the child is my child
— my only child, and the hope of my house.'

She looked at him wildly. 'Who are you, then?' she
said, her voice sinking almost to a whisper.

'I am his father,' he answered; when I looked to hear
him state his name and titles. 'And as his father, I thank
and bless you for all that you have done for him.'

'His mother?' she whispered, open-eyed with awe.

'His mother is dead. She died three years ago,' he
answered gravely. 'And now tell me your name, for I
must go.'

'You must go!' she exclaimed. 'You will go — you can
go — and your child lost and wandering?'

'Yes,' he replied, with a dignity which silenced her, 'I
can, for I have other and greater interests to guard than
those of my house, and I dare not be negligent. He may
be found to-morrow, but what I have to do to-day cannot
be done to-morrow. See, take that,' he continued more

gently, laying a heavy purse on the table before her. 'It is for you, for your own use — for your dowry, if you have a lover. And remember always that, in the house of Hugo of Leuchtenstein, at Cassel, or Marburg, or at the Schloss by Leuchtenstein, you will find a home and shelter, and stout friends whenever you need them. Now give me your name.'

She stared at him dumfounded and was silent. I told him Marie Wort of Munich, at present in attendance on the Countess of Heritzburg; and he set it down in his tablets.

'Good,' he said. And then in his stern, grave fashion he turned to me. 'Master Steward,' he said, in a measured tone which nevertheless stirred my blood, 'are you an ambitious man? If so, search for my child, and bring him to Cassel or Marburg, or my house, and I will fulfil your ambition. Would you have a command, I will see to it; or a farm, it shall be yours. You can do for me, my friend,' he continued strenuously, laying his hand on my arm, ' what in this stress of war and statecraft I cannot do for myself. I have a hundred at my call, but they are not here; and by to-night I must be ten leagues hence, by to-morrow night beyond the Main. Yet God, I believe,' he went on, uncovering himself and speaking with reverent earnestness, ' who brought me to this place, and permitted me to hear again of my son, will not let His purpose fail because He calls me elsewhere.'

And he maintained this grave composure to the last. A man more worthy of his high repute, not in Hesse only, but in the Swedish camp, at Dresden, and Vienna, I thought that I had never seen. Yet still under the mask I discerned the workings of a human heart. His eye, as he turned to go, wandered round the room; I knew that it was seeking some trace of his boy's presence. On the threshold he halted suddenly; I knew that he was listening. But no sound rewarded him. He nodded sternly to me and went out.

I followed to hold his stirrup. The Finland riders, sitting upright in their saddles, looked as if they had not moved an eyelash in our absence. As I had left them so I found them. He gave a short, sharp word of command; a sudden jingling of bridles followed; the troop walked forward, broke into a trot, and in a twinkling disappeared down the road in a cloud of dust.

Then, and not till then, I remembered that I had not said a word to him about my lady's position. His personality and the loss of the child had driven it from my mind. Now it recurred to me; but it was too late, and after stamping up and down in vexation for a while, I turned and went into the house.

Marie Wort had fallen back into the old position at the table, and was sitting with her face on her arms, sobbing bitterly. I went up to her and saw the purse lying by her side.

' Come,' I said, trying awkwardly to cheer her, ' the child will be found, never fear. When my lady returns she will send to the general, and he will have it cried through the camp. It is sure to be found. And you have made a powerful friend.'

But she took no heed of me. She continued to weep; and her sobs hurt me. She seemed so small and lonely and helpless that I had not the heart to leave her by herself in the house and go out into the sunshine to search. And so — I scarcely know how it came about — in a moment she was sobbing out her grief on my shoulder and I was whispering in her ear.

Of love? of our love? No, for to have spoken of that while she wept for the child, would have seemed to me no better than sacrilege. And, besides, I think that we took it for granted. For when her sobs presently ceased, and she lay quiet, listening, and I found her soft dark hair on my shoulder, I kissed it a hundred times; and still she lay silent, her cheek against my rough coat. Our eyes had spoken morning and evening, at dawn when we met, and at night when we parted; and now that this matter of the chain was settled, it seemed fitting that she should come to me for comfort — without words.

At length she drew herself away from me, her cheek dark and her eyes downcast. 'Not now,' she said, gently stopping me — for then I think I should have spoken. ' Will you please to go out and search ? No, I will not grieve.'

' But your purse!' I reminded her. She was leaving it on the table, and it was not safe there. 'You should put it in a place of safety, Marie.'

She took it up and very simply placed it in my hands. ' He said it was for my — dowry,' she whispered, blushing. And then she fled away shamefaced to her room.

CHAPTER XVIII.

A SUDDEN EXPEDITION.

I DID not after that suffer the grass to grow under my feet. I went out, and with my own eyes searched the fields at the back, and every ditch and water-hole. I had the loss cried in the camp, my lady on her return offered a reward, we sent even to the nearer villages, we patrolled the roads, we omitted nothing that could by any chance avail us. Yet evening fell, and night, and found us still searching; and no nearer, as far as we could see, to success. The child was gone mysteriously. Left to play alone for two minutes in the stillness of the afternoon, he had vanished as completely as if the earth had opened and swallowed him.

Baffled, we began to ask, while ·Marie sat pale and brooding in a corner, or now and again stole to the door to listen, who could have taken him and with what motive ? There were men and women in the camp capable of anything. It seemed probable to some that these had stolen the child for the sake of his clothes. Others suggested witchcraft. But in my own mind, I leaned to neither of these theories. I suspected, though I dared not utter the thought, that the general had done it. Without knowing how much of the story Count Hugo had confided to him, I took it as certain that the father had said enough to apprise him of the boy's value. And this being so, what more probable than that the general, whom I was prepared to credit with any atrocity, had taken instant steps to possess himself of the child?

My lady said and did all that was kind on the occasion, and for a few hours it occupied all our thoughts. At the end of that time, however, about sunset, General Tzerclas rode to the door, and with him, to my surprise, the Waldgrave. They would see her, and detained her so long that when she sent for me on their departure, I was sore on Marie's account, and inclined to blame her as indifferent to our loss. But a single glance at her face put another colour on the matter. I saw that something had occurred to excite and disturb her.

'Martin,' she said earnestly, 'I am going to employ you on an errand of importance. Listen to me and do not interrupt me. General Tzerclas starts to-morrow with the larger part of his forces to intercept one of Wallenstein's convoys, which is expected to pass twelve leagues to the south of this. There will be sharp fighting, I am told, and my cousin, the Waldgrave Rupert, is going. He is not at present — I mean, I am afraid he may do something rash. He is young,' my lady continued with dignity and a heightened colour, 'and I wish he would stay here. But he will not.'

I guessed at once that this affair of the convoy was the business which had brought Count Hugo to the camp. And I was beginning to consider what advantage we might make of it, and whether the general's absence might not afford us both a pretext for departure and the opportunity, when my lady's next words dispelled my visions.

'I want you,' she said slowly, 'to go with him. He has a high opinion of you, and will listen to you.'

'The general?' I cried in amazement.

'Who spoke of him?' she exclaimed angrily. 'I said the Waldgrave Rupert. I wish you to go with him to see that he does not run any unnecessary risk.'

I coughed dryly, and stood silent.

'Well?' my lady said with a frown. 'Do you understand?'

'I understand, my lady,' I answered firmly; 'but I cannot go.'

'*You cannot go!* when I send you!' she murmured, unable, I think, to believe her ears. 'Why not, sirrah? Why not, if you please?'

'Because my first duty is to your excellency,' I stammered. 'And as long as you are here, I dare not — and will not leave you!'

'As long as I am here!' she retorted, red with anger and surprise. 'You have still that maggot in your head, then? By my soul, Master Martin, if we were at home I would find means to drive it out! But I know what it is! What you really want is to stay by the side of that puling girl! Oh, I am not blind,' my lady continued viciously, seeing that she had found at last the way to hurt me. 'I know what has been going on.'

'But Count Leuchtenstein ——' I muttered.

'Don't bring him in!' my lady cried, in such a voice that I dared go no farther. 'General Tzerclas has told me of him. I understand what is between them, and you do not. Presumptuous booby!' she continued, flashing at me a glance of scorn, which made me tremble. 'But I will thwart you! Since you will not leave me, I will go myself. I will go, but Mistress Marie shall stay here till we return.'

'But if there is to be fighting?' I said humbly.

'Ah! So you have changed your note, have you!' she cried triumphantly. I had seldom seen her more moved. 'If there is to be fighting' — she mocked my tone. 'Well, there is to be, but I shall go. And now do you go, and have all ready for a start at daybreak, or it will be the worse for

you! One of my women will accompany me. Fraulein
Anna will stay here with your — other mistress!'

She pointed to the door as she spoke, and once more
charged me to be ready; and I went away dazed. Everything seemed on a sudden to be turned upside down — the
child lost, my lady offended, the Waldgrave desperate, the
general in favour. It was hard to see which way my duty
lay. I would fain have stayed in the camp a day to make
farther search for the child, but I must go. I would gladly
have got clear of the camp, but we were to travel in the
general's company. As to leaving Marie, my lady wronged
me. I knew of no special danger which threatened the girl,
nor any reason why she should not be safe where she was.
If the child were found she would be here to receive it.

On the other hand, there was my discovery of the beggar's
fate, from the immediate consequences of which Count
Hugo's arrival had saved me. This sudden expedition
should favour me there; the general would have his hands
full of other things, and Ludwig be hard put to it to gain
his ear. I might now, if I pleased, discover the matter to
my lady, and open her eyes. But I had no proof; even if
time permitted, and I could take the Countess to that part
of the camp, I could not be sure that the body was still
there. And to accuse General Tzerclas of such a thing
without proof would be to court my own ruin.

While I was puzzling over this, I saw the Waldgrave
outside, and, thinking to profit by his advice, I went to meet
him. But I found him in a peculiar mood, talking, laughing,
and breaking into snatches of song; all with a wildness and
abandon that frightened while they puzzled me. He laughed
at my doubts, and walking up and down, while his servants
scoured his breast-piece and cleaned his harness by the
light of a lantern, he persisted in talking of nothing but
the expedition before us and the pleasure of striking a blow
or two.

'We are rusting, man!' he cried feverishly, clapping me
on the back. 'You have the rust on you yet, Martin.
But —

"Clink, clink, clink !
     Sword and stirrup and spur !
     Ride, ride, ride,
     Fast as feather or fur ! "

To-morrow or the next day we will have it off.'
'You have heard about the child, my lord,' I said gravely,
trying to bring him back to the present.
'I have heard that Von Werder, the dullest man at a
board I ever met, turns out to be Hugo of Leuchtenstein,
whom God preserve !' he answered recklessly. 'And that
your girl's brat of a brother turns out to be his brat ! And
no sooner is the father found than the son is lost; and
that both have gone as mysteriously as they came. But
Himmel! man, what's the odds when we are going to fight
to-morrow ! What compares with that? Ça! ça! steady
and the point !'
I thought of Marie ; and it seemed to me that there were
other things in the world besides fighting. For love makes
a man both brave and a coward. But the argument would
scarcely have been to the Waldgrave's mind, and, seeing
that he would neither talk nor hear reason, I left him and
went away to make my preparations.
But on the road next day I noticed that though now and
then he flashed into the same wild merriment, he was on
the whole as dull as he had been gay. Our party rode at
the head of the column, that we might escape the dust and
have the best of the road, the general and his principal
officers accompanying us and leaving the guidance of the
march to inferiors. Our force consisted of about six hundred
horse and four hundred foot ; and as we were to return to
the camp, we took with us neither sutlers nor ordinary baggage, while camp followers were interdicted under pain of
death. Yet the amount of our impedimenta astonished me.
Half a dozen sumpter horses were needed to carry the general's tent and equipage ; his officers required a score more.
The ammunition for the foot soldiers, who were sufficiently
burdened with their heavy matchlocks, provided farther

loads; and in fine, while supposed to be marching in light
fighting order, we had something like a hundred pack-
horses in our train. Then there were men to lead them,
and cooks and pages and foot-boys and the general's band,
and but that our way lay through woodland tracks and by-
routes, I verily believe that we should have had his coach
and dwarf also.

The sight of all these men and horses in motion was so
novel and exhilarating, and the morning air so brisk, that I
soon recovered from my parting with Marie, and began to
take a more cheerful view of the position. I came near to
sympathizing with my lady, whose pleasure and delight
knew no bounds. The long lines of horsemen winding
through the wood, the trailing pikes and waving pennons,
gratified her youthful fancy for war; while as our march
lay through the forest, she was shocked by none of those
traces of its ravages which had appalled us on first leaving
Heritzburg. The general waited on her with the utmost
attention, riding by her bridle-rein and talking with her by
the hour together. Whenever I looked at them I noticed
that her eye was bright and her colour high, and I guessed
that he was unfolding the plan of ambition which I was
sure he masked under a cold and reserved demeanour.
Alas! I could think of nothing more likely to take my
lady's fancy, no course more sure to enlist her sympathy
and interest. But I was helpless; I could do nothing. And
for the Waldgrave, if he still had any power he would not
use it.

My lady gave him opportunities. Several times I saw
her try to draw him into conversation, and whenever
General Tzerclas left her for a while she turned to the
younger man and would have talked to him. But he seemed
unable to respond. When he was not noisily gay, he rode
like a mute. He seemed half sullen, half afraid; and she
presently gave him up, but not before her efforts had caught
Tzerclas' eye. The general had been called for some
purpose to the rear of the column, and on his return found

The general waited on her with the utmost attention, riding by her bridle-rein

the two talking, my lady's attitude such that it was very evident she was the provocant. He did not try to resume his place, but fell in behind them; and riding there, almost, if not quite, within earshot, cast such ugly glances at them as more than confirmed me in the belief that in his own secret way he loved my mistress; and that, after a more dangerous fashion than the Waldgrave.

This was late in the afternoon, and another hour brought us who marched at the head of the column to our camping-ground for the night. We lay in a rugged, wooded valley, not very commodious, but chosen because only one high ridge divided it from a second valley, through which the main road and the river had their course. Our instructions were that the convoy, which was bound for Wallenstein's army then marching on Nuremberg, would pass through this second valley some time during the following day; but until the hour came for making the proper dispositions, all persons in our force were forbidden to mount the intervening ridge under pain of death. We had even to do without fires — lest the smoke should betray our presence — and for this one night lay under something like the strict discipline which I had expected to find prevailing in a military camp. The only fire that was permitted cooked the general's meal, which he shared with my lady and the Waldgrave and the principal officers.

Even so the order caused trouble. The pikemen and musketeers did not come in till an hour before midnight, when they trudged into camp dusty and footsore and murmuring at their leaders. When, in this state, they learned that fires were not to be lighted, disgust grew rapidly into open disobedience. On a sudden, in half a dozen quarters at once, flames flickered up, and the camp, dark before, became peopled in a moment with strange forms, whose eighteen-foot weapons and cumbrous headpieces flung long shadows across the valley.

We had lain down to rest, but at the sound of the altercation and the various cries of 'Pikes! Pikes!' and

'Mutiny!' which broke out, we came out of our lairs in the bracken to learn what was happening. Calling young Jacob and three or four of the Heritzburg men to my side, I ran to my lady to see that nothing befell her in the confusion. The noise had roused her, and we found her at the door of her tent looking out. The newly-kindled fires, flaming and crackling on the sloping sides of the valley, lit up a strange scene of disorder — of hurrying men and plunging horses, for the alarm had extended to the horse lines — and for a moment I thought that the mutiny might spread and cut the knot of our difficulties, or whelm us all in the same ruin.

I had scarcely conceived the thought, when the general passed near us on his way from his tent, whence he had just been called; and at the sight my new-born hopes vanished. He was bare-headed; he carried no arms, and had nothing in his hand but a riding-switch. But the stern, grim aspect of his face, in which was no mercy and no quailing, was worth a thousand pikes. The firelight shone on his pale, olive cheek and brooding eyes, as he went by us, not seeing us; and after that I did not doubt what would happen, although for a moment the tumult of oaths and cries seemed to swell rather than sink, and I saw more than one pale-lipped officer climbing into his saddle that he might be able to fly, if necessary.

The issue agreed with my expectations. The heart of the disorder lay in a part of the camp separated from our quarters by a brook, but near enough in point of distance; so that we saw, my lady and all, pretty clearly what followed. For a moment, for a few seconds, during which you could hear a pin drop through the camp, the general stood, his life in the balance, unarmed in the midst of armed men. But he had that set courage which seems to daunt the common sort and paralyse the finger on the trigger; and he prevailed. The knaves lowered their weapons and shrank back cowering before him. In a twinkling the fires were beaten out by a hundred eager feet, and the general strode back to us through the silent, obsequious camp.

He distinguished my lady standing at the door of her tent, and stepped aside. 'I am sorry that you have been disturbed, Countess,' he said politely. 'It shall not occur again. I will hang up a dozen of those hounds to-morrow, and we shall have less barking.'

'You are not hurt?' my lady asked, in a voice unlike her own.

He laughed, deigning no answer in words. Then he said, 'You have no fire? Camp rules are not for you. Pray have one lit.' And he went on to his tent.

I had the curiosity to pass near it when my lady retired. I found a dozen men, cuirassiers of his privileged troop, peeping and squinting under the canvas which had been hung round the fire. I joined them and looked; and saw him lying at length, wrapped in his cloak, reading 'Cæsar's Campaigns' by the light of the blaze, as if nothing had happened.

CHAPTER XIX.

IN A GREEN VALLEY.

HE was as good as his word. Before the sun had been up an hour six of the mutineers, chosen by lot from a hundred of the more guilty, dangled from a great tree which over-hung the brook, and were already forgotten — so short are soldiers' memories — in the hurry and bustle of a new undertaking. The slope of the ridge which divided us from the neighbouring valley was quickly dotted with parties of men making their way up it, through bracken and furze which reached nearly to the waist; while the horse under Count Waska rode slowly off to make the circuit of the hill and enter the next valley by an easier road.

13

My lady chose to climb the hill on foot, in the track of the pikemen, though the heavy dew, which the sun had not yet drunk up, soon drenched her skirts, and she might, had she willed it, have been carried to the top on men's shoulders. The fern and long grass delayed her and made our progress slow, so that the general's dispositions were in great part made when we reached the summit. Busy as he still was, however, he had eyes for us. He came at once and placed us in a small coppice of fir trees that crowned one of the knobs of the ridge. From this point, where he took up his own position, we could command, ourselves unseen, the whole valley, the road, and river — the scene of the coming surprise — and see clearly, what no one below could discern, where our footmen lay in ambush in parties of fifty; the pikemen among some black thorns, close to the north end of the valley, the musketmen a little farther within and almost immediately below us. The latter, prone in the fern, looked, viewed from above, like lines of sheep feeding, until the light gleamed on a gun-barrel or sword-hilt and dispelled the peaceful illusion.

The sun had not yet risen above the hill on which we stood, and the valley below us lay cool and green and very pleasant to the eye. About a league in length, it was nowhere, except at its southern extremity, where it widened into a small plain, more than half a mile across. At its northern end, below us, and a little to the right, it diminished to a mere wooded defile, through which the river ran over rocks and boulders, with a dull roar that came plainly to our ears. A solitary house of some size, with two or three hovels clustered about it, stood near the middle of the valley; but no smoke rose from the chimney, no cock crowed, no dog barked. And, looking more closely, I saw that the place was deserted.

So quiet it seemed in this peaceful Thuringian valley, I shuddered when I thought of the purpose which brought us hither; and I saw my lady's face grow sad with a like reflection. But General Tzerclas viewed all with another

mind. The stillness, the sunshine, the very song of the
lark, as it rose up and up and up above us, and, still un-
wearied, sang its song of praise, touched no chord in his
breast. The quietude pleased him, but only because it
favoured his plans; the lark's hymn, because it covered
with a fair mask his lurking ambush; the sunshine,
because it seemed a good augury. His keen and vigilant
eye, the smile which curled his lip, the set expression of
his face, showed that he saw before him a battle-field and
no more; a step upwards — a triumph, a victory, and that
was all.

I blamed him then. I confess now, I misjudged him.
He who leads on such occasions risks more than his life,
and bears a weight of responsibility that may well crush
from his mind all moods or thoughts of weather. At least,
I did him, I had to do him, this justice: that he betrayed
no anxiety, uttered no word of doubt or misgiving. Standing with his back against a tree and his eyes on the
northern pass, he remained placidly silent, or talked at
his ease. In this he contrasted well with the Waldgrave,
who continually paced up and down in the background, as
if the fir-grove were a prison and he a captive waiting to be
freed.

'At what hour should they be here?' my lady asked
presently, breaking a long silence.

She tried to speak in her ordinary tone, but her voice
sounded uncertain. A woman, however brave, is a woman
still. It began to dawn upon her that things were going to
happen which it might be unpleasant to see, and scarcely
more pleasant to remember.

'I am afraid I cannot say,' the general answered lightly.
'I have done my part; I am here. Between this and night
they should be here too.'

'Unless they have been warned.'

'Precisely,' he answered, 'unless they have been warned.'

After that my lady composed herself anew, and the day
wore on, in desultory conversation and a grim kind of

picnic. Noon came, and afternoon, and the Countess grew nervous and irritable. But General Tzerclas, though the hours, as they passed without event, without bringing that for which he waited, must have tried him severely, showed to advantage throughout. He was ready to talk, satisfied to be silent. Late in the day, when my lady, drowsy with the heat, dozed a little, he brought out his Cæsar, and read in it, as if nothing depended on the day, and he were the most indifferent of spectators. She awoke and found him reading, and, for a time, sat staring at him, wondering where she was. At last she remembered. She sat up with a start, and gazed at him.

' Are we still waiting ? ' she said.

'We are still waiting,' he answered, closing his book with a smile. 'But,' he continued, a moment later, ' I think I hear something now. Keep. back a little, if you please, Countess.'

We all stood up among the trees, listening, and presently, though the murmuring of the river in the pass prevented us hearing duller sounds, a sharp noise, often repeated, came to our ears. It resembled the snapping of sticks under foot.

'Whips!' General Tzerclas muttered. 'Stand back, if you please.'

The words were scarcely out of his mouth before a handful of horsemen appeared on a sudden in the road below us. They came on like tired men, some with their feet dangling, some sitting sideways on their horses. Many had kerchiefs wound round their heads, and carried their steel caps at the saddle-bow ; others nodded in their seats, as if asleep. They were abreast of our pikemen when we first saw them, and we watched them advance, until a couple of hundred yards brought them into line with the musketmen. These, too, they passed without suspicion, and so went jolting and clinking down the valley, every man with a bundle at his crupper, and strange odds and ends banging and swinging against his horse's sides.

Two hundred paces behind them the first waggon appeared dragged slowly on by four labouring horses, and guarded by a dozen foot soldiers — heavy-browed fellows, lounging along beside the wheels, with their hands in their breeches pockets. Their long, trailing weapons they had tied at the tail of the waggon. Close on their heels came another waggon creaking and groaning, and another, and another, with a drowsy, stumbling train of teamsters and horse-boys, and here and there an officer or a knot of men-at-arms. But the foot soldiers had mostly climbed up into the waggons, and lay sprawling on the loads, with arms thrown wide, and heads rolling from side to side with each movement of the straining team.

We watched eighty of these waggons go by; the first must have been a mile and more in front of the last. After them followed a disorderly band of stragglers, among whom were some women. Then a thick, solid cloud of dust, far exceeding all that had gone before, came down the pass. It advanced by fits and starts, now plunging forward, now halting, while the heart of it gave forth a dull roaring sound that rose above the murmur of the river.

'Cattle!' General Tzerclas muttered. 'Five hundred head, I should say. There can be nothing behind that dust. Be ready, trumpeter.'

The man he addressed stood a few paces behind us; and at intervals along the ridge others lay hidden, ready to pass the signal to an officer stationed on the farthest knob, who as soon as he heard the call would spring up, and with a flag pass the order to the cavalry below him.

The suspense of the moment was such, it seemed an age before the general gave the word. He stood and appeared to calculate, now looking keenly towards the head of the convoy, which was fast disappearing in a haze of dust, now gazing down at the bellowing, struggling, wavering mass below us. At length, when the cattle had all but cleared the pass, he raised his hand and cried sharply —

'Now!'

The harsh blare of the trumpet pierced the upper stillness in which we stood. It was repeated — repeated
again; then it died away shrilly in the distance. In its
place, hoarse clamour filled the valley below us. We
pressed forward to see what was happening.

The surprise was complete; and yet it was a sorry sight
we saw down in the bottom, where the sunshine was dying,
and guns were flashing, and men were chasing one another
in the grey evening light. Our musketmen, springing out
of ambush, had shot down the horses of the last half-dozen
waggons, and, when we looked, were falling pell-mell upon
the unlucky troop of stragglers who followed. These, flying
all ways, filled the air with horrid screams. Farther to the
rear, our pikemen had seized the pass, and penning the
cattle into it rendered escape by that road hopeless. Forward, however, despite the confusion and dismay, things
were different. Our cavalry did not appear — the dust prevented us seeing what they were doing. And here the
enemy had a moment's respite, a moment in which to
think, to fly, to stand on their defence.

And soon, while we looked on breathless, it was evident
that they were taking advantage of it. Possibly the general had not counted on the dust or the lateness of the
hour. He began to gaze forward towards the head of the
column, and to mutter savagely at the footmen below us,
who seemed more eager to overtake the fugitives and strip
the dead, than to press forward and break down opposition.
He sent down Ludwig with orders; then another.

But the mischief was done already, and still the cavalry
did not appear; being delayed, as we afterwards learned,'
by an unforeseen brook. Some one with a head on his
shoulders had quickly drawn together all those among the
enemy who could fight, or had a mind to fight. We saw
two waggons driven out of the line, and in a moment overturned; in a twinkling the panic-stricken troopers and
teamsters had a haven in which they could stand at bay.

Its value was soon proved. A company of our mus-

keteers, pursuing some stragglers through the medley of
flying horses and maddened cattle which covered the
ground near the pass, came upon this rude fortress, and
charged against it, recklessly, or in ignorance. In a moment a volley from the waggons laid half a dozen on the
ground. The rest fell back, and scattered hither and
thither. They were scarcely dispersed before a handful
of the enemy's officers and mounted men came riding back
from the front. Stabbing their horses in the intervals
between the waggons, they took post inside. Every moment others, some with arms and some without, came
straggling up. When our cavalry at last arrived on the
scene, there were full three hundred men in the waggon
work, and these the flower of the enemy. All except one
had dismounted. This one, a man on a white charger,
seemed to be the soul of the defence.

Our horse, flushed with triumph and yelling loudly, came
down the line like a torrent, sabreing all who fell in their
way. Half rode on one side of the convoy and half on the
other. They had met with no resistance hitherto, and
expected none, and, like the musketmen, were on the barricade before they knew of its existence. In the open, the
stoutest hedgehog of pikes could scarcely have resisted
a charge driven home with such blind recklessness; but
behind the waggons it was different. Every interstice
bristled with pike-heads, while the musketmen poured in
a deadly fire from the waggon-tops. For a few seconds the
place belched flame and smoke. Two or three score of the
foremost assailants went down horse and man. The rest,
saving themselves as best they could, swerved off to either
side amid a roar of execrations and shouts of triumph.

My lady, trembling with horror, had long ago retired.
She would no longer look. The Waldgrave, too, was gone ;
with her, I supposed. Half the general's attendants had
been sent down the hill, some with one order, some with
another. In this crisis — for I saw clearly that it was a
crisis, and that if the defenders could hold out until dark-

ness fell, the issue must be doubtful — I turned to look at our commander. He was still cool, but his brow was dark with passion. At one moment he stepped forward as if to go down into the *mêlée ;* the next he repressed the impulse. The level rays of the sun which just caught the top of the hill shone in our eyes, while dust and smoke began to veil the field. We could still make out that the cavalry were sweeping round and round the barricade, pouring in now and then a volley of pistol shots ; but they appeared to be suffering more loss than they caused.

Given a ring of waggons in the open, stoutly defended by resolute men, and I know nothing more difficult to reduce. Gazing in a kind of fascination into the depths where the smoke whirled and eddied, as the steam rolls this way and that on a caldron, I was wondering what I should do were I in command, when I saw on a sudden what some one was doing ; and I heard General Tzerclas utter an oath of relief. Back from the front of the convoy came three waggons, surrounded and urged on by a mob of footmen ; jolting and bumping over the uneven ground, and often nearly overturned, still they came on, and behind them a larger troop of men. Finally they came almost abreast of the enemy's position, and some thirty paces to one side of it. There perforce they stayed, for the leading horses fell shot ; but it was near enough. In an instant our men swarmed up behind them and began to fire volleys into the enemy's fortress, while the horse moving to and fro at a little distance forbade any attempt at a sally.

'That man has a head on his shoulders!' General Tzerclas muttered between his teeth. 'That is Ludwig! Now we have them!'

But I saw that it was not Ludwig ; and presently the general saw it too. I read it in his face. The man who had brought up the waggons, and who could still be seen expos-ing himself, mounted and bare-headed in the hottest of the fire, ordering, threatening, inciting, leading, so that we could almost hear his voice where we stood, was the Waldgrave! His blue velvet cloak and bright fair head were unmistakable, though darkness was fast closing over the fight, and it was only at intervals that we could see anything through the pall of smoke.

'Vivat Weimar!' I cried involuntarily, a glow of warmth and pride coursing through my veins. In that moment I loved the young man as if he had been my son.

The next I fell from the clouds. What would my lady say if anything happened to him? What should I say if I stood by and saw him fall? And he with no headpiece, breast or back! It was madness of him to expose himself! I started forward, stung by the thought, and before I knew what I was doing — for, in fact, I could have done no good — I was on the slope and descending the hill. Almost at the same moment the general gave the word to those who remained with him, and began to descend also. The hill was steep there, and it took us five minutes to reach the scene of action.

If I had foolishly thought that I could do anything, I was disappointed. By this time the battle was over. Manning every waggon within range, and pouring in a steady fire, our sharp-shooters had thinned the ranks behind the barricade. The enemy's fire had first slackened, and then ceased. A little later, one wing, unable to bear the shower of shot, had broken and tried to fly, and in a moment our pikemen had gained the work.

We heard the flight and pursuit go wailing up the valley, but the disorder, and darkness, and noise at the foot of the hill where we found ourselves, were such that I stood scared and bewildered, uncertain which way to turn or whither to go. On every side of me men were stripping the dead, the wounded were crying for water, and cattle and horses, wounded or maddened, were rushing up and down among broken waggons and prostrate loads. Such eyes of cruelty and greed glared at me out of the gloom, such shouts cursed me across dead men that I drew my sword and carried it drawn. But the scene robbed me of

half my faculties ; I did not know which way to turn ; I
did not know what to do ; and until I came upon Ludwig,
I wandered aimlessly about, looking for the Waldgrave
without plan or system.   It was my first experience of the
darker side of war, and it surpassed in horror anything I
had imagined or thought possible.

Ludwig, badly wounded in the leg, I found under a
waggon.   I had stood beside him some time without seeing
him, and he had not spoken.   But when I moved away I
suppose he recognized my figure or step, for when I had
gone a few paces I heard a hoarse voice calling my name.   I
went cautiously back to the waggon, and after a moment's
search detected him peering from under it with a white,
fierce face, which reminded me of a savage creature at bay.

' Hallo ! ' I said.   ' Why did you not speak before, man ? '

' Get me some water,' he whispered painfully.   ' Water,
for the love of Heaven ! '

I told him that I had no flask or bottle, or I should
before this have fetched some for others.   He gave me his,
and I was starting off when I remembered that he might
know how the Waldgrave had fared.   I asked him.

' He led the pursuit,' he muttered.   ' He is all right.'
Then, as I was again turning away, he clutched my arm
and continued, ' Have you a pistol ? '

' Yes,' I said.

' Lend it to me until you come back,' he gasped.   ' If
these vultures find me they will finish me.   I know them.
That is better.   I shall win through yet.'

I marked where his waggon stood, and left him.   The
river was distant less than a quarter of a mile, but it lay
low, and the banks were steep ; and in the darkness it was
not easy to find a way down to the water.   Succeeding at
last — and how still and peaceful it seemed as I bent over
the gently flowing surface and heard the plash and gurgle
of the willows in the stream ! — I filled my bottle and
climbed back to the plain level.   Here I found a change in
progress.   At intervals up and down the valley great fires

had been kindled. Some of these, burning high already, lit up the wrecked convoy and the dark groups that moved round it, and even threw a red, uncertain glare far up the slopes of the hills. Aided by the light, I hastened back, and finding Ludwig without much difficulty, held the bottle to his lips. He seemed nearly gone, but the draught revived him marvellously.

When he had drunk I asked him if I could do anything else for him. He looked already more like himself.

'Yes,' he said, propping his back against the wheel and speaking with his usual hardihood. 'Tell our little general where I am. That is all. I shall do now we have light. I am not afraid of these skulkers any longer. But here, friend Martin. You asked about your Waldgrave just now?'

'Yes,' I said. 'Has he returned ?'

'He never went,' he replied coolly. 'But if I had told you when you first asked me, you would not have gone for water for me. He is down. He fell, as nearly as I can remember, on the farther side of the second fire from here.'

With a curse I ran from him, raging, and searched round that fire and the next, like one beside himself. Many of the dead lay stripped to the skin, so that it was necessary to examine faces. And this ghastly task, performed with trembling fingers and by an uncertain light, took a long time. There were men prowling about with knives and bundles, whom I more than once interrupted in their work ; but the sight of my pistol, and my face — for I was full of fierce loathing and would have shot them like rats — drove them off wherever I came. Not once but many times the wounded and dying begged me to stay by them and protect them ; but my water was at an end and my time was not my own. I left them, and ran from place to place in a fever of dread, which allowed of no rest or relaxation. At last, when I had well-nigh given up hope, I found him lying half-stripped among a heap of dead and wounded, at the farthest corner of the barricade.

All his finery was gone, and his handsome face and fair
hair were stained and bedabbled with dust and blood. But
he was not dead. I could feel his heart beating faintly in
his breast; and though he lay senseless and showed no
other signs of life, I was thankful to find hope remained.
I bore him out tenderly, and laid him down by himself and
moistened his lips with the drainings of my flask. But
what next? I could not leave him; the plunderers who
had already robbed him might return at any moment.
And yet, without cordials, and coverings, and many things
I had not, the feeble spark of life left in him must go out.
I stood up and looked round in despair. A lurid glare, a
pitiful wailing, a passing of dark figures filled the valley.
A hundred round us needed help; a hundred were beyond
help. There were none to give it.

I was about to raise him in my arms and carry him in
search of it — though I feared the effect of the motion on
his wounds — when, to my joy and relief, the measured
tramp of footsteps broke on my ears, and I distinguished
with delight a party of men approaching with torches.
A few mounted officers followed them, and two waggons
creaked slowly behind. They were collecting the wounded.

I ran to meet them. 'Quick!' I cried breathlessly.
'This way!'

'Not so fast!' a harsh voice interposed; and, looking
up, I saw that the general himself was directing the party.
'Not so fast, my friend,' he repeated. 'Who is it?' and
leaning forward in his saddle, he looked down at me.

'The Waldgrave Rupert,' I answered impatiently. 'He
is hurt almost to death. But he is alive, and may live,
your excellency. Only direct them to come quickly.'

Sitting on his horse in the full glare of the torches, he
gazed down at me, his face wearing a strange expression of
hesitation. 'He is alive?' he said at last.

'Yes, at present. But he will soon be dead if we do not
go to him,' I retorted. 'This way! He lies yonder.'

'Lead on!' the general said.

I obeyed, and a moment brought our party to the spot, where the Waldgrave still lay insensible, his face pale and drawn, his eyes half open and disclosing the whites. Under the glare of the torches he looked so like a corpse and so far beyond aid, that it was not until I had again thrust my hand into his breast, and felt the movement of his heart that I was reassured.

As for the general, after looking down at him for awhile, he said quietly, 'He is dead.'

'Not so, your excellency,' I answered, rising briskly from my knees. 'He is stunned. That is all.'

'He is dead,' the general replied coldly. 'Leave him. We must help those first who need help.'

They were actually turning away. They had moved a couple of paces before I could believe it. Then I sprang to the general's rein.

'You mistake, your excellency!' I cried, my voice shrill with excitement. 'In Heaven's name, stop! He is alive! I can feel his breathing. I swear that he is alive!' I was trembling with emotion and terror.

'He is dead!' he said harshly. 'Stand back!'

Then I understood. In a flash his wicked purpose lay bared before me, and I knew that he was playing with me; I read in the cold, derisive menace of his eye that he knew the Waldgrave lived, that he knew he might live, might survive, might see the dawn, and that he was resolved that he should not. The perspiration sprang out on my brow. I choked with indignation.

'Mein Gott!' I cried breathless, 'and but for him you would have been beaten.'

'Stand back!' he muttered through his closed teeth; and his eyes flickered with rage. 'Are you tired of your life, man?'

'Ay, if you live!' I roared; and I shook his rein so that his horse reared and almost unseated him. But still I clung to it. 'Come back! Come back!' I cried, mad with passion, wild with indignation at treachery so vile,

so cold-blooded, 'or I will heave you from your horse, you
villain ! I will ——'

I stumbled as I spoke over a broken shaft of a waggon,
and in a moment half a dozen strong arms closed round
me. I was down and up again and again down. I fought
savagely, passionately, at the last desperately, having that
cold, sneering face before me, and knowing that it was for
my life. But they were many to one. They crushed me
down and knelt on me, and presently I lay panting and
quiet. One of the men who held me had unsheathed his
dagger and stood looking to the general for a signal. I
closed my eyes expecting the blow, and involuntarily drew
in my breast, as if that poor effort might avert the stroke.

But the general did not give the signal. He sat gazing
down at me with a ruthless smile on his face. 'Tie him
up,' he said slowly, when he had enjoyed his triumph to
the full. 'Tie him up tightly. When we get back to the
camp we will have a shooting-match, and he shall find us
sport. You knave!' he continued, riding up to me in a
paroxysm of anger, and slashing me across the face with
his riding-whip so cruelly that the flesh rose in great
wheals, and I fell back into the men's arms blind and
shuddering with pain, 'I have had my eye on you ! But
you will work me no more mischief. Throw him into the
waggon there,' he continued. 'Tie up his mouth if he
makes a noise. Has any one seen Ludwig ?'

CHAPTER XX.

MORE HASTE, LESS SPEED.

THE dawn came slowly. Night, loth to unveil what the
valley had to show, hung there long after the wooded
knobs that rose along the ridge had begun to appear, looking like grey and misty islands in a sea of vapour. Many
cried for the light — what night passes that some do not ?

— but none more impatiently than a woman, whose unquiet figure began with the first glimmer to pace the top of the hill. Sometimes she walked to and fro with her face to the sky; sometimes she stood and peered into the depths where the fires still glowed fitfully; or again listened with shrinking ears to the wailing that rose out of the darkness.

It was the Countess. She had lain down, because they had bidden her do so, and told her that nothing could be done while night lasted. But with the first dawn she was on foot, so impatient that her own people dared not come near her, so imperious that the general's troopers crept away abashed.

The fight in the valley and the dreadful things she had seen and heard at nightfall had shaken her nerves. The absence of her friends had finished the work. She was almost distraught this morning. If this was war — this merciless butchery, this infliction of horrible pain on man and beast — their screams still rang in her ears — she had seen enough. Only let her get her friends back, and escape to some place where these things would not happen, and she asked no more.

The light, as it grew stronger, the sun, as it rose, filling the sky with glory, failed to comfort her; for the one disclosed the dead, lying white and stripped in the valley below, like a flock of sheep grazing, the other seemed by its very cheerfulness to mock her. She was raging like a lioness, when the general at last appeared, and came towards her, his hat in his hand.

His eye had still the brightness, his cheek the flush of victory. He had lain much of the night, thinking his own thoughts, until he had become so wrapped in himself and his plans that his shrewdness was for once at fault, and he failed to read the signs in her face which his own soldiers had interpreted. He was all fire and triumph; she, sick of bloodshed and ambition. For the first time since they had come together, she was likely to see him as he was.

'Countess,' he said, as he stopped before her, 'you will

do yourself harm, I fear. You were on foot, I am told, before it was light.'

'It is true,' she said, shuddering and restraining herself by an effort.

'It was foolish,' he replied. 'You may be sure that as soon as anything is heard the news will be brought to you. And to be missing is not to be dead — necessarily.'

'Thank you,' she answered, her lip quivering. She flashed a look of scorn at him, but he did not see it. Her hands opened and closed convulsively.

'He was last seen in the pursuit,' the general continued smoothly, flattering himself that in suppressing his own triumphant thoughts and purposes and talking her talk he was doing much. 'A score or more of them got away together. It is quite possible that they carried him off a prisoner.'

'And Martin?' she said in a choking voice. She could not stand still, and had begun already to pace up and down again. He walked beside her.

He shrugged his shoulders. 'I know nothing about him,' he said, scarcely concealing a sneer. 'The man went where he was not sent. I hope for the best, but——' He spread out his hands and shook his head.

'Oh!' she said. She was bursting with indignation. The sight of the dead lying below had stirred her nature to its depths. She felt intuitively the shallowness of his sympathy, the selfishness of his thoughts. She knew that he had it on his lips to talk to her of his triumph, and hated him for it. The horror which the day-old battle-field sometimes inspires in the veteran was on her. She was trembling all over, and only by a great effort kept herself from tears and fainting.

'The man is useful to you?' he said after a pause. He felt that he had gone wrong.

She bowed in silence.

'Almost necessary, I suppose?'

She bowed again. She could not speak. It was wonder

ful. Yesterday she had liked this man, to-day she almost
hated him.

But he knew nothing of that, as he looked round with
pride. Below, in the valley, parties of men were going to
and fro with a sparkle and sheen of pikes. Now and
again a trumpet spoke, giving an order. On the hill, not
far from where they walked, a group of officers who had
ascended with him sat round a fire watching the preparation of breakfast. And of all he was the lord. He had
only to raise a finger to be obeyed. He saw before him a
vista of such battles and victories, ending — God knows
in what. The Emperor's throne was not above the dreams
of such a man. And it moved him to speak.

The flush on his cheek was deeper when he turned to her
again. 'Yes, I suppose he was necessary to you,' he said,
' but it should not be so. The Countess of Heritzburg
should look elsewhere for help than to a servant. Let me
speak plainly, Countess,' he continued earnestly. ' It is
becoming I should so speak, for I am a plain man. I am
neither Baron, Count, nor Prince, Margrave, nor Waldgrave. I have no title but my sword, and no heritage save
these who follow me. Yet, if I cannot with the help of
the one and the other carve out a principality as long and
as wide as Heritzburg, I am not John Tzerclas !'

' Poor Germany!' the Countess said with a faint smile.

He interpreted the words in his own favour, and shrugged
his shoulders. ' *Væ victis !*' he said proudly. ' There was
a time when your ancestors took Heritzburg with the
strong hand. Such another time is coming. The future is
for those who dare, for those who can raise themselves
above an old and sinking system, and on its ruins build
their fortunes. Of these men I intend to be one.'

The Countess was an ambitious woman. At another
time she might have heard his tale with sympathy. But
at this moment her heart was full of anxiety for others,
and she saw with perfect clearness the selfishness, the
narrowness, the hardness of his aims. She was angry, too,

14

that he should speak to her now — with the dead lying
unburied, and the lost unfound, and strewn all round them
the ghastly relics of the fight. She looked at him hardly,
but she did not say a word ; and he, following the exultant
march of his own thoughts, went on.

'Albert of Wallenstein, starting from far less than I
stand here, has become the first man in Germany,' he
said, heedless of her silence — 'Emperor in all but the
name. Your uncle and mine, from a country squire, became
Marshal and Count of the Empire, and saw the greatest
quail before him. Ernest of Mansfeld, he was base-born
and crook-backed too, but he lay softly and ruled men all
his days, and left a name to tremble at. Countess,' the
general continued, speaking more hurriedly, and addressing
himself, though he did not know it, to the feeling which
was uppermost in her mind, 'you may think that in saying
what I am going to say, I am choosing an untimely moment;
that with this round us, and the air scarce free from powder,
I am a fool to talk of love. But' — he hesitated, yet
waved his hand abroad with a proud gesture, as if to show
that the pause was intentional — 'I think I am right.
For I offer you no palace, no bed of down, but only myself
and my sword. I ask you to share a soldier's fortunes,
and be the wife and follow the fate of John Tzerclas.
May it be ? '

His form seemed to swell as he spoke. He had an air
half savage, half triumphant as he turned to her with that
question. The joy of battle was still in his veins; he
seemed but half sober, though he had drunk nothing. A
timid woman might have succumbed to him, one of lesser
soul might have shrunk before him; but the Countess
faced him with a pride as great as his own.

'You have spoken plainly,' she said, undaunted. 'Perhaps you will pardon me if I speak plainly too.'

'I ask no more, sweet cousin,' he answered.

'Then let me remind you,' she replied, 'that you have
said much about John Tzerclas, and little about the Coun-

tess of Heritzburg. You have given excellent reasons why you should speak here, but none why I should answer. For shame, sir,' the Countess continued tremulously, letting her indignation appear. 'I lost last night my nearest relative and my old servant. I am still distracted with anxiety on their account. Yet, because I stand alone, unprotected, and with none of my kin by my side, you choose this time to press your suit. For shame, General Tzerclas!'

'Himmel!' he exclaimed, forgetting himself in his annoyance — the fever of excitement was still in his blood — 'do you think the presence of that dandified silken scarf would have kept me silent? No, my lady!'

She looked at him for a moment, astonished. The contemptuous reference to the Waldgrave, the change of tone, opened her eyes still wider.

'I think you do not understand me,' she said coldly.

'I do more; I love you,' he answered hotly. And his eyes burned as he looked at her. 'You are fit to be a queen, my queen! And if I live, sweet cousin, I will make you one!'

'Let that go by,' she said contemptuously, bearing up against his look of admiration as well as she could and continuing to move, so that he had to walk also. 'What you do not understand is my nature — which is, not to desert my friends when they are in trouble, nor to play when those who have served me faithfully are missing.'

'I can help neither the one nor the other,' he answered. But his brow began to darken, and he stood silent a moment. Then he broke out in a different tone. 'By Heaven!' he said, 'I am in no mood for play. And I think that you are playing with me!'

'I do not understand you!' she said. Her tone should have frozen him.

'I have asked a question. Will you answer me yes or no,' he persisted. 'Will you be my wife, or will you not?'

She did not blench. 'This is rather rough wooing, is it not?' she said with fine scorn.

'This is a camp, and I am a soldier.'

She shrugged her shoulders. 'I do not think I like rough ways,' she said.

He controlled himself by a mighty effort. 'Pardon me,' he said with a sickly smile, which sat ill on his flushed and angry face. 'Perhaps I am somewhat spoiled, and forget myself. But, like the man in the Bible, I am accustomed to say to some, "Go," and they go, and to others, "Do it," and it is done. And woe to those who disobey me. Possibly this makes me a rough wooer. But, Countess, the ways of the world are rough; the times are rough. We do not know what to-morrow will bring forth, and whatever we want we want quickly. More, sweetheart,' he continued, drawing a step nearer to her and speaking in a voice he vainly strove to modulate, 'a little roughness before marriage is better than ill-treatment afterwards. I have known men who wooed on their knees bring their wives to theirs very quickly after the knot was tied. I am not of that kind.'

My lady's heart sickened. Despite the assurance of his last words, she saw the man as he was; she read his will in his eyes; and though his sudden frankness was in reality the result of overmastering excitement, she had the added horror of supposing it to be dictated by her friendless position and the absence of the last men who might have protected her. She knew that her only hope lay in her courage, and, though her heart leapt under her bodice, she faced him boldly.

'You wish for an answer?' she asked.

'I have said so,' he answered.

'Then I shall not give you one now,' she replied with a quiet smile. 'You see, general, I am not one of those to whom you can say "Go," and they go, and "Do," and it is done. I must choose my own time for saying yes or no. And this time' — she continued, looking round, and suffering a little shudder to escape her, as she pointed to the valley below — 'I do not like. I am no coward, but I do not love the smell of blood. I will take time to consider your offer, if you please; and, meanwhile, I think you gallant gentleman enough not to press me against my will.'

She had a fan in her hand, and she began to walk again; she held it up, between her face and the sun, which was still low. He walked by her side, his brow as black as thunder. He read her thoughts so far correctly that he felt the evasion boded him no good; but the influence of her courage and pride was such that he shrank from throwing down the mask altogether, or using words which only force could make good. True, it wanted only a little to urge him over the edge, but her lucky star and bold demeanour prevailed for the time, and perhaps the cool, fresh air had sobered him.

'I suppose a lady's wish must be law,' he muttered, though still he scowled. 'But I hope that you will not make a long demand on my patience.'

'That, too, you must leave to me,' she replied with a flash of coquetry, which it cost her much to assume. 'This morning I am so full of anxiety, that I scarcely know what I am saying. Surely your people must know by this time if they — they are among the dead?'

'They are not,' he answered sulkily.

'Then they must have been captured?' she said, a tremor in her voice.

He nodded. At that moment a man came up to say that breakfast was ready. The general repeated the message to her.

'With your leave I will take it with my women,' she answered with presence of mind. 'I slept ill, and I am poor company this morning,' she added, smiling faintly.

The ordeal over, she could scarcely keep her feet. She longed to weep. She felt herself within an inch of swooning.

He saw that she had turned pale, and he assented with a tolerable grace. 'Let me give you my hand to your fire,' he said anxiously.

'Willingly,' she answered.

It was the last effort of her diplomacy, and she hated herself for it. Still, it won her what she wanted — peace, a respite, a little time to think.

Yet as she sat and shivered in the sunshine, and made believe to eat, and tried to hide her thoughts, even from her women, a crushing sense of her loneliness took possession of her. She had read often and often, with scarce a quickening of the pulse, of men and women in tragic straits — of men and women brought face to face with death, nay, choosing it. But she had never pictured their feelings till now — their despair, their shrinkings, their bitter lookings back, as the iron doors closed upon them. She had never considered that such facts might enter into her own life.

Now, on a sudden, she found herself face to face with inexorable things, with the grim realities that have closed, like the narrowing walls of the Inquisition dungeons, on many a gay life. In the valley below they were burying men like rotten sheep. The Waldgrave was gone, captured or killed. Martin was gone. She was alone. Life seemed a cheap and uncertain thing, death very near. Pleasure — folly — a dancing on the grave.

Of her own free will she had placed herself in the power of a man who loved her, and whom she now hated with an untimely hatred, that was half fear and half loathing. In his power! Her heart stood still, and then beat faster, as she framed the thought. The sunshine, though it was summer, seemed to fall grey and pale on the hill sward; the morning air, though the day was warm, made her shiver. The trumpet call, the sharp command, the glitter of weapons, that had so often charmed her imagination, startled her now. The food was like ashes in her mouth; she could not swallow it. She had been blind, and now she must pay for her folly.

She had passed the night in the lee of one of the wooded knolls that studded the ridge, and her fire had been kindled there. The nearest group of soldiers — Tzerclas' staff, whose harsh voices and reckless laughter came to her ears at intervals — had their fire full a hundred paces away. For a moment she entertained the desperate idea that she might slip away, alone, or with her women, and, passing from clump to clump, might gain the valley from which she had ascended, and, hiding in the woods, get somehow to Cassel. The smallest reflection showed her that the plan was not possible, and it was rejected as soon as formed. But a moment later she was tempted to wish that she had put it into effect. An officer made his appearance, with his hat in his hand and an air of haste, and wished to know, with the general's service, whether she could be ready in an hour.

'For what ? ' she asked, rising. She had been sitting on the grass.

'To start, your excellency,' he replied politely.

'To start!' she exclaimed, taken by surprise. 'Whither, sir ? '

'On the return journey. To the camp.'

The blood rushed to her face. 'To the camp ? ' she repeated. 'But is the general going to start this morning ? Now ? '

'In an hour, madam.'

'And leave the Waldgrave Rupert — and my servant ? ' she cried, in a voice of burning indignation. 'Are they to be abandoned ? It is impossible ! I will see the general. Where is he ? ' she continued impetuously.

'He is in the valley,' the man answered.

'Then take me to him,' she said, stepping forward. 'I will speak to him. He cannot know. He has not thought.'

But the officer stood silent, without offering to move. The Countess's eyes flashed. 'Do you hear, sir ? ' she cried. 'Lead on, if you please. I asked you to take me to him.'

'I heard, madam,' he replied in a low voice, 'and I

crave your pardon. But this is an army, and I am part of it. I can take orders only from General Tzerclas. I have received them, and I cannot go beyond them.'

For a moment the Countess stood glaring at him, her face on fire with wrath and indignation. She had been so long used to command, she was of a nature so frank and imperious, that she trembled on the verge of an outburst that could only have destroyed the little dignity it was still possible for her to retain. Fortunately in the nick of time her eyes met those of a group of officers who stood at a distance, watching her. She thought that she read amusement in their gaze, and a pride greater than that which had impelled her to anger came to her aid. She controlled herself by a mighty effort. The colour left her cheeks as quickly as it had flown to them. She looked at the man coldly and disdainfully.

' True,' she said, 'you do well to remind me. It is not easy to remember that in war many things must give way. You may go, sir. I shall be ready.'

But as she stood and saw her horses saddled, her heart sank like lead. All the misery of her false position came home to her. She felt that now she was alone indeed, and powerless. She was leaving behind her the only chance that remained of regaining her friends. She was going back to put herself more completely, if that were possible, in the general's hands. Yet she dared not resist! She dared not court defeat! As her only hope and reserve lay in her wits and in the prestige of her rank and beauty, to lower that prestige by an unavailing struggle, by an unwomanly display, would be to destroy at a blow half her defences.

The Countess saw this; and though her heart ached for her friends, and her eyes often turned back in unavailing hope, she mounted with a serene brow. Her horses had been brought to the top of the hill, and she rode down by a path which had been discovered. When she had gone a league on the backward road she came upon the foremost part of the captured convoy; which was immediately halted and drawn aside, that she might pass more conveniently and escape the noise and dust it occasioned. Among the rest were three waggons laden with wounded. Awnings had been spread to veil them from the sun, and she was spared the sight of their sufferings. But their moanings and cries, as the waggons jolted and creaked over the rough road, drove the blood from her cheeks. She passed them quickly — they were many and she was one, and she could do nothing — and rode on, little thinking who lay under the awnings, or whose eyes followed her as she went.

CHAPTER XXI.

AMONG THE WOUNDED.

WHEN a man lies fettered at the bottom of a jolting waggon, and, unable to help himself, is made a pillow for wounded wretches, whose feverish struggles go near to stifling him; and when to these miseries are added the heat of a sultry night, thirst, and the near prospect of death, passion soon dies down. Anger gives place to pain and the chill of apprehension. The man begins to know himself again — forgets his enemies, thinks of his friends.

It was so with me. The general's back was not turned before I ceased to cry out; and that gained me the one alleviation I had — that I was not gagged. They piled the waggon with bleeding, groaning men, — of our side, of course, for no quarter was given to the other, — and I shuddered as each mangled wretch came in. Still, I had my mouth free. If I could not move, I could breathe, and hear what passed round me. I could see the dark night sky lit up by the glare of the fires, or, later, watch the stars shining coldly and indifferently down on this scene of pain and misery.

When the waggon was full they drove us, jolting and

wailing, to an appointed place, and took out some, leaving
only enough to cover the floor thickly. And then, ah me!
the night began. That which at first had been an incon-
venience, became in time intolerable pain. The ropes cut
into my flesh, the boards burned my back; we were so
closely packed, and I was so tightly bound that I could not
move a limb. Every moment the wounded cried for water,
and those in pain wailed and lamented, while all night the
wolves howled round the camp. In one corner, a man
whose eyes were injured babbled unceasingly of his mother
and his home. Hour by hour, for the frenzy held him all
night, he rolled his head, and chattered, and laughed! In
the morning he died, and we thanked God for it.

The peasant and the soldier sup the real miseries of war;
the noble and the officer, whose it is to dare death in the
field, but rarely, very rarely to lie wounded under the
burning sun or through the freezing night, only taste
them. A place of arms falls; there is quarter for my
lord and a pass and courtesy for my lady, but edge and
point for the common herd. To risk all and get nothing
—or a penny a day, unpaid—is the lot of most.

When morning at last dawned, I was half dead. My
head seemed bursting; my hands were purple with the
tightness of my bonds. Deep groans broke from me. I
moved my eyes—the only things I could move—in an
agony. Round me I heard the sick thanking God as the
light grew stronger, and muttering words of hope. But
the light helped me little. Where I lay, trussed like a
fowl, I could see nothing except the sky—whence the sun
would soon add to my miseries—and the heads of the two
men who sat propped against the waggon boards next
to me.

I took one of these to be dead, for he had slipped to one
side, and the arm with which he had stayed himself against
the floor of the waggon stood out stiff and stark. The other
man had the comfort of the corner; there was a cloak
under him and a pad behind him. But his head was sunk

on his breast, and for a while I thought him dead too, and
had a horrible dread that he would slide over on to my face
and stifle me. But he did not, and by-and-by, when the
sun had risen, and I felt that I could bear it no longer, he
woke up and raised his fierce, white face and groaned.

It was Ludwig. He stared at me for a minute or more
in a dazed, stupid fashion. Then he moved his leg and
cried out with pain. After that he looked at me more
sensibly, and by-and-by spoke.

'Donner, man!' he said. 'What is it? You look like a
ripe mulberry.'

I tried to answer him, but my lips and throat were
so parched and swollen I could only murmur. He saw my
lips move, however, and guessed how it was with me.

'They have tied you up with a vengeance!' he said with
a grim smile. 'Here, Franz! Willibrod! Who is there?
Come, some one. Do you hear, you lazy knaves?' he
continued in a hoarse croak. 'When I am about again I
will find some of you quicker heels!'

A man just risen came grumbling to the side of the
waggon. Ludwig bade him climb in and loosen my bonds,
and set me up against the side.

'And take away that carrion!' he added brutally. 'Dead
men pay no fares. That is better. Ay, give him some
water. He will come round.'

I did presently, though for a time the blood flowing where
it had been before restrained, caused me horrible pain, and
my tongue, when I tried to thank him, seemed to be too
large for my mouth. But I could now sit up, and stretch
my limbs, and even raise my hands to my mouth. Hope
returned. My thoughts flew back to Marie Wort. Her
pale face and large eyes rose before my eyes, and filled
them with tears. Then there was my lady. And the
Waldgrave. Doubtless he, poor fellow, was dead. But the
rest lived — lived, and would soon look to me, look to any
one for help. On that I became myself again. I shook off
the pain and lethargy and despair of the night, and took up

the burden of life. If my wits could save us, or, failing
them, some happy accident, I would not be wanting. I had
still a day or two, and all the chances of a journey.

Ludwig gave me food and a drink from his flask. I
thanked him again.

'You are a man!' he said, shrugging his shoulders. 'It
was a pity you would knot your own rope. As for these
chicken-hearted tremblers,' he continued, squinting askance
at our companions, 'a fico for them! To call themselves
soldiers and pule like women! Faugh! I am sick of them!'

For my part, the sights I saw from the waggon seemed
more depressing. In every direction parties were moving,
burying our dead, putting wounded horses out of their
misery, collecting plunder. One division was at work
driving the poor lowing cattle, already over-driven, back
the way they had come, through the pass and up the river
bank. Another was righting such of the waggons as had
been overturned, or dragging them out of the nether part
of the valley. Everywhere men were working, shouting,
swearing, spurning the dead. All showed that the general
did not mean to linger, but would secure his booty by a
timely retreat to his camp.

They came by-and-by and horsed our waggon and turned
us round, and presently we took our place in the slow,
creaking procession, and began to move up the pass. I
looked everywhere for my lady, but could see nothing of
her. The noise was prodigious, the dust terrible, the glare
intolerable. I was thankful when some kind heart brought
a waggon cloth and stretched it over us. After that things
were better; and between the heat and the monotony of
the motion I fell asleep, and slept until the afternoon was
well advanced.

Then a singular thing occurred. The waggon which followed ours was drawn by four horses abreast, whose heads
as they plodded wearily along at the tail of our waggon
were so close to us that we could see easily into the vehicle,
which was full of wounded men, and covered with an awn-

ing. We could see easily, I say; but the steady cloud of
dust through which we moved and the white glare of the
sunlight gave to everything so phantom-like an appearance
that it was hard to say whether we were looking on real
things.

Be that as it may, the first thing I saw when I awoke
and rubbed my eyes, was the Waldgrave's face! He lay in
the front part of the waggon, his head on the side-board.
Thinking I dreamed, or that the dust deceived me, I rubbed
my eyes again and looked. Still it was he. His eyes were
closed. He was pale, where the dust did not hide all
colour; his head moved with the motion of the wheels.
But he seemed to be alive, for even while I looked, a man
who sat by him leaned forward and moistened his forehead
with water.

Trembling with excitement, I touched Ludwig on the
shoulder. 'Look!' I said. 'The Waldgrave!'

He looked and nodded. 'Yes,' he said, chuckling. 'Now
you see what you have done for yourself. And all for
nothing!'

'But who took him up?' I persisted.

'The general,' he answered sententiously. 'Who else?'

'Why?' I cried in a fever. 'Why did he do it?'

Ludwig shrugged his shoulders. 'He knows his own
business,' he said. 'I suppose that he found he had life
in him.'

'Did he take him up at once? After I was seized?'

'Of course. Whether he will live or no is another
matter.'

The helpless way in which the dusty, bedraggled head
rolled as the waggon jolted, warned me of that. Still, he
was alive. He might live; and I longed to be beside him,
to tend and nurse him, to make the most of the least hope.
But my eyes fell on my fettered hands; and when I looked
again he had disappeared. He had sunk down in the cart,
and was out of sight. I was left to wonder whether he was
dead, or had only changed his posture for another more

comfortable. And the dust growing ever thicker, and the sun-glare less as the day advanced, I presently lost sight even of the waggon.

We lay that night in a coppice on the left bank of the river. Each waggon halted where it stood at sunset, so that there was no common camp, but all along the road a line of bivouacs. But for the cloud of anxiety which darkened my mind, and the cords which bound my hands and constantly reminded me of my troubles, I might have enjoyed the comparative quietness of that night, the evening coolness, the soft green light, the freshness of leaf and bough, which lapped us round and seemed so much the more refreshing, as we had passed the day in a fever of heat and dust. But the unexpected sight of the Waldgrave had excited me ; and I confess that as we came nearer to the camp, the tremors I felt on my own account grew more violent. I recalled with a shudder the shooting-match at which I had been present, and the leather targets. I drew vivid pictures of another shooting-match in the same valley — of my lady looking on in ignorance, of minutes of suspense, of a sudden pang, a gagged scream, of hours of lingering torture.

Against such dreams the silence and beauty of the night were powerless, and the morning found me wakeful and unrefreshed, divided between reluctance to desert my lady and the instinct which bade me make an attempt at escape by the way, and while the chances of the journey were still mine. How I might have acted had a favourable opportunity presented itself, I cannot say ; but as things went, I did nothing, and a little before sunset on the third day we gained the camp.

Then, I confess, I wished with all my heart that I had taken any chance, however slight. At sight of the familiar lines, the dusty, littered roads, the squalid crowds that came out to meet us, my gorge rose. The very smell of the place which I had so hated gave me qualms. I turned hot and cold as we rumbled slowly through the throng and one pointed me out to another, and I saw round me again the dark, lowering faces, the unsexed women, the horde of vile sutlers and footboys. They surged round the waggon, jeering and staring; and if I had shrunk from them when my hands were free, I loathed them still more now that I lay a prisoner and any moment might place me at their mercy.

I had seen nothing of the Waldgrave or the waggon which carried him for nearly two days, but as we passed through the gates I caught sight of the latter moving slowly on, a little way in front of us. Both waggons halted inside the camp while the wounded were taken out. I prepared to follow, but was bidden to stay. Then I began to realize my position. When the waggon bore me on alone — alone, though two or three pikemen and a rabble of gibing, grinning horse-boys marched beside me — I felt my blood run cold, and found my only consolation in the fact that the other waggon still went in front, and seemed to be bound for the same goal.

' What are you going to do with me ? ' I asked one of the ruffians who guarded me.

' Prison,' he answered laconically.

And a strange prison it was. On the verge of the camp, near the river, where a snug farmhouse had once stood, rose four gaunt walls, blackened with smoke. The roof was gone — burned off; but the rooftree, charred and sootbegrimed, still ran from gable to gable. A strong, high gate filled the room of the door; the windows had been bricked up. When I saw the waggon which preceded me halt before this melancholy place, I looked out between hope and fear — fearing some act of treachery, hoping to see the Waldgrave. But the blackguard crowd which surrounded the doorway was so great that it hid everything; and I had to curb my impatience until in turn my waggon stopped in the midst of them.

A mocking voice called to me to descend, and though I liked the look of the place little, and the aspect of the gang still less, I had no choice but to obey. I scrambled down, and passed as quickly as I could down the lane opened for me. A row of more villainous faces it has seldom been my fate to see, but the last on the right by the gate was so much the worst, that it caught my eye instantly. It was seamed with scars and bloated with drink, and it wore a ferocious grin. I was not surprised when the knave, a huge pike-man, dealt me, as I passed, a brutal shove with his knee, which sent me staggering into the enclosure, where I fell all at length on my face.

The blow hurt my hip cruelly, and yet the sight of that drunken, ugly giant filled me with a rush of joy and hope that effaced all other feelings. I forgot my fellow-prisoners, I forgot even the Waldgrave — who to be sure was there, sitting doubled up against the wall, and looking very white and sick. For the man with the seamed face was Drunken Steve of Heritzburg, whom we had left behind us in the castle, to be cured of his wounds. I had punished him a dozen times; almost as often my lady had threatened to drive him from the place and her service. Always he had had the name of a sullen, wilful fellow. But I had found him staunch as any tyke in time of need. For dogged fidelity and a ferocious courage, proof against the utmost danger, I knew that I could depend on him against the world; while the prompt line of conduct he had adopted at sight of me led me to hope something from wits which drink had not yet deadened.

It was well I had this spark of hope, for I found the Waldgrave so ill as to be beyond comfort or counsel, and without it I should have been in a parlous state. The place of our confinement was roofless, ill-smelling, strewn with refuse and filth, a mere dog-yard. A little straw alone protected us from the soil. Everything we did was watched through the open bars of the gate; and bad as this place was, we shared it with two soldiers, who lay, heavily shackled, in one corner, and sullenly eyed my movements.

I did what I could for the Waldgrave, and then, as dark-ness fell, I sat down with my back to the wall and thought over our position — miserably enough. Half an hour passed, and I was beginning to nod, when a slight noise as of a rat gnawing a board caught my ear. I raised my head and listened ; the sound came from the gate. I stood up and crept towards it. As I expected, I found Steve on guard outside. Even in the darkness it was impossible to mistake his huge figure.

'Hush!' he muttered. 'Is it you, master ? '

' Yes,' I replied in the same tone. ' Are you alone ? '

'For the moment,' he answered hoarsely. 'Not for long. So speak quickly. What is to be done ? '

Alas! that was more than I could say. 'What of my lady ? ' I replied vaguely. 'Is she here ? In the camp ? '

' To be sure.'

' And Marie Wort ? The Papist girl ? '

' Yes, yes.'

'Then you must see Marie,' I answered. 'She will know my lady's mind. Until we know that, we can do nothing. Do not tell her where I am — it may hurt the girl ; or of the Waldgrave, but learn how they are. If things are bad with my lady, bid them gain time. You understand ? '

' Yes, yes,' he grunted. 'And that is to be all, is it ? You will have nothing done to-night ? '

' What, here ? '

' To be sure.'

' No, no,' I replied, trembling for the man's rashness. ' We can do nothing here until horses are got and placed for us, and the pass-word learned, and provisions gathered, and half a dozen other things.'

' Donner ! I don't know how all that is to be done,' he muttered despondently.

' Nor I,' I said with a shiver. ' You have not heard anything of a — a shooting-match, have you ? '

' It is for Sunday,' he answered.

' And to-day is Tuesday,' I said. ' Steve ! you will not lose time ? '

' No, no.'

15

'You will see her in the morning? In the morning, lad,'
I continued feverishly, clinging to the bars and peering out
at him. 'I must get out of this before Sunday! And this
is Tuesday! Steve!'
'Hush!' he answered. 'They are coming back.'

CHAPTER XXII.

GREEK AND GREEK.

WHAT my lady's thoughts were during her long ride back
to the camp, I do not know. But I have heard her say that
when she rode into the village, a day and a half in advance
of the dusty, lumbering convoy, she could scarcely believe
that it was the place she had left, the place in which she
had lived for a fortnight. And this, though all remained
the same. So much does the point from which we look at
things alter their aspect.

The general had sent on the news of the Waldgrave's
loss by messenger, that she might be spared the pain of
telling it; and Fraulein Max and Marie Wort were waiting
on the wooden platform before the house when she rode
wearily in. The sight of those two gave her a certain
sense of relief and home coming, merely because they were
women and wore petticoats. But that was all. The village,
the reeking camp, the squalid soldiery, the whining beggars
filled her — now that her eyes were opened and she saw this
ugly face of war stripped of the glamour with which her
fancy had invested it — with fear and repulsion. She
wondered that she could ever have liked the place and been
gay in it, or drawn pleasure from the amusements which
now seemed poor and tawdry.

Fraulein Max ran down into the road to meet her, and
when she had dismounted, covered her with tearful caresses.
But the Countess, after receiving her greetings, still looked
round wistfully as if she missed some one; and then in a

moment moved from her, and mounting the steps went
swiftly to the dark corner by the porch whither Marie
Wort had run, and where she now stood leaning against
the house with her face to the wall.

My lady, whom few had ever seen unbend, took the girl in
her arms, and laid her head on her shoulder and stroked
her hair pitifully.

'Hush, hush, child!' she murmured, her eyes wet with
tears. 'Poor child, poor child! Is it so very bad?'
But Marie could only sob.

They went into the house in a moment after that, those
three, with the waiting-women. And then a change came
over the Countess. Fraulein Max blinked to see it. My
lady who, outside, had been so tender, began, before her
riding cloak was off, to walk up and down like a caged wolf,
with hard eyes and cheeks burning with indignation. Fraulein Max spoke to her timidly — said that the meal was
ready, that my lady's woman was waiting, that my lady
must be tired. But the Countess put her by almost with
an oath. For hours she had been playing a part, a thing
her proud soul loathed. For hours she had hidden, not her
sorrow only and her anger, but her anxieties, her fears, her
terrors. Now she must be herself or die.

Besides, the thing pressed! She had her woman's wits,
and might stave off the general's offer for a few days, for
a week. But a week — what was that? No wonder that
she looked on the four helpless women round her, and
realised that these were her only helpers now, her only
protection; no wonder that she cried out.

'I have been a fool!' she said, looking at them with
burning eyes. 'A fool! When Martin warned me, I would
not listen; when the Waldgrave hinted, I laughed at him.
I was bewitched, like a silly fool in her teens! Don't
contradict me!' And she stamped her foot impatiently.
Fraulein Max had raised her hand.

'I don't,' the Fraulein answered. 'I don't understand
you.'

'Do you understand that empty chair?' my lady answered bitterly. 'Or that empty stool?'

Fraulein Anna blinked more and more. 'But war,' she said mildly — 'a necessary evil, Voetius calls it — war, Countess ——'

'Oh!' my lady cried in a fury. 'As carried on by these, it is a horror, a fiendish thing! I did not know before. Now I have seen it. Wait, wait, girl, until it takes those you love, and threatens your own safety, and then talk to me of war!'

But Fraulein Anna set her face mutinously. 'Still, I do not understand,' she said slowly, winking her short-sighted eyes like an owl in the daylight. 'You talk as if we had cause not only to grieve — as we have, indeed — but to fear. Are we not safe here? General Tzerclas ——'

'Bah!' the Countess cried, trembling with emotion. 'Don't let me hear his name! I hate him. He is false. False, girl. I do not trust him; I do not believe him; and I would to Heaven we were out of his hands!'

Even Marie Wort, sitting white and quiet in a corner, looked up at that. As for Fraulein Max, she passed her tongue slowly over her lips, but did not answer; and for a moment there was silence in the room. Then Marie said very softly, 'Thank God!'

My lady turned to her roughly. 'Why do you say that?' she said.

'Because of what I have learned since you left us,' the girl answered, in a frightened whisper. 'There was a man who lived in this house, my lady.'

'Yes, yes,' the Countess muttered eagerly. 'I remember he begged of me, and General Tzerclas gave him money. That was one of the things that blinded me.'

'He hung him afterwards,' the girl whispered in a shaking voice. 'By the river, in the south-east corner of the camp.'

The Countess stared at her incredulously, rage and horror in her face. 'That man whom I saw?' she cried. 'It is not possible! You have been deceived.'

But Marie Wort shook her head. 'It is true,' she said simply.

'Then Heaven help us all!' the Countess whispered in a thrilling tone. 'For we are in that man's power!'

There was a stricken silence after that, which lasted some minutes. The room seemed to grow darker, the house more silent, the road on which they looked through the unglazed window more dusty, squalid, dreary — dreary with the summer dreariness of drought. One of the waiting-women began to cry. The other stood bolt upright, looking out with startled eyes, and lips half open.

'Yes, all,' the Countess presently went on, her voice hard and composed. 'He has asked me to be his wife. He has honoured me so far.' She laughed a thin, mirthless laugh. 'If I am willing, therefore, well. If I am not — still he will wed me. After that he will keep us here in the midst of these horrors. Or he will march to Heritz-burg, and then God help Heritzburg and my people!'

Fraulein Anna passed her tongue over her lips again, and shifted her hands in her lap. She was paler than usual. But she did not speak.

'The child?' the Countess said presently, in a different tone. 'Has it been recovered?'

Marie shook her head; and a moment later threw her kerchief over her face and went out. They heard her sobs as she went along the passage.

My lady frowned. 'If we could get a message to Count Leuchtenstein,' she murmured thoughtfully. 'But I do not know where he is. He may return to seek the child, · however; and that is our best chance, I think.'

They brought food in after that, and the council broke up. It is to be feared that the Countess found herself little the better for its advice.

In the evening the general called to learn whether she was much fatigued; and she fancied she detected in his manner a masterfulness and a familiarity from which it had been free. But her suspicions rendered her so prone to read between the lines, that it is possible that she saw some things that were not there. Her own feelings she succeeded in masking, except in one matter. He brought Count Waska with him; and it occurred to her, in her fear and helplessness, that she might enlist the Bohemian on her side. Such schemes come to women, even to proud women; and though Waska, half sportsman and half sot, and in body a mountain of flesh, was an unlikely knight-errant, she plied him so craftily, that when the two were gone she sat for an hour in a state of exaltation, believing that here a new and unexpected way to safety might open. The Bohemian was second in command, though at a great interval. He was popular, and in some points a gentleman. Could she excite in him jealousy, discontent, even passion, her position was such that she was in no mood to stand on scruples.

But when the general came next day, *he did not bring Waska;* nor the day after. And he showed so plainly that he saw through the design, and suspected her, that he left her white and furious. Indeed it was a question who was left by this interview the more excited, my lady, who saw the circle growing ever narrower round her, and read with growing clearness the man's determination to win her at all costs and by all means; or the general, whose passion every day augmented, who saw in her both the woman he desired and the heiress, and would fain, if he could, have won her heart as well as her person.

The possession of power tempts to the use of it, and he began to lose patience. He had a screw in readiness, he fancied, that would bend even that proud neck and humble those knees. A day or two more he would give her, and then he would turn it. Hate itself is not more cruel than love despised!

But he did not count on her influence over him. The day or two passed, and another day or two, and still she kept him amused and kept him at bay. Sometimes he saw through her wiles, and came near to vowing that he would

not give her another hour. Will she, nill she, she should
wed him. But then the glamour of her presence and her
beauty blinded him again. And so a week went slowly
by; each day won, at what a cost of pride, of courage, of
‎‑self-respect!

At the end of that time my lady's face had grown so
white and drawn under the strain, that when she sat alone
she looked years older than her age. The light still
flashed in her eyes; they had grown only the larger. But
her cheeks and her lips had lost their colour, her hair its
gloss. When no one was watching her, she glanced round
her like a hunted animal. When anything crossed her, she
flew into fearful rages with her women. They were so
useless, so helpless! She was like a scorpion I have
heard of, that, ringed round with fire, stings all within its
reach.

How many nights she tossed, sleepless; how often she
went over the odds against her; grasped at this idea or
that; thought of horses and roads, ways and means, the
distance to Cassel, or the chances of Leuchtenstein's return,
I cannot say; but I can guess. At last, during one of
these night vigils, something happened. She was lying,
torturing herself with the thought that to this constant
putting off there could only be one end, when ‑she heard
sneaking footsteps moving in the passage. The wall which
divided it from her room ran beside her bed, and, lying
still, she heard the rustling of garments against the boards.

Something like this she had feared in her worst moments; and on the instant she sat up and listened, her
heart beating wildly. Since her return the two waiting-
women had lain in her room. She could hear them breathing now. But beside and above that, she could hear the
stealthy rustling sound she had heard before. Then it
ceased.

She rose trembling. The windows were shuttered, and
the lamp which commonly burned in a basin had gone out.
The room, therefore, was quite dark. Without awaking

the women she stole across the floor to the door, and there set her ear to the panels and listened. But she heard nothing except the distant shout of a reveller, and the mournful howling of one of the pack of curs that infested the camp; all was still.

Still she crouched there listening, and presently her patience was rewarded. Some one entered by the outer door, and went quickly along the passage, the boards creaking so loudly that it was a wonder the women were not aroused. The footsteps went straight to the room where Fraulein Max and Marie Wort slept. Some one had been out and returned!

There was a hint of treachery here, and my lady stood up, her face growing hard. Which of the two was it? In a moment she had her answer. A dozen times in the last week Marie had puzzled her; a dozen times the Papist girl's easy resignation had angered her. She had caught her more than once smiling — smiling childish smiles that would not be repressed. This was the secret, then!

The Countess grew hot, and in a moment was out of her room and at the door of that other room. A taper still burned there; its light showed through the cracks. Without hesitation she thrust the door open, and entering surprised Marie Wort in the very act. The girl was standing in the middle of the floor taking off a cloak. Guilt and fear were written on her face.

' You wicked girl!' the Countess cried, her eyes blazing.

Then she stopped. For Marie, instead of retreating before her, pointed with a warning finger to a second empty pallet; and my lady looking round saw with astonishment that Fraulein Max was missing.

'What does this mean?' the Countess muttered in a different tone.

Marie, trembling and listening, put her finger to her lips. 'Hush, hush, my lady,' she whispered. 'She must not find you here! She must not, indeed. I heard her go out, and I followed. I have heard all.'

'All?' the Countess stammered, and she began to tremble.

'Yes,' the girl answered. Then 'Go, go! my lady,' she cried. She was shaking with agitation, and looked round as if for a way of escape. But there was no second door to the room. 'If she finds you here we are lost. Go back, and in the morning ——'

She stopped abruptly, and her eyes grew wide. The Countess listening too, and catching the infection of her fear, heard a board creak below.

For a moment the two stood in the middle of the floor, gazing into one another's eyes. Then Marie, with a sudden movement, thrust my lady down on her pallet, and with the other hand put out the light.

They lay, scarcely daring to breathe, and heard Fraulein Anna grope her way in, and stand awhile, silent and listening, as if she found something suspicious in the extinction of the light. But the taper — it was a mere rushlight — had done this before, and Marie stirred so naturally, that Fraulein Max's doubts passed away. She put off her cloak quickly, and presently — but not, as it seemed to the Countess, until an hour had elapsed — they heard her begin to breathe regularly. A few minutes more and they had no doubt she slept. Then Marie touched my lady's arm, and the latter, rising softly, stole out of the room.

The adventure left the Countess's thoughts in a whirl. She hated double-dealing as much as any one, and she could scarcely contain herself before Fraulein Max. It was as much as she could do to wear a smooth face for an hour, until a chance occasion, which fortunately came early in the day, left her alone with Marie. Then she turned, almost fiercely, on the girl.

'What is this?' she said. 'What does it all mean? Himmel! Tell me! Tell me quickly!'

Marie Wort looked at her with tears in her eyes. 'You should be able to guess, my lady,' she said sadly. 'There is a traitor among us.'

'Fraulein Anna?'

Marie nodded. 'She is in his pay,' she said simply.

'His? The general's?'

'Yes,' Marie answered, speaking quickly, with her eyes on the door. 'She met him last night, and told him what you feel about him.'

The Countess drew a deep breath. Her face turned a shade paler. She sat up straight in her chair. 'All?' she said huskily.

Marie nodded.

'And he?'

'He said he would have an answer to-day. Then I left. I did not hear any more.'

The Countess sat for a minute as if turned to stone. Here was an end of putting off — of smiles, and pleasant words, and the little craftinesses which had hitherto served her. Stern necessity, hard fate were before her. She was of a high courage, but terror was fast mastering her, when Marie touched her on the arm.

'If you can put him off, until this evening,' the girl muttered, 'I think something may be done.'

'What?'

'Something. I do not know what,' the girl answered in a troubled tone.

The Countess rose suddenly. 'Ah! I would like to choke her!' she cried hoarsely. She stretched out her arms.

'Hush, hush, my lady!' Marie whispered. The Countess's violence frightened her. 'I think, if you can put him off until to-night, we may contrive something.'

'We? You and I?' my lady said in scorn. But as she looked at the other's pale, earnest face, her own softened, her tone changed. 'Well, it shall be as you wish,' she said, letting her arms drop. 'You are a better plotter than I am. But I fear Fraulein Cat, Fraulein Snake, Fraulein Fox will prove the best of all!'

Marie's frightened face showed that she thought this possible, but she said no more, and would give my lady no explanation, though the Countess pressed for it. It was decided in the end that the Countess should plead sudden illness, and use that pretext both to avoid Fraulein Max, and postpone her interview with the general until the evening.

He came at noon, and the Countess heard his horses pawing and fretting in the road, and she sat up in her darkened room with a white face. What if he would not accept the excuse? If he *would* see her? What if the moment had come in which his will and hers must decide the struggle? She rose and stood listening, as fierce in her beauty as any trapped savage creature. Her heart beat wildly, her bosom heaved. But in a moment she heard the horses move away, and presently Marie came in to tell her that he would wait till evening.

'No longer?' the Countess asked, hiding her face in the pillow.

'Not an hour, he said,' Marie answered, indicating by a gesture that the door was open, and that Fraulein Max was listening. 'He was — different,' she whispered.

'How?' my lady muttered.

'He swore at me,' Marie answered in the same tone. 'And he spoke of you — somehow differently.'

The Countess laughed, but far from joyously. 'I suppose to-night — I must see him?' she said. She tried as she spoke to press herself more deeply into the pillows, as if she might escape that way. Her flesh crept, and she shivered though she was as hot as fire.

Once or twice in the hours which followed she was almost beside herself. Sometimes she prayed. More often she walked up and down the room like one in a fever. She did not know on what she was trusting, and she could have struck Marie when the girl, appealed to again and again, would explain nothing, and name no quarter from which help might come. All the afternoon the camp lay grilling in the sunshine, and in the shuttered room in the middle of it my lady suffered. Had the house lain by the river she might have tried to escape; but the camp girdled it on three sides, and on the fourth, where a swampy inlet guarded one flank of the village, a deep ditch as well as the morass forbade all passage.

She remained in her room until she heard the unwelcome sounds which told of the general's return. Then she came into the outer room, her eyes glittering, a red spot on either cheek, all pretence at an end. Her glance withered Fraulein Max, who sat blinking in a corner with a very evil conscience. And to Marie Wort, when the girl came near her on the pretence of adjusting her lace sleeves, she had only one word to say.

'You slut!' she hissed, her breath hot on the girl's cheek. 'If you fail me I will kill you. Begone out of my sight!'

The child, excited before, broke down at that, and, bursting into a fit of weeping, ran out. Her sobs were still in the air when General Tzerclas entered.

The Countess's face was flushed, and her bearing, full of passion and defiance, must have warned him what to expect, if he felt any doubt before. The sun was just setting, the room growing dusk. He stood awhile, after saluting her, in doubt how he should come to the point, or in admiration; for her scorn and anger only increased her beauty and his feeling for her. At length he pointed lightly to the women, who kept their places by the door.

'Is it your wish, fair cousin,' he said slowly, 'that I should speak before these, or will you see me alone?'

'Your spy, that cat there,' my lady answered, carried away by her temper, 'may go! The women will stay.'

Fraulein Max, singled out by that merciless finger, sprang forward, her face mottled with surprise and terror. For a second she hesitated. Then she rushed towards her friend, as if she would embrace her.

'Countess!' she cried. 'Rotha! Surely you are mad! You cannot think that I would —— '

My lady turned, and in a flash struck her fiercely on the

cheek with her open hand. ' Liar !' she cried; 'go to your
master, you whipped hound !'

The Dutch woman recoiled with a cry of pain, and
sobbing wildly went back to her place. The general
laughed harshly.

' You hold with me, sweetheart,' he said. ' Discipline
before everything. But you have not my patience.'

She looked at him — angry with him, angry with herself,
her hand to her bosom — but she did not answer.

' For you must allow,' he continued — his tone and his
eyes still bantered her — ' that I have been patient. I have
been like a man athirst in the desert; but I have waited
day after day, until now I can wait no longer, sweetheart.'

' So you tamper with my — with that woman ! ' she said
scornfully.

The general shrugged his shoulders and laughed grimly.
' Why not ? ' he said. ' What are waiting-women and the
like made for, if not to be bribed — or slapped ? '

She hated him for that sly hit — if never before ; but
she controlled herself. She would throw the burden on
him.

He read the thought, and it led him to change his tone.
There was a gloomy fire in his eyes, and smouldering
passion in his voice, when he spoke again.

' Well, Countess,' he said, ' I am here for your answer.'

' To what ? '

' To the question I asked you some time ago,' he rejoined,
dwelling on her with sullen eyes. ' I asked you to be my
wife. Your answer ? '

' Prythee ! ' she said proudly, ' this is a strange way of
wooing.'

' It is not of my choice that I woo in company,' he
answered, shrugging his shoulders. ' My answer; that is
all I want — and you.'

' Then you shall have the first, and not the last,' she
exclaimed on a sudden impulse. ' No, no — a hundred
times no ! If you do not see that by pressing me now,'

she continued impetuously, 'when I am alone, friendless, and unprotected, you insult me, you should see it, and I do.'

For a moment there was silence. Then he laughed; but his voice, notwithstanding his mastery over it and in spite of that laugh, shook with rage and resentment. 'As I expected,' he said. 'I knew last night that you hated me. You have been playing a part throughout. You loathe me. Yes, madam, you may wince,' he continued bitterly, 'for you shall still be my wife; and when you are my wife we will talk of that.'

'Never!' she said, with a brave face; but her heart beat wildly, and a mist rose before her eyes.

He laughed. 'My legions are round me,' he said. 'Where are yours?'

'You are a gentleman,' she answered with an effort. 'You will let me go.'

'If I do not?'

'There are those who will know how to avenge me.'

He laughed again. 'I do not know them, Countess,' he said contemptuously. 'For Hesse Cassel, he has his hands full at Nuremberg, and will be likely, when Wallenstein has done with him, to need help himself. The King of Sweden — the brightest morning ends soonest in rain — and he will end at Nuremberg. Bernhard of Weimar, Leuchtenstein, all the fanatics fall with him. Only the banner of the Free Companies stands and waves ever the wider. Be advised,' he continued grimly. 'Bend, Countess, or I have the means to break you.'

'Never!' she said.

'So you say now,' he answered slowly. 'You will not say so in five minutes. If you care nothing for yourself, have a care for your friends.'

'You said I had none,' she retorted hoarsely.

'None that can help you,' he replied; 'some that you can help.'

She started and looked at him wildly, her lips apart,

her eyes wide with hope, fear, expectation. What did he mean? What could he mean by this new turn? Ha! She had her face towards the window, and dark as the room was growing — outside the light was failing fast — he read the thought in her eyes, and nodded.

'The Waldgrave?' he said lightly. 'Yes, he is alive, Countess, at present; and your steward also.'

'They are prisoners?' she whispered, her cheeks grown white.

'Prisoners ; and under sentence of death.'

'Where?'

'In my camp.'

'Why?' she muttered. But alas! she knew ; she knew already.

'They are hostages for your good behaviour,' he answered in his cold, mocking tone. 'If their principal satisfies me, good ; they will go free. If not, they die — to-morrow.'

'To-morrow?' she gasped.

'To-morrow,' he answered ruthlessly. 'Now I think we understand one another.'

She threw up her hand suddenly, as if she were about to vent on him all the passions which consumed her — the terror, rage, and shame which swelled in her breast. But something in his gibing tone, something in the set lines of his figure — she could not see his face — checked her. She let her hand fall in a gesture of despair, and shrank into herself, shuddering. She looked at him as at a serpent — that fascinated her. At last she murmured —

'You will not dare. What have they done to you?'

'Nothing,' he answered. 'It is not their affair; it is yours.'

For a moment after that they stood confronting one another while the sound of the women sobbing in a corner, and the occasional jingle of a bridle outside, alone broke the silence. Behind her the room was dark ; behind him, through the open windows, lay the road, glimmering pale through the dusk. Suddenly the door at her back opened,

and a bright light flashed on his face. It was Marie Wort
bringing in a lamp. No one spoke, and she set the lamp
on the table, and going by him began to close the shutters.
Still the Countess stood as if turned to stone, and he stood
watching her.

'Where are they?' she moaned at last, though he had
already told her.

'In the camp,' he said.

'Can I — can I see them?' she panted.

'Afterwards,' he answered, with the smile of a fiend;
'when you are my wife.'

That added the last straw. She took two steps to the
table, and sitting down blindly, covered her face with her
hands. Her shoulders began to tremble, her head sank
lower and lower on the table. Her pride was gone.

'Heaven help us!' she whispered in a passion of grief.
'Heaven help us, for there is no help here!'

'That is better,' he said, eyeing her coldly. 'We shall
soon come to terms now.'

In his exultation he went a step nearer to her. He was
about to touch her — to lay his hand on her hair, believing
his evil victory won, when suddenly two dark figures rose
like shadows behind her chair. He recoiled, dropping his
hand. In a moment a pistol barrel was thrust into his face.
He fell back another step.

'One word and you are a dead man!' a stern voice hissed
in his ear. Then he saw another barrel gleam in the lamplight, and he stood still.

'What is this?' he said, looking from one to the other, his
voice trembling with rage.

'Justice!' the same speaker answered harshly. 'But
stand still and be silent, and you shall have your life. Give
the alarm, and you die, general, though we die the next
minute. Sit down in that chair.'

He hesitated. But the two shining barrels converging
on his head, the two grim faces behind them, were convinc-
ing; in a moment he obeyed.

CHAPTER XXIII.

THE FLIGHT.

ONE of the men — it was I — muttered something to Marie, and she snuffed the wick, and blew up the light. In a moment it filled the room, disclosing a strange medley of levelled weapons, startled faces, and flashing eyes. In one corner Fraulein Max and the two women cowered behind one another, trembling and staring. At the table sat my lady, with dull, dazed eyes, looking on, yet scarcely understanding what was happening. On either side of her stood Steve and I, covering the general with our pistols, while the Waldgrave, who was still too weak for much exertion, kept guard at the door.

Tzerclas was the first to speak. ' What is this foolery ? ' he said, scowling unutterable curses at us. ' What does this mean ? '

' This ! ' I said, producing a piece of hide rope. ' We are going to tie you up. If you struggle, general, you die. If you submit, you live. That is all. Go to work, Steve.'

There was a gleam in Tzerclas' eye, which warned me to stand back and crook my finger. His face was black with fury, and for an instant I thought that he would spring upon us and dare all. But prudence and the pistols prevailed. With an evil look he sat still, and in a trice Steve had a loop round his arms and was binding him to the heavy chair.

I knew then that as far as he was concerned we were safe; and I turned to bid the women get cloaks and food, adjuring them to be quick, since every moment was precious. ' Bring nothing but cloaks and food and wine,' I said. ' We have to go a league on foot and can carry little.'

The Countess heard my words, and looked at me with growing comprehension. ' The Waldgrave ? ' she muttered. ' Is he here ? '

16

He came forward from the door to speak to her; but
when she saw him, and how pale and thin he was, with
great hollows in his cheeks and his eyes grown too large
for his face, she began to cry weakly, as any other woman
might have cried, being overwrought. I bade Marie, who
alone kept her wits, to bring her wine and make her take
it; and in a minute she smiled at us, and would have
thanked us.

'Wait!' I said bluntly, feeling a great horror upon me
whenever I looked towards the general or caught his eye.
'You may have small cause to thank us. If we fail, Heaven
and you forgive us, my lady, for this man will not. If we
are retaken —— '

'We will not be retaken!' she cried hardily. 'You have
horses?'

'Five only,' I answered. 'They are all Steve could get,
and they are a league away. We must go to them on foot.
There are eight of us here, and young Jacob and Ernst are
watching outside. Are all ready?'

My lady looked round; her eye fell on Fraulein Max, who
with a little bundle in her arms had just re-entered and
stood shivering by the door. The Dutch girl winced under
her glance, and dropping her bundle, stooped hurriedly to
pick it up.

'That woman does not go!' the Countess said suddenly.

I answered in a low tone that I thought she must.

'No!' my lady cried harshly — she could be cruel sometimes — 'not with us. She does not belong to our party.
Let her stay with her paymaster, and to-morrow he will
doubtless reward her.'

What reward she was likely to get Fraulein Max knew
well. She flung herself at my lady's feet in an agony of
fear, and clutching her skirts, cried abjectly for mercy; she
would carry, she would help, she would do anything, if she
might go! Knowing that we dared not leave her since
she would be certain to release the general as soon as our
backs were turned, I was glad when Marie, whose heart

was touched, joined her prayers to the culprit's and won a reluctant consent.

It has taken long to tell these things. They passed very quickly. I suppose not more than a quarter of an hour elapsed between our first appearance and this juncture, which saw us all standing in the lamplight, laden and ready to be gone ; while the general glowered at us in sullen rage, and my lady, with a new thought in her mind, looked round in dismay.

She drew me aside. 'Martin,' she said, 'his orderly is waiting in the road with his horse. The moment we are gone he will shout to him.'

'We have provided for that,' I answered, nodding. Then assuring myself by a last look round that all were ready, I gave the word. 'Now, Steve !' I said sharply.

In a twinkling he flung over the general's head a small sack doubled inwards. We heard a stifled oath and a cry of rage. The bars of the strong chair creaked as our prisoner struggled, and for a moment it seemed as if the knots would barely hold. But the work had been well done, and in less than half a minute Steve had secured the sack to the chair-back. It was as good as a gag, and safer. Then we took up the chair between us, and lifting it into the back room, put it down and locked the door upon our captive.

As we turned from it Steve looked at me. 'If he catches us after this, Master Martin,' he said, 'it won't be an easy death we shall die !'

'Heaven forbid !' I muttered. 'Let us be off !'

He gave the word and we stole out into the darkness at the back of the house, Steve, who had surveyed the ground, going first. My lady followed him ; then came the Wald- grave ; after him the two women and Fraulein Max, with Jacob and Ernst ; last of all, Marie and I. It was no time for love-making, but as we all stood a minute in the night, while Steve listened, I drew Marie's little figure to me and kissed her pale face again and again ; and she clung to me,

trembling, her eyes shining into mine. Then she put me
away bravely; but I took her bundle, and with full hearts
we followed the others across the field at the back and
through the ditch.

That passed, we found ourselves on the edge of the
village, with the lights of the camp forming five-sixths of
a circle round us. In one direction only, where the swamp
and creek fringed the place, a dark gap broke the ring of
twinkling fires. Towards this gap Steve led the way, and
we, a silent line of gliding figures, followed him. The
moon had not yet risen. The gloom was such that I could
barely make out the third figure before me; and though all
manner of noises — the chorus of a song, the voice of a
scolding hag, even the rattle of dice on a drumhead — came
clearly to my ears, and we seemed to be enclosed on all
sides, the darkness proved an effectual shield. We met no
one, and five minutes after leaving the house, reached the
bank of the little creek I have mentioned.

Here we paused and waited, a group of huddled figures,
while Steve groped about for a plank he had hidden.
Before us lay the stream, behind us the camp. At any
moment the alarm might be raised. I pictured the outcry,
the sudden flickering of lights, the galloping this way and
that, the discovery. And then, thank Heaven! Steve
found his plank, and in the work of passing the women
over I forgot my fears. The darkness, the peril — for the
water on the nearer side was deep — the nervous haste of
some, and the terror of others, made the task no easy one.
I was hot as fire and wet to the waist before it was over,
and we all stood ankle-deep in the ooze which formed the
farther bank.

Alas! our troubles were only beginning. Through this
ooze we had to wade for a mile or more, sometimes in
doubt, always in darkness; now plashing into pools, now
stumbling over a submerged log, often up to our knees in
mud and water. The frogs croaked round us, the bog
moaned and gurgled; in the depth of the marsh the bit-

terns boomed mournfully. If we stood a moment we sank. It was a horrible time; and the more horrible, as through it all we had only to turn to see the camp lights behind us, a poor half-mile or so away.

None but desperate men could have exposed women to such a labour; nor could any but women without hope and at their wit's end have accomplished it. As it was, Fräulein Max, who never ceased to whimper, twice sank down and would go no farther, and we had to pluck her up roughly and force her on. My lady's women, who wept in their misery, were little better. Wet to the waist, draggled, and worn out by the clinging slime and the reek of the marsh, they were kept moving only with difficulty; so that, but for Steve's giant strength and my lady's courage, I think we should have stayed there till daylight, and been caught like birds limed on a bough.

As it was, we plunged and strove for more than an hour in that place, the dark sky above us, the quaking bog below, the women's weeping in our ears. Then, at last, when I had almost given up hope, we struggled out one by one upon the road, and stood panting and shaking, astonished to find solid ground under our feet. We had still two miles to walk, but on dry soil; and though at another time the task might have seemed to the women full of adventure and arduous, it failed to frighten them after what we had gone through. Steve took Fräulein Anna, and I one of the women. My lady and the Waldgrave went hand in hand; the one giving, I fancy, as much help as the other. For Marie, her small, white face was a beacon of hope in the darkness. In the marsh she had never failed or fainted. On the road the tears came into my eyes for pity and love and admiration.

At length Steve bade us stand, and leaving us in the way, plunged into the denser blackness of a thicket, which lay between it and the river. I heard him parting the branches before him, and stumbling and swearing, until presently the sounds died away in the distance, and we remained shivering and waiting. What if the horses were gone? What if they had strayed from the place where he had tethered them early in the day, or some one had found and removed them? The thought threw me into a cold sweat.

Then I heard him coming back, and I caught the ring of iron hoofs. He had them! I breathed again. In a moment he emerged, and behind him a string of shadows — five horses tied head and tail.

'Quick!' he muttered. He had been long enough alone to grow nervous. 'We are two hours gone, and if they have not yet discovered him they must soon! It is a short start, and half of us on foot!'

No one answered, but in a moment we had the Waldgrave, my lady, Fraulein, and one of the women mounted. Then we put up Marie, who was no heavier than a feather, and the lighter of the women on the remaining horse; and Steve hurrying beside the leader, and I, Ernst, and Jacob bringing up the rear, we were well on the road within two minutes of the appearance of the horses. Those who rode had only sacking for saddles and loops of rope for stirrups; but no one complained. Even Fraulein Max began to recover herself, and to dwell more upon the peril of capture than on aching legs and chafed knees.

The road was good, and we made, as far as I could judge, about six miles in the first hour. This placed us nine miles from the camp; the time, a little after midnight. At this point the clouds, which had aided us so far by increasing the darkness of the night, fell in a great storm of rain, that, hissing on the road and among the trees, in a few minutes drenched us to the skin. But no one complained. Steve muttered that it would make it the more difficult to track us; and for another hour we plodded on gallantly. Then our leader called a halt, and we stood listening.

The rain had left the sky lighter. A waning moon, floating in a wrack of watery clouds to westward, shed a faint gleam on the landscape. To the right of us it disclosed a bare plain, rising gradually as it receded, and offering no cover. On our left, between us and the river, it was different. Here a wilderness of osiers — a grey willow swamp that in the moonlight shimmered like the best Utrecht — stretched as far as we could see. The road where we stood rose a few feet above it, so that our eyes were on a level with the highest shoots; but a hundred yards farther on the road sank a little. We could see the water standing on the track in pools, and glimmering palely.

'This is the place,' Steve muttered. 'It will be dawn in another hour. What do you think, Master Martin?'

'That we had better get off the road,' I answered. 'Take it they found him at midnight; the orderly's patience would scarcely last longer. Then, if they started after us a quarter of an hour later, they should be here in another twenty minutes.'

'It is an aguey place,' he said doubtfully.

'It will suit us better than the camp,' I answered.

No one else expressed an opinion, and Steve, taking my lady's rein, led her horse on until he came to the hollow part of the road. Here the moonlight disclosed a kind of water-lane, running away between the osiers, at right angles from the road. Steve turned into it, leading my lady's horse, and in a moment was wading a foot deep in water. The Waldgrave followed, then the women. I came last, with Marie's rein in my hand. We kept down the lane about one hundred and fifty paces, the horses snorting and moving unwillingly, and the water growing ever deeper. Then Steve turned out of it, and began to advance, but more cautiously, parallel with the road.

We had waded about as far in this direction, sidling between the stumps and stools as well as we could, when he came again to a stand and passed back the word for me. I waded on, and joined him. The osiers, which were interspersed here and there with great willows, rose above our heads and shut out the moonlight. The water gurgled

black about our knees. Each step might lead us into a
hole, or we might trip over the roots of the osiers. It was
impossible to see a foot before us, or anything above us
save the still, black rods and the grey sky.

'It should be in this direction,' Steve said, with an accent
of doubt. 'But I cannot see. We shall have the horses
down.'

'Let me go first,' I said.

'We must not separate,' he answered hastily.

'No, no,' I said, my teeth beginning to chatter. 'But
are you sure that there is an eyot here?'

'I did not go to it,' he answered, scratching his head.
'But I saw a clump of willows rising well above the level,
and they looked to me as if they grew on dry land.'

He stood a moment irresolutely, first one and then another of the horses shaking itself till the women could
scarcely keep their seats.

'Why do we not go on?' my lady asked in a low voice.

'Because Steve is not sure of the place, my lady,' I said.
'And it is almost impossible to move, it is so dark, and
the osiers grow so closely. I doubt we should have
waited until daylight.'

'Then we should have run the risk of being intercepted,'
she answered feverishly. 'Are you very wet?'

'No,' I said, though my feet were growing numb, 'not
very. I see what we must do. One of us must climb into
a willow and look out.'

We had passed a small one not long before. I plashed
my way back to it, along the line of shivering women, and,
pulling myself heavily into the branches, managed to
scramble up a few feet. The tree swayed under my
weight, but it bore me.

The first dawn was whitening the sky and casting a faint,
reflected light on the glistening sea of osiers, that seemed
to my eyes — for I was not high enough to look beyond it
— to stretch far and away on every side. Here and there
a large willow, rising in a round, dark clump, stood out

above the level; and in one place, about a hundred paces away on the riverside of us, a group of these formed a shadowy mound. I marked the spot, and dropped gently into the water.

'I have found it,' I said. 'I will go first, and do you bring my lady, Steve. And mind the stumps. It will be rough work.'

It was rough work. We had to wind in and out, leading and coaxing the frightened horses, that again and again stumbled to their knees. Every minute I feared that we should find the way impassable or meet with a mishap. But in time, going very patiently, we made out the willows in front of us. Then the water grew more shallow, and this gave the animals courage. Twenty steps farther, and we passed into the shadow of the trees. A last struggle, and, plunging one by one up the muddy bank, we stood panting on the eyot.

It was such a place as only despair could choose for a refuge. In shape like the back of some large submerged beast, it lay in length about forty paces, in breadth half as many. The highest point was a poor foot above the water. Seven great willows took up half the space; it was as much as our horses, sinking in the moist mud to the fetlock, could do to find standing-room on the remainder. Coarse grass and reeds covered it; and the flotsam of the last flood whitened the trunks of the willows, and hung in squalid wisps from their lower branches.

For the first time we saw one another's faces, and how pale and woe-begone, mudstained and draggled we were! The cold, grey light, which so mercilessly unmasked our refuge, did not spare us. It helped even my lady to look her worst. Fraulein Anna sat a mere lifeless lump in her saddle. The waiting-women cried softly; they had cried all night. The Waldgrave looked dazed, as if he barely understood where he was or why he was there.

To think over-much in such a place was to weep. Instead, I hastened to get them all off their horses, and with Steve's help and a great bundle of osiers and branches which we cut, I made nests for them in the lower boughs of the willows, well out of reach of the water. When they had all taken their places, I served out food and a dram of Dantzic waters, which some of us needed; for a white mist, drawn up from the swamp by the rising sun, began to enshroud us, and, hanging among the osiers for more than an hour, prolonged the misery of the night.

Still, even that rolled away at last — about six o'clock — and let us see the sun shining overhead in a heaven of blue distance and golden clouds. Larks rose up and sang, and all the birds of the marsh began to twitter and tweet. In a trice our mud island was changed to a bower — a place of warmth and life and refreshment — where light and shade lay on the dappled floor, and the sunshine fell through green leaves.

Then I took the cloaks, and the saddles, and everything that was wet, and spread them out on branches to dry; and leaving the women to make themselves comfortable in their own way and shift themselves as they pleased, we two, with the Waldgrave and the two servants, went away to the other end of the eyot.

'I shall sleep,' Steve said drowsily. The insects were beginning to hum. The horses stood huddled together, swishing their long tails.

'You think they won't track us?' I asked.

'Certain,' he said. 'There are six hundred yards of mud and water, eel-holes, and willow shoots between us and the road.'

The Waldgrave assented mechanically; it seemed so to me too. And by-and-by, worn out with the night's work, I fell asleep, and slept, I suppose, for a good many hours, with the sun and shade passing slowly across my face, and the bees droning in my ears, and the mellow warmth of the summer day soaking into my bones. When I awoke I lay for a time revelling in lazy enjoyment. The oily plop of a water-rat, as it dived from a stump, or the scream of a dis-

We were alone. . . . I whispered in her ear . . .

tant jay, alone broke the laden silence. I looked at the
sun. It lay south-west. It was three o'clock then.
A light touch fell on my knee. I started, looked down,
and for a moment stared in sleepy wonder. A tiny bunch of
blue flowers, such as I could see growing in a dozen places
on the edge of the island, lay on it, tied up with a thread of
purple silk. I started up on my elbow, and — there, close
beside me, with her cheeks full of colour, and the sunshine
finding golden threads in her dark hair, sat Marie, toying
with more flowers.

'Ha!' I said foolishly. 'What is it?'

'My lady sent me to you,' she answered.

'Yes,' I asked eagerly. 'Does she want me?'

But Marie hung her head, and played with the flowers.
'I don't think so,' she whispered. 'She only sent me to
you.'

Then I understood. The Waldgrave had gone to the
farther end. Steve and the men were tending the horses
half a dozen paces beyond the screen of willow-leaves. We
were alone. A rat plashed into the water, and drove Marie
nearer to me; and she laid her head on my shoulder, and I
whispered in her ear, till the lashes sank down over her
eyes and her lips trembled. If I had loved her from the
first, what was the length and height and breadth of my
love now, when I had seen her in darkness and peril, sunshine and storm, strong when others failed, brave when
others flinched, always helpful, ready, tireless! And she
so small! So frail, I almost feared to press her to me; so
pale, the blood that leapt to her cheeks at my touch seemed
a mere reflection of the sunlight.

I told her how Steve had made the guards at the prison
drunk with wine bought with her dowry; how the horses
he had purchased and taken out of the camp by twos and
threes had been paid for from the same source; and how
many ducats had gone for meats and messes to keep the
life, that still ran sluggishly, in the Waldgrave's veins.
She listened and lay still.

'So you have no dowry now, little one,' I said, when I had told her all. 'And your gold chain is gone. I believe you have nothing but the frock you stand up in. Why, then, should I marry you?'

I felt her heart give a great leap under my hand, and a shiver ran through her. But she did not raise her head, and I, who had thought to tease her into looking at me, had to put back her little face till it gazed into mine. 'Why?' I said; 'why?'—drawing her closer and closer to me.

Then the colour came into her face like the sunlight itself. 'Because you love me,' she whispered, shutting her eyes.

And I did not gainsay her.

CHAPTER XXIV.

MISSING!

WE lay in the osier bed two whole days and a night, during which time two at least of us were not unhappy, in spite of peril and hardship. We left it at last, only because our meagre provision gave out, and we must move or starve. We felt far from sure that the danger was over, for Steve, who spent the second day in a thick bush near the road, saw two troops of horse go by; and others, we believed, passed in the night. But we had no choice. The neighbourhood was bleak and bare. Such small homesteads as existed had been eaten up, and lay abandoned. If we had felt inclined to venture out for food, none was to be had. And, in fine, though we trembled at the thought of the open road, and my heart for one grew sick as I looked from Marie to my lady, and reckoned the long tale of leagues which lay between us and Cassel, the risk had to be run.

Steve had discovered a more easy though longer way out of the willow-bed, and two hours before midnight on the second night, he and I mounted the women and prepared to set out. He arranged that we should go in the same order in which we had come : that he should lead the march, and I bring up the rear, while the Waldgrave, who was still far from well, and whose continued lack of vigour troubled us the more as we said little about it, should ride with my lady.

The night seemed likely to be fine, but the darkness, the sough of the wind as it swept over the plain, and the melancholy plashing of the water as our horses plodded through it, were not things of a kind to allay our fears. When we at last left our covert, and reaching the road stood to listen, the fall of a leaf made us start. Though no sounds but those of the night came to our ears — and some of these were of a kind to reassure us — we said 'Hush!' again and again, and only moved on after a hundred alarums and assurances.

I walked by Marie, with my hand on the withers of her horse, but we did not talk. The two waiting-women riding double were before us, and their muttered fears alone broke the silence which prevailed at the end of the train. We went at the rate of about two leagues an hour, Steve and I and the men running where the roads were good, and everywhere and at all times urging the horses to do their best. The haste of our movements, the darkness, our constant alarm, and the occasional confusion when the rear pressed on the van at an awkward place, had the effect of upsetting the balance of our minds ; so that the most common impulse of flight — to press forward with ever-increasing recklessness — began presently to possess us. Once or twice I had to check the foremost, or they would have outrun the rear ; and this kind of race brought us gradually into such a state of alarm, that by-and-by, when the line came to a sudden stop on the brow of a gentle descent, I could hardly restrain my impatience.

'What is it ? ' I asked eagerly. 'Why are we stopping ? ' Surely the road is good enough here.'

No one answered, but it was significant that on the instant one of the women began to cry.

'Stop that folly!' I said. 'What is in front there? Cannot some one speak?'

'The Waldgrave thinks that he hears horsemen before us,' Fraulein Max answered.

In another moment the Waldgrave's figure loomed out of the darkness. 'Martin,' he said — I noticed that his voice shook — 'go forward. They are in front. Man alive, be quick!' he continued fiercely. 'Do you want to have them into us?'

I left my girl's rein, and pushing past the women and Fraulein, joined Steve, who was standing by my lady's rein. 'What is it?' I said.

'Nothing, I think,' he answered in an uncertain tone.

I stood a moment listening, but I too could hear nothing. I began to argue with him. 'Who heard it?' I asked impatiently.

'The Waldgrave,' he answered.

I did not like to say before my lady what I thought — that the Waldgrave was not quite himself, nor to be depended upon; and instead I proposed to go forward on foot and learn if anything was amiss. The road ran straight down the hill, and the party could scarcely pass me, even in the gloom. If I found all well, I would whistle, and they could come on.

My lady agreed, and, leaving them halted, I started cautiously down the hill. The darkness was not extreme; the cloud drift was broken here and there, and showed light patches of sky between; I could make out the shapes of things, and more than once took a clump of bushes for a lurking ambush. But halfway down, a line of poplars began to shadow the road on our side, and from that point I might have walked into a regiment and never seen a man. This, the being suddenly alone, and the constant rustling of the leaves overhead, which moved with the slightest air, shook my nerves, and I went very warily, with my heart in my mouth and a cry trembling on my lips.

Still I had reached the hillfoot before anything happened. Then I stopped abruptly, hearing quite distinctly in front of me the sound of footsteps. It was impossible that this could be the sound that the Waldgrave had heard, for only one man seemed to be stirring, and he moved stealthily; but I crouched down and listened, and in a moment I was rewarded. A dark figure came out of the densest of the shadow and stood in the middle of the road. I sank lower, noiselessly. The man seemed to be listening. It flashed into my head that he was a sentry; and I thought how fortunate it was that I had come on alone.

Presently he moved again. He stole along the track towards me, stooping, as I fancied, and more than once standing to listen, as if he were not satisfied. I sank down still lower, and he passed me without notice, and went on, and I heard his footsteps slowly retreating until they quite died away.

But in a moment, before I had risen to my full height, I heard them again. He came back, and passed me, breathing quickly and loudly. I wondered if he had detected our party and was going to give the alarm; and I stood up, anxious and uncertain, at a loss whether I should follow him or run back.

At that instant a fierce yell broke the silence, and rent the darkness as a flash of lightning might rend it. It came from behind me, from the brow of the hill; and I started as if I had been struck. Hard on it a volley of shouts and screams flared up in the same direction, and while my heart stood still with terror and fear of what had happened, I heard the thunder of hoofs come down the road, with a clatter of blows and whips. They were coming headlong — my lady and the rest. The danger was behind them, then. I had just time to turn and get to the side of the road before they were on me at a gallop.

I could not see who was who in the darkness, but I

caught at the nearest stirrup, and, narrowly escaping being ridden down, ran on beside the rider. The horses, spurred down the slope, had gained such an impetus that it was all I could do to keep up. I had no breath to ask questions, nor state my fear that there was danger ahead also. I had to stride like a giant to keep my legs and run.

Some one else was less lucky. We had not swept fifty yards from where I joined them, when a dark figure showed for a moment in the road before us. I saw it; it seemed to hang and hesitate. The next instant it was among us. I heard a shrill scream, a heavy fall, and we were over it, and charging on and on and on through the darkness.

To the foot of the hill and across the bottom, and up the opposite slope. I do not know how far we had sped, when Steve's voice was heard, calling on us to halt.

'Pull up! pull up!' he cried, with an angry oath. 'It is a false alarm! What fool set it going? There is no one behind us. Donner und Blitzen! where is Martin?'

The horses were beginning to flag, and gladly came to a trot, and then to a walk.

'Here! I panted.

'Himmel! I thought we had ridden you down!' he said, leaving my lady's side. His voice shook with passion and loss of breath. 'Who was it? We might all have broken our necks, and for nothing!'

The Waldgrave — it was his stirrup I had caught — turned his horse round. 'I heard them — close behind us!' he panted. There was a note of wildness in his voice. My elbow was against his knee, and I felt him tremble.

'A bird in the hedge,' Steve said rudely. 'It has cost some one dear. Whose horse was it struck him?'

No one answered. I left the Waldgrave's side and went back a few paces. The women were sobbing. Ernst and Jacob stood by them, breathing hard after their run. I thought the men's silence strange. I looked again. There was a figure missing; a horse missing.

'Where is Marie?' I cried.

She did not answer. No one answered; and I knew. Steve swore again. I think he had known from the beginning. I began to tremble. On a sudden my lady lifted up her voice and cried shrilly —

'Marie! Marie!'

Again no answer. But this time I did not wait to listen. I ran from them into the darkness the way we had come, my legs quivering under me, and my mouth full of broken prayers. I remembered a certain solitary tree fronting the poplars, on the other side of the way, which I had marked mechanically at the moment of the fall — an ash, whose light upper boughs had come for an instant between my eyes and the sky. It stood on a little mound, where the moorland began to rise on that side. I came to it now, and stopped and looked. At first I could see nothing, and I trod forward fearfully. Then, a couple of paces on, I made out a dark figure, lying head and feet across the road. I sprang to it, and kneeling, passed my hands over it. Alas! it was a woman's.

I raised the light form in my arms, crying passionately on her name, while the wind swayed the boughs overhead, and, besides that and my voice, all the countryside was still. She did not answer. She hung limp in my arms. Kneeling in the dust beside her, I felt blindly for a pulse, a heart-beat. I found neither — neither; the woman was dead.

And yet it was not that which made me lay the body down so quickly and stand up peering round me. No; something else. The blood drummed in my ears, my heart beat wildly. The woman was dead; but she was not Marie.

She was an old woman, sixty years old. When I stooped again, after assuring myself that there was no other body near, and peered into her face, I saw that it was seamed and wrinkled. She was barefoot, and her clothes were foul and mean. She had the reek of one who slept in ditches and washed seldom. Her toothless gums grinned

17

at me. She was a horrible mockery of all that men love
in women.

When I had marked so much, I stood up again, my head
reeling. Where was the man I had seen scouting up and
down ? Where was Marie ? For a moment the wild idea
that she had become this thing, that death or magic had
transformed the fair young girl into this toothless hag, was
not too wild for me. An owl hooted in the distance, and I
started and shivered and stood looking round me fearfully.
Such things were ; and Marie was gone. In her place this
woman, grim and dead and unsightly, lay at my feet. What
was I to think ?

I got no answer. I raised my voice and called, trembling,
on Marie. I ran to one side of the road and the other and
called, and still got no answer. I climbed the mound on
which the ash-tree stood, and sent my voice thrilling
through the darkness of the bottom. But only the owl
answered. Then, knowing nothing else I could do, I went
down wringing my hands, and found my lady standing over
the body in the road. She had come back with Steve and
the others.

I had to listen to their amazement, and a hundred guesses
and fancies, which, God help me ! had nothing certain in
them, and gave me no help. The men searched both sides
of the road, and beat the moor for a distance, and tried to
track the horse — for that was missing too, and there lay
my only hope — but to no purpose. At last my lady came
to me and said sorrowfully that nothing more could be done.

'In the morning !' I cried jealously.

No one spoke, and I looked from one to another. The
men had returned from the search, and stood in a dark
group round the body, which they had drawn to the side of
the road. It wanted an hour of daylight yet, and I could
not see their faces, but I read in their silence the answer
that no one liked to put into words.

'Be a man !' Steve muttered, after a long pause. 'God
help the girl. But God help us too if we are found here !'

Still my lady did not speak, and I knew her brave heart too well to doubt her, though she had been the first to talk of going. 'Get to horse,' I said roughly.

'No, no,' my lady cried at last. 'We will all stay, Martin.'

'Ay, all stay or all go!' Steve muttered.

'Then all go!' I said, choking down the sobs that would rise. And I turned first from the place.

I will not try to state what that cost me. I saw my girl's face everywhere — everywhere in the darkness, and the eyes reproached me. That she of all should suffer, who had never fainted, never faltered, whose patience and courage had been the women's stay from the first — that she should suffer! I thought of the tender, weak body, and of all the things that might happen to her, and I seemed, as I went away from her, the vilest thing that lived.

But reason was against me. If I stayed there and waited on the road by the old crone's body until morning, what could I do? Whither could I turn? Marie was gone and already might be half a dozen miles away. So the bonds of custom and duty held me. Dazed and bewildered, I lacked the strength that was needed to run counter to all. I was no knight-errant, but a plain man, and I reeled on through the last hour of the night and the first grey streaks of dawn, with my head on my breast and sobs of despair in my throat.

CHAPTER XXV.

NUREMBERG.

IF it had been our fate after that to continue our flight in the same weary fashion we had before devised, lying in woods by day, and all night riding jaded horses, until we passed the gates of some free city, I do not think that I could have gone through with it. Doubtless it was my duty to go with my lady. But the long hours of daylight in-

action, the slow brooding tramp, must have proved intolerable. And at some time or other, in some way or other, I
must have snapped the ties that bound me.

But, as if the loss of my heart had rid us of some spell
cast over us, by noon of that day we stood safe. For, an
hour before noon, while we lay in a fir-wood not far from
Weimar, and Jacob kept watch on the road below, and the
rest slept as we pleased, a party of horse came along the
way, and made as if to pass below us. They numbered
more than a hundred, and Jacob's heart failed him, lest
some ring or buckle of our accoutrements should sparkle
and catch their eyes. To shift the burden he called us, and
we went to watch them.

'Do they go north or south?' I asked him as I rose.

'North,' he whispered.

After that they were nothing to me, but I went with the
rest. Our lair was in some rocks overhanging the road.
By the time we looked over, the horsemen were below us,
and we could see nothing of them; though the sullen tramp
of their horses, and the jingle of bit and spur, reached us
clearly. Presently they came into sight again on the road
beyond, riding steadily away with their backs to us.

'That is not General Tzerclas?' my lady muttered anxiously.

'Nor any of his people!' Steve said with an oath.

That led me to look more closely, and I saw in a moment
something that lifted me out of my moodiness. I sprang on
the rock against which I was leaning and shouted long and
loudly.

'Himmel!' Steve cried, seizing me by the ankle. 'Are
you mad, man?'

But I only shouted again, and waved my cap frantically.
Then I slipped down, sobered. 'They see us,' I cried.
'They are Leuchtenstein's riders. And Count Hugo is with
them. You are safe, my lady.'

She turned white and red, and I saw her clutch at the rock
to keep herself on her feet. 'Are you sure?' she said.

The troop had halted and were wheeling slowly and in perfect order.

'Quite sure, my lady,' I answered, with a touch of bitterness in my tone. Why had not this happened yesterday or the day before? Then my girl would have been saved. Now it came too late! Too late! No wonder I felt bitterly about it.

We went down into the road on foot, a little party of nine — four women and five men. The horsemen, as they came up, looked at us in wonder. Our clothes, even my lady's, were dyed with mud and torn in a score of places. We had not washed for days, and our faces were lean with famine. Some of the women were shoeless and had their hair about their ears, while Steve was bare-headed and bare-armed, and looked so huge a ruffian the stocks must have yawned for him anywhere. They drew up and gazed at us, and then Count Hugo came riding down the column and saw us.

My lady went forward a step. 'Count Leuchtenstein,' she said, her voice breaking; she had only seen him once, and then under the mask of a plain name. But he was safety, honour, life now, and I think that she could have kissed him. I think for a little she could have fallen into his arms.

'Countess!' he said, as he sprang from his horse in wonder. 'Is it really you? Gott im Himmel! These are strange times. Waldgrave! Your pardon. Ach! Have you come on foot?'

'Not I. But these brave men have,' my lady answered, tears in her voice.

He looked at Steve and grunted. Then he looked at me and his eyes lightened. 'Are these all your party?' he said hurriedly.

'All,' my lady answered in a low voice.

He did not ask farther, but he sighed, and I knew that he had looked for his child. 'I came north upon a reconnaissance, and was about to turn,' he said. 'I am thankful that I did not turn before. Is Tzerclas in pursuit of you?'

'I do not know,' my lady answered, and told him shortly of our flight, and how we had lain two days and a night in the osier-bed.

'It was a good thought,' he said. 'But I fear that you are half famished.' And he called for food and wine, and served my lady with his own hands, while he saw that we did not go without. 'Campaigner's fare,' he said. 'But you come of a fighting stock, Countess, and can put up with it.'

'Shame on me if I could not,' she answered.

There was a quaver in her voice, which showed how the rencontre moved her, how full her heart was of unspoken gratitude.

'When you have finished, we will get to horse,' he said. 'I must take you with me to Nuremberg, for I am not strong enough to detach a party. But this evening we will make a long halt at Hesel, and secure you a good night's rest.'

'I am sorry to be so burdensome,' my lady said timidly.

He shrugged his shoulders without compliment, but I did not hear what he answered. For I could bear no more. Marie seemed so forgotten in this crowd, so much a thing of the past, that my gorge rose. No word of her, no thought of her, no talk of a search party! I pictured her forlorn, helpless little figure, her pale, uncomplaining face — I and no one else; and I had to go away into the bushes to hide myself. She was forgotten already. She had done all for them, I said to myself, and they forgot her.

Then, in the thicket screened from the party, I had a thought — to go back and look for her, myself. Now my lady was safe, there was nothing to prevent me. I had only to lie close among the rocks until Count Hugo left, and then I might plod back on foot and search as I pleased. In a flash I saw the poplars, and the road running beneath the ash-tree, and the woman's body lying stiff and stark on the sward. And I burned to be there.

Left to myself I should have gone too. But the plan was no sooner formed than shattered. While I stood, hotfoot to be about it, and pausing only to consider which way I could steal off most safely, a rustling warned me that some one was coming, and before I could stir, a burly trooper broke through the bushes and confronted me. He saluted me stolidly.

'Sergeant,' he said, 'the general is waiting for you.'

'The general?' I said.

'The Count, if you like it better,' he answered. 'Come, if you please.'

I followed him, full of vexation. It was but a step into the road. The moment I appeared, some one gave the word 'Mount!' A horse was thrust in front of me, two or three troopers who still remained afoot swung themselves into the saddle; and I followed their example. In a trice we were moving down the valley at a dull, steady pace — southwards, southwards. I looked back, and saw the fir trees and rocks where we had lain hidden, and then we turned a corner, and they were gone. Gone, and all round me I heard the measured tramp of the troop-horses, the swinging tones of the men, and the clink and jingle of sword and spur. I called myself a cur, but I went on, swept away by the force of numbers, as the straw by the current. Once I caught Count Hugo's eye fixed on me, and I fancied he had a message for me, but I failed to interpret it.

Steve rode by me, and his face too was moody. I suppose that we should all of us have thanked God the peril was past. But my lady rode in another part with Count Leuchtenstein and the Waldgrave; and Steve yearned, I fancy, for the old days of trouble and equality, when there was no one to come between us.

I saw Count Hugo that night. He sent for me to his quarters at Hesel, and told me frankly that he would have let me go back had he thought good could come of it.

'But it would have been looking for a needle in a bundle

of hay, my friend,' he continued. 'Tzerclas' men would
have picked you up, or the peasants killed you for a soldier,
and in a month perhaps the girl would have returned safe
and sound, to find you dead.'

'My lord!' I cried passionately, 'she saved your child.
It was to her as her own!'

'I know it,' he answered with gravity, which of itself
rebuked me. 'And where is my child?'

I shook my head.

'Yet I do not give up my work and the task God and
the times have given me, and go out looking for it!' he
answered severely. 'Leaving Scot, and Swede, and Pole,
and Switzer to divide my country. For shame! You have
your work too, and it lies by your lady's side. See to it
that you do it. For the rest I have scouts out, who know
the country; if I learn anything through them you shall
hear it. And now of another matter. How long has the
Waldgrave been like this, my friend?'

'Like this, my lord?' I muttered stupidly.

He nodded. 'Yes, like this,' he repeated. 'I have
heard him called a brave man. Coming of his stock, he
should be; and when I saw him in Tzerclas' camp he had
the air of one. Now he starts at a shadow, is in a trance
half his time, and a tremor the other half. What ails
him?'

I told him how he had been wounded, fighting bravely,
and that since that he had not been himself.

Count Hugo rubbed his chin gravely. 'It is a pity,' he
said. 'We want all—every German arm and every German head. We want you. Man alive!' he continued,
roused to anger, I suppose, by my dull face, 'do you know
what is in front of you?'

'No, my lord,' I said in apathy.

He opened his mouth as if to hurl a volley of words at
me. But he thought better of it and shut his lips tight.
'Very well,' he said grimly. 'Wait three days and you
will see.'

But in truth, I had not to wait three days. Before sunset of the next I began to see, and, downcast as I was, to
prick up my ears in wonder. Beyond Romhild and between that town and Bamberg, the great road which runs
through the valley of the Pegnitz, was such a sight as I
had never seen. For many miles together a column of
dust marked its course, and under this went on endless
marching. We were but a link in a long chain, dragging
slowly southwards. Now it was a herd of oxen that passed
along, moving tediously and painfully, driven by half-naked
cattle-men and guarded by a troop of grimy horse. Now it
was a reinforcement of foot from Fulda, rank upon rank of
shambling men trailing long pikes, and footsore, and parched
as they were, getting over the ground in a wonderful fashion.
After them would come a long string of waggons, bearing
corn, and hay, and malt, and wines; all lurching slowly
forward, slowly southward; often delayed, for every quarter of a mile a horse fell or an axle broke, yet getting
forward.

And then the most wonderful sight of all, a regiment of
Swedish horse passed us, marching from Erfurt. All their
horses were grey, and all their head-pieces, backs and
breasts of black metal, matched one another. As they
came on through the dust with a tramp which shook the
ground, they sang, company by company, to the music of
drums and trumpets, a hymn, 'Versage nicht, du Häuflein
klein!' Behind them a line of light waggons carried their
wives and children, also singing. And so they went by us,
eight hundred swords, and I thought it a marvel I should
never see beaten.

When they were gone out of sight, there were still droves
of horses and mighty flocks of sheep to come, and cargoes
of pork, and more foot and horse and guns. Some companies wore buff coats and small steel caps, and carried
arquebuses; and some marched smothered in huge head-
pieces with backs and breasts to match. And besides all
the things I have mentioned and the crowds of sutlers

and horse-boys that went with them, there were muni-
tion waggons closely guarded, and pack-horses laden with
powder, and always and always waggons of corn and hay.
And all hurrying, jostling, crawling southwards. It
seemed to me that the world was marching southwards;
that if we went on we must fall in at the end of this with
every one we knew. And the thought comforted me.

Steve put it into words after his fashion. 'It must be a
big place we are going to,' he said, about noon of the second
day, 'or who is to eat all this? And do you mark, Master
Martin? We meet no one coming back. All go south.
This place Nuremberg that they talk of must be worth
seeing.'

'It should be,' I said.

And after that the excitement of the march began to
take hold of me. I began to think and wonder, and look
forward, with an eagerness I did not understand, to the
issues of this.

We lay a night at Bamberg, where the crowd and confusion and the stress of people were so great that Steve
would have it we had come to Nuremberg. And certainly
I had never known such a hurly-burly, nor heard of it
except at the great fair at Dantzic. The night after we
lay at Erlangen, which we found fortified, trenched, and
guarded, with troops lying in the square, and the streets
turned into stables. From that place to Nuremberg was
a matter of ten miles only; but the press was so great on
the road that it took us a good part of the day to ride from
one to the other. In the open country on either side of the
way strong bodies of horse and foot were disposed. It
seemed to me that here was already an army and a camp.

But when late in the afternoon we entered Nuremberg
itself, and viewed the traffic in the streets, and the endless
lines of gabled houses, the splendid mansions and bridges,
the climbing roofs and turrets and spires of this, the greatest city in Germany, then we thought little of all we had
seen before. Here thousands upon thousands rubbed

shoulders in the streets ; here continuous boats turned
the river into solid land. Here we were told were baked
every day a hundred thousand loaves of bread; and I saw
with my own eyes a list of a hundred and thirty-eight bake-
houses. The roar of the ways, choked with soldiers and
citizens, the babel of strange tongues, the clamour of bells and
trumpets, deafened us. The constant crowding and pushing
and halting turned our heads. I forgot my grief and my
hope too. Who but a madman would look to find a single
face where thousands gazed from the windows ? or could
deem himself important with this swarming, teeming hive
before him ? Steve stared stupidly about him; I rode
dazed and perplexed. The troopers laughed at us, or
promised us greater things when we should see the
Swedish Lager outside the town, and Wallenstein's great
camp arrayed against it. But I noticed that even they, as
we drew nearer to the heart of the city, fell silent at times,
and looked at one another, surprised at the great influx of
people and the shifting scenes which the streets presented.

For myself and Steve and the men, we were as good as
nought. A house in the Ritter-Strasse was assigned to my
lady for her quarters — no one could lodge in the city without the leave of the magistrates ; and we were glad to get
into it and cool our dizzy heads, and look at one another.
Count Hugo stayed awhile, standing with my lady and the
Waldgrave in one of the great oriels that overlooked the
street. But a mounted messenger, sent on from the Town
House, summoned him, and he took horse again for the
camp. I do not know what we should have done without·
him at entering. The soldiers, who crowded the streets,
showed scant respect for names, and would as soon have
jostled my lady as a citizen's wife; but wherever he came
hats were doffed and voices lowered, and in the greatest
press a way was made for him as by magic.

For that night we had seen enough. I thought we had
seen all, or that nothing in my life would ever surprise me
again. But next day my lady went up to the Burg on the

hill in the middle of the city to look abroad, and took Steve
and myself with her. And then I found that I had not seen
the half. The city, all roofs and spires and bridges, girt
with a wall of seventy towers, roared beneath us ; and that
I had expected. But outside the wall I now saw a second
city of huts and tents, with a great earthwork about it, and
bastions and demilunes and picquets posted.

This was the Swedish Lager. It lay principally to the
south of the city proper, though on all sides it encircled it
more or less. They told me that there lay in it about
forty thousand soldiers and twenty thousand horses, and
twenty thousand camp followers ; but the number was constantly increasing, death and disease notwithstanding, so
that it presently stood as high as sixty thousand fighting
men and half as many followers, to say nothing of the
garrison that lay in the city, or the troops posted to guard
the approaches. It seemed to me, gazing over that mighty
multitude from the top of the hill, that nothing could
resist such a force; and I looked abroad with curiosity
for the enemy.

I expected to view his army cheek by jowl with us; and
I was disappointed when I saw beyond our camp to southward, where I was told he lay, only a clear plain with the
little river Rednitz flowing through it. This plain was a
league and more in width, and it was empty of men.
Beyond it rose a black wooded ridge, very steep and
hairy.

My lady explained that Wallenstein's army lay along
this ridge — seventy thousand men, and forty thousand
horses, and Wallenstein himself. His camp we heard was
eight miles round, the front guarded by a line of cannon,
and taking in whole villages and castles. And now I
looked again I saw the smoke hang among the trees. They
whispered in Nuremberg that no man in that army took
pay ; that all served for booty ; and that the troopers that
sacked Magdeburg and followed Tilly were, beside these,
gentle and kindly men.

'God help us!' my lady cried fervently. 'God help this great city! God help the North! Never was such a battle fought as must be fought here!'

We went down very much sobered, filled with awe and wonder and great thoughts, the dullest of us feeling the air heavy with portents, the more clerkly considering of Armageddon and the Last Fight. Briefly — for thirteen years the Emperor and the Papists had hustled and harried the Protestants; had dragooned Donauwörth, and held down Bohemia, and plundered the Palatinate, and crushed the King of Denmark, and wherever there was a weak Protestant state had pressed sorely on it. Then one short year before I stood on the Burg above the Pegnitz, the Protestant king had come out of the North like a thunderbolt, had shattered in a month the Papist armies, had run like a devouring fire down the Priests' Lane, rushed over Bohemia, shaken the Emperor on his throne!

But could he maintain himself? That was now to be seen. To the Emperor's help had come all who loved the old system, and would have it that the south was Germany; all who wished to chain men's minds and saw their profit in the shadow of the imperial throne; all who lived by license and plunder, and reckoned a mass to-day against a murder to-morrow. All these had come, from the great Duke of Friedland grasping at empire, to the meanest freebooter with peasant's blood on his hands and in his veins; and there they lay opposite us, impregnably placed on the Burgstall, waiting patiently until famine and the sword should weaken the fair city, and enable them to plunge their vulture's talons into its vitals.

No wonder that in Nuremberg the citizens could be distinguished from the soldiers by their careworn faces; or that many a man stood morning and evening to gaze at the carved and lofty front of his house — by St. Sebald's or behind the new Cathedral — and wondered how long the fire would spare it. The magistrates who had staked all — their own and the city's — on this cast, went about with

stern, grave faces and feared almost to meet the public eye.
With a doubled population, with a huge army to feed, with
order to keep, with houses and wives and daughters of their
own to protect, with sack and storm looming luridly in the
future, who had cares like theirs ?

One man only, and him I saw as we went home from the
Burg. It was near the foot of the Burg hill, where the
strasse meets three other ways.   At that time Count Tilly's
crooked, dwarfish figure and pale horse's face, and the great
hat and boots which seemed to swallow him up, were fresh
in my mind; and sometimes I had wondered whether this
other great commander were like him.   Well, I was to
know; for through the crowd at the junction of these four
roads, while we stood waiting to pass, there came a man on
a white horse, followed by half a score of others on horse-
back ; and in a moment I knew from the shouting and the
way women thrust papers into his hands that we saw the
King of Sweden.

He wore a plain buff coat and a grey flapped hat with a
feather; a tall man and rather bulky, his face massive and
fleshy, with a close moustache trimmed to a point and a
small tuft on his chin.   His aspect was grave; he looked
about him with a calm eye, and the shouting did not seem
to move him.   They told me that it was Bañer, the Swedish
General, who rode with him, and our Bernard of Weimar
who followed.   But my eye fell more quickly on Count
Leuchtenstein, who rode after, with the great Chancellor
Oxenstierna; in him, in his steady gaze and serene brow
and wholesome strength, I traced the nearest likeness to
the king.

And so I first saw the great Gustavus Adolphus.   It was
said that he would at times fall into fits of Berserk rage,
and that in the field he was another man, keen as his sword,
swift as fire, pitiless to those who flinched, among the foremost in the charge, a very thunderbolt of war.   But as I
saw him taking papers from women's hands at the end of
the Burg Strasse, he had rather the air of a quiet, worthy

prince — of Coburg or Darmstadt, it might be, — no dresser and no brawler; nor would any one, to see him then, have thought that this was the lion of the north who had dashed the pride of Pappenheim and flung aside the firebrands of the south. Or that even now he had on his shoulders the burden of two great nations and the fate of a million of men.

CHAPTER XXVI.

THE FACE AT THE WINDOW.

AFTER this it fared with us as it fares at last with the driftwood that chance or the woodman's axe has given to a forest stream in Heritzburg. After rippling over the shallows and shooting giddily down slopes — or perchance lying cooped for days in some dark bend, until the splash of the otter or the spring freshet has sent it dancing on in sunshine and shadow — it reaches at last the Werra. It floats out on the bosom of the great stream, and no longer tossed and chafed by each tiny pebble, feels the force of wind and stream — the great forces of the world. The banks recede from sight, and one of a million atoms, it is borne on gently and irresistibly, whither it does not know.

So it was with us. From the day we fell in with Count Leuchtenstein and set our faces towards Nuremberg, and in a greater degree after we reached that city, we embarked on a wider current of adventure, a fuller and less selfish life. If we had still our own cares and griefs, hopes and perils — as must be the case, I suppose, until we die — we had other common ones which we shared with tens of thousands, rich and poor, gentle and simple. We had to dread sack and storm; we prayed for relief and safety in company with all who rose and lay down within the walls. When a hundred waggons of corn slipped through the Croats and came in, or Duke Bernard of Weimar beat up a corner of the Burgstall and gave Wallenstein a bad night, we ran out into the streets to tell and hear the news. Similarly, when tidings came that Tzerclas with his two thousand ruffians had burned the King of Sweden's colours, put on green sashes, and marched into the enemy's camp, we were not alone in our gloomy anticipations. We still had our private adventures, and I am going to tell them. But besides these, it should be remembered that we ran the risks, and rose every morning fresh to the fears, of Nuremberg. When bread rose to ten, to fifteen, to twenty times its normal price ; when the city, where many died every day of famine, plague, and wounds, began to groan and heave in its misery ; when through all the country round the peasants crawled and died among the dead; when Wallenstein, that dark man, heedless of the fearful mortality in his own camp, still sat implacable on the heights and refused all the king's invitations to battle, we grew pale and gloomy, stern-eyed and thin-cheeked with the rest. We dreamed of Magdeburg as they did ; and as the hot August days passed slowly over the starving city and still no end appeared, but only with each day some addition of misery, we felt our hearts sink in unison with theirs.

And we had to share, not their lot only, but their labours. We had not been in the town twenty-four hours before Steve, Jacob, and Ernst were enrolled in the town militia ; to me, either out of respect to my lady, or on account of my stature, a commission as lieutenant was granted. We drilled every morning from six o'clock until eight in the fields outside the New Gate; the others went again at sunset to practise their weapons, but I was exempt from this drill, that the women might not be left alone. At all times we had our appointed rendezvous in case of alarm or assault. The Swedish veterans strolled out of the camp and stood to laugh at our clumsiness. But the excellent order which prevailed among them made them favourites, and we let them laugh, and laughed again.

The Waldgrave, who had long had Duke Bernard's promise, received a regiment of horse, so that he lay in the camp and should have been a contented man, since his strength had come back to him. But to my surprise he showed signs of lukewarmness. He seemed little interested in the service, and was often at my lady's house in the Ritter Strasse, when he would have been better at his post. At first I set this down to his passion for my lady, and it seemed excusable ; but within a week I stood convinced that this no longer troubled him. He paid scant attention to her, but would sit for hours looking moodily into the street. And I — and not I alone —began to watch him closely.

I soon found that Count Hugo was right. The once gallant and splendid young fellow was a changed man. He was still comely and a brave figure, but the spirit in him was quenched. He was nervous, absent, irritable. His eyes had a wild look; on strangers he made an unfavourable impression. Doubtless, though his wounds had healed, there remained some subtle injury that spoiled the man ; and often I caught my lady looking at him sadly, and knew that I was not the only one with cause for mourning.

But how strange he was we did not know until a certain day, when my lady and I were engaged together over some accounts. It was evening, and the three men were away drilling. The house was very quiet. Suddenly he flung in upon us with a great noise, his colour high, his eyes glittering. His first action was to throw his feathered hat on one chair, and himself into another.

'I 've seen him !' he said. 'Himmel ! he is a clever fellow. He will worst you, cousin, yet — see if he does not. Oh, he is a clever one !'

'Who ?' my lady said, looking at him in some displeasure.

'Who ? Tzerclas, to be sure !' he answered, chuckling.

'You have seen him !' she exclaimed, rising.

'Of course I have !' he answered. 'And you will see him too, one of these days.'

18

My lady looked at me, frowning. But I shook my head.
He was not drunk.

'Where?' she asked, after a pause. 'Where did you see
him, Rupert?'

'In the street — where you see other men,' he answered,
chuckling again. 'He should not be there, but who is to
keep him out? He is too clever. He will get his way in
the end, see if he does not!'

'Rupert!' my lady cried in wrathful amazement, 'to
hear you, one would suppose you admired him.'

'So I do,' he replied coolly. 'Why not? He has all the
wits of the family. He is as cunning as the devil. Take
a hint, cousin; put yourself on the right side. He will
win in the end!' And the Waldgrave rose restlessly from
his chair, and, going to the window, began to whistle.

My lady came swiftly to me, and it grieved me to see the
pain and woe in her face.

'Is he mad?' she muttered.

I shook my head.

'Do you think he has really seen him?' she whispered.
We both stood with our eyes on him.

'I fear so, my lady,' I said with reluctance.

'But it would cost *him* his life,' she muttered eagerly,
'if he were found here!'

'He is a bold man,' I answered.

'Ah! so was he — once,' she replied in a peculiar tone,
and she pointed stealthily to the unconscious man in the
window. 'A month ago he would have taken him by the
throat anywhere. What has come to him?'

'God knows,' I answered reverently. 'Grant only he
may do us no harm!'

He turned round at that, humming gaily, and went out,
seeming almost unconscious of our presence; and I made
as light of the matter to my lady as I could. But Tzerclas
in the city, the Waldgrave mad, or at any rate not sane,
and last, but not least, the strange light in which the latter
chose to regard the former, were circumstances I could not

easily digest. They filled me with uneasy fears and sur-
mises. I began to perambulate the crowd, seeking furtively
for a face; and was entirely determined what I would do if
I found it. The town was full, as all besieged cities are,
of rumours of spies and treachery, and of reported over-
tures made now to the city behind the back of the army,
and now to the army to betray the city. A single word of
denunciation, and Tzerclas' life would not be worth three
minutes' purchase — a rope and the nearest butcher's hook
would end it. My mind was made up to say the word.

I suppose I had been going about in this state of vigi-
lance three days or more, when something, but not the
thing I sought, rewarded it. At the time I was on my way
back from morning drill. It was a little after eight, and
the streets and the people wore an air bright, yet haggard.
Night, with its perils, was over; day, with its privations,
lay before us. My mind was on the common fortunes, but
I suppose my eyes were mechanically doing their work, for
on a sudden I saw something at a window, took perhaps
half a step, and stopped as if I had been shot.

I had seen Marie's face! Nay, I still saw it, while a man
might count two. Then it was gone. And I stood gasping.

I suppose I stood so for half a minute, waiting, with the
blood racing from my heart to my head, and every pulse in
my body beating. But she did not reappear. The door of
the house did not open. Nothing happened.

Yet I had certainly seen her; for I remembered particulars — the expression of her face, the surprise that had
leapt into her eyes as they met mine, the opening of the
lips in an exclamation.

And still I stood gazing at the window and nothing
happened.

At last I came to myself, and I scanned the house. It
was a large house of four stories, three gables in width.
The upper stories jutted out; the beams on which they
rested were finely carved, the gables were finished off with
rich, wooden pinnacles. In each story, the lowest ex-

cepted, were three long, low windows of the common
Nuremberg type, and the whole had a substantial and
reputable air.

The window at which I had seen Marie was farthest
from the door, on the first floor. To go to the door I had
to lose sight of it, and perhaps for that reason I stood the
longer. At last I went and knocked, and waited in a fever
for some one to come. The street was a thoroughfare.
There were a number of people passing. I thought that
all the town would go by before a dragging foot at last
sounded inside, and the great nail-studded door was opened
on the chain. A stout, red-faced woman showed herself
in the aperture.

'What is it?' she asked.

'You have a girl in this house, named Marie Wort,' I
answered breathlessly. 'I saw her a moment ago at the
window. I know her, and I wish to speak to her.'

The woman's little eyes dwelt on me stolidly for a space.
Then she made as if she would shut the door. 'For
shame!' she said spitefully. 'We have no girls here.
Begone with you!'

But I put my foot against the door. 'Whose house is
this?' I said.

'Herr Krapp's,' she answered crustily.

'Is he at home?'

'No, he is not,' she retorted; 'and if he were, we have
no baggages here.' And again she tried to shut the door,
but I prevented her.

'Where is he?' I asked sternly.

'He is at morning drill, if you must know,' she snapped;
'and his two sons. Now, will you let me shut my door?
Or must I cry out?'

'Nonsense, mother!' I said. 'Who is in the house
besides yourself?'

'What is that to you?' she replied, breathing short.

'I have told you,' I said, trying to control my anger.
'I——'

But, quick as lightning, the door slammed to and cut me short. I had thoughtlessly moved my foot. I heard the woman chuckle and go slipshod down the passage, and though I knocked again in a rage, the door remained closed.

I fell back and looked at the house. An elderly man in a grave, sober dress was passing, among others, and I caught his eye.

'Whose house is that?' I asked him.

'Herr Krapp's,' he answered.

'I am a stranger,' I said. 'Is he a man of substance?'

The person I addressed smiled. 'He is a member of the Council of Safety,' he said dryly. 'His brother is prefect of this ward. But here is Herr Krapp. Doubtless he has been at St. Sebald's drilling.'

I thanked him, and made but two steps to Herr Krapp's side. He was the other's twin — elderly, soberly dressed, his only distinction a sword and pistol in his girdle and a white shoulder sash.

'Herr Krapp?' I said.

'The same,' he answered, eying me gravely.

'I am the Countess of Heritzburg's steward,' I said. I began to see the need of explanation. 'Doubtless you have heard that she is in the city?'

'Certainly,' he answered. 'In the Ritter Strasse.'

'Yes,' I replied. 'A fortnight ago she missed a young woman, one of her attendants. She was lost in a night adventure,' I continued, my throat dry and husky. 'A few minutes ago I saw her looking from one of your windows.'

'From one of my windows?' he exclaimed in a tone of surprise.

'Yes,' I said stiffly.

He opened his eyes wide. 'Here?' he said. He pointed to his house.

I nodded.

'Impossible!' he replied, shutting his lips suddenly. 'Quite impossible, my friend. My household consists of my two sons and myself. We have a housekeeper only, and two lads. I have no young women in the house.'

'Yet I saw her face, Herr Krapp, at your window,' I answered obstinately.

'Wait,' he said ; 'I will ask.'

But when the old housekeeper came she had only the same tale to tell. She was alone. No young woman had crossed the threshold for a week past. There was no other woman there, young or old.

'You will have it that I have a young man in the house next !' she grumbled, shooting scorn at me.

'I can assure you that there is no one here,' Herr Krapp said civilly. 'Dorcas has been with me many years, and I can trust her. Still if you like you can walk through the rooms.'

But I hesitated to do that. The man's manner evidenced his sincerity, and in face of it my belief wavered. Fancy, I began to think, had played me a trick. It was no great wonder if the features which were often before me in my dreams, and sometimes painted themselves on the darkness while I lay wakeful, had for once taken shape in the daylight, and so vividly as to deceive me. I apologised. I said what was proper, and, with a heavy sigh, went from the door.

Ay, and with bent head. The passing crowd and the sunshine and the distant music of drum and trumpet grated on me. For there was yet another explanation. And I feared that Marie was dead.

I was still brooding sadly over the matter when I reached home. Steve met me at the door, but, feeling in no mood for small talk just then, I would have passed him by and gone in, if he had not stopped me.

'I have a message for you, lieutenant,' he said.

'What is it ? ' I asked without curiosity.

'A little boy gave it to me at the door,' he answered. 'I was to ask you to be in the street opposite Herr Krapp's half an hour after sunset this evening.'

I gasped. 'Herr Krapp's!' I exclaimed. Steve nodded, looking at me queerly. 'Yes; do you know him?' he said.

'I do now,' I muttered, gulping down my amazement. But my face was as red as fire, the blood drummed in my ears. I had to turn away to hide my emotion. 'What was the boy like?' I asked.

But it seemed that the lad had made off the moment he had done his errand, and Steve had not noticed him particularly. 'I called after him to know who sent him,' he added, 'but he had gone too far.'

I nodded and mumbled something, and went on into the house. Perhaps I was still a little sore on my girl's account, and resented the easy way in which she had dropped out of others' lives. At any rate, my instinct was to keep the thing to myself. The face at the window, and then this strange assignation, could have only one meaning; but, good or bad, it was for me. And I hugged myself on it, and said nothing even to my lady.

The day seemed long, but at length the evening came, and when the men had gone to drill and the house was quiet, I slipped out. The streets were full at this hour of men passing to and fro to their drill-stations, and of women who had been out to see the camp, and were returning before the gates closed. The bells of many of the churches were ringing; some had services. I had to push my way to reach Herr Krapp's house in time; but once there the crowd of passers served my purpose by screening me, as I loitered, from farther remark; while I took care, by posting myself in a doorway opposite the window, to make it easy for any one who expected me to find me.

And then I waited with my heart beating. The clocks were striking a half after seven when I took my place, and for a time I stood in a ferment of, excitement, now staring with bated breath at the casement, where I had seen Marie, now scanning all the neighbouring doorways, and then again letting my eyes rove from window to window both

of Krapp's house and the next one on either side. As the
latter were built with many quaint oriels, and tiny dormers,
and had lattices in side-nooks, where one least looked to
find them, I was kept expecting and employed. I was
never quite sure, look where I would, what eyes were upon
me.

But little by little, as time passed and nothing happened,
and the strollers all went by without accosting me, and no
faces save strange ones showed at the windows, the heat of
expectation left me. The chill of disappointment took its
place. I began to doubt and fear. The clocks struck
eight. The sun had been down an hour. Half that time
I had been waiting.

To remain passive was no longer bearable, and sick of
caution, I stepped out and began to walk up and down the
street, courting rather than avoiding notice. The traffic
was beginning to slacken. I could see farther and mark
people at a distance; but still no one spoke to me, no one
came to me. Here and there lights began to shine in the
houses, on gleaming oak ceilings and carved mantels. The
roofs were growing black against the paling sky. In nooks
and corners it was dark. The half-hour sounded, and still
I walked, fighting down doubt, clinging to hope.

But when another quarter had gone by, doubt became
conviction. I had been fooled! Either some one who had
seen me loitering at Krapp's in the morning and heard my
tale had gone straight off, and played me this trick; or —
Gott im Himmel! — or I had been lured here that I might
be out of the way at home.

That thought, which should have entered my thick head
an hour before, sped me from the street, as if it had been a
very catapult. Before I reached the corner I was running;
and I ran through street after street, sweating with fear.
But quickly as I went, my thoughts outpaced me. My
lady was alone save for her women. The men were drilling,
the Waldgrave was in the camp. The crowded state of the
streets at sunset, and the number of strangers who thronged

the city favoured certain kinds of crime; in a great crowd, as in a great solitude, everything is possible.

I had this in my mind. Judge, then, of my horror, when, as I approached the Ritter Strasse, I became aware of a dull, roaring sound; and hastening to turn the corner, saw a large mob gathered in front of our house, and filling the street from wall to wall. The glare of torches shone on a thousand upturned faces, and flamed from a hundred case-ments. At the windows, on the roofs, peering over balco-nies and coping-stones and gables, and looking out of door-ways were more faces, all red in the torchlight. And all the time as the smoking light rose and fell, the yelling, as it seemed to me, rose and fell with it — now swelling into a stern roar of exultation, now sinking into an ugly, snarl-ing noise, above which a man might hear his neighbour speak.

I seized the first I came to — a man standing on the skirts of the mob, and rather looking on than taking part. 'What is it?' I said, shaking him roughly by the arm. 'What is the matter here?'

'Hallo!' he answered, starting as he turned to me. 'Is it you again, my friend?'

I had hit on Herr Krapp! 'Yes!' I cried breathlessly. 'What is it? what is amiss?'

He shrugged his shoulders. 'They are hanging a spy,' he answered. 'Nothing more. Irregular, but wholesome.'

I drew a deep breath. 'Is that all?' I said.

He eyed me curiously. 'To be sure,' he said. 'What did you think it was?'

'I feared that there might be something wrong at my lady's,' I said, beginning to get my breath again. 'I left her alone at sunset. And when I saw this crowd before the house I — I could almost have cut off my hand. Thank God, I was mistaken!'

He looked at me again and seemed to reflect a moment. Then he said, 'You have not found the young woman you were seeking?'

I shook my head.

'Well, it occurred to me afterwards — but at which window did you see her?'

'At a window on the first floor; the farthest from the door,' I answered.

'The second from the door end of the house?' he asked.

'No, the third.'

He nodded with an air of quiet triumph. 'Just so!' he said. 'I thought so afterwards. But the fact is, my friend, my house ends with the second gable. The third gable-end does not belong to it, though doubtless it once did.'

'No?' I exclaimed. And for a moment I stood taken aback, cursing my carelessness. Then I stammered, 'But this third gable — I saw no door in it, Herr Krapp.'

'No, the door is in another street,' he answered. 'Or rather it opens on the churchyard at the back of St. Austin's. So you may have seen her after all. Well, I wish you well,' he continued. 'I must be going.'

The crowd was beginning to separate, moving away by twos and threes, talking loudly. The lights were dying down. He nodded and was gone; while I still stood gaping. For how did the matter stand? If I had really seen Marie at the window — as seemed possible now — and if nothing turned out to be amiss at home, then I had not been tricked after all, and the message was genuine. True she had not kept her appointment. But she might be in durance, or one of a hundred things might have frustrated her intention.

Still I could do nothing now except go home, and cutting short my speculations, I forced myself through the press, and with some labour managed to reach the door. As I did so I turned to look back, and the sight, though the people were moving away fast, was sufficiently striking. Almost opposite us in a beetling archway, the bowed head and shoulders of a man stood up above the common level. There was a little space round him, whence men held back; and the red glow of the smouldering links which the executioners had cast on the ground at his feet, shone upwards on his swollen lips and starting eyeballs. As I looked, the body seemed to writhe in its bonds; but it was only the wind swayed it. I went in shuddering.

On the stairs I met Count Hugo coming down, and knew the moment I saw him that there was something wrong. He stopped me, his eyes full of wrath.

'My man,' he said sternly, 'I thought that you were to be trusted! Where have you been? What have you been doing? *Donner!* Is your lady to be left at dark with no one to man this door?'

Conscience-stricken, I muttered that I hoped nothing had gone amiss.

'No, but something easily might!' he answered grimly. 'When I came here I found three as ugly looking rogues whispering and peering in your doorway as man could wish to see! Yes, Master Martin, and if I had not ridden up at that moment I will not answer for it, that they would not have been in! It is a pity a few more knaves are not where that one is,' he continued sourly, pointing through the open door. 'We could spare them. But do you see and have more care for the future. Or, mein Gott, I will take other measures, my friend!'

So it had been a ruse after all! I went up sick at heart.

CHAPTER XXVII.

THE HOUSE IN THE CHURCHYARD.

THE heat which Count Leuchtenstein had thrown into the matter surprised me somewhat when I came to think of it, but I was soon to be more surprised. I did not go to my lady at once on coming in, for on the landing the sound of voices and laughter met me, and I learned that there were still two or three young officers sitting with her who had

outstayed Count Hugo. I waited until they were gone —
clanking and jingling down the stairs; and then, about the
hour at which I usually went to take orders before retiring,
I knocked at the door.

Commonly one of the women opened to me. To-night
the door remained closed. I waited, knocked again, and
then went in. I could see no one, but the lamps were flickering, and I saw that the window was open.

At that moment, while I stood uncertain, she came in
through it; and blinded, I suppose, by the lights, did not
see me. For at the first chair she reached just within the
window, she sat down suddenly and burst into tears!

'Mein Gott!' I cried clumsily. I should have known
better; but the laughter of the young fellows as they
trooped down the stairs was still in my ears, and I was
dumfounded.

She sprang up on the instant, and glared at me through
her tears. 'Who are — how dare you? How dare you
come into the room without knocking?' she cried violently.

'I did knock, my lady,' I stammered, 'asking your
pardon.'

'Then now go! Go out, do you hear?' she cried, stamping her foot with passion. 'I want nothing. Go!'

I turned and crept towards the door like a beaten hound.
But I was not to go; when my hand was on the latch, her
mood changed.

'No, stay,' she said in a different tone. 'You may come
back. After all, Martin, I had rather it was you than any
one else.'

She dried her tears as she spoke, standing up very
straight and proud, and hiding nothing. I felt a pang as I
looked at her. I had neglected her of late. I had been
thinking more of others.

'It is nothing, Martin,' she said after a pause, and when
she had quite composed her face. 'You need not be
frightened. All women cry a little sometimes, as men
swear,' she added, smiling. ·

'You have been looking at that thing outside,' I said, grumbling.

'Perhaps it did upset me,' she replied. 'But I think it was that I felt — a little lonely.'

That sounded so strange a complaint on her lips, seeing that the echo of the young sparks' laughter was barely dead in the room, that I stared. But I took it, on second thoughts, to refer to Fraulein Max, whom she had kept at a distance since our escape, never sitting down with her, or speaking to her except on formal occasions ; and I said bluntly —

'You need a woman friend, my lady.'

She looked at me keenly, and I fancied her colour rose. But she only answered, 'Yes, Martin. But you see I have not one. I am alone.'

'And lonely, my lady ? '

'Sometimes,' she answered, smiling sadly.

'But this evening ? ' I replied, feeling that there was still something I did not understand. 'I should not have thought you would be feeling that way. I have not been here, but when I came in, my lady ——'

'Pshaw !' she answered with a laugh of disdain. 'Those boys, Martin? They can laugh, fight, and ride; but for the rest, pouf ! They are not company. However, it is bedtime, and you must go. I think you have done me good. Good night. I wish — I wish I could do you good,' she added kindly, almost timidly.

To some extent she had. I went away feeling that mine was not the only trouble in the world, nor my loneliness the only loneliness. She was a stranger in a besieged city, a woman among men, exposed, despite her rank, to many of a woman's perils; and doubtless she had felt Fraulein Max's defection and the Waldgrave's strange conduct more deeply than any one watching her daily bearing would have supposed. So much the greater reason was there that I should do my duty loyally, and putting her first to whom I owed so much, let no sorrow of my own taint my service.

But God knows there is one passion that defies argu·
ment. The house next Herr Krapp's had a fascination
for me which I could not resist; and though I did not
again leave my lady unguarded, but arranged that Steve
should stop at home and watch the door, four o'clock the
next afternoon saw me sneaking away in search of St.
Austin's. Of course I soon found it; but there I came
to a check. Round the churchyard stood a number of
quiet family houses, many-gabled and shaded by limes, and
doubtless once occupied by reverend canons and preben-
daries. But no one of these held such a position that
it could shoulder Herr Krapp's, or be by any possibility
the house I wanted. The churchyard lay too far from the
street for that.

I walked up the row twice before I would admit this;
but at last I made it certain. Still Herr Krapp must know
his own premises, and not much cast down, I was going to
knock at a chance door and put the question, when my
eyes fell on a man who sat at work in the churchyard.
He wore a mason's apron, and was busily deepening the
inscription on a tablet let into the church wall. He seemed
to be the very man to know, and I went to him.

'I want a house which looks into the Neu Strasse,' I
said. 'It is the next house to Herr Krapp's. Can you
direct me to the door?'

He looked at me for a moment, his hammer suspended.
Then he pointed to the farther end of the row. 'There is
an alley,' he said in a hoarse, croaking voice. 'The door
is at the end.'

I thought his occupation an odd one, considering the
state of the city; but I had other things to dwell on, and
hastened off to the place he indicated. Here, sure enough,
I found the mouth of a very narrow passage which, starting between the last house and a blind wall, ran in the
required direction. It was a queer place, scarcely wider
than my shoulders, and with two turns so sharp that I
remember wondering how they brought their dead out.

In one part it wound under the timbers of a house; it was dark and somewhat foul, and altogether so ill-favoured a path that I was glad I had brought my arms.

In the end it ran into a small, paved court, damp but clean, and by comparison light. Here I saw the door I wanted facing me. Above it the house, with its narrow front of one window on each floor, and every floor jutting out a little, gave a strange impression of gloomy height. The windows were barred and dusty, the plaster was mildewed, the beams were dark with age. Whatever secrets, innocent or the reverse, lay within, one thing was plain — this front gave the lie to the other.

I liked the aspect of things so little that it was with a secret tremor I knocked, and heard the hollow sound go echoing through the house. So certain did I feel that something was wrong, that I wondered what the inmates would do, and whether they would lie quiet and refuse to answer, or show force and baffle me that way. No foreign windows looked into the little court in which I stood; three of the walls were blind. The longer I gazed about me, the more I misdoubted the place.

Yet I turned to knock again; but did not, being anticipated. The door slid open under my hand, slowly wide open, and brought me face to face with an old toothless hag, whose bleared eyes winked at me like a bat's in sunshine. I was so surprised both by her appearance and the opening of the door, that I stood tongue-tied, staring at her and at the bare, dusty, unswept hall behind her.

'Who lives here?' I blurted out at last.

If I had stopped to choose my words I had done no better. She shook her head and pointed first to her ears, and then to her lips. The woman was deaf and dumb!

I would not believe it at the first blush. I tried her again. 'Who lives here, mother?' I cried more loudly.

She smiled vacuously, showing her toothless gums. And that was all.

Still I tried again, shouting and making signs to her to

fetch whoever was in the house. The sign she seemed to understand, for she shook her head violently. But that helped me no farther.

All the time the door stood wide open. I could see the hall, and that it contained no furniture or traces of habitation. The woman was alone, therefore a mere caretaker. Why should I not enter and satisfy myself?

I made as if I would do so. But the moment I set my foot across the threshold the old crone began to mow and gibber so horribly, putting herself in my way, that I fell back cowed. I had not the heart to use force to her, alone as she was, and in her duty. Besides, what right had I to thrust myself in? I should be putting myself in the wrong if I did. I retired.

She did not at once shut the door, but continued to tremble and make faces at me awhile as if she were cursing me. Then with her old hand pressed to her side, she slowly but with evident passion clanged the door home.

I stood a moment outside, and then I retreated. I had been driven to believe Herr Krapp. Why should I not believe this old creature? Here was an empty house, and so an end. And yet — and yet I was puzzled.

As I went through the churchyard, I passed my friend the mason, and saw he had a companion. If he had looked up I should have asked him a question or two. But he did not, and the other's back was towards me. I walked on.

In the silent street, however, three minutes later, a sudden thought brought me to a stand. An empty house? Was there not something odd in this empty house, when quarters were so scarce in Nuremberg, and even my lady had got lodgings assigned to her as a favour and at a price? The town swarmed with people who had taken refuge behind its walls. Where one had lain two lay now. Yet here was an empty house!

In a twinkling I was walking briskly towards the Neu Strasse, determined to look farther into the matter. It was again the hour of evening drill; the ways were crowded, the bells of the churches were ringing. Using some little care as I approached Herr Krapp's, I slipped into a doorway, which commanded it from a distance, and thence began to watch the fatal window.

If the old hag had not lied with her dumb lips I should see no one; or at best should only see her.

Half an hour passed; an hour passed. Hundreds of people passed, among them the man I had seen talking with the mason in the churchyard. I noticed him, because he went by twice. But the window remained blank. Then on a sudden, as the light began to fail, I saw the Waldgrave at it.

The Waldgrave?

'Gott im Himmel!' I muttered, the blood rushing to my face. What was the meaning of this? What was the magic of this cursed window? First I had seen my love at it. Then the Waldgrave.

While I stood thunderstruck, he was gone again, leaving the window blank and black. The crowd passed below, chattering thoughtlessly. Groups of men with pikes and muskets went by. All seemed unchanged. But my mind was in a whirl. Rage, jealousy, and wonder played with it. What did it all mean? First Marie, then the Waldgrave! Marie, whom we had left thirty leagues away in the forest; the Waldgrave, whom I had seen that morning.

I stood gaping at the window, as if it could speak, and gradually my mind regained its balance. My jealousy died out, hope took its place. I did not think so ill of the Waldgrave as to believe that knowing of Marie's existence he would hide it from me, and for that reason I could not explain or understand how he came to be in the same house with her. But it was undeniable that his presence there encouraged me. There must be some middle link between them; perhaps some one controlling both. And then I thought of Tzerclas.

The Waldgrave had seen him in the town, and had even spoken to him. What if it were he who occupied this

19

house close by the New Gate, with a convenient secre-
tive entrance, and used it for his machinations? Marie
might well have fallen into his hands. She might be in
his power now, behind the very walls on which I gazed.

From that moment I breathed and lived only to see the
inside of that house. Nothing else would satisfy me. I
scanned it with greedy eyes, its steep gable, its four windows one above another, its carved weather-boards. I
might attack it on this side; or by way of the alley and
door. But I quickly discarded the latter idea. Though I
had seen only the old woman, I judged that there were
defenders in the background, and in the solitude of the
alley I might be easily despatched. It remained to enter
from the front, or by way of the roof. I pondered a moment, and then I went across to Herr Krapp's and knocked.

He opened the door himself. I almost pushed my way in.
'What do you want, my friend?' he said, recoiling before
me, and looking somewhat astonished.

'To get into your neighbour's house,' I answered bluntly.

CHAPTER XXVIII.

UNDER THE TILES.

HE had a light in his hand, and he held it up to my face.
'So?' he said. 'Is that what you would be at? But you
go fast. It takes two to that, Master Steward.'

'Yes,' I answered. 'I am the one, and you are the other,
Herr Krapp.'

He turned from me and closed the door, and, coming back,
held the light again to my face. 'So you still think that it
was your lady's woman you saw at the window?'

'I am sure of it,' I answered.

He set down his light on a chair and, leaning against the
wall, seemed to consider me. After a pause, 'And you have
been to the house?'

'I have been to the house — fruitlessly.'

'You learned nothing ? '

'Nothing.'

'Then what do you want to do now ? ' he asked, softly rubbing his chin.

'To see the inside of it.'

'And you propose —— ? '

'To enter it from yours,' I answered. 'Surely you have some dormer, some trap-door, some roof-way, by which a bold man may get from this house to the next one.'

He shook his head. 'I know of none,' he said. 'But that is not all. You are asking a strange thing. I am a peaceful man, and, I hope, a good neighbour; and this which you ask me to do cannot be called neighbourly. However, I need say the less about it, because the thing cannot be done.'

'Will you let me try ? ' I cried.

He seemed to reflect. In the end he made a strange answer. 'What time did you call at the house ? ' he said.

'Perhaps an hour ago — perhaps more.'

'Did you see any one in the churchyard as you passed ? '

'Yes,' I said, thinking; 'there was a man at work there. I asked him the way.'

Herr Krapp nodded, and seemed to reflect again. 'Well,' he said at last, 'it is a strong thing you ask, my friend. But I have my own reasons for suspecting that all is not right next door, and therefore you shall have your way as far as looking round goes. But I do not think that you will be able to do anything.'

'I ask no more than that,' I said, trembling with eagerness.

He looked at me again as he took up the light. 'You are a big man,' he said, 'but are you armed ? Strength is of little avail against a bullet.'

I showed him that I had a brace of pistols, and he turned towards the stairs. 'Dorcas is in the kitchen,' he said. 'My sons are out, and so are the lads. Nevertheless, I am not very proud of our errand; so step softly, my friend, and do not grumble if you have your labour for your pains.'

He led the way up the stairs with that, and I followed him. The house was very silent, and the higher we ascended the more the silence grew upon us, until, in the empty upper part, every footfall seemed to make a hollow echo, and every board that creaked under our tread to whisper that we were about a work of danger. When we reached the uppermost landing of all, Herr Krapp stopped, and, raising his light, pointed to the unceiled rafters.

'See, there is no way out,' he said. 'And if you could get out, you could not get in.'

I nodded as I looked round. Clearly, this floor was not much used. In a corner a room had been at some period roughly partitioned off; otherwise the place was a huge garret, the boards covered with scraps of mortar, the corners full of shadows and old lumber and dense cobwebs. In the sloping roof were two dormer windows, unglazed but shuttered; and, beside the great yawning well of the staircase by which we had ascended, lay a packing-box and some straw, and two or three old rotting pallets tied together with ropes. I shivered as I looked round. The place, viewed by the light of our one candle, had a forlorn, depressing aspect. The air under the tiles was hot and close; the straw gave out a musty smell.

I was glad when Herr Krapp went to one of the windows and, letting down the bar, opened the shutters. On the instant a draught, which all but extinguished his candle, poured in, and with it a dull, persistent noise unheard before — the murmur of the city, of the streets, the voice of Nuremberg. I thrust my head out into the cool night air, and rejoiced to see the lights flickering in the streets below, and the shadowy figures moving this way and that. Above the opposite houses the low sky was red; but the chimneys stood out black against it, and in the streets it was dark night.

I took all this in, and then I turned to the right and

looked at the next house. I saw as much as I expected; more, enough to set my heart beating. The dormer window next to that from which I leaned, and on a level with it, was open; if I might judge from the stream of light which poured through it, and was every now and then cut off as if by a moving figure that passed at intervals between the casement and the candle. Who or what this was I could not say. It might be Marie; it might not. But at the mere thought I leaned out farther, and greedily measured the distance between us.

Alas! between the dormer-gable in which I stood and the one in the next house lay twelve feet of steep roof, on which a cat would have been puzzled to stand. Its edge towards the street was guarded by no gutter, ledge, or coping-stone, but ended smoothly in a frail, wooden water-pipe, four inches square. Below that, yawned a sheer, giddy drop, sixty feet to the pavement of the street. I drew in my head with a shiver, and found Herr Krapp at my elbow.

'Well,' he said, 'what do you see?'

'The next window is open,' I answered. 'How can I get to it?'

'Ah!' he replied dryly, 'I did not undertake that you should.' He took my place at the window and leaned out in his turn. He had set the candle in a corner where it was sheltered from the draught. I strode to it, and moved it a little in sheer impatience — I was burning to be at the window again. As I came back, crunching the scraps of mortar underfoot, my eyes fell on a bit of old dusty rope lying coiled on the floor, and in a second I saw a way. When Herr Krapp turned from the window he missed me.

'Hallo!' he cried. 'Where are you, my friend?'

'Here,' I answered, from the head of the stairs.

As he advanced, I came out of the darkness to meet him, staggering under the bundle of pallets which I had seen lying by the stair-head. He whistled.

'What are you going to do with those?' he said.

'By your leave, I want this .rope,' I answered.
'What will you do with it ? ' he asked soberly.   He was
one of those even-tempered men to whom excitement, irritation, fear, are all foreign.

'Make a loop and throw it over the little pinnacle on
the top of yonder dormer,' I answered briefly, 'and use it
for a hand-rail.'

'Can you throw it over ? '

'I think so.'

'The pinnacle will hold ? '

'I hope so.'

He shrugged his shoulders, and stood for a moment
staring at me as I unwound the rope and formed a noose.
At length : 'But the noise, my friend ? ' he said. 'If you
miss the first time, and the second, the rope falling and
sliding over the tiles will give the alarm.'

'Two cats ran along the ridge a while ago,' I answered.
'Once, and, perhaps, twice, the noise will be set down to
them.   The third time I must succeed.'

I thought it likely that he would forbid the attempt ;
but he did not.   On the contrary, he silently took hold of
my belt, that I might lean out the farther and use my hands
with greater freedom.   Against the window I placed the
bundle of pallets ; setting one foot on them and the other
heel on the pipe outside, I found I could whirl the loop
with some chance of success.

Still, it was an anxious moment.   As I craned over the
dark street and, poising myself, fixed my eyes on the black,
slender spirelet which surmounted the neighbouring window,
I felt a shudder more than once run through me.   I shrank
from looking down.   At last I threw : the rope fell short.
Luckily it dropped clear of the window, and came home
again against the wall below me, and so made no noise.
The second time I threw with better heart ; but I had the
same fortune, except that I nearly overbalanced myself,
and, for a moment, shut my eyes in terror.   The third
time, letting out a little more rope, I struck the pinnacle,

but below the knob. The rope fell on the tiles, and slid down them with some noise, and for a full minute I stood motionless, half inside the room and half outside, expecting each instant to see a head thrust out of the other window. But no one appeared, no one spoke, though the light was still obscured at intervals ; and presently I took courage to make a fourth attempt. I flung, and this time the rope fell with a dull thud on the tiles, and stopped there : the noose was round the pinnacle.

Gently I drew it tight, and then, letting it hang, I slipped back into the room, where we had before taken the precaution to put out the light. Herr Krapp asked me in a whisper if the rope was fast.

' Yes,' I said. ' I must secure this end to something.'

He passed it round the hinge of the left-hand shutter and made it safe. Then for a moment we stood together in the darkness.

' All right ? ' he said.

' All right,' I answered hoarsely.

The next moment the thing was done. I was outside, the rope in my hands, my feet on the bending pipe, the cool night air round my temples — below me, sheer giddiness, dancing lights, and blackness. For the moment I tottered. I balanced myself where I stood, and clung to the rope, shutting my eyes. If the pinnacle had given way then, I must have fallen like a plummet and been killed. One crash against the wall below, one grip at the rope as it tore its way through my fingers — and an end !

But the pinnacle held, and in a few seconds I gained wit and courage. One step, then another, and then a third, taken warily, along the pipe, as I have seen rope-walkers take them at Heritzburg fair, and I was almost within reach of my goal. Two more, and, stooping, I could touch, with my right hand, the tiles of the little gable, while my left, raised above my head, still clutched the rope.

Then came an anxious moment. I had to pass under the rope, which was between me and the street, and between me and the window also — the window, my goal. I did it; but in my new position I found a new difficulty, and a grim one, confronting me. Standing outside the rope now, with my right hand clinging to it, I could not, with all my stretching, reach with my other hand any part of the window, or anything of which I could get a firm grip. The smooth tiles and crumbling mortar of the little gable gave no hold, while the rope, my grip on which I dared not for my life relax, prevented me stooping sufficiently to reach the sill or the window-case.

It was a horrible position. I stood still, sweating, trembling, and felt the wooden pipe bend and yield under me. Behind me, the depth, the street, yawned for me; before me, the black roof, shutting off the sky. My head reeled, my fingers closed on the ropes like claws; for a second I shut my eyes, and thought I was falling. In that moment I forgot Marie — I forgot everything, except the pavement below, the cruel stones, the depth; I would have given all, coward that I was, to be back in Herr Krapp's room.

Then the fit passed, and I stood, thinking. To take my hand from the rope would be to fall — to die. But could I lower the rope so that, still holding it, I could reach the sill, or the hinges, or some part of the window-case that would furnish a grip? I could think of only one way, and that a dangerous one; but I had no choice, nor any time to lose, if I would keep my head. I drew out my knife, and, leaning forward on the rope, with one knee on the tiles, I began to sever the cord as far away to my right as I could reach. This was to cut off my retreat — my connection with the window I had left; but I dared not let myself think much of that or of anything. I hacked away in a frenzy, and in a twinkling the rope flew apart, and I slipped forward on the tiles, clutching the piece that remained to me in a grasp of iron.

So far, good! I was trembling all over, but I was safe, and I lost not a moment in passing the loose end twice round the fingers of my right hand. This done, only one

thing remained to be done — only one thing: to lean over
the abyss, trusting all my weight to the frail cord, and to
grope for the sill. Only that! Well, I did it. My hair
stood up straight as the pinnacle groaned and bent under
my weight; my eyes must have been astare with terror;
all my flesh crept. I clung to the face of the gable like a
fly, but I did it! I reached the sill, clutched it, loosed the
rope, and in a moment was lying on my breast, half in and
half out of the window — safe!

I do not know how long I hung there, recovering my
breath and strength, but I suppose only a minute or two,
though it seemed to me an hour. A while before I should
have thought such a position, without foothold, above the
dizzy street, perilous enough. Now it seemed to be safety.
Nevertheless, as I grew cooler I began to think of getting
in, of whom I should find there, of the issue of the attempt.
And presently, lifting one leg over the sill, I stretched out
a hand and drew aside a scanty curtain which hid the room
from view. It was this curtain that, rising and falling with
the draught, had led me to picture a figure moving to and
fro.

There was no one to be seen, and for a moment I fancied
that the room was empty. The light was on the other side,
and my act disclosed nothing but a dusky corner under a
sloping roof. The next instant, however, a harsh voice,
which shook the rafters, cried, with an oath —

'What is that ?'

I let the curtain fall and, as softly as I could, scrambled
over the sill. My courage came back in face of a danger
more familiar; my hand grew steady. As I sat on the sill,
· I drew out a pistol; but I dared not cock it.

'Speak, or I shoot!' cried the same voice. 'One, two !
Was it the wind — Himmel — or one of those cats ?'

I remained motionless. The speaker, whose voice I
seemed to know, was clearly uncertain and a little sleepy.
I hoped that he would not rouse the house and waste a
shot on no better evidence; and I sat still in the smallest

compass into which I could draw myself. I could see the light through the curtain, a makeshift thing of thin stuff, unbleached — and I tried to discern his figure, but in vain. At last I heard him sink back, grumbling uneasily.

I waited a few minutes, until his breathing became more regular, and then, with a cautious hand, I once more drew the curtain aside. As I had judged, the light stood on the floor, by the end of the pallet. On the pallet, his head uneasily pillowed on his arm, while the other hand almost touched the butt of a pistol which lay beside the candle, sprawled the man who had spoken — a swarthy, reckless-looking fellow, still in his boots and dressed. His attitude as he slept, alone in this quiet room, no less than the presence of the light and pistol, spoke of danger and suspicion. But I did not need the one sign or the other to warn me that my hopes and fears were alike realized. The man was Ludwig!

I dropped the curtain again, and sat thinking. I could not hope to overcome such a man without a struggle and noise that must alarm the house; and yet I must pass him, if I would do any good. My only course seemed to be to slip by him by stealth, open the door in the same manner, and gain the stairs. After that the house would be open to me, and it would go hard with any one who came between me and Marie. - I did not doubt now that she was there.

I waited until his more regular breathing seemed to show that he slept, and then, after softly cocking my pistol, I set my feet to the floor, and began to cross it. Unluckily my nerves were still ajar with my roof-work. At the third step a board creaked under me; at the same moment I caught a glimpse of a huge, dark figure at my elbow, and though this was only my shadow, cast on the sloping roof by the candle, I sprang aside in a fright. The noise was enough to awaken the sleeper. As my eyes came back to him he opened his and saw me, and, raising himself, in a trice groped for his pistol. He could not on the instant find it, however, and I had time to cover him with mine.

'Have done!' I hissed. 'Be still, or you are a dead man!'

'Martin Schwartz!' he cried, with a frightful oath.

'Yes,' I rejoined; 'and mark me, if you raise a finger, I fire.'

He glared at me, and so we stood a moment. Then I said, 'Push that pistol to me with your foot. Don't put out your hand, or it will be the worse for you.'

He looked at me for a moment, his face distorted with rage, as if he were minded to disobey at all risks; then he drew up his foot sullenly and set it against the pistol. I stepped back a pace and for an instant took my eyes from his — intending to snatch up the firearm as soon as it was out of his reach. In that instant he dashed out the light with his foot; I heard him spring up — and we were in darkness.

The surprise was complete, and I did not fire; but I had the presence of mind, believing that he had secured his pistol, to change my position — almost as quickly as he changed his. However, he did not fire; and so there we were in the pitchy darkness of the room, both armed, and neither knowing where the other stood.

I felt every nerve in my body tingle; but with rage, not fear. I dared not change my position again, lest a creaking board should betray me, now all was silent; but I crouched low in the darkness with the pistol in one hand and my knife drawn in the other, and listened for his breathing. The same consideration — we were both heavy men — kept him motionless also; and I remember to this day, that as we waited, scarcely daring to breathe — and for my part each moment expecting the flash and roar of a shot — one of the city clocks struck slowly and solemnly ten.

The strokes ceased. In the room I could not hear a sound, and I felt nervously round me with my knife; but without avail. I crouched still lower, lower, with a beating heart. The curtain obscured the window, there was no

moon, no light showed under the door. The darkness was
so complete that, but for a kind of fainter blackness that
outlined the window, I could not have said in what part of
the room I stood.

Suddenly a sharp loud 'thud' broke the silence. It
seemed to come from a point so close to me that I almost
fired on that side before I could control my fingers. The
next moment I knew that it was well I had not. It was
Ludwig's knife flung at a venture — and now buried, as I
guessed, an inch deep in the door — which had made the
noise. Still, the action gave me a sort of inkling where
he was, and, noiselessly facing round a trifle, I raised my
pistol, and waited for some movement that might direct
my aim.

I feared that he had a second knife; I hoped that in
drawing it from its sheath he would make some noise.
But all was still. Sharpen my ears as I might, I could
hear nothing; strain my eyes as I might, I could see no
shadow, no bulk in the darkness. A silence as of death
prevailed. I could scarcely believe that he was still in the
room. My courage, hot and fierce at first, began to wane
under the trial. I felt the point of his knife already in my
back; I winced and longed to be sheltered by the wall,
yet dared not move to go to it. In another minute I think
I should have fired at a sheer venture, rather than bear the
strain longer; but at last a sound broke on my ear. The
sound was not in the room, but in the house below. Some
one was coming up the stairs.

The step reached a landing, and I heard it pause; a
stumble, and it came on again up the next flight. Another
pause, this time a longer one. Then it mounted again,
and gradually a faint line of light shone under the door. I
felt my breath come quickly. One glance at the door,
which was near me on the right hand, and I peered away
again, balancing the pistol in my hand. If Ludwig cried
out or spoke, I would fire in the direction of the voice.
Between two foes I was growing desperate.

Before I could recover myself a pair of strong arms closed
round mine and bound them to my sides.

The step came on and stopped at the door; still Ludwig held his peace. The new-comer rapped; not loudly, or I think I should have started and betrayed myself — to such a point were my feelings wound up — but softly and timidly. I set my teeth together and grasped my knife. Ludwig on his part kept silence; the person outside, getting no answer, knocked again, and yet again, each time more loudly. Still no answer. Then I heard a hand touch the latch. It grated. A moment of suspense, and a flood of light burst in — close to me on my right hand — dazzling me. I looked round quickly, in fear; and there, in the doorway, holding a taper in her hand, I saw Marie — Marie Wort!

While I stood open-mouthed, gazing, she saw me, the light falling on me. Her lips opened, her breast heaved, I think she must have seen my danger; but if so the shriek she uttered came too late to save me. I heard it, but even as I heard it a sudden blow in the back hurled me gasping to my knees at her feet. Before I could recover myself a pair of strong arms closed round mine and bound them to my sides. Breathless and taken at advantage I made a struggle to rise; but I heaved and strained without avail. In a moment my hands were tied, and I lay helpless and a prisoner.

After that I was conscious only of a tumult round me; of a woman shrieking, of loud trampling, and lights and faces, among these Tzerclas' dark countenance, with a look of fiendish pleasure on it. Even these things I only noted dully. In the middle of all I was wool-gathering. I suppose I was taken downstairs, but I remember nothing of it; and in effect I took little note of anything until, my breath coming back to me, I found myself being borne through a doorway — on the ground floor, I think — into a lighted room. A man held me by either arm, and there were three other men in the room.

CHAPTER XXIX.

IN THE HOUSE BY ST. AUSTIN'S.

Two of these men sat facing one another at a great table covered with papers. As I entered they turned their faces to me, and on the instant one sprang to his feet with an exclamation of rage that made the roof ring.

'General!' he cried passionately, 'what — what devil's trick is this? Why have you brought that man here?'

'Why?' Tzerclas answered easily, insolently. 'Does he know you?' He had come in just before us. He smiled; the man's excitement seemed to amuse him.

'By ——, he does!' the other exclaimed through his teeth. 'Are you mad?'

'I think not,' the general answered, still smiling. 'You will understand in a minute. But his business can wait. First ' — he took up a paper and scanned it carefully — ' let us complete this list of —— '

'No!' the stranger replied impetuously. And he dashed the paper back on the table and looked from one to another like a wild beast in a trap. He was a tall, very thin, hawk-nosed man, whom I had seen once at my lady's — the commander of a Saxon regiment in the city's service, with the name of a reckless soldier. 'No!' he repeated, scowling, until his brows nearly met his moustachios. 'Not another gun, not another measurement will I give, until I know where I stand! And whether you are the man I think you, general, or the blackest double-dyed liar that ever did Satan's work!'

The general laughed grimly — the laugh that always chilled my blood. 'Gently, gently,' he said. 'If you must know, I have brought him into this room, in the first place, because it is convenient, and in the second, because —— '

'Well?' Neumann snarled, with an ugly gleam in his eyes.

'Because dead men tell no tales,' Tzerclas continued quietly. 'And our friend here is a dead man. Now, do you see? I answer for it, you run no risk.'

'Himmel!' the other exclaimed; in a different tone, however. 'But in that case, why bring him here at all? Why not despatch him upstairs?'

'Because he knows one or two things which I wish to know,' the general answered, looking at me curiously. 'And he is going to make us as wise as himself. He has been drilling in the south-east bastion by the orchard, you see, and knows what guns are mounted there.'

'Cannot you get them from the fool in the other room?' Neumann grunted.

'He will tell nothing.'

'Then why do you have him hanging about here day after day, risking everything? The man is mad.'

'Because, my dear colonel, I have a use for *him* too,' Tzerclas replied. Then he turned to me. 'Listen, knave,' he said harshly. 'Do you understand what I have been saying?'

I did, and I was desperate. I remembered what I had done to him, how we had outwitted, tricked, and bound him; and now that I was in his power I knew what I had to expect; that nothing I could say would avail me. I looked him in the face. 'Yes,' I said.

'You had the laugh on your side the last time we met,' he smiled. 'Now it is my turn.'

'So it seems,' I answered stolidly.

I think it annoyed him to see me so little moved. But he hid the feeling. 'What guns are in the orchard bastion?' he asked.

I laughed. 'You should have asked me that,' I said, 'before you told me what you were going to do with me. The dead tell no tales, general.'

'You fool!' he replied. 'Do you think that death is the

worst you have to fear? Look round you! Do you see
these windows? They are boarded up. Do you see the
door? It is guarded. The house? The walls are thick,
and we have gags. Answer me, then, and quickly, or I
will find the way to make you. What guns are in the
orchard bastion?'

He took up a paper with the last word and looked at me
over it, waiting for my answer. For a moment not a sound
broke the silence of the room. The other men stood all at
gaze, watching me, Neumann with a scowl on his face.
The lights in the room burned high, but the frowning masks
of boards that hid the windows, the litter of papers on the
table, the grimy floor, the cloaks and arms cast down on it
in a medley — all these marks of haste and secrecy gave
a strange and lowering look to the chamber, despite its
brightness. My heart beat wildly like a bird in a man's
hand. I feared horribly. But I hid my fear; and suddenly
I had a thought.

'You have forgotten one thing,' I said.

They started. It was not the answer they expected.

'What?' Tzerclas asked curtly, in a tone that boded ill
for me — if worse were possible.

'To ask how I came into the house.'

The general looked death at Ludwig. 'What is this,
knave?' he thundered. 'You told me that he came in by
the window?'

'He did, general,' Ludwig answered, shrugging his
shoulders.

'Yes, from the next house,' I said coolly. 'Where my
friends are now waiting for me.'

'Which house?' Tzerclas demanded.

'Herr Krapp's.'

I was completely in their hands. But they knew, and I
knew, that their lives were scarcely more secure than mine;
that, given a word, a sign, a traitor among them — and they
were all traitors, more or less — all their boarded windows
and locked doors would avail them not ten minutes against

the frenzied mob. That thought blanched more than one cheek while I spoke; made more than one listen fearfully and cast eyes at the door; so that I wondered no longer, seeing their grisly faces, why the room, in spite of its brightness, had that strange and sombre look. Treachery, fear, suspicion, all lurked under the lights.

Tzerclas alone was unmoved; perhaps because he had something less to fear than the faithless Neumann. ' Herr Krapp's ? ' he said scornfully. ' Is that all ? I will answer for that house myself. I have a man watching it, and if danger threatens from that direction, we shall know it in good time. He marks all who go in or out.'

'You can trust him ?' Neumann muttered, wiping his brow.

'I am trusting him,' the general answered dryly. ' And I am not often deceived. This man and the puling girl upstairs tricked me once; but they will not do so again. Now, sirrah ! ' and he turned to me afresh, a cruel gleam in his eyes. 'That bird will not fly. To business. Will you tell me how many guns are in the orchard bastion?'

'No !' I cried. I was desperate now.

' You will not ? '

' No ! '

' You talk bravely,' he answered. ' But I have known men talk as bravely, and whimper and tremble like flogged children five minutes later. Ludwig — ah, there is no fire. Get a bit of thin whip-cord, and twist it round his head with your knife-handle. But first,' he continued, devouring me with his hard, smiling eyes, ' call in Taddeo. You will need another man to handle him neatly.'

At the word my blood ran cold with horror, and then burning hot. My gorge rose; I set my teeth and felt all my limbs swell. There was a mist of blood before my eyes, as if the cord were already tight and my brain bursting. I heaved in my bonds and heard them crack and crack. But, alas ! they held.

' Try again ! ' he said, sneering at me.

20

'You fiend!' I burst out in a fury. 'But I defy you. Do your worst, I will balk you yet!'

He looked at me hard. Then he smiled. 'Ah!' he said. 'So you think you will beat me. Well, you are an obstinate knave, I know; and I have not much time to spare. Yet I shall beat you. Ludwig,' he continued, raising his voice, though his smiling eyes did not leave me. 'Is Taddeo there?'

'He is coming, general.'

'Then bid him fetch the girl down! Yes, Master Martin,' he continued with a ruthless look, 'we will see. I have a little account against her too. Do not think that I have kept her all this time for nothing. We will put the cord not round your head — you are a stubborn fool, I know — but round hers, my friend. Round her pretty little brow. We will see if that will loosen your tongue.'

The room reeled before my eyes, the lights danced, the men's faces, some agrin, some darkly watchful, seemed to be looking at me through a mist that dimmed everything. I cried out wild oaths, scarcely knowing what I said, that he would not, that he dared not.

He laughed. 'You think not, Master Martin?' he said. 'Wait until the slut comes. Ludwig has a way of singeing their hands with a lamp — that will afford you, I think, the last amusement you will ever enjoy!'

I knew that he spoke truly, and that he and his like had done things as horrible, as barbarous, a hundred times in the course of this cursed war! I knew that I had nothing to expect from their pity or their scruples. And the frenzy of passion, which for a moment had almost choked me, died down on a sudden, leaving me cold as the coldest there and possessed by one thought only, one hope, one aim — to get my hands free for a moment and kill this man. The boarded windows, the guarded doors, the stern faces round me, the silence of the gloomy house all forbade hope; but revenge remained. Rather than Marie should suffer, rather than that childish frame should be racked by their

cruel arts, I would tell all, everything they wanted. But if
by any trick or chance I went afterwards free for so much
as a second, I would choke him with my naked hands !

I waited, looking at the door, my mind made up. The
moments passed like lead. So apparently thought some
one else, for suddenly on the silence came an interruption.
'Is this business going to last all night?' Neumann burst
out impatiently. 'Hang the man out of hand, if he is to be
hanged !'

'My good friend, revenge is sweet,' Tzerclas answered,
with an ugly smile. 'These two fooled me a while ago ;
and I have no mind to be fooled with impunity. But it
will not take long. We will singe her a little for his
pleasure — he will like to hear her sing — and then we will
hang him for her pleasure. After which ——'

'Do what you like !' Neumann burst out, interrupting
him wrathfully. 'Only be quick about it. If the girl is
here —— '

'She is coming. She is coming now,' Tzerclas answered.

I had gone through so much that my feelings were
blunted. I could no longer suffer keenly, and I waited for
her appearance with a composure that now surprises me.
The door opened, Taddeo came in. I looked beyond him,
but saw no one else ; then I looked at him. The ruffian
was trembling. His face was pale. He stammered
something.

Tzerclas made but one stride to him. 'Dolt !' he cried,
'what is it ?'

'She is gone !' the man stuttered.

'Gone ?'

'Yes, your excellency.'

For an instant Tzerclas stood glaring at him. Then like
lightning his hand went up and his pistol-butt crashed
down on the man's temple. The wretch threw up his
arms and fell as if a thunderbolt had struck him — senseless, or lifeless ; no one asked which, for his assailant, like
a beast half-sated, stood glaring round for a second victim.

But Ludwig, who had come down with Taddeo, knew his master, and kept his distance by the door. The other two men shrank behind me.

'Well ?' Tzerclas cried, as soon as passion allowed him to speak. 'Are you dumb? Have you lost your tongue? What is it that liar meant?'

'The girl is away,' Ludwig muttered. 'She got out through a window.'

'Through what window?'

'The window of my room, under the roof,' the man answered sullenly. 'The one — through which that fool came in,' he continued, nodding towards me.

'Ah !' the general cried, his voice hissing with rage. 'Well, we have still got him. How did she go?'

'Heaven knows, unless she had wings,' Ludwig answered. 'The window is at the top of the house, and there is neither rope nor ladder there, nor foothold for anything but a bird. She is gone, however.'

The general ground his teeth together. 'There is some cursed treachery here !' he said.

The Saxon colonel laughed in scorn. 'Maybe !' he retorted in a mocking tone, 'but I will answer for it, that there is something else, and that is cursed mismanagement! I tell you what it is, General Tzerclas,' he continued fiercely. 'With your private revenges, and your public plots, and your tame cats who are mad, and your wild cats who have wings — you think yourself a very clever man. But Heaven help those who trust you !'

The general's eyes sparkled. 'And those who cross me ?' he cried in a voice that made his men tremble. 'But there, sir, what ground of complaint have you? The girl never saw you.'

'No, but that man has seen me !' Neumann retorted, pointing to me. 'And who knows how soon she may be back with a regiment at her heels? Then it will be "Save yourselves !" and he will be left to hang me.'

The general laughed without mirth. 'Have no fear !' he

said. 'We will hang him out of hand. Ludwig, while we collect these papers, take the other two men and string him up in the hall. When they break in they shall find some one to receive them!'

I had thought that the agony of death was passed; but I suppose that the news of Marie's escape had awakened my hopes as well as rekindled my love of life; for at these words, I felt my courage run from me like water. I shrank back against the wall, my limbs trembling under me, my heart leaping as if it would burst from my breast. I felt the rope already round my neck, and when the men laid hold on me, I cried out, almost in spite of myself, that I would tell what guns there were in the orchard bastion, that I knew other things, that——

'Away with him!' Tzerclas snarled, stamping his foot passionately. He was already hurrying papers together, and did not give me a glance. 'String him up, knaves, and see this time that you obey orders. We must be gone, so pull his legs.'

I would have said something more; I would have tried again. Even a minute, a minute's delay meant hope. But my voice failed me, and they hustled me out. I am no coward, and I had thought myself past fear; but the flesh is weak. At this pinch, when their hands were on me, and I looked round desperately and found no one to whom I could appeal — while hope and rescue might be so near and yet come too late — I shrank. Death in this vile den seemed horrible. My knees trembled; I could scarcely stand.

The hall into which they dragged me was the same dusty, desolate place into which, little foreseeing what would happen there, I had looked over the deaf hag's shoulder. Ludwig's candle only half dispersed the darkness which reigned in it. Two of the men held me while he went to and fro with the light raised high above his head.

'Ha! here it is!' he said at last. 'I thought that there was a hook. Bring him here, lads.'

They forced me, resisting feebly, to the place. The candle stood beside him; he was forming a noose. The light, which left all behind them dark, lit up the men's harsh faces; but I read no pity there, no hope, no relenting; and after a hoarse attempt to bribe them with promises of what my lady would give for my life, I stood waiting. I tried to pray, to think of Marie, of my soul and the future; but my mind was taken up with rage and dread, with the wild revolt against death, and the rush of indignation that would have had me scream like a woman!

On a sudden, out of the darkness grew a fourth face that looked at me, smiling. It was no more softened by ruth or pity than the others were; the laughing eyes mocked me, the lip curled as with a jest. And yet, at sight of it, I gasped. Hope awoke. I tried to speak, I tried to implore his help, I tried —— But my voice failed me, no words came. The face was the Waldgrave's.

Yet he nodded as if I had spoken. 'Yes,' he said, smiling more broadly, 'I see, Martin, that you are in trouble. You should have taken my advice in better time. I told you that he would get the better of you.'

Ludwig, who had not seen him before he spoke, dropped the rope, and stood, stupefied, gazing at him. I cried out hoarsely that they were going to hang me.

'No, no, not as bad as that!' he said lightly, between jest and earnest. 'But I gave you fair warning, you know, Martin. Oh, he is ——'

Waldgrave, Waldgrave!' I panted, trying to get to him; but the men held me back. 'They will hang me! They will! It is no joke. In God's name, save me, save me! I saved you once, and ——'

'Chut, chut!' he replied easily. 'Of course I will save you. I will go to the general and arrange it now. Don't be afraid. My sweet cousin must not lose her steward. Why, you are shaking like an aspen, man. But I told you, did I not? Oh, he is the —— Wait, fellow,' he continued to Ludwig, 'until I come back. Where is your master?'

'Upstairs,' Ludwig answered sullenly, an ugly gleam in his eyes.

The Waldgrave turned from me carelessly, and went towards the stairs, which were at the end of the hall. Ludwig, as he did so, picked up the rope with a stealthy gesture. I read his mind, and called pitifully to the Waldgrave to stop.

'They will hang me while you are away,' I cried. 'And he is not upstairs! They are lying to you. He is in the room on the left.'

The Waldgrave halted and came back, his handsome face troubled. Ludwig, looking as if he would strike me, swore under his breath.

'Upstairs, your excellency, upstairs!' he cried. 'You will find him there. Why should I ——'

'Hush!' one of the other men said, and I felt his grasp on my arm relax. 'What is that, captain — that noise?'

But Ludwig was intent on the Waldgrave. 'Upstairs!' he continued to cry, waving his hand in that direction. 'I assure you, my lord ——'

'Steady!' the man who had cut him short before exclaimed. 'They are at the door, Ludwig. Listen, man, listen, or we shall be taken like wolves in a trap!'

This time Ludwig condescended to listen, scowling. A noise like that made by a rat gnawing at wood could be heard. My heart beat fast and faster. The man who had given the alarm had released my arm altogether. The other held me carelessly.

With a yell which startled all, I burst suddenly from him and sprang past the Waldgrave. Bound as I was, I had the start and should have been on the stairs in another second, when, with a crash and a blinding glare, a shock, which loosened the very foundations of the house, flung me on my face.

I lay a moment, gasping for breath, wondering where I was hurt. Out of the darkness round me came a medley of groans and shrieks. The air was full of choking smoke, through which a red glare presently shone, and grew gradually brighter. I could see little, understand less of what was happening; but I heard shots and oaths, and once a rush of charging feet passed over me.

After that, growing more sensible, I tried to rise, but a weight lay on my legs — my arms were still tied — and I sank again. I took the fancy then that the house was on fire and that I should be burned alive; but before I had more than tasted the horror of the thought, a crowd of men came round me, and rough hands plucked me up.

'Here is another of them!' a voice cried. 'Have him out! To the churchyard with him! The trees will have a fine crop!'

'Halloa! he is tied up already!' a second chimed in.

I gazed round stupidly, meeting everywhere vengeful looks and savage faces.

A butcher, with his axe on his shoulder, hauled at me. 'Bring him along!' he shouted. 'This way, friends! Hurry him. To the churchyard!'

My wits were still wool-gathering, and I should have gone quietly; but a man pushed his way to the front and looked at me. 'Stop! stop!' he cried in a voice of authority. 'This is a friend. This is the man who got in by the roof. Cut the ropes, will you? See how his hands are swollen. That is better. Bring him out into the air. He will revive.'

The speaker was Herr Krapp. In a moment a dozen friendly arms lifted me up and carried me through the crowd, and set me down in the little court. The cool night air swept my brow. I looked up and saw the stars shining in the quiet heaven, and I leant against the wall, sobbing like a woman.

CHAPTER XXX.

THE END OF THE DAY.

LUDWIG was found dead in the hall, slain on the spot by
the explosion of the petard which had driven in the door.
His two comrades, less fortunate, were taken alive, and,
with the hag who kept the house, were hanged within the
hour on the elms in St. Austin's churchyard. The Waldgrave and Neumann, both wounded, the former by the
explosion and the latter in his desperate resistance, were
captured and held for trial. But Tzerclas, the chief of all,
arch-tempter and arch-traitor, vanished in the confusion of
the assault, and made his escape, no one knew how. Some
said that he went by way of a secret passage known only to
himself; some, that he had a compact with the devil, and
vanished by his aid; some, that he had friends in the
crowd who sheltered him. For my part, I set down his
disappearance to his own cool wits and iron nerves, and
asked no further explanation.

For an hour the little dark court behind the ill-omened
house seethed with a furious mob. No sooner were one
party satisfied than another swept in with links and
torches and ransacked the house, tore down the panels,
groped through the cellars, and probed the chimneys; all
with so much rage, and with gestures so wild and extrava-
gant, that an indifferent spectator might have thought them
mad. Nor were those who did these things of the lowest
class; on the contrary, they were mostly burghers and
traders, solid townsfolk and their apprentices, men who,
with wives and daughters and sweethearts, could not sleep
at night for thoughts of storm and sack, and in whom the
bare idea that they had amongst them wretches ready to
open the gates, was enough to kindle every fierce and cruel
passion.

I stood for a time unnoticed, gazing at the scene in a kind of stupor, which the noise and tumult aggravated. Little by little, however, the cool air did its work; memory and reason began to return, and, with anxiety awaking in my breast, I looked round for Herr Krapp. Presently I saw him coming towards me with a leather flask in his hand.

'Drink some of this,' he said, looking at me keenly. 'Why so wild, man?'

'The girl?' I stammered. I had not spoken before since my release, and my voice sounded strange and unnatural.

'She is safe,' he answered, nodding kindly. 'I was at my window when she swung herself on to the roof by the rope which you left hanging. Donner! you may be proud of her! But she was distraught, or she would not have tried such a feat. She must inevitably have fallen if I had not seen her. I called out to her to stand still and hold fast; and my son, who had come upstairs, ran down for a twelve-foot pike. We thrust that out to her, and, holding it, she tottered along the pike to my window, where I caught her skirts, and we dragged her in in a moment.'

I shuddered, remembering how I had suffered, hanging above the yawning street. 'I suppose that it was she who warned you and sent you here?' I said.

'No,' he answered. 'This house had been watched for two days, though I did not tell you so. We had been suspicious of it for a week or more, or I should not have helped you into a neighbour's house as I did. However, all is well that ends well; and though we have not got that bloodthirsty villain to hang, we have stopped his plans for this time.'

He was just proposing that, if I now felt able, I should return to my lady's, when a rush of people from the house almost carried me off my feet. In a moment we were pushed aside and squeezed against the wall. A hoarse yell, like the cry of a wild beast, rose from the crowd, a hundred hands were brandished in the air, weapons appeared as if by magic. The glare of torches, falling on the raging sea of men, picked out here and there a scared face, a wandering eye ; but for the most part the mob seemed to feel only one passion — the thirst for blood.

'What is it ? ' I shouted in Herr Krapp's ear.

'The prisoners,' he answered. 'They are bringing them out. Your friend the Waldgrave, and the other. They will need a guard.'

And truly it was a grim thing to see men make at them, striking over the shoulders of the guard, leaping at them wolf-like, with burning eyes and gnashing teeth, striving to tear them with naked hands. Down the narrow passage to the churchyard the soldiers had an easy task ; but in the open graveyard, whither Herr Krapp and I followed slowly, the party were flung this way and that, and tossed to and fro — though they were strong men, armed,.and numbered three or four score — like a cork floating on rapids. Their way lay through the Ritter Strasse, and I went with them so far. Though it was midnight, the town, easily roused from its feverish sleep, was up and waking. Scared faces looked from windows, from eaves, from the very roofs. Men who had snatched up their arms and left their clothes peered from doorways. The roar of the mob, as it swayed through narrow ways, rose and fell by turns, now loud as the booming of cavern-waves, now so low that it left the air quivering.

When it died away at last towards the Burg, I took leave of Herr Krapp, and hurried to my lady's, passing the threshold in a tumult of memories, of emotions, and thankfulness. I could fancy that I had lived an age since I last crossed it — eight hours before. The house, like every other house, was up. Herr Krapp had sent the news of my escape before me, and I looked forward with a tremulous, foolish expectation that was not far from tears to the first words two women would say to me.

But though men and women met me with hearty greetings on the threshold, on the stairs, on the landing, and Steve clapped me on the back until I coughed again, *they* did not appear. It was after midnight, but the house was still lighted as if the sun had just set, and I went up to the long parlour that looked on the street. My heart beat, and my face grew hot as I entered; but I might have spared myself. There was only Fraulein Max in the room.

She came towards me, blinking. 'So Sancho Panza has turned knight-errant,' she said with a sneer, 'as well as Governor?'

I did not understand her, and I asked gently where my lady was.

She laughed in her gibing way. 'You beg for a stone and expect bread,' she said. 'You care no more where my lady is than where I am! You mean, where is your Romanist chit, with her white face and wheedling ways.'

I saw that she was bursting with spite; that Marie's return and the stir made about it had been too much for her small, jealous nature, and I was not for answering her. She was out of favour; let her spit, her venom would be gone the sooner. But she had not done yet.

'Of course she has had some wonderful adventurés!' she continued, her face working with malice and ill-nature. 'And we are all to admire her. But to a lover does she not seem somewhat *blandula, vagula?* Here to-day and gone to-morrow. *Dolus latet in generalibus,* the Countess says' — and here the Dutch girl mimicked my lady, her eyes gleaming with scorn. 'But *dolus latet in virginibus,* too, Master Martin, as you will find some day! Oh, a great escape, a heroic escape, — but from her friends!'

'If you mean to infer, Fraulein —' I said hotly.

'Oh, I infer nothing. I leave you to do that!' she replied, smirking. 'But pigs go back to the dirt, I read. You know where you found her and the brat!'

'I know where we should all be to-day,' I cried, trembling with indignation, 'if it had not been for her!'

'Perhaps not worse off than we are now,' she snapped. 'However, keep your eyes shut, if it pleases you.'

My raised voice had reached the Countess's chamber, and as Fraulein Max, giggling spitefully, went out through one door the other opened and stood open. My anger melted away. I stood trembling, and looking, and waiting.

They came in together, my lady with her arm round Marie, the two women I loved best in the world. I have heard it said that evil runs to evil as drops of water to one another. But the saying is equally true of good. Little had I thought, a few weeks back, that my lady would come to treat the outcast girl from Klink's as a friend ; nor I believe were there ever two people less alike, and yet both good, than these two. But that óne quality — which is so quick to see its face mirrored in another's heart — had brought them close together, and made each to recognise the other; so that, as they came in to me, there was not a line of my lady's figure, not a curve of her head, not a glance of her proud eyes, that was not in sympathy with the girl who clung to her — Romanist stranger, low born as she was. I looked and worshipped, and would have changed nothing. I found the dignity of the one as beautiful as the dependence of the other.

Not a word was spoken. I had wondered what they would say to me — and they said nothing. But my lady put her into my. arms, and she clung to me, hiding her face.

The Countess laughed, yet there were tears in her voice. 'Be happy,' she said. 'Child, from the day you were lost he never forgave me. Martin, see where the rope has cut her wrist. She did it to save you.'

'And myself!' Marie whispered on my breast.

'No!' my lady said. 'I will not have it so ! You will spoil both him and my love-story. *Per tecta, per terram*, you have sought one another. You have gone down *sub orco*. You have bought one another back from death, as Alcestis bought her husband Admetus. At the first it was a gold chain that linked you together, soon —— '

I felt Marie start in my arms. She freed herself gently, and looked at my lady with trouble in her eyes. 'Oh,' she said, 'I had forgotten !'

'What?' the Countess said. 'What have you forgotten?'
'The child!' Marie replied, clasping her hands. 'I
should have told you before!'

'You have had no time to tell us much!' my lady answered smiling. 'And you are trembling like an aspen
now. Sit down, girl. Sit down at once!' she continued
imperatively. 'Or, no! You shall go to your bed, and we
will hear it in the morning.'

But Marie seemed so much distressed by this that my
lady did not insist; and in a few minutes the girl had told
us a tale so remarkable that consideration of her fatigue
was swallowed up in wonder.

'It was the night I was lost,' she said; 'the night when
the alarm was given on the hill, and we rode down it. I
clung to my saddle — it was all I could do — and remember
only a dreadful shock, from which I recovered to find myself lying in the road, shaken and bruised. Fear of those
whom I believed to be behind us was still in my mind,
and I rose, giddy and confused, my one thought to get off
the road. As I staggered towards the bank, however, I
stumbled over something. To my horror I found that it
was a woman. She was dead or senseless, but she had a
child in her arms; it cried as I felt her face. I dared not
stay, but, on the impulse of the moment — I could not move
the woman, and I expected our pursuers to ride down the
hill each instant — I snatched the child up and ran into
the brushwood. After that I only remember stumbling
blindly on through bog and fern, often falling in my haste,
but always rising and pushing on. I heard cries behind
me, but they only spurred me to greater exertions. At
last I reached a little wood, and there, unable to go farther,
I sank down, exhausted, and, I suppose, lost my senses, for
I awoke, chilled and aching, in the first grey dawn. The
leaves were black overhead, but the white birch trunks
round me glimmered like pale ghosts. Something stirred
in my arms. I looked down, and saw the face of my child
— the child I found in the wood by Vach.'

'What!' the Countess cried, rising and staring at her. 'Impossible! Your wits were straying, girl. It was some other child.'

But Marie shook her head gently. 'No, my lady,' she said. 'It was my child.'

'Count Leuchtenstein's ? '

'Yes, if the child I found was his.'

'But how — did it come where you found it?' the Countess asked.

'I think that the woman whom I left in the road was the poor creature who used to beg at our house in the camp,' Marie answered, hesitating somewhat — 'the wife of the man whom General Tzerclas hung, my lady. I saw her face by a glimmer of light only, and, at the moment, I thought nothing. Afterwards it flashed across me that she was that woman. If so, I think that she stole the child to avenge herself. She thought that we were General Tzerclas' friends.'

' But then where *is* the child?' my lady exclaimed, her eyes shining. I was excited myself ; but the delight, the pleasure which I saw in her face took me by surprise. I stared at her, thinking that I had never seen her look so beautiful.

Then, as Marie answered, her face fell. 'I do not know,' my girl said. 'After a time I found my way back to the road, but I had scarcely set foot on it when General Tzerclas' troopers surprised me. I gave myself up for lost; I thought that he would kill me. But he only gibed at me, until I almost died of fear, and then he bade one of his men take me up behind him. They carried me with them to the camp outside this city, and three days ago brought me in and shut me up in that house.'

'But the child?' my lady cried. 'What of it?'

' He took it from me,' Marie said. ' I have never seen it since, but I think that he has it in the camp.'

'Does he know whose child it is ?'

'I told him,' Marie replied. 'Otherwise they might have let it die on the road. It was a burden to them.'

The Countess shuddered, but in a moment recovered her-self. '"While there is life there is hope,"' she said. 'Martin, here is more work for you. We will leave no stone unturned. Count Leuchtenstein must know, of course, but I will tell him myself. If we could get the child back and hand it safe and sound to its father, it would be —— Perhaps the Waldgrave may be able to help us ?'

'I think that he will need all his wits to help himself,' I said bluntly.

'Why ?' my lady questioned, looking at me in wonder.

'Why ?' I cried in astonishment. 'Have you heard nothing about him, my lady ?'

'Nothing,' she said.

'Not that he was taken to-night, in Tzerclas' company,' I answered, 'and is a prisoner at this moment at the Burg, charged, along with the villain Neumann, with a plot to admit the enemy into the city ?'

My lady sat down, her face pale, her aspect changed, as the countryside changes when the sun goes down. 'He was *there*,' she muttered — 'with Tzerclas ?'

I nodded.

'The Waldgrave Rupert — my cousin ?' she murmured, as if the thing passed the bounds of reason.

'Yes, my lady,' I said, as gently as I could. 'But he is mad. I am assured that he is mad. He has been mad for weeks past. We know it. We have known it. Besides, he knew nothing, I am sure, of Tzerclas' plans.'

'But — he was *there!*' she cried. 'He was one of those two men they carried by ? One of those!'

'Yes,' I said.

She sat for a moment stricken and silent, the ghost of herself. Then, in a voice little above a whisper, she asked what they would do to him.

I shrugged my shoulders. To be candid, I had not given the Waldgrave much thought, though in a way he had saved my life. Now, the longer I considered the matter, the less

room for comfort I found. Certainly he was mad. We
knew him to be mad. But how were we to persuade
others? For weeks his bodily health had been good; he
had carried himself indoors and out-of-doors like a sane
man; he had done duty in the trenches, and mixed, though
grudgingly, with his fellows, and gone about the ordinary
business of life. How, in the face of all this, could we
prove him mad, or make his judges, stern men, fighting
with their backs to the wall, see the man as we saw him?

'I suppose that there will be a trial?' my lady said at
last, breaking the silence.

I told her yes — at once. 'The town is -in a frenzy of
rage,' I continued. 'The guards had a hard task to save
them to-night. Perhaps Prince Bernard of Weimar —— '

'Don't count on him,' my lady answered. 'He is as
hard as he is gallant. He would hang his brother if he
thought him guilty of such a thing as this. No; our only
hope is in ' — she hesitated an instant, and then ended the
sentence abruptly — 'Count Leuchtenstein. You must go
to him, Martin, at seven, or as soon after as you can catch
him. He is a just man, and he has watched the Waldgrave
and noticed him to be odd. The court will hear him.
If not, I know no better plan.'

Nor did I, and I said I would go; and shortly afterwards I took my leave. But as I crept to my bed at last,
the clocks striking two, and my head athrob with excitement and gratitude, I wondered what was in my lady's
mind. Remembering the Waldgrave's gallant presence
and manly grace, recalling his hopes, his courage, and his
overweening confidence, as displayed in those last days at
Heritzburg, I could feel no surprise that so sad a downfall
touched her heart. But — was that all? Once I had
deemed him the man to win her. Then I had seen good
cause to think otherwise. Now again I began to fancy
that his mishaps might be crowned with a happiness which
fortune had denied to him in his days of success.

CHAPTER XXXI.

THE TRIAL.

LATE as it was when I fell asleep — for these thoughts long kept me waking — I was up and on my way to Count Leuchtenstein's before the bells rang seven. It was the 17th of August, and the sun, already high, flashed light from a hundred oriels and casements. Below, in the streets, it sparkled on pikeheads and steel caps; above, it glittered on vane and weather-cock; it burnished old bells hung high in air, and decked the waking city with a hundred points of splendour. Everywhere the cool brightness of early morning met the eye, and spoke of things I could not see — the dew on forest leaves, the Werra where it shoals among the stones.

But as I went I saw things that belied the sunshine, things to which I could not shut my eyes. I met men whose meagre forms and shrunken cheeks made a shadow round them; and others, whose hungry vulture eyes, as they prowled in the kennel for garbage, seemed to belong to belated night-birds rather than to creatures of the day. Wan, pinched women, with white-faced children, signs of the deeper distress that lay hidden away in courts and alleys, shuffled along beside the houses; while the common crowd, on whose features famine had not yet laid its hand, wore a stern pre-occupied look, as if the gaunt spectre stood always before their eyes — visible, and no long way off.

In the excitement of the last few days I had failed to note these things or their increase; I had gone about my business thinking of little else, seeing nothing beyond it. Now my eyes were rudely opened, and I recognised with a kind of shock the progress which dearth and disease were making, and had made, in the city. North and south and east and west of me, in endless multitude, the roofs and spires of Nuremberg rose splendid and sparkling in the sunshine. North and south, and east and west, in city and lager lay scores of thousands of armed men, tens of thousands of horses — a host that might fitly be called invincible; and all come together in its defence. But, in corners, as I went along I heard men whisper that Duke Bernard's convoy had been cut off, that the Saxon forage had not come in, that the Croats were gripping the Bamberg road, that a thousand waggons of corn had reached the imperial army. And perforce I remembered that an army must not only fight but eat. The soldiers must be fed, the city must be fed. I began to see that if Wallenstein, secure in his impregnable position on the hills, declined still to move or fight, the time would come when the Swedish King must choose between two courses, and either attack the enemy on the Alta Veste against all odds of position, or march away and leave the city to its fate. I ceased to wonder that care sat on men's faces, and seemed to be a feature of the streets. The passion which the mob had displayed in the night, no longer surprised me. The hungry man is no better than a brute.

Opposite Count Leuchtenstein's lodgings they were quelling a riot at a bakehouse, and the wolfish cries and screams rang in my ears long after I had turned into the house. The Count had been on night service, and was newly risen, and not yet dressed, but his servant consented to admit me. I passed on the stairs a grey-haired sergeant, scarred, stiff, and belted, who was waiting with a bundle of lists and reports. In the ante-chamber two or three gentlemen in buff coats, who talked in low, earnest voices and eyed me curiously as I passed, sat at breakfast. I noted the order and stillness which prevailed everywhere in the house, and nowhere more than in the Count's chamber ; where I found him dressing before a plain table, on which a small, fat Bible had the place of a pouncet-box, and a pair of silver-mounted pistols figured instead of a scent-case. Not that the appointments of the room were mean. On a little stand beside the Bible was the chain of gold walnuts which I had good cause to remember; and this was balanced on the other side by a miniature of a beautiful woman, set in gold and surmounted by a coat-of-arms.

He was vigorously brushing his grey hair and moustachios when I entered, and the air, which the open window freely admitted, lent a brightness to his eyes and a freshness to his complexion that took off ten of his years. He betrayed some surprise at seeing me so early; but he received me with good nature, congratulated me on my adventure, the main facts of which had reached him, and in the same breath lamented Tzerclas' escape.

'But we shall have the fox one of these days,' he continued. 'He is a clever scoundrel, and thinks to be a Wallenstein. But the world has only space for one monster at a time, friend Steward. And to be anything lower than Wallenstein, whom I take to be unique, — to be a Pappenheim, for instance, — a man must have a heart as well as a head, or men will not follow him. However, you did not come to me to discuss Tzerclas,' he continued genially. 'What is your errand, my friend?'

'To ask your excellency's influence on behalf of the Waldgrave Rupert.'

He paused with his brushes suspended. 'On your own account?' he asked; and he looked at me with sudden keenness.

'No, my lord,' I answered. 'My lady sent me. She would have come herself, but the hour was early; and she feared to let the matter stand, lest summary measures should be taken against him.'

'It is likely very summary measures will be taken!' he answered dryly, and with a sensible change in his manner; his voice seemed to grow harsher, his features more rigid. 'But why,' he continued, looking at me again, 'does not the Countess leave him in Prince Bernard's hands? He is his near kinsman.'

'She fears, my lord, that Prince Bernard may not——'

'Be inclined to help him?' the Count said. 'Well, and I think that that is very likely, and I am not surprised. See you how the matter stands? This young gallant should have been, since his arrival here, foremost in every skirmish; he should have spent his days in the saddle, and his nights in his cloak, and been the first to mount and the last to leave the works. Instead of that, he has shown himself lukewarm throughout, Master Steward. He has done no credit to his friends or his commission; he has done everything to lend colour to this charge; and, by my faith, I do not know what can be done for him — nor that it behoves us to do anything.'

'But he is not guilty of this, if your excellency pleases,' I said boldly. The Count's manner of speaking of him was hard and so nearly hostile that my choler rose a little.

'He has not done his duty!'

'Because he has not been himself,' I replied.

'Well, we have enough to do in these evil days to protect those who are!' he answered sharply. 'Besides, this matter is a city matter. It is in the citizens' hands, and I do not know what we have to do with it. Look now,' he continued, almost querulously, 'it is an invidious thing to meddle with them. We of the army are risking our lives and no more, but our hosts are risking all — wives and daughters, sweethearts, and children, and homes! And I say it is an awkward thing meddling with them. For Neumann the sooner they hang the dog the better; and for this young spark I can think of nothing that he has done that binds us to go out of our way to save him. Marienbad! What brought him into that den of thieves?'

'My lord,' I said, taken aback by his severity — 'since he received a wound some months back he has not been himself.'

'He has been sufficiently himself to hang about a woman's apron-strings,' the Count answered with a flash of querulous contempt, 'instead of doing his duty. However, what you say is true. I have seen it myself. But, again, why

does not your lady leave Prince Bernard to settle the
matter ? '

'She fears that he may not be sufficiently interested.'

He turned away abruptly; unless I was mistaken, he
winced. And in a moment a light broke in upon me.
The peevishness and irritability with which he had received the first mention of the Waldgrave's name had
puzzled me. I had not expected such a display in a man
of his grave, equable nature, of his high station, his great
name. I had given him credit for a less churlish spirit
and a judgment more evenly balanced. And I had felt
surprised and disappointed.

Now, on a sudden, I saw light — in an unexpected quarter. For a moment I could have laughed both at myself
and at him. The man was jealous; jealous, at his age and
with his grey hairs ! At the first blush of the thing I could
have laughed, the feeling and the passion it implied seemed
alike so preposterous. There on the table before me stood
the miniature of his first wife, and his child's necklace.
And the man himself was old enough to be my lady's
father. What if he was tall and strong; and still vigorous though grey-haired ; and a man of great name. When
I thought of the Waldgrave — of his splendid youth and
gallant presence, his gracious head and sunny smile, and
pictured this staid, sober man beside him, I could have
found it in my heart to laugh.

While I stood, busy with these thoughts, the Count
walked the length of the room more than once with his
head bent and his shoulder turned to me. At length he
stopped and spoke; nor could my sharpened ear now detect
anything unusual in his voice.

'Very well,' he said, his tone one of half-peevish resignation, 'you have done your errand. I think I understand,
and you may tell your mistress — I will do what I can.
The King of Sweden will doubtless remit the matter to
the citizens, and there will be some sort of a hearing
to-day. I will be at it. But there is a stiff spirit abroad,

and men are in an ugly mood — and I promise nothing. But I will do my best. Now go, my friend. I have business.'

With that he dismissed me in a manner so much like his usual manner that I wondered whether I had deceived myself. And I finally left the room in a haze of uncertainty. However, I had succeeded in the object of my visit; that was something. He had taken care to guard his promise, but I did not doubt that he would perform it. For there are men whose lightest word is weightier than another's bond; and I took it, I scarcely know why, that the Count belonged to these.

Nevertheless, I saw things, as I went through the streets, that fed my doubts. While famine menaced the poorer people, the richer held a sack, with all the horrors which Magdeburg had suffered, in equal dread. The discovery of Neumann's plot had taught them how small a matter might expose them to that extremity ; and as I went along I saw scarcely a burgher whose face was not sternly set, no magistrate whose brow was not dark with purpose.

Consequently, when I attended my lady to the Rath-haus at two o'clock, the hour fixed for the inquiry, I was not surprised to find these signs even more conspicuous. The streets were thronged, and ugly looks and suspicious glances met us on all sides, merely because it was known that the Waldgrave had been much at my lady's house. We were made to feel that Nuremberg was a free city, and that we were no more than its guests. It is true, no one insulted us; but the crowd which filled the open space before the Town-house eyed us with so little favour that I was glad to think that the magistrates with all their independence must still be guided by the sword, and that the sword was the King of Sweden's.

My lady, I saw, shared my apprehensions. But she came of a stock not easily daunted, and would as soon have dreamed of putting out one of her eyes because it displeased a chance acquaintance, as of deserting a friend because the Nurembergers frowned upon him. Her eyes sparkled and her colour rose as we proceeded; the ominous silence which greeted us only stiffened her carriage. By the time we reached the Rath-haus I knew not whether to fear more from her indiscretion, or hope more from her courage.

The Court sat in private, but orders that we should be admitted had been given; and after a brief delay we were ushered into the hall of audience — a lofty, panelled chamber, carved and fretted, having six deep bays, and in each a window of stained glass. A number of scutcheons and banners depended from the roof; at one end a huge double eagle wearing the imperial crown pranced in all the pomp of gold and tinctures; and behind the court, which consisted of the Chief Magistrate and four colleagues, the sword of Justice was displayed. But that which struck me far more than these things, was the stillness that pre- vailed; which was such that, though there were a dozen persons present when we entered, the creaking of our boots as we walked up the floor, and the booming of distant cannon, seemed to be equally audible.

The Chief Magistrate rose and received my lady with due ceremony, ordering a chair to be placed for her, and requesting her to be seated at the end of the dais-table, behind which he sat. I took my stand at a respectful dis- tance behind her; and so far we had nothing to complain of; but I felt my spirits sensibly dashed both by the still- ness and the sombre and almost forbidding faces of the five judges. Two or three attendants stood by the doors, but neither the King of Sweden nor any of his officers were present. I looked in vain for Count Leuchtenstein; I could see nothing of him or of the prisoners. The solemn air of the room, the silence, and the privacy of the pro- ceedings, all contributed to chill me. I could fancy myself before a court of inquisitors, a Vehm-Gericht, or that famous Council of Ten which sits, I have heard, at Venice; but for any of the common circumstances of such tribunals as are usual in Germany, I could not find them.

I think that my lady was somewhat taken aback too; but she did not betray it. After courteously thanking the Council for granting her an audience, she explained that her object in seeking it was to state certain facts on behalf of the Waldgrave Rupert of Weimar, her kinsman, and to offer the evidence of her steward, a person of respectability.

'We are quite willing to hear your excellency,' the Chief Magistrate answered in a grave, dry voice. 'But perhaps you will first inform us to what these facts tend? It may shorten the inquiry.'

'Some weeks ago,' my lady answered with dignity, 'the Waldgrave Rupert was wounded in the head. From that time he has not been himself.'

'Does your excellency mean that he is not aware of his actions?'

'No,' my lady answered quietly. 'I do not go as far as that.'

'Or that he is not aware in what company he is?' the magistrate persisted.

'Oh no.'

'Or that he is ignorant at any time where he is?'

'No, but——'

'One moment!' the Chief Magistrate stopped her with a courteous gesture. 'Pardon me. In an instant, your excellency—to whom I assure you that the Court are obliged, since we desire only to do justice — will see to what my questions lead. I crave leave to put one more, and then to put the same question to your steward. It is this: Do you admit, Countess, that the Waldgrave Rupert was last night in the house with Tzerclas, Neumann, and the other persons inculpated?'

'Certainly,' my lady answered. 'I am so informed. I did not know that that was in question,' she added, looking round with a puzzled air.

'And you, my friend?' The Chief Magistrate fixed me with his small, keen eyes. 'But first, what is your name?'

'Martin Schwartz.'

'Yes, I remember. The man who was saved from the villains. We could have no better evidence. What do you say, then? Was the Waldgrave Rupert last night in this house — the house in question?'

'I saw him in the house,' I answered warily. 'In the hall. But he was not in the room with Tzerclas and Neumann — the room in which I saw the maps and plans.'

'A fair answer,' the Burgomaster replied, nodding his head, 'and your evidence might avail the accused. But the fact is — it is to this point we desire to call your excellency's attention,' he continued, turning with a dusty smile to my lady — 'the Waldgrave steadily denies that he was in the house at all.'

'He denies that he was there?' my lady said. 'But was he not arrested in the house?'

'Yes,' the Chief Magistrate answered dryly, 'he was.' And he looked at us in silence.

'But — what does he say?' my lady asked faintly.

'He affects to be ignorant of everything that has occurred in connection with the house. He pretends that he does not know how he comes to be in custody, that he does not know many things that have lately occurred. For instance, three days ago,' the Burgomaster continued with a chill smile, 'I had the honour of meeting him at the King of Sweden's quarters and talking with him. He says to-day that I am a stranger to him, that we did not meet, that we did not talk, and that he does not know where the King of Sweden's quarters are.'

'Then,' my lady said sorrowfully, 'he is worse than he was. He is now quite mad.'

'I am afraid not,' the magistrate replied, shaking his head gravely. 'He is sane enough on other points. Only he will answer no questions that relate to this conspiracy, or to his guilt.'

'He is not guilty,' the Countess cried impetuously. 'Believe me, however strangely he talks, he is incapable of such treachery!'

'Your excellency forgets — that he was in this house!'
'But with no evil intentions!'
'Yet denies that he was there!' the Burgomaster con-
cluded gravely.

That silenced my lady, and she sat rolling her kerchief
in her hands. Against the five impassive faces that confronted her, the ten inscrutable eyes that watched her;
above all, against this strange, this inexplicable denial, she
could do nothing! At last —

'Will you hear my steward?' she asked — in despair, I
think.

'Certainly,' the Burgomaster answered. 'We wish to do
so.'

On that I told them all I knew; in what terms I had
heard Neumann and General Tzerclas refer to the Waldgrave; how unexpected had been his appearance in the
hall; how this interference had saved my life; and, finally,
my own conviction that he was not privy to Tzerclas'
designs.

The Court heard me with attention; the Burgomaster
put a few questions, and I answered them. Then, afraid to
stop — for their faces showed no relenting — I began to
repeat what I had said before. But now the Court remained silent; I stumbled, stammered, finally sank into
silence myself. The air of the place froze me; I seemed
to be talking to statues.

The Countess was the first to break the spell. 'Well?'
she cried, her voice tremulous, yet defiant.

The Burgomaster consulted his colleagues, and for the
first time something of animation appeared in their faces.
But it lasted an instant only. Then the others sat back in
their chairs, and he turned to my lady.

'We are obliged to your excellency,' he said gravely and
formally. 'And to your servant. But the Court sees no
reason to change its decision.'

'And that is?' The Countess's voice was husky. She
knew what was coming.

'That both prisoners suffer together.'

For an instant I feared that my lady would do something unbecoming her dignity, and either.break into womanish sobs and lamentations, or stoop to threats and insistence that must be equally unavailing. But she had learned in command the man's lesson of control; and never had I seen her more equal to herself. I knew that her heart was bounding wildly; that her breast was heaving with indignation, pity, horror; that she saw, as I saw, the fair head for which she pleaded, rolling in the dust. But with all — she controlled herself. She rose stiffly from her seat.

'I am obliged to you for your patience, sir,' she said, trembling but composed. 'I had expected one to aid me in my prayer, who is not here. And I can say no more. On his head be it. Only — I trust that you may never plead with as good a cause — and be refused.'

They rose and stood while she turned from them; and the two court ushers with their wands went before her as she walked down the hall. The silence, the formality, the creaking shoes, the very gules and purpure that lay in pools on the floor — I think that they stifled her as they stifled me; for when she reached the open air at last and I saw her face, I saw that she was white to the lips.

But she bore herself bravely; the surly crowd, that filled the Market Square and hailed our appearance with a harsh murmur, grew silent under her scornful eye, and partly out of respect, partly out of complaisance, because they now felt sure of their victim, doffed their caps to her and made room for us to pass. Every moment I expected her to break down : to weep or cover her face. But she passed through all proudly, and walked, unfaltering, back to our lodging.

There on the threshold she did pause at last, just when I wished. her to go on. She stood and turned her head, listening.

'What is that ?' she said.

But with all—she controlled herself. She rose
stillly from her seat.

.

'Cannon,' I answered hastily. 'In the trenches, my lady.'

'No,' she said quietly. 'It is shouting. They have read the sentence.'

She said no more, not another word ; and went in quietly and upstairs to her room. But I wondered and feared. Such composure as this seemed to be unnatural, almost cruel. I could not think of the Waldgrave myself without a lump coming in my throat. I could not face the sunshine. And Steve and the men, when they heard, were no better. We stood inside the doorway in a little knot, and looked at one another mournfully. A man who passed — and did not know the house or who we were — stopped to tell us that the sentence would be carried out at sunset ; and, pleased to have given us the news, went whistling down the stale, sunny street.

Steve growled out an oath. 'Who are these people,' he said savagely, 'that they should say my lady nay ? When the Countess stoops to ask a life — Himmel ! — is she not to have it ? '

'Not here,' I said, shaking my head.

'And why not ? '

'Because we are not at Heritzburg now,' I answered sadly.

'But — are we nobody here ? ' he growled in a rage. 'Are we going to sit still and let them kill my lady's own cousin ? '

I shrugged my shoulders. 'We have done all we can,' I said.

'But there is some one can say nay to these curs ! ' he cried. And he spat contemptuously into the street. He had a countryman's scorn of townsfolk. 'Why don't we take the law into our own hands, Master Martin ? '

'It is likely,' I said. 'One against ten thousand ! And for the matter of that, if the people are angry, it is not without cause. Did you see the man under the archway ? '

Steve nodded. 'Dead,' he muttered.

'Starved,' I said. 'He was a cripple. First the cripples. Then the sound men. Life is cheap here.'

Steve swore another oath. 'Those are curs. But our man — why don't we go to the King of Sweden? I suppose he is a sort of cousin to my lady?'

'We have as good as gone to him,' I answered. At another time I might have smiled at Steve's notion of my lady's importance. 'We have been to one equally able to help us. And he has done us no good. And for the matter of that, there is not time to go to the camp and back.'

Steve began to fume and fret. The minutes went like lead. We were all miserable together. Outside, the kennel simmered in the sun, the low rumble of the cannon filled the air. I hated Nuremberg, the streets, the people, the heat. I wished that I had never seen a stone of it.

Presently one of the women came down stairs to us. 'Do you know if there has been any fighting in the trenches to-day?' she asked.

'Nothing to speak of,' I answered. 'As far as I have heard. Why?'

'The Countess wishes to know,' she said. 'You have not heard of any one being killed?'

'No.'

'Nor wounded?'

'No.'

She nodded and turned away. I called after her to know the reason of her questions, but she flitted upstairs without giving me an answer, and left us looking at one another. In a second, however, she was down again.

'My lady will see no one,' she said, with a face of mystery. 'You understand, Master Martin? But — if any come of importance, you can take her will.'

I nodded. The woman cast a lingering look into the street and went upstairs again.

CHAPTER XXXII.

A POOR GUERDON.

I HAD slept scantily the night before, and the excitement of the last twenty-four hours had worn me out. I was grieved for the gallant life so swiftly ebbing, and miserable on my lady's account; but sorrow of this kind is a sleepy thing, and the day was hot. I did not feel about the Waldgrave as I had about Marie ; and gradually my head nodded, and nodded again, until I fell fast asleep, on the seat within the door.

A man's voice, clear and penetrating, awoke me. 'Let him be,' it said. ' Hark you, fellow, let him be. He was up last night ; I will announce myself.'

I was drowsy and understood only half of what I heard ; and I should have taken the speaker at his word, and turning over dropped off again, if Steve had not kicked me and brought me to my feet with a cry of pain. I stood an instant, bewildered, dazzled by the sunlight, nursing my ankle in my hand. Then I made out where I was, and saw through the arch of the entrance Count Leuchtenstein dismounting in the street. As I looked, he threw the reins to a trooper who accompanied him, and turned to come in.

' Ah, my friend,' he said, nodding pleasantly, 'you are awake. I will see your mistress.'

I was not quite myself, and his presence took me aback. I stood looking at him awkwardly. ' If your excellency will wait a moment,' I faltered at last, 'I will take her pleasure.'

He glanced at me a moment, as if surprised. Then he laughed. ' Go,' he said. ' I am not often kept waiting.'

I was glad to get away, and I ran upstairs ; and knocking hurriedly at the parlour door, went in. My lady, pale and frowning, with a little book in her hand, got up hastily —

from her knees, I thought. Marie Wort, with tears on her cheeks, and Fraulein Max, looking scared, stood behind her.

The Countess looked at me, her eyes flashing. 'What is it?' she asked sharply.

'Count Leuchtenstein is below,' I said.

'Well?'

'He wishes to see your excellency.'

'Did I not say that I would see no one?'

'But Count Leuchtenstein?'

She laughed a shrill laugh full of pain — a laugh that had something hysterical in it. 'You thought that I would see *him?*' she cried. 'Him, I suppose, of all people? Go down, fool, and tell him that even here, in this poor house, my doors are open to my friends and to them only! Not to those who profess much and do nothing! Or to those who bark and do not bite! Count Leuchtenstein? Pah, tell him —— Silence, woman!' This to Marie, who would have interrupted her. 'Tell him what I have told you, man, word for word. Or no' — and she caught herself up with a mocking smile, such as I had never seen on her face before. 'Tell him this instead — that the Countess Rotha is engaged with the Waldgrave Rupert, and wants no other company! Yes, tell him that — it will bite home, if he has a conscience! He might have saved him, and he would not! Now, when I would pray, which is all women can do, he comes here! Oh, I am sick! I am sick!'

I saw that she was almost beside herself with grief; and I stood irresolute, my heart aching for her. What I dared not do, Marie did. She sprang forward, and seizing the Countess's hand, knelt beside her, covering it with kisses.

'Oh, my lady!' she cried through her tears. 'Don't be so hard. See him. See him. Even at this last moment.'

With an inarticulate cry the Countess flung her off so forcibly that the girl fell to the ground. 'Be silent!' my lady cried, her eyes on fire. 'Or go to your prayers, wench. To your prayers! And do you begone! Begone, and on your peril give my message, word for word!'

I saw nothing for it but to obey; and I went down full of dismay. I could understand my lady's grief, and that I had come upon her at an inopportune moment. But the self-control which she had exhibited before the Court rendered the violence of her rage now the more surprising. I had never seen her in this mood, and her hardness shocked me. I felt myself equally bewildered and grieved.

I found Count Leuchtenstein waiting on the step, with his face to the street. He turned as I descended. 'Well?' he said, smiling. 'Am I to go up, my friend?'

I saw that he had not the slightest doubt of my answer, and his cheerfulness kindled a sort of resentment in my breast. He seemed to be so well content, so certain of his reception, so calm and strong — and, at this very moment — for the sunshine had left the street and was creeping up the tiles — they might be leading out the Waldgrave! I had liked my lady's message very little when she gave it to me; now I rejoiced that I could sting him with it.

'My lady is not very well,' I said. 'The sentence on the Waldgrave has upset her.'

He smiled. 'But she will receive me?' he said.

'Craving your excellency's indulgence, I do not think that she will receive any one.'

'You told her that I was here?'

'Yes, your excellency. And she said ——'

His face fell. 'Tut! tut!' he exclaimed. 'But I come on purpose to —— What did she say, man?'

The smile was gone from his lips, but I caught it lurking in his eyes; and it hardened me to do her bidding. 'I was to tell your excellency that she could not receive you,' I said, 'that she was engaged with the Waldgrave.'

He started and stared at me, his expression slowly passing from amazement to anger. 'What!' he exclaimed at last, in a cutting tone. 'Already?' And his lip curled with a kind of disgust. 'You have given me the message exactly, have you?'

'Yes, your excellency,' I said, quailing a little. But

22

servants know when to be stupid, and I affected stupidity, fixing my eyes on his breast and pretending to see nothing. He turned, and for a moment I thought that he was going without a word. Then on the steps he turned again. 'You have heard the news, then?' he said sourly. He had already regained his self-control.

'Yes, my lord.'

'Ah! Well, you lose no time in your house,' he replied grimly. 'Call my horse!'

I called the man, who had wandered a little way up the street, and he brought it. As I held the Count's stirrup for him to mount, I noticed how heavily he climbed to his saddle, and that he settled himself into it with a sigh; but the next moment he laughed, as at himself. I stood back expecting him to say something more, or to leave some message, but he did not even look at me again; he touched his horse with the spur, and walked away steadily. I stood and watched him until he reached the end of the street — until he turned the corner and disappeared.

Even then I still stood looking after him, partly sorry and partly puzzled, for quite a long time. It was only when I turned to go in that I missed Steve and the men, and began to wonder what had become of them. I had left them with the Count at the door — they were gone now. I looked up and down, I could see them nowhere. I went in and asked the women; but they were not with them. The sunset gun had just gone off, and one of the girls was crying hysterically, while the others sat round her, white and frightened. This did not cheer me, nor enliven the house. I came out again, vowing vengeance on the truants; and there in the entrance, facing me, standing where the Count had stood a few minutes before, I saw the last man I looked to see!

I gasped and gave back a step. The sun was gone, the evening light was behind the man, and his face was in the shadow. His figure showed dark against the street. 'Ach Gott!' I cried, and stood still, stricken. It was the Waldgrave!

'Martin !' he said.

I gave back another step. The street was quiet, the house like the grave. For a moment the figure did not move, but stood there gazing at me. Then —

'Why, Martin!' he cried. 'Don't you know me?'

Then, not until then, I did — for a man and not a ghost; and I caught his hand with a cry of joy. 'Welcome, my lord, welcome!' I said, grown hot all over. 'Thank God that you have escaped!'

'Yes,' he said, and his tone was his own old tone, 'thank God; Him first, and then my friends. Steve and Ernst I have seen already; they heard the news from the Count's man, and came to meet me, and I have sent them on an errand, by your leave. And now, where is my cousin?'

'Above,' I answered. 'But——'

'But what?' he said quickly.

'I think that I had better prepare her.'

'She does not know?'

'No, your excellency. Nor did I, until I saw you.'

'But Count Leuchtenstein has been here. Did he not tell you?' he asked in surprise.

'Not a word!' I answered. And then I stopped, conscience-stricken. 'Himmel! I remember now,' I said. 'He asked me if we had heard the news; and I, like a dullard, dreaming that he meant other news, and the worst, said yes!'

The Waldgrave shrugged his shoulders. 'Well, go to her now, and tell her,' he said. 'I want to see her; I want to thank her. I have a hundred things to say to her. Quick, Martin, for I am laden with debts, and I choke to pay some of them.'

I ran upstairs, marvelling. On the lobby I met Fraulein Max coming down. 'What is it?' she asked impatiently.

'The Waldgrave! He has been released! He is here!' I cried in a breath.

She stared at me while a man might count ten. Then to my astonishment she laughed aloud. 'Who released him?' she asked.

'The magistrates,' I said. 'I suppose so. I don't know.
I had not given the matter a thought.
' Not Count Leuchtenstein ? '
I started. ' So ! ' I muttered, staring at her in my turn.
' It must have been he. The Waldgrave said something
about him. And he must have come here to tell us.'
' And you gave him my lady's message ? '
' Alas ! yes.'
Fraulein Max laughed again, and kept on laughing, until
I grew hot all over, and could have struck her for her
malice. She saw at last that I was angry, and she stopped.
' Tut ! tut ! ' she said, ' it is nothing. But that disposes of
the old man. Now for the young one. He is here ? '
' Yes.'
' Then why do you not show him up ? '
' She must be prepared,' I muttered.
She laughed again; this time after a different fashion.
' Oh you fools of men ! ' she said. ' She must be prepared ?
Do you think that women are made of glass and that a
shock breaks them ? That she will die of joy ? Or would
have died of grief ? Send him up, gaby, and I will prepare
her ! Send him up.'
I supposed that she knew women's ways, and I gave in to
her, and sent him up; and I do not know that any harm
was done. But, as a result of this, I was not present when
my lady and the Waldgrave met, and I only learned by
hearsay what happened.

*   *   *   *   *   *

An hour or two later, when the bustle of shrieks and
questions had subsided, and the excitement caused by his
return had somewhat worn itself out, Marie slipped out to
me on the stairs, and sat with me in the darkness, talking.
The gate of curious ironwork which guarded the house
entrance was closed for the night; but the moon was
up, and its light, falling through the scrollwork, lay like a
pale, reedy pool at our feet. The men were at supper, the
house was quiet, the city was for a little while still. Not a

foot sounded on the roadway; only sometimes a skulking dog came ghost-like to the bars and sniffed, and sneaked noiselessly away.

I have said that we talked, but in truth we sat long silent, as lovers have sat these thousand years, I suppose, in such intervals of calm. The peace of the night lapped us round; after the perils and hurry, the storm and stress of many days, we were together and at rest, and content to be silent. All round us, under the covert of darkness, under the moonlight, the city lay quaking; dreading the future, torn by pangs in the present; sleepless, or dreaming of death and outrage, ridden by the nightmare of Wallenstein. But for the moment we recked nothing of this, nothing of the great camp round us, nothing of the crash of nations. We were of none of these. We had one another, and it was enough; loved one another, and the rest went by. For the moment we tasted perfect peace; and in the midst of the besieged city, were as much alone, as if the moonlight at our feet had been, indeed, a forest pool high in the hills over Heritzburg.

Does some old man smile? Do I smile myself now, though sadly? A brief madness, was it? Nay; but what if then only we were sane, and for a moment saw things as they are — lost sight of the unreal and awoke to the real? I once heard a wise man from Basle say something like that at my lady's table. The men, I remember, stared; the women looked thoughtful.

For all that, it was Marie who on this occasion broke the trance. The town clock struck ten, and at the sound hundreds, I dare swear, turned on their pillows, thinking of the husbands and sons and lovers whom the next light must imperil. My girl stirred.

'Ah!' she murmured, 'the poor Countess! Can we do nothing?'

'Do?' I said. 'What should we do? The Waldgrave is back, and in his right mind; which of all the things I have ever known, is the oddest. That a man should lose his senses under one blow, and recover them under another, and remember nothing that has happened in the interval — it almost passes belief.'

' Yet it is true.'

' I suppose so,' I answered. ' The Waldgrave was mad — I can bear witness to it — and now he is sane. There is no more to be said.'

' But the Countess, Martin ? '

' Well, I do not know that she is the worse,' I answered stupidly. ' She sent off the Count with a flea in his ear, and a poor return it was. But she can explain it to him, and after all, she has got the Waldgrave back, safe and sound. That is the main thing.'

Marie sighed, and moved restlessly. ' Is it ? ' she said. ' I wish I knew.'

' What ? ' I asked, drawing her little head on to my shoulder.

' What my lady wishes ? '

' Eh ? '

' Which ? '

My jaw fell. I stared into the darkness open-mouthed. ' Why,' I exclaimed at last, ' he is sixty — or fifty-five at least, girl ! '

Marie laughed softly, with her face on my breast. ' If she loves him,' she murmured. ' If she loves him.' And she hung on me.

I sat amazed, confounded, thinking no more of Marie, though my arm was round her, than of a doll. ' But he is fifty-five,' I said.

' And if you were fifty-five, do you think that I should not love you ? ' she whispered. ' When you are fifty-five, do you think that I shall not love you ? Besides, he is strong, brave, famous — a man ; and she is not a girl, but a woman. If the Count be too old, is not the Waldgrave too young ? '

' Yes,' I said cunningly. ' But why either ? '

' Because love is in the air,' Marie answered ; and I knew

that she smiled, though the gloom hid her face. 'Because there is a change in her. Because she knows things and sees things and feels things of which she was ignorant before. And because — because it is so, my lord.'

I whistled. This was beyond me. ' And yet you don't know which ? ' I said.

' No ; I suspect.'

' Well — but the Waldgrave ? ' I exclaimed. ' Why, mädchen, he is one of the handsomest men I have ever seen. An Apollo ! A Fairy Prince ! It is not possible that she should prefer the other.'

Marie laughed. ' Ah ! ' she said, 'if men chose all the husbands, there would be few wives.'

* * * * * *

CHAPTER XXXIII.

TWO MEN.

THE Waldgrave's return to his old self, and to the frankness and gaiety that, when we first knew him at Heritzburg, had surrounded him with a halo of youth, was perhaps the most noteworthy event of all within my experience. For the return proved permanent, the transformation was perfect. The moodiness, the crookedness, the crafty humours that for weeks had darkened and distorted the man's nature — so that another and a worse man seemed to look out of his eyes and speak with his mouth — were gone, leaving no cloud or remembrance. He had been mad ; he was now as sane as the best. Only one peculiarity remained — and for a few days a little pallor and weakness — of all the things that had befallen him between his first wound and his second, he could remember nothing, not a jot or tittle ; nor could any amount of allusion or questioning bring these things back to him. After many attempts we desisted ; but there were always some who, from this date, regarded him with a certain degree of awe — as a man who had been for a time in the flesh, and yet not of it.

With sanity returned also all the wholesome ambitions and desires that had formerly moved the man; and amongst these his passion for my lady. He lay at our house that night, and spent the next two days there, recovering his strength; and I had more than one oppor-tunity of marking the assiduity with which he followed all the Countess's movements with his eyes, the change which his voice underwent when he spoke to her, and his manner when he came into her presence. In a word, he seemed to take up his love where he had dropped it — at the point it had reached when he rode down into the green valley and secured his rival's victory at so great a cost; at the point at which Tzerclas' admiration and my lady's rebuff had at once strengthened and purified it.

Now Tzerclas was gone from the field — magically, as it seemed to the Waldgrave. And, magically also — for he knew nothing of its flight — time had passed; days and weeks running into months — a sufficiency of time, he hoped, to remove unfavourable impressions from her mind, to obliterate the memory of that unhappy banquet, and replace him on the pinnacle he had occupied at Heritzburg.

But he soon found that, though Tzerclas was gone and the field seemed open, all was not to be had for the asking. My lady was kind; she had a smile for him, and pleasant words, and a ready ear. But before he had been in the house twenty-four hours, he came and confided to me that something was wrong. The Countess was changed; was pettish as he had never seen her before; absent and thoughtful, traits equally new; restless — and placid dignity had been one of her chief characteristics.

'What is it, Martin?' he said, knitting his brows and striding to and fro in frank perplexity. 'It cannot be that, after all that has passed, she is fretting for that villain Tzerclas?'

'After risking her life to escape from him?' I answered dryly. 'No, I think not, my lord.'

'If I ever set eyes on him again I will end him!' the Waldgrave cried, still clinging, I think, to his idea, and exasperated by it. He strode up and down a time or two, and did not grow cooler. 'If it is not that, what is it?' he said at last.

'There are not many light hearts in Nuremberg,' I suggested. 'And of those, few are women's. There must be an end of this soon.'

'You think it is that?' he said.

'Why not?' I answered. 'I am told that the horses are dying by hundreds in the camp. The men will die next. In the end the King will have to march away, or see his army perish piecemeal. In either case the city will pay for all. Wallenstein will swoop down on it, and make of it another and greater Magdeburg. That is a poor prospect for the weak and helpless.'

'It is those rascally Croats!' the Waldgrave groaned. 'They cover the country like flies — are here and there and nowhere all in the same minute, and burn and harry and leave us nothing. We have no troops of that kind.'

'There was plundering in the Wert suburb last night,' I said. 'The King blames the Germans.'

'Soldiers are bad to starve,' the Waldgrave answered.

'Yes; they will see the townsfolk suffer first,' I rejoined, with a touch of bitterness. 'But look whichever way you please, it is a gloomy outlook, my lord, and I do not wonder that my lady is down-hearted.'

He nodded, but presently he said something that showed that he was not satisfied. 'The Countess used to be of a bolder spirit,' he muttered. 'I don't understand it.'

I did not know how to answer him, and fortunately, at that moment, Marie came down to say that my lady proposed to visit Count Leuchtenstein, and that I was to go to her. The Waldgrave heard, and raced up before me, crying out that he would go too. I followed. When I reached the parlour I found them confronting one another, my lady standing in the oriel with her back to the street.

'But would it not be more seemly?' the Waldgrave was saying as I entered. 'As your cousin, and ———'

'I would rather go alone,' the Countess replied curtly.

'To the camp?' he exclaimed. 'He is not in his city quarters.'

'Yes, to the camp,' my lady answered, with a spark of anger in her eyes.

On that he stood, fidgety and discomfited, and the Countess gave me her orders. But he could not believe that she did not need him, and the moment she was silent, he began again.

'You do not want me; but you do not object to my company, I suppose?' he said airily. 'I have to thank the Count, cousin, and I must go to-day or to-morrow. There is no time like the present, and if you are going now ———'

'I should prefer to go alone,' my lady said stiffly.

His face fell; he stood looking foolish. 'Oh, I did not know,' he stammered at last; 'I thought ———'

'What?' the Countess said.

'That you liked me well enough — to — to be glad of my company,' he answered, half offended, half in deprecation.

'I liked you well enough to abase myself for you!' my lady retorted cruelly. And I dare say that she said more, but I did not hear it. I had to go down and prepare for her visit.

When I next saw him, he was much subdued. He seemed to be turning something over in his mind, and by-and-by he asked me a question about Count Leuchtenstein. I saw which way his thoughts were tending, or fancied that I did; but it was not my business to interfere one way or the other, and I answered him and made no comment. The horses were at the door then, and in a moment my lady came down, looking pale and depressed. The Waldgrave went humbly to her, and put her into her saddle, touching her foot as if it had been glass; and I mounted Marie, who was to attend her. I expected that my lady — who had a very tender heart under her queenly manner — would say something to him before we started; but she seemed to be quite taken up with her thoughts, and to be barely conscious, if conscious at all, of his presence. She said 'Thank you,' but it was mechanically. And the next moment we were moving, Ernst making up the escort.

My eyes soon furnished me with other matter for thought than the Waldgrave. Throughout the city the summer drought had dried up the foliage of the trees; and the grass, where it had not been plucked by the poor and boiled for food, had been eaten to the roots by starving cattle. The whole city under the blaze of sunshine wore an arid, dusty, parched appearance, and seemed to reflect on its face the look of dreary endurance which was worn by too many of the countenances we observed in the streets. Pain creeps by instinct to some dark and solitary place; but here was a whole city in pain, gasping and suffering under the pitiless sunshine; and the contrast between the blue sky above and the scene below added indescribably to the gloom and dreariness of the latter. I know that I got a horror of sunshine there that lasted for many a month after.

Either twenty-four hours had aggravated the pinch of famine, which was possible, or I had a more open mind to perceive it. I marked more hollow cheeks than ever, more hungry eyes, more faces with the glare of brutes. And in the bearing of the crowd that filled the streets — though no business was done, no trade carried on — I thought that I saw a change. Wherever it was thickest, I noticed that men walked in one of two ways, either hurrying along feverishly and in haste, as if time were of the utmost value, or moving listlessly, with dragging feet and lacklustre eyes, as if nothing had any longer power to stir them. I even noticed that the same men went in both ways within the space of a minute, passing in a second and apparently without intention from feverish activity to the moodiness of despair.

And no wonder. Not only famine, but pestilence had tightened its grasp on the city; and from this the rich had as much to fear as the poor. As we drew near the walls the smell of carrion, which had hitherto but spoiled the air, filled the nostrils and sickened the whole man. In some places scores of horses lay unburied, while it was whispered that in obscure corners death had so far outstripped the grave-diggers that corpses lay in the houses and the living slept with the dead. There was fighting in front of the bakers' shops in more than one place — my lady had to throw money before we could pass; in the kennels women screamed and fought for offal; from the open doors of churches prayers and wailing poured forth; at the gates, where gibbets, laden with corpses, rose for a warning, multitudes stood waiting and listening for news. And on all, dead and living, the sun shone hotly, steadily, ruthlessly, so that men asked with one voice, 'How long? How long?'

In the camp, which had just received huge reinforcements of men and horses, we found order and discipline at least. Rows of kettles and piles of arms proclaimed it, and lines of pennons that stretched almost as far as the eye could reach. But here, too, were knitted brows, and gloomy looks, and loud murmurings, that grew and swelled as we passed. Count Leuchtenstein's quarters were on the border of the Swedish camp, near the Finland regiments, and not far from the King's. A knot of officers, who stood talking in front of them and knew my lady, came to place themselves at her service. But the offer proved ·to be abortive, for the first thing she learned was that the Count was absent. He had gone at dawn in the direction of Altdorf to cover the entrance of a convoy.

I felt that she was grievously disappointed, for whether she loved him or not, I could understand the humiliation under which she smarted, and would smart until she had set herself right with him. But she veiled her chagrin admirably, and, lightly refusing the offer of refreshment, turned

her horse's head at once, so that in a twinkling we were on
our road home again.

By the way, I saw only what I had seen before. But the
Countess, whose figure began to droop, saw, I think, with
other eyes than those through which she had looked on the
outward journey. Her thoughts no longer occupied, she
saw in their fulness the ravages which famine and plague
were making in the town, once so prosperous. When she
reached her lodgings her first act was to send money, of
which we had no great store, to the magistrates, that a free
meal in addition to the starvation rations might be given
to the poor; and her next, to declare that henceforth she
would keep the house.

Accordingly, instead of going again to the Count's, she
sent me next day with a letter. I found the camp in an
uproar, which was fast spreading to the city. A rumour
had just got wind that the King was about to break up his
camp and give battle to the enemy at all hazards; and so
many were riding and running into the city with the news
that I could scarcely make head against the current.

Arriving at last, however, I was fortunate enough to find
the Count in his quarters and alone. My lady had charged
me — with a blushing cheek but stern eyes — to deliver the
letter with my own hands, and I dismounted. I thought that
I had nothing to do but deliver it; I foresaw no trouble. But
at the last moment, as a trooper led me through the ante-
chamber, who should appear at my side but the Waldgrave!

'You did not expect to see me?' he said, nodding grimly.

'No, my lord,' I answered.

'So I thought,' he rejoined. 'But before you give the
Count that letter, I have a word to say to him.'

I looked at him in astonishment. What had the letter
to do with him? My first idea was that he had been
drinking, for his colour was high and his eye bright. But
a second glance showed that he was sober, though excited.
And while I hesitated the trooper held up the curtain, and
perforce I marched in.

Count Leuchtenstein, wearing his plain buff suit, sat writing at a table. His corselet, steel cap, and gauntlets lay beside him, and seemed to show that he had just come in from the field. He looked up and nodded to me; I had been announced before. Then he saw the Waldgrave and rose; reluctantly, I fancied. I thought, too, that a shade of gloom fell on his face; but as the table was laden with papers and despatches and maps and lists, and the sight reminded me that he bore on his shoulders all the affairs of Hesse, and the responsibility for the boldest course taken by any German prince in these troubles, I reflected that this might arise from a hundred causes.

He greeted the Waldgrave civilly nevertheless; then he turned to me. 'You have a letter for me, have you not, my friend?' he said.

'Yes, my lord,' I answered.

'But,' the Waldgrave interposed, 'before you read it, I have a word to say, by your leave, Count Leuchtenstein.'

I think I never saw a man more astonished than the Count. 'To me?' he said.

'By your leave, yes.'

'In regard to — this letter?'

'Yes.'

'But what do you know about this letter?'

'Too much, I am afraid,' the Waldgrave answered; and I am bound to say that, putting aside the extraordinary character of his interference, he bore himself well. I could detect nothing of wildness or delusion in his manner. His face glowed, and he threw back his head with a hint of defiance; but he seemed sane. 'Too much,' he continued rapidly, before the Count could stop him; 'and, before the matter goes farther, I will have my say.'

The Count stared at him. 'By what right?' he said at last.

'As the Countess Rotha's nearest kinsman,' the Waldgrave answered.

'Indeed?' I could see that the Count was hard put to

it to keep his temper; that the old lion in him was stirring, and would soon have way. But for the moment he controlled himself. 'Say on,' he cried.

'I will, in a few words,' the Waldgrave answered. 'And what I have to say amounts to this : I have become aware — no matter how — of the bargain you have made, Count Leuchtenstein, and I will not have it.'

'The bargain!' the Count ejaculated; 'you will not have it!'

'The bargain; and I will not have it!' the Waldgrave rejoined.

Count Leuchtenstein drew a deep breath, and stared at him like a man demented. 'I think that you must be mad,' he said at last. 'If not, tell me what you mean.'

'What I say,' the Waldgrave answered stubbornly. 'I forbid the bargain to which I have no doubt that that letter relates.'

'In Heaven's name, what bargain ? ' the Count cried.

'You think that I do not know,' the Waldgrave replied, with a touch of bitterness; 'it did not require a Solomon to read the riddle. I found my cousin distrait, absent, moody, sad, preoccupied, unlike herself. She had moved heaven and earth, I was told, to save me; in the last resort, had come to you, and you saved me. Yet when she saw me safe, she met me as much in sorrow as in joy. The mere mention of your name clouded her face ; and she must see you, and she must write to you, and all in a fever. I say, it does not require a Solomon to read this riddle, Count Leuchtenstein.'

'You think ? ' said the Count, bluntly. 'I do not yet know what you think.'

'I think that she sold herself to you to win my pardon,' the Waldgrave answered.

For a moment I did not know how Count Leuchtenstein would take it. He stood gazing at the Waldgrave, his hand on a chair, his face purple, his eyes starting. At length, to my relief and the Waldgrave's utter dismay and shame, he sank into the chair and broke into a hoarse shout of laughter — laughter that was not all merriment, but rolled in its depths something stern and sardonic.

The Waldgrave changed colour, glared and fumed; but the Count was pitiless, and laughed on. At last: 'Thanks, Waldgrave, thanks,' he said. 'I am glad I let you go on to the end. But pardon me if I say that you seem to do the Lady Rotha something less than justice, and yourself something more.'

'How?' the Waldgrave stammered. He was quite out of countenance.

'By flattering yourself that she could rate you so highly,' Count Leuchtenstein retorted, 'or fall herself so low. Nay, do not threaten me,' he continued with grim severity. 'It was not I who brought her name into question. I never dreamed of, never heard of, never conceived such a bargain as you have described; nor, I may add, ever thought of the Lady Rotha except with reverence and chivalrous regard. Have I said enough?' he continued, rising, and speaking with growing indignation, with eyes that seemed to search the culprit; 'or must I say too, Waldgrave, that I do not traffic in men's lives, nor buy women's favours, nor sell pardons? That such power as God and my master have given me I use to their honour and not for my own pleasure? And, finally, that this, of which you accuse me, I would not do, though to do it were to prolong my race through a dozen centuries? For shame, boy, for shame!' he continued more calmly. 'If my mind has gone the way you trace it, I call it back to-day. I have done with love; I am too old for aught but duty, if love can lead even a young man's mind so far astray.'

The Waldgrave shivered; but the position was beyond words, and he essayed none. With a slight movement of his hand, as if he would have shielded himself, or deprecated the other's wrath, he turned towards the door. I saw his face for an instant; it was pale, despairing — and with reason. He had exposed my lady. He had exposed himself. He had invited such a chastisement as must for ever bring the blood to his cheeks. And his cousin: what would she say? He had lost her. She would never forgive him — never! He groped blindly for the opening in the curtain.

His hand was on it — and I think that, for all his manhood, the tears were very near his eyes — when the other called after him in an altered tone.

'Stay!' Count Leuchtenstein said. 'We will not part thus. I can see that you are sorry. Do not be so hasty another time, and do not be too quick to think evil. For the rest, our friend here will be silent, and I will be silent.'

The Waldgrave gazed at him, his lips quivering, his eyes full. At last: 'You will not tell — the Countess Rotha?' he said almost in a whisper.

The Count looked down at his table, and pettishly pushed some papers together. For an instant he did not answer. Then he said gruffly, — 'No. Why should she know? If she chooses you, well and good; if not, why trouble her with tales?'

'Then!' the Waldgrave cried with a sob in his voice, 'you are a better man than I am!'

The Count shrugged his shoulders rather sadly. 'No,' he said, ' only an older one.'

CHAPTER XXXIV.

SUSPENSE.

FOR a little while after the Waldgrave had retired, Count Leuchtenstein stood turning my lady's letter over in his hands, his thoughts apparently busy. I had leisure during this time to compare the plainness of his dress with the greatness of his part, to which his conduct a moment before had called my attention ; and the man with his reputation. No German had at this time so much influence with

23

the King of Sweden as he; nor did the world ever doubt
that it was at his instance that the Landgrave, first of all
German princes, flung his sword into the Swedish scale.
Yet no man could be more unlike the dark Wallenstein,
the crafty Arnim, the imperious Oxenstierna, or the sleepless French cardinal, whose star has since risen — as I
have heard these men described; for Leuchtenstein carried
his credentials in his face. An honest, massive downright-
ness and a plain sagacity seemed to mark him, and commend him to all who loved the German blood.

My eyes presently wandered from him, and detected
among the papers on the table the two stands I had seen
in his town quarters — the one bearing his child's necklace, the other his wife's portrait. Doubtless they lay on
the table wherever he went — among assessments and im-
posts, regimental tallies and state papers. I confess that
my heart warmed at the sight; that I found something
pleasing in it; greatness had not choked the man. And
then my thoughts were diverted: he broke open my lady's
letter, and turning his back on me began to read.

I waited, somewhat impatiently. He seemed to be a
long time over it, and still he read, his eyes glued to the
page. I heard the paper rustle in his hands. At last he
turned, and I saw with a kind of shock that his face was
dark and flushed. There was a strange gleam in his eyes
as he looked at me. He struck the paper twice with his
hand.

'Why was this kept from me?' he exclaimed. 'Why?
Why?'

'My lord!' I said in astonishment. 'It was delivered to
me only an hour ago.'

'Fool!' he answered harshly, bending his bushy eye-
brows. 'When did that girl get free?'

'That girl?'

'Ay, that girl! Girl, I said. What is her name? Marie
Wort?'

This is Saturday. Wednesday night,' I said.

'Wednesday night? And she told you of the child then; of my child — that this villain has it yonder! And you kept it from me all Thursday and Friday — Thursday and Friday,' he repeated with a fierce gesture, 'when I might have done something, when I might have acted! Now you tell me of it, when we march out to-morrow, and it is too late. Ah! It was ungenerous of her — it was not like her!'

'The Countess came yesterday in person,' I muttered.

'Ay, but the day before!' he retorted. 'You saw me in the morning! You said nothing. In the evening I called at the Countess's lodgings; she would not see me. A mistake was it? Yes, but grant the mistake; was it kind, was it generous to withhold *this?* If I had been as remiss as she thought me, as slack a friend — was it just, was it womanly? In Heaven's name, no! No!' he repeated fiercely.

'We were taken up with the Waldgrave's peril,' I muttered, conscience-stricken. 'And yesterday, my lady ——'

'Ay, yesterday!' he retorted bitterly. 'She would have told me yesterday. But why not the day before? The truth is, you thought much of your own concerns and your lady's kin, but of mine and my child — nothing! Nothing!' he repeated sternly.

And I could not but feel that his anger was justified. For myself, I had clean forgotten the child; hence my silence at my former interview. For my lady, I think that at first the Waldgrave's danger and later, when she knew of his safety, remorse for the part she had played, occupied her wholly, yet, every allowance made, I felt that the thing had an evil appearance; and I did not know what to say to him.

He sighed, staring absently before him. At last, after a prolonged silence, 'Well, it is too late now,' he said. 'Too late. The King moves out to-morrow, and my hands are full, and God only knows the issue, or who of us will be living three days hence. So there is an end.'

'My lord!' I cried impulsively. 'God forgive me, I forgot.'

He shrugged his shoulders with a grand kind of patience. 'Just so,' he said. 'And now, go back to your mistress. If I live I will answer her letter. If not — it matters not.'

I was terribly afraid of him, but my love for Marie had taught me some things; and though he waved me to the door, I stood my ground a moment.

'To you, my lord, no,' I said. 'Nothing. But to her, if you fall without answering her letter —— '

'What?' he said.

'You can best judge from the letter, my lord.'

'You think that she would suffer?' he answered harshly, his face growing red again. 'Well, what say you, man? Does she not deserve to suffer? Do you know what this delay may cost me? What it may mean for my child? Mein Gott,' he continued, raising his voice and striking his hand heavily on the table, 'you try me too far! Your mistress was angry. Have I no right to be angry? Have I no right to punish? Go! I have no more to say.'

And I had to go, then and there, enraged with myself, and fearful that I had said too much in my lady's behalf. I had invited this last rebuff, and I did not see how I should dare to tell her of it, or that I had exposed her to it. I had made things worse instead of better, and perhaps, after all, the message he had framed might not have hurt her much, or fallen far short of her expectations.

I should have troubled myself longer about this, but for the increasing bustle and stir of preparation that had spread by this time from the camp to the city; and filling the way with a throng of people whom the news affected in the most different ways, soon diverted my attention. While some, ready to welcome any change, shouted with joy, others wept and wrung their hands, crying out that the city was betrayed, and that the King was abandoning it. Others again anticipated an easy victory, looked on the frowning heights of the Alta Veste as already conquered, and divided Wallenstein's spoils. Everywhere I saw men laughing, wailing, or shaking hands; some eating of their private hoards, others buying and selling horses, others again whooping like lunatics.

In the city the shops, long shut, were being opened, orderlies were riding to and fro, crowds were hurrying to the churches to pray for the King's success; a general stir of relief and expectancy was abroad. The sunshine still fell hot on the streets, but under it life moved and throbbed. The apathy of suffering was gone, and with it the savage gloom that had darkened innumerable brows. From window and dormer, from low door-ways, from carven eaves and gables, gaunt faces looked down on the stir, and pale lips prayed, and dull eyes glowed with hope.

While I was still a long way off I saw my lady at the oriel watching for me. I saw her face light up when she caught sight of me ; and if, after that, I could have found any excuse for loitering in the street, or putting off my report, I should have been thankful. But there was no escape. In a moment the animation of the street was behind me, the silence of the house fell round me, and I stood before her. She was alone. I think that Marie had been with her ; if so, she had sent her away.

' Well ? ' she said, looking keenly at me, and doubtless drawing her conclusions from my face. 'The Count was away ? '

' No, my lady.'

'Then — you saw him ? ' with surprise.

' Yes.'

' And gave him the letter ? '

' Yes, my lady.'

' Well ' — this with impatience, and her foot began to tap the floor — 'did he give you no answer ? '

'No, my lady.'

She looked astonished, offended, then troubled. 'Neither in writing nor by word of mouth ? ' she said faintly.

'Only — that the King was about to give battle,' I stammered; 'and that if he survived, he would answer your
excellency.'

She started, and looked at me searchingly, her colour
fading gradually. 'That was all!' she said at last,
a quaver in her voice. 'Tell me all, Martin. Count
Leuchtenstein was offended, was he not?'

'I think that he was hurt, your excellency,' I confessed.
'He thought that the news about his child — should have
been sent to him sooner. That was all.'

'All!' she ejaculated; and for a moment she said no
more, but with that word, which thrilled me, she began to
pace the floor. 'All!' she repeated presently. 'But I —
yes, I am justly punished. I cannot confess to him; I will
confess to you. Your girl would have had me tell him
this, or let her tell him this. She pressed me; she went
on her knees to me that evening. But I hardened my
heart, and now I am punished. I am justly punished.'

I was astonished. Not that she took it lightly, for there
was that in her tone as well as in her face that forbade the
thought; but that she took it with so little passion, without tears or anger, and having been schooled so seldom in
her life bore this schooling so patiently. She stood for a
time after she had spoken, looking from the window with a
wistful air, and her head drooping; and I fancied that she
had forgotten my presence. But by-and-by she began to
ask questions about the camp, and the preparations, and
what men thought of the issue, and whether Wallenstein
would come down from his heights or the King be driven
to the desperate task of assaulting them. I told her all
that I had heard. Then she said quietly that she would
go to church; and she sent me to call Fraulein Max to go
with her.

I found the Dutch girl sitting in a corner with her back
to the windows, through which Marie and the women were
gazing at the bustle and uproar and growing excitement of
the street. She was reading in a great dusty book, and did

not look up when I entered. Seeing her so engrossed, I had the curiosity to ask her, before I gave her my lady's message, what the book was.

' " The Siege of Leyden," ' she said, lifting her pale face for an instant, and then returning to her reading. 'By Bor.'

I could not refrain from smiling. It seemed to me so whimsical that she could find interest in the printed page, in this second-hand account of a siege, and none in the actual thing, though she had only to go to the window to see it passing before her eyes. Doubtless she read in Bor how men and women thronged the streets of Leyden to hear each new rumour; how at every crisis the bells summoned the unarmed to church; how through long days and nights the citizens waited for relief — and she found these things of interest. But here were the same portents passing before her eyes, and she read Bor !

'You are busy, I am afraid,' I said.

'I am using my time,' she answered primly.

'I am sorry,' I rejoined; 'for my lady wants you to go to church with her.'

She shut up her book with peevish violence, and looked at me with her weak eyes. 'Why does not your Papist go with her?' she said spitefully. 'And then you could do without me. As you do without me when you have secrets to tell ! But I suppose you have brought things to such a pass now that there is nothing for it but church. And so I am called in !'

'I have given my lady's message,' I said patiently.

'Oh, I know that you are a faithful messenger!' she replied mockingly. 'Who writes love letters grows thin ; who carries them, fat. You are growing a big man, Master Martin.'

CHAPTER XXXV.

ST. BARTHOLOMEW'S DAY.

THAT was a night that saw few in Nuremberg sleep soundly. Under the moon the great city lay waiting; watching and fasting through the short summer night. Hour by hour the solemn voices of sentinels, tramping the walls and towers, told the tale of time; to men, who, hearing it, muttered a prayer, and, turning on the other side, slept again; to women, who lay, trembling and sleepless, their every breath a prayer. For who would see the next night? Who that went out would come in? How many, parting at dawn, would meet again? The howling of the dogs that, wild as wolves, roved round the camp and scratched in the shallow graveyards, made dreary answer.

Many there were, even then I remember, who thought the King foolhardy, and preached patience; and would have had him still sit quiet and play the game of starvation against his enemy, even to the bitter end. But these were of the harder sort — men who, with brain, might have been Wallensteins. And few of them knew the real state of things. I say nothing of the city. Who died there in those months, in holes and corners and dark places, the magistrates may have known, no others. But in the camp, for many days before the King marched out, a hundred men died of plague and want every day; so that in the sum, twenty thousand men entered his lines who never left them. Moderate men set the loss of the city at ten thousand more. Add to these items that the plague was increasing, that all stores of food were nearly exhausted, that if the issue were longer delayed the cavalry would have no horses on which to advance or retreat, and it will be clear, I think, that the King, whose judgment had never yet deceived him, was right in this also. Or, if he erred, it was on the side of mercy.

At dawn all the northern walls and battlements were covered with white-faced women, come together to see the army leave the camp, in which it had lain so many weeks. I went up with my lady to the Burg, whence we could command, not only the city with its necklace of walls and towers, but the camp encircling it like another and greater city, encompassed in its turn with gates and ramparts and bastions. And, beyond this, we had an incomparable view of the country; of our own stream, the Pegnitz, gliding away through the level plain, to fall presently into the Rednitz; of the Rednitz, a low line of willows, running athwart the western meadows; and beyond this, a league and a half away, of the frowning heights of the Alta Veste, where Wallenstein hung, vulture-like, waiting to pounce on the city.

As the sun rose behind us, the shadow of the Burg on which we stood fell almost to the foot of the distant heights, and covered, as with a pall, the departing army, which was beginning to pass out of the camp by the northern and western gates. At the same time the level beams shone on the dark brow of the Alta Veste, and caught there the flash of lurking steel. I think that the hearts of many among us sank at the omen.

If so, it was not for long, for the sun rose swiftly in the summer sky and, as it overtopped our little eminence, showed us an innumerable host pressing out of the camp in long lines, like ants from a hill. While we gazed, they began to swarm on the plain between the city and the Rednitz. The colours of a thousand waving pennons, the sheen of a forest of lances, the duller gleam of cannon crawling slowly along the roads, caught the sun and the eye; but between them moved other and darker masses — the regiments of East and West Gothland, the Småland horse, Stalhanske's Finns, the Yellow and Blue regiments, the sombre, steady veterans of the Swedish force, marching with a neatness and wheeling with a precision, noticeable even at that distance.

Doubtless it was a grand and splendid sight, this marching out of a hundred thousand men — for the army fell little short of that prodigious number — under the first captain of the age, to fight before the walls of the richest city in the world. And I have often taken blame to myself and regretted that I did not regard it with closer attention, and imprint it more carefully on my memory. But at the time I was anxious. Somewhere in that great host rode the Waldgrave and Count Leuchtenstein ; and I looked for them, though I had no hope of finding them. Then little things continually diverted the mind. A single waggon, which broke down at the gate below us, and could not for a time be removed, swelled into a matter that obstructed my view of the whole army ; an officer, whose horse ran away in an orchard at our feet, became, for a moment, more important than a hundred banners. When I had done with these trifles, the sun had climbed halfway up the sky, and the foremost troops were already crossing the Rednitz by Furth, with a sound of trumpets and the flashing of corselets.

A cannon shot, and then another, and then long rolling thunder from the heights, over which a pillar of smoke began to gather. My lady sighed. Below us, in the streets, on the walls, on the towers, women and men fell on their knees and prayed aloud. Across the plain horsemen galloped this way or that, hurrying the laggards through the dust. The great battle was beginning.

And then on a sudden the firing ceased; the pillar of smoke on the heights melted away ; the rear-guard and the cloud of dust in which it moved, rolled farther and farther towards the Rednitz and Furth — and still the guns remained silent. It was noon by this time ; soon it was afternoon. But the suspense was so great that no one went away to eat; and still the silence prevailed.

Towards two o'clock I persuaded the Countess to go to

her lodgings to eat; but within the hour she was back again. An officer on the Burg, who had a perspective glass, reported that Wallenstein was moving; that cannon and troops could be seen passing through the trees on the Alta Veste, as if he were descending to meet the King; and for a time our excitement rose to the highest pitch. But before sunset, news came that he was quiet; that the King was forming a new camp beyond the Rednitz, and almost under the enemy's guns; and that the battle would take place on the morrow.

The morrow! It seemed to some of us, it was always the morrow. Yet I think that we slept better that night. Earliest dawn saw us again on the Burg, staring and strain-ing our eyes westwards. But minutes passed, hours passed, the sun rose and declined, and still no sound of battle reached us. Women, with pinched faces, clutched babies to their breasts; men, pale and stern, gazed into the dis-tance. Those who had murmured that the King was too hasty, murmured now that he dallied; for every day the grip of famine grew tighter, its signs more marked. This evening all my lady's horses were requisitioned and carried off, to mount the King's staff, it was said, of whom some were going afoot.

A third day rose on the anxious city, and yet a fourth, and still the armies stood inactive. Communication with the new camp was easy, but as each day, and all day, a battle was expected, such news as we heard rather height-ened than relieved our fears. On this fourth morning, I received a message from the Waldgrave, asking me to come to him in the camp; that he had something to say to me, and could not leave.

I was not unwilling to see for myself how things stood there; and I determined to go. I did not tell the Countess, however, nor Marie, thinking it useless to alarm them; but I left Steve in charge, and, bidding him be on his guard, promised to be back by noon at the latest. As I had no horse, I had to do the journey on foot, and soon was down

in the plain myself, threading the orchards and plodding
along the trampled roads, where so many thousands had
preceded me. The ground in some spots was actually
ploughed up; dust covered everything; the trees were
bruised, the fences broken down. Old boots and shattered
pike-staves marked the route, and here and there — saddest
sight of all — dead horses, fast breeding the plague. The
sky, for the first time for days, was clouded, and ·making the
most of the coolness I gained the river bank by nine o'clock,
and crossing found myself close to the new camp.

The army had just marched out, yet the lines seemed full.
The King had strictly forbidden all women and camp-
followers to cross the Rednitz ; but an army in these days
needs so many drivers and sutlers that I found myself one
among thousands. I asked for the Waldgrave, and got as
many answers as there were men within hearing. One said
that he was with his regiment of horse on the left flank ;
another, that he was with Duke Bernard's staff ; a third, that
he was not with the army at all. Despairing of hearing
anything in the confusion, I was in two minds about turning
back ; but in the end I took heart of grace and determined
to seek him in the field.

Fortunately, the last regiments had barely cleared the
lines, and a few minutes' rapid walking set me abreast of
the rearmost, which was hastening into position. Here
also at the first glance I saw nothing but confusion ; but a
second resolved the mass into two parts, and then I saw
that the King's army lay in two long lines facing the
heights. An interval of about three hundred paces divided
the lines, but behind each was a small reserve. In the
first were most of the German regiments, the second being
composed of Finns, Swedes, and Northerners. The cavalry
were grouped on the flanks, and seemed stronger on the
left flank. In the rear of all, as well as in gaps left
between the pikes and musketmen, were the King's ord-
nance — drakes, serpents, falcons, and cartows, with the
light two- and four-pounders for which he was famous.

Such an array — so many thousand men, gay with steel, and a thousand pennons — seemed to the eye to be invincible ; and I looked for the enemy. He was not to be seen, but fronting the lines at a distance of three or four hundred paces rose the Alta Veste — a steep, rugged hill, scarred and seamed, and planted thickly with pines and jagged stumps and undergrowth. Here and there among the trees great rocks peeped out, or dark holes yawned. The dry beds of two torrents furrowed this natural glacis ; and opposite these I noticed that our strongest regiments were placed. But of the enemy I could see nothing, except here and there a sparkle of steel among the trees ; I could hear nothing, except now and then the fall of a stone, that, slipping under an unseen foot, fell from ledge to ledge until it reached the plain.

Everywhere the hush of expectation stirred the heart ; for in the presence of that great host silence seemed a thing supernatural. As the regiment I had joined, the last to arrive, wheeled into position in the middle of the right wing, I asked one of the officers, who stood near me, if the enemy had retired.

' Wait ! ' he said grimly — he spoke with a foreign accent — ' and you will see. But to what regiment do you belong, comrade ? '

'To none here,' I said.

He looked astonished, and asked me what I was doing there, then.

I had my lips apart to answer him, when a trumpet sounded, and in an instant, all along the line, the Swedish cannon began to fire, shaking the earth and filling the air round us with smoke, that in a twinkling hid everything. This lasted for two or three minutes with a deafening noise ; but as far as I could hear, the enemy were still silent. I was wondering what would happen next, and hoping that they had given up the position, when my new friend touched my arm and pointed to the front. I peered through the smoke, and saw dimly that the regiment before us, a German brigade about eight hundred strong, was moving on at a run and making for the hill. A minute elapsed, the smoke rolled between. I listened, trembling. Afterwards I learned that at the same moment two other parties sprang forward and dashed to the assault.

Then, at last, with an ear-splitting roar that seemed to silence our guns, the enemy spoke. The hill in front, hidden the second before by smoke, became in a moment visible, lit up by a thousand darting flames. Dark masses seemed to topple down, rocks hung midway in air, and involuntarily I stepped back and uttered a cry of horror. Out of that hell of fire came an answering wail of shrieks and curses — the feeble voice of man!

'Ach Gott!' I said, trembling. My hair stood on end.

'Steady, comrade, steady!' muttered the man who had before spoken to me. 'Presently it will be our turn.'

He had scarcely spoken, when a man came riding along the front with his hat in his hand. He rode a white horse, and wore no back or breast, nor, as far as I could see, any armour.

'Steady, Swedes, steady!' he cried in a loud voice — he was a big, stout man with a fine presence. 'Your time will come by-and-by. Then remember Breitenfeld!'

It was the King of Sweden. In a moment he was gone, passing along the lines; and I drew breath again, wondering what would happen next. I had not long to wait. Men came straggling back across our front, some wounded, some helping their comrades along, all with faces ghastly under the powder-stains. And then like magic a new regiment stood before us, where the other had stood. Again the King's guns pealed along the line, again I heard the hoarse cry 'Vorwärts!' waited a minute, and once more the hill seemed to be rent by the explosion. From every cave and ledge guns flashed forth, lighting up the smoke. The roar died away again — slowly, from west to east — in cries and shrieks; and presently a few men, scores where there had been hundreds, came wandering back like ghosts through the reek.

'This looks ill!' I muttered. I was no longer scared. The gunpowder was getting into my head.

'Pooh!' my friend answered. 'This is only the beginning. It will take men to fill that gap. Wait till our turn comes.'

By this time the Waldgrave and my errand were forgotten, and I thought only of the battle. I watched two more assaults, saw two more regiments hurl themselves vainly against the fiery breast of the hill; then came a diversion. As the scattered fragments of the last came reeling back, a sudden roar of many voices startled me. The ground seemed to shake, and right across our front came a charge of horse — out of the smoke and into the smoke! In an instant our stragglers were trodden down, cut up, and swept away, before our eyes and within shot of us.

The men round me uttered shouts of rage. The line swayed, there was an instant's confusion. Then a harsh voice cried above the tumult, 'Steady, Gothlanders, steady! Pikes forward! Blow your matches! Steady! steady!' and in a twinkling, with a crash, such as the ninth wave makes when it falls on a pebbly beach, the horse were on us. I had a glimpse through the smoke of rearing breasts, and floating manes, and grinning teeth, and of men's faces grim and white, held low behind the steel; and I struck out blindly with my half-pike. Still they came on, and something hit me on the chest and I fell: but instantly a clash of long pikes met over my body, and I scrambled to my feet unhurt! Then a dozen spurts of flame leapt out round me, and the horsemen seemed to melt away.

Into the smoke; but before I had time to know that they were gone, they had wheeled and were back again like the wind, led by a man on a black horse, who came on so gallantly to the very pike-points, that I thought it must be Pappenheim himself. He wore the black breastplate and helmet of Pappenheim's cuirassiers; and it was only when his horse reared up on end within a pike's length of me, and he fired his pistol among us, wounding two men, that

I espied under the helmet the stern face and flashing eyes
of Tzerclas. He recognised me at the same moment, and
hurling his empty pistol in my face, tried to spur his horse
over me. But the long pikes meeting before me kept him
off, his men vanished, some falling, some flying, and in a
moment he stood almost alone.

Even then his courage did not fail him. Scornfully eyeing our line from end to end, he hurled a bitter taunt at us,
and wheeling his horse coolly, prepared to ride off. I
think that we should have let him go, in pure admiration
of his courage. But a wounded man on whom he trod
houghed the horse with his sword. In a moment he was
down, and two men running out of the line, fixed him to
the earth with their pikes.

I confess, for myself, I would have spared him for his
courage; and I ran to him to see if he was dead. He was
not quite gone. He recognised me, and tried to speak.
Forgetting the dangers round me, the uproar and tumult,
the dim figures of men and horses flying through the
smoke, I knelt down by him.

'What is it?' I said. After all, he was my lady's cousin.

'Tell him — tell him — the child! He will never get
it!' he breathed. With each word the blood-stained froth
rose to his lips, and he clutched my hand in a cold grip.

He strove to say something more, and raised himself
with a last effort on his elbow. 'Tell her,' he gasped, his
dark face distorted — 'tell her — I — I ——'

No more. His eyes turned, his head fell back. He was
dead. What he would have said of my lady, whether he
would have sent her a message or what, no man will know
here. But I fancied it like the man, who might have been
great had he ever given a thought to others, that his last
word was — "I."

His head was scarcely down before I had to run back
within the pikes. A fresh charge of horse swept over him,
we received them with a volley; they broke, and a Swedish
regiment, the West Gothland horse, rode them down.

Meanwhile our manœuvres had brought us insensibly into
the first line. I found that we were close under the hill,
and I was not surprised when a handful of horse whirled
up to us out of the *mêlée*, and one, disengaging himself
from the others, rode along our front. It was the King.
His face was stained with powder, his horse was bleeding,
a ball had ripped up his boot; it was said that he had been
placing and pointing cannon with his own hands. But as
the regiment greeted him with a hoarse cheer, he smiled as
if he had been in a ball-room.

He raised his hand for silence; such silence as could be
obtained where every moment men shot off a cannon, and
at no great distance a mortal combat was in progress.

'Men of Gothland!' he cried, in a clear, ringing voice,
'it is your turn now! You are my children. Take me
this hill! Be steady, strike home, flinch not! Show these
Germans what you can do! The word is, God with us.
Remember St. Bartholomew's, and Forward! Forward!
Forward!'

My heart beat furiously; but there was no retreat.
Rather than be left standing on the ground, I would have
died there. In a moment we were moving on elbow to
elbow, with a stern, heavy step. Some one struck up a
Swedish psalm, and to the thunder of its rhythm we strode
on — on to the very foot of the hill; on, until we reached
the rough shale, and the rugged steep stood above us.
With a gallant shout an officer . flung his hat on to the
slope, a score of Ritt-Meisters sprang forward together;
and then for a moment we and all things seemed to stand
still. The wood above us belched fire, the eyes were
blinded, the ears stunned, rocks and stones rolled down,
all creation seemed to be falling on us in fearful ruin.
Men were hurled this way and that, or fell in their places,
or, reeling to and fro, clutched one another. For an instant, I say, we stood still.

But for an instant only. Then with a shout of rage
the Swedes sprang forward, and grasping boughs, stumps,

rocks, swung themselves up, doing such things in their
fury as no cool man could do. A row of jagged stakes
barred the way; men set their naked breasts against them,
and others climbed over on their shoulders. Bleeding,
wounded, singed, torn by splinters, all who lived climbed.
To get up — up — up — higher, in face of the storm of shot
and iron; up, over the bursting mines and through the
smoke; up, to where they stood and butchered us, was the
only instinct left.

And we did get up — to a bastion, jutting from the hillside, where a company of picked men with pikes and three
cannons waited for us behind a breastwork. They thought
to stop us, and stood firm; our men were mad. Flinging
themselves against the mouths of the cannon, they scaled
the work in a moment, and left not one defender alive!

God with us!

Stern and high the shout rang out; but breath was everything, and the scarp still rose above us and the shot still
tore our ranks! On! Up a torrent bed now, round one
corner and another, to where we were a little out of the
line of fire, and an overhanging shoulder covered us. Here
we had room to take breath; and for the first time, some
hope of life, of ultimate escape, entered my breast. The
officer who led us — I learned afterwards that he was the
great General Torstensohn — cried, ' Well done, Swedes! '
and with the confidence of giants we were once more breast-
ing the ascent, when a withering volley, poured in at short
range, checked the head of the column. Before we could
recover way, a body of pikes rushed to meet us, and in an
instant, having the vantage of the ground, rolled us, still
fighting desperately, down the steep. The general was
swept away, the Ritt-Meisters were down. Once we ral-
lied, but ineffectually. The enemy were reinforced, and in
a moment the rout was complete.

At the moment the tide turned and our men fell back, I
happened to be against the rock-wall, in something of a
niche; and the stream passed me by. I had two slight

wounds, and I stood an instant, giddy and confused, taking breath. The instant showed me my comrades in the act of being slaughtered one by one, and a great horror seized me. I found no hope anywhere. Below were the cruel pikes, in a moment their savage bearers would be reascending; above were the enemy. But above, if I climbed on, I might live a little while; and in that desperate hope I scrambled out of the torrent bed and up the sheer hill on the right. Two or three saw me from the torrent bed, and fired at me; and others shouted, and began to follow. But I only pressed on, right up the scarp, which was there like the side of a house.

A dozen times I all but fell back; still in a fever of dread I kept on. The sweat poured down me; I had no hope or aim, I thought only of the pikes behind. Presently I came to a jutting shoulder that all but overhung me; to pass it seemed to be impossible. But in my frenzy I did the impossible. I swung myself from root to root; where one stone gave, I clutched another, and yet another; I hung on with tooth and nail. I flattened myself against the rock. I heard the pursuers rail and curse, heard the bullets strike the earth round me, and then in a moment I was up.

Up; but only to come instantly on a wall crossing the steep and barring my way, and to find a dozen pikes levelled at my breast. Desperate, giving up hope at last — I had long dropped my weapon — I cried mechanically, ' God with us !' and threw up my arms.

I nearly fell backwards — for what did it matter? But the men were quick. In a moment one had me by the collar. And God! They were friends! They were friends, and I was saved.

One of the first faces that I saw, as I leaned breathless against the wall, unable for the time to answer the questions that poured upon me, was the Waldgrave's — the Waldgrave's, with the light of battle in his eyes, a laugh of triumph on his lips. He was wounded, bandaged, blackened, his fair hair singed; but he was happy. Presently I understood why; and why I was safe and among friends.

'A little earlier,' he said — he seemed in his exaltation not a whit surprised to see me — 'and you would have had a different reception, Martin. We only turned them out of this an hour ago!'

All his superior officers had fallen, and his had been the voice that had cheered on the forlorn, to which he was attached — acting from the right flank — and heartened them, just when all seemed lost, to make one more effort, ending in the capture of this sconce. Joined to the mass of the hill only by a narrow neck, it commanded the enemy's position.

'We only want cannon!' he said, and in a moment I was as one of the garrison. 'Three guns, and the day is ours. When will they come? When will they come?'

'You have sent for them?'

'I have sent a dozen times.'

And he sent as many times more; while we, a mere handful, tired and worn and famished, but every man with a hero's thoughts, leaned against the breastwork, and gazed down into the plain, where, under the smoke, pigmy troops rushed to and fro, and Nuremberg's fate hung in the balance. In an hour it would be night. And still no reinforcements came, no cannon.

Thrice the enemy tried to drive us out. But the neck was narrow, and, pressed along their front by three assaults, they came on half-heartedly and fell back lightly; and we held it. In the mean time, it became more and more clear that elsewhere the day was going against us. Until night fell, and through long hours of darkness, forlorn after forlorn was flung against the heights — in vain. Regiment after regiment, the core of the Swedish army, came on undaunted, only to be repulsed with awful loss; with the single exception of the Waldgrave's little sconce not a foot of the hill was captured.

About nine o'clock reinforcements reached us, and some food, but no guns. Two hours later the King drew sullenly back into his lines, and the attack ceased. Even then we looked to see the fight resumed with the dawn ; we looked still for victory and revenge. We could not believe that all was over. But towards three o'clock in the morning rain fell, rendering the slopes slippery and impassable ; and with the first flush of sunrise came an order from Prince Bernard directing us to withdraw.

Perhaps the defeat fell as lightly on the Waldgrave as on any man, though to him it was a huge disappointment. For he alone of all had made his footing good. I thought that it was that which made him look so cheerful ; but while the rank and file were falling in, he came to me.

'Well, Martin,' he said. 'We are both veterans now.'

I laughed. The rain had ceased. The sun was getting up, and the air was fresh. Far off in the plain the city sparkled with a thousand gems. I thought of Marie, I thought of life, and I thanked God that I was alive.

'I have an errand for you,' he continued, a laugh in his eyes. 'Come and see what we took yesterday, besides this sconce.'

At the back of the work were two low huts, that had perhaps been guardrooms or officers' quarters. He led the way into one, bending his head as he passed under the low lintel.

'An odd place,' he said.

'Yes, my lord.'

'Yes, but I mean — an odd place for what I found here,' he rejoined. 'Look, man.'

There were two low bunks in the hut, and on these and on the floor lay a medley of soldiers' cloaks, pouches, weapons, and ammunition. There was blood on the one wall and the door was shattered, and in a corner, thrown one on another, were two corpses. The Waldgrave took no heed of these, but stepped to the corner bunk and drew away a cloak that lay on it. Something — the sound in

that place scared me as a cannon-shot would not have —
began to wail. On the bed, staring at us between tears
and wonder, lay a child.

'So !' I said, and stared at it.

'Do you know it ?' the Waldgrave asked.

'Know it ? No,' I answered.

'Are you sure ?' he replied, smiling. 'Look again.'

'Not I !' I said. 'How did it come here ? A child ! A
baby ! It is horrible.'

He shrugged his shoulders. 'We found it in this hut;
in that bed. A man to whom we gave quarter said it
was —— '

'No !' I shouted.

'Yes,' he answered, nodding.

'Tzerclas' child ! Count Leuchtenstein's child ! Do you
mean it ?' I cried.

He nodded. 'Tzerclas' child, the man said. The other's
child, I guess. Nay, I am certain. It knows your girl's
name.'

'Marie's ? '

The Waldgrave nodded. 'Take it up,' he said. 'And
take charge of it.'

But I only stared at it. The thing seemed too wonderful
to be true. I told the Waldgrave of Tzerclas' death, and of
what he had muttered about the child.

'Yes, he was a clever man,' the Waldgrave answered.
'But, you see, God has proved too clever for him. Come,
take it, man.'

I took it. 'I had better carry it straight to the Count's
quarters ?' I said.

The Waldgrave paused, looked away, then looked at me.
'No,' he said at last, and slowly, 'take it to Lady Rotha.
Let her give it to him.'

I understood him, I guessed all he meant; but I made no
answer, and we went out together. The rain was still in
the air, but the sky was blue, the distance clear. The spire
of the distant city shone like my lady's amethysts. Below
us the dead lay in thousands. But we were alive.

CHAPTER XXXVI.

A WINGLESS CUPID.

THAT was a dreary procession that a little before noon on the 25th of August wound its way back into Nuremberg. The King, repulsed but not defeated, remained in his camp beyond the Rednitz, and with trumpets sounding and banners displayed, strove vainly to tempt his wily antagonist into the plain. Those who returned on this day, therefore, carrying with them the certain news of ill-fortune, were the wounded and the useless, a few prisoners, two or three envoys, half a dozen horse-dealers, and a train of waggons bearing crippled and dying men to the hospital.

Of this company I made one, and I doubt if there were six others who bore in their breasts hearts as light, or who could look on the sunny roofs and peaked gables of the city with eyes as cheerful. Prince Bernard had spoken kindly to me ; the King had sent for me to inquire where I last saw General Torstensohn ; I had stood up a man amongst men ; and I deemed these things cheaply bought at the cost of a little blood. On the other hand, the horrors of the day were still so fresh in my mind that my heart overflowed with thankfulness and the love of life ; feelings which welled up anew whenever I looked abroad and saw the Rednitz flowing gently between the willows, or looked within and pictured the Werra rippling swiftly down the shallows under cool shade of oak and birch and alder.

Add to all these things one more. I had just learned that Count Leuchtenstein lived and was unhurt, and on the saddle before me under a cloak I bore his son. More than one asked me what booty I had taken, where others had found only lead or steel, that I hugged my treasure so closely and smiled to myself. But I gave them no answer.

I only held the child the tighter, and pushing on more quickly, reached the city a little after twelve.

I say nothing of the gloomy looks and sad faces that I encountered at the gate, of the sullen press that would hardly give way, or of the thousand questions I had to parry. I hardened my heart, and, disengaging myself as quickly as I could, I rode straight to my lady's lodgings; and it was fortunate that I did so. For I was only just in time. As I dismounted at the door — receiving such a welcome from Steve and the other men as almost discovered my treasure, whether I would or no — I saw Count Leuchtenstein turn into the street by the other end and ride slowly towards me, a trooper behind him.

The men would have detained me. They wanted to hear the news and the details of the battle, and where I had been. But I thrust my way through them and darted in.

Quick as I was, one was still quicker, and as I went out of the light into the cool darkness of the entrance, flew down the stairs to meet me, and, before I could see, was in my arms, covering me with tears and laughter and little cries of thanksgiving. How the child fared between us I do not know, for for a minute I forgot it, my lady, the Count, everything, in the sweetness of that greeting; in the clinging of those slender arms round my neck, and the joy ‚of the little face given up to my kisses.

But in a moment, the child, being, I suppose, half choked between us, uttered a feeble cry; and Marie sprang back, startled and scared, and perhaps something more.

‘What is it?’ she cried, beginning to tremble. ‘What have you got?’

I did not know how to tell her on the instant, and I had no time to prepare her, and I stood stammering.

Suddenly, ‘Give it to me!’ she cried in a strange voice.

But I thought that in the fulness of her joy and surprise she might swoon or something, and I held back. ‘You won't drop it,’ I said feebly, ‘when you know what it is?’

Her eyes flashed in the half light. 'Fool!' she cried —
yes, though I could scarcely believe my ears. 'Give it to
me.'

I was so taken aback that I gave it up meekly on the
spot. She flew off with it into a corner, and jealously
turned her back on me before she uncovered the child;
then all in a moment she fell to crying, and laughing,
crooning over it and making strange noises. I heard the
Count's horse at the door, and I stepped to her.

'You are sure that it *is* your child?' I said.

'*Sure?*' she cried; and she darted a glance at me that
for scorn outdid all my lady's.

After that I had no doubt left. 'Then bring it to the
Countess, my girl,' I said. 'He is here. And it is she
who should give it to him.'

'Who is here?' she cried sharply.

'Count Leuchtenstein.'

She stared at me for a moment, and then suddenly
quailed and broke down, as it were. She blushed crimson;
her eyes looked at me piteously, like those of a beaten
dog.

'Oh,' she said, 'I forgot that it was you!'

'Never mind that,' I said. 'Take the child to my lady.'

She nodded, in quick comprehension. As the Count
crossed the threshold below, she sped up the stairs, and
I after her. My lady was in the parlour, walking the
length of it impatiently, with a set face; but whether the
impatience was on my account, because I had delayed below
so long, or on the Count's, whose arrival she had probably
seen from the window, I will not say, for as I entered and
before she could speak, Marie ran to her with the child
and placed it in her arms.

My lady turned for a moment quite pale. 'What is it?'
she said faintly, holding it from her awkwardly.

Marie cried out between laughing and crying, 'The
child! The child, my lady.'

'And Count Leuchtenstein is on the stairs,' I said.

The colour swept back into the Countess's face in a flood and covered it from brow to neck. For a moment, taken by surprise, she forgot her pride and looked at us shyly, timidly. 'Where — where did you recover it?' she murmured.

'The Waldgrave recovered it,' I answered hurriedly, 'and sent it to your excellency, that you might give it to Count Leuchtenstein.'

'The Waldgrave!' she cried.

'Yes, my lady, with that message,' I answered strenuously.

The Countess looked to Marie for help. I could hear steps on the stairs — at the door; and I suppose that the two women settled it with their eyes. For no words passed, but in a twinkling Marie snatched the child, which was just beginning to cry, from the Countess and ran away with it through an inner door. As that door fell to, the other opened, and Ernst announced Count Leuchtenstein.

He came in, looking embarrassed, and a little stiff. His buff coat showed marks of the corselet — he had not changed it — and his boots were dusty. It seemed to me that he brought in a faint reek of powder with him, but I forgot this the next moment in the look of melancholy kindness I espied in his eyes — a look that enabled me for the first time to see him as my lady saw him.

She met him very quietly, with a heightened colour, but the most perfect self-possession. I marvelled to see how in a moment she was herself again.

'I rejoice to see you safe, Count Leuchtenstein,' she said. 'I heard early this morning that you were unhurt.'

'Yes,' he answered. 'I have not a scratch, where so many younger men have fallen.'

'Alas! there will be tears on many hearths,' my lady said.

'Yes. Poor Germany!' he answered. 'Poor Germany! It is a fearful thing. God forgive us who have to do with the making of war. Yet we may hope, as long as our young men show such valour and courage as some showed yesterday; and none more conspicuously than the Wald-grave Rupert.'

'I am glad,' my lady said, colouring, 'that he justified your interference on his behalf, Count Leuchtenstein. It was right that he should; and right that I should do more — ask your pardon for the miserable ingratitude of which my passion made me guilty a while ago.'

'Countess !' he cried.

'No,' she said, stopping him with a gesture full of dignity. 'You must hear me out, for now that I have confessed, we are quits. I behaved ill — so ill that I deserved a heavy punishment. You thought so — and inflicted it!'

Her voice dropped with the last words. He turned very red, and looked at her wistfully; but I suppose that he dared not draw conclusions. For he remained silent, and she resumed, more lightly.

'So Rupert did well yesterday?' she said. 'I am glad, for he will be pleased.'

'He did more than well!' Count Leuchtenstein answered, with awkward warmth. 'He distinguished himself in the face of the whole army. His courage and coolness were above praise. As we have —— ' The Count paused, then blundered on hastily — 'quarrelled, dare I say, Countess, over him, I am anxious to make him the ground of our reconciliation also. I have formed the highest opinion of him; and I hope to advance his interests in every way.'

My lady raised her eyebrows. 'With me?' she said quaintly.

The Count fidgeted, and looked very ill at ease. 'May I speak quite plainly?' he said at last.

'Surely,' the Countess answered.

'Then it can be no secret to you that he has — formed an attachment to you. It would be strange if he had not,' the Count added gallantly.

'And he has asked you to speak for him?' my lady exclaimed, in an odd tone.

'No, not exactly. But——'

'You think that it—it would be a good match for me,' she said, her voice trembling, but whether with tears or laughter, I could not tell. 'You think that, being a woman, and for the present houseless, and almost friendless, I should do well to marry him?'

'He is a brave and honest man,' the Count muttered, looking all ways—and looking very miserable. 'And he loves you!' he added with an effort.

'And you think that I should marry him?' my lady persisted mercilessly. 'Answer me, if you please, Count Leuchtenstein, or you are a poor ambassador.'

'I am not an ambassador,' he replied, thus goaded. 'But I thought——'

'That I ought to marry him?'

'If you love him,' the Count muttered.

My lady took a turn to the window, looked out, and came back. When she spoke at last, I could not tell whether the harshness in her voice was real or assumed.

'I see how it is,' she said, 'very clearly, Count Leuchtenstein. I have confessed, and I have been punished; but I am not forgiven. I must do something more, it seems. Wait!'

He was going to protest, to remonstrate, to deny; but she was gone, out through the door, to return on the instant with something in her arms. She took it to the Count and held it out to him.

'See!' she said, her voice broken by sobs; 'it is your child. God has given it back again. God has given it to you, because you trusted in Him. It is your child.'

He stood as if turned to stone. 'Is it?' he said at last, in a low, strained voice. 'Is it? Then thank God for His mercy to my house. But how—shall I know it?'

'The girl knows it. Marie knows it,' my lady cried, 'and the child knows her. And Martin—Martin will tell you how it was found—how the Waldgrave found it.'

'The Waldgrave?' the Count cried.

'Yes, the Waldgrave,' she answered; 'and he sent it to me to give to you.'

Then I went to him and told him all I knew; and Marie, who, like my lady, was laughing through her tears, took the child, and showed him how it knew her, and remembered my name and my lady's, and had this mark and that mark, and so forth, until he was convinced; and while in that hour all Nuremberg outside our house mourned and lamented, within, I think, there were as thankful hearts as anywhere in the world, so that even Steve, when he came peeping through the door to see what was the matter, went blubbering down again.

Presently Count Leuchtenstein said something handsome to Marie about her care of the child, and slipping off a gold chain that he was wearing, threw it round her neck, with a pleasant word to me. Marie, covered with blushes, took this as a signal to go, and would have left the child with his father; but the boy objected strongly, and the Count, with a laugh, bade her take him.

'If he were a little older!' he said. 'But I have not much accommodation for a child in my quarters. Next week I am going to Cassel, and then ——'

'You will take him with you?' my lady said.

The Count looked at the closing door, as it fell to behind Marie, and when the latch dropped, he spoke. 'Countess,' he said bluntly, 'have I misunderstood you?'

My lady's eyes fell. 'I do not know,' she said softly.

'I should think not. I have spoken very plainly.'

'I am almost an old man,' he said, looking at her kindly, 'and you are a young woman. Have you been amusing yourself at my expense?'

The Countess shook her head. 'No,' she said, with a gleam of laughter in her eyes; 'I have done with that. I began to amuse myself with General Tzerclas, and I found it so perilous a pleasure that I determined to forswear it. Though,' she added, looking down and playing with her bracelet, 'why I should tell you this, I do not know.'

'Because — henceforth I hope that you will tell me everything,' the Count said suddenly.

' Very well,' my lady answered, colouring deeply.

' And will be my wife ? '

' I will — if you desire it.'

The Count walked to the window and returned. 'That is not enough,' he said, looking at her with a smile of infinite tenderness. 'It must not be unless *you* desire it; for I have all to gain, you little or nothing. Consider, child,' he went on, laying his hand gently on her shoulder as she sat, but not now looking at her. 'Consider; I am a man past middle age. I have been married already, and the portrait of my child's mother stands always on my table. Even of the life left to me — a soldier's life — I can offer you only a part ; the rest I owe to my country, to the poor and the peasant who cry for peace, to my master, than whom God has given no State a better ruler, to God Himself, who places power in my hands. All these I cannot and will not desert. Countess, I love you, and men can still love when youth is past. But I would far rather never feel the touch of your hand or of your lips than I would give up these things. Do you understand ? '

' Perfectly,' my lady said, looking steadfastly before her, though her heaving breast betrayed her emotion. ' And I desire to be your wife, and to help you in these things as the greatest happiness God can give me.'

The Count stooped gently and kissed her forehead. ' Thank you,' he said.

*   *   *   *   *   *

I have very little to add. All the world knows that the King of Sweden, unable to entice Wallenstein from his lines, remained in his camp before Nuremberg for fifteen days longer, during which period the city and the army suffered all the extremities of famine and plague. After that, satisfied that he had so far reduced the Duke of Friedland's strength that it no longer menaced the city, he marched away with his army into Thuringia; and there, two months later, on the immortal field of Lützen, defeated his enemy, and fell, some say by a traitor's hand, in the moment of victory; leaving to all who ever looked upon his face the memory of a sovereign and soldier without a rival, modest in sunshine and undaunted in storm. I saw him seven times and I say this.

And all the world knows in what a welter of war and battles and sieges and famines we have since lain, so that no man foresees the end, and many suppose that happiness has quite fled from the earth, or at least from German soil. Yet this is not so. It is true in comparison with the old days, when my lady kept her maiden Court at Heritz-burg, and our greatest excitement was a visit from Count Tilly, we lead a troubled life. My lady's eyes are often grave, and the days when she goes with her two brave boys to the summit of the Schloss and looks southward with a wistful face, are many; many, for the Count, though he verges on seventy, still keeps the field and is a tower in the councils of the north. But with all that, the life is a full one — full of worthy things and help given to others, and a great example greatly set, and peace honestly if vainly pursued. And for this and for other reasons, I believe that my lady, doing her duty, hoping and praying and training her children, is happy; perhaps as happy as in the old days when Fraulein Anna prosed of virtue and felicity and Voetius.

The Waldgrave Rupert, still the handsomest of men, but sobered by the stress of war, comes to see us in the intervals of battles and sieges. On these occasions the children flock round him, and he tells tales — of Nordlingen, and Leipzig, and the leaguer of Breysach; and blue eyes grow stern, and chubby faces grim, and shell-white teeth are ground together, while Marie sits pale and quaking, devouring her boys with hungry mother's eyes. But they do not laugh at her now; they have not since the day when the Waldgrave bade them guess who was the bravest person he had ever known.

'Father!' my lady's sons cried. And Marie's, not to be outdone, cried the same.

But the Waldgrave shook his head. 'No,' he said, 'try again.'

My youngest guessed the King of Sweden.

'No.' the Waldgrave answered him. 'Your mother.

THE END.

A List of Recent Fiction

Published by ✒ ✒ ✒ ✒ ✒ ✒

Longmans, Green, & Co.,

15 East 16th Street ✒ New York.

By Stanley J. Weyman.

A GENTLEMAN OF FRANCE. Illustrated. 12mo, cloth, $1.25..

THE HOUSE OF THE WOLF. A Romance. Illustrated. 12mo, cloth, $1.25.

UNDER THE RED ROBE. With 12 full-page Illustrations. 12mo, cloth, $1.25.

MY LADY ROTHA. A Romance. With 8 full-page Illustrations. 12mo, cloth, $1.25.

By H. Rider Haggard.

THE PEOPLE OF THE MIST. Illustrated. 12mo, cloth, $1.25.

HEART OF THE WORLD. Illustrated. 12mo, cloth, $1.25.

By A. Conan Doyle.

MICAH CLARKE. Author's Edition. Illustrated. 12mo, cloth, $1.25.

THE CAPTAIN OF THE POLESTAR, and Other Tales. Illustrated. 12mo, cloth, $1.25.

By Mrs. Parr.

CAN THIS BE LOVE? Illustrated. 12mo, cloth, $1.25.

By Edna Lyall.

DOREEN. The Story of a Singer. 12mo, cloth, $1.50.

THE AUTOBIOGRAPHY OF A SLANDER. Illustrated. 12mo. cloth, $1.50.

By Mrs. Walford.

THE MATCHMAKER. 12mo, cloth, $1.50.

LONGMANS' PAPER LIBRARY.

Issued Quarterly at 50 cents each.

No. 1. NADA THE LILY. By H. RIDER HAGGARD. *Copyright Edition.* With all the original Illustrations.

No. 2. THE ONE GOOD GUEST. By Mrs. L. B. WALFORD.

No. 3. KEITH DERAMORE. By the Author of "Miss Molly."

No. 4. A FAMILY TREE, and Other Stories. By BRANDER MATTHEWS.

No. 5. A MORAL DILEMMA. By ANNIE THOMPSON.

No. 6. GERALD FFRENCH'S FRIENDS. By GEORGE H. JESSOP.

No. 7. SWEETHEART GWEN. By WILLIAM TIREBUCK.

LONGMANS' DOLLAR NOVELS.

By H. Rider Haggard.
MONTEZUMA'S DAUGHTER. Illustrated. 12mo, cloth, $1.00.
NADA THE LILY. Illustrated. 12mo, cloth, $1.00.

By Miss L. Dougall.
WHAT NECESSITY KNOWS. A Novel. 12mo, cloth, $1.00.
BEGGARS ALL. A Novel. 12mo, cloth, $1.00.

By E. W. Hornung.
THE UNBIDDEN GUEST. An Australian Story. 12mo, cloth, $1.00.

By Francis Forster.
MAJOR JOSHUA. A Novel. 12mo, cloth, $1.00.

By John Trafford Clegg.
DAVID'S LOOM. A Story of Rochdale Life in the Early Years of the Nineteenth Century. 12mo, cloth, $1.00.

By Mrs. L. B. Walford.
THE ONE GOOD GUEST. 12mo, cloth, $1.00.
' PLOUGHED,' and Other Stories. 12mo, cloth, $1.00.

By May Kendall.
SUCH IS LIFE. A Novel. 12mo, cloth, $1.00.

By William Tirebuck.
SWEETHEART GWEN. A Welsh Idyl. 12mo, cloth, $1.00.

By the Author of " Miss Molly."
KEITH DERAMORE. 12mo, cloth, $1.00.

By Annie Thompson.
A MORAL DILEMMA. 12mo, cloth, $1.00.

By Julian Sturgis.
AFTER TWENTY YEARS, and Other Stories. 12mo, cloth, $1.00.

By C. J. Cutliffe Hyne.
THE NEW EDEN. Illustrated. 12mo, cloth, $1.00.

UNDER THE RED ROBE.

A ROMANCE.

By STANLEY J. WEYMAN,

AUTHOR OF "A GENTLEMAN OF FRANCE," "THE HOUSE OF THE WOLF," ETC.

With 12 Full-page Illustrations by R. Caton Woodville.
12mo, Linen Cloth, Ornamental, $1.25.

"Mr. Weyman is a brave writer, who imagines fine things and describes them splendidly. There is something to interest a healthy mind on every page of his new story. Its interest never flags, for his resource is rich, and it is, moreover, the kind of a story that one cannot plainly see the end of from Chapter I. . . . the story reveals a knowledge of French character and French landscape that was surely never acquired at second hand. The beginning is wonderfully interesting."—NEW YORK TIMES.

"As perfect a novel of the new school of fiction as 'Ivanhoe' or 'Henry Esmond' was of theirs. Each later story has shown a marked advance in strength and treatment, and in the last Mr. Weyman . . . demonstrates that he has no superior among living novelists. . . . There are but two characters in the story—his art makes all other but unnoticed shadows cast by them—and the attention is so keenly fixed upon one or both, from the first word to the last, that we live in their thoughts and see the drama unfolded through their eyes."—N. Y. WORLD.

"It was bold to take Richelieu and his time as a subject and thus to challenge comparison with Dumas's immortal musketeers; but the result justifies the boldness. . . . The plot is admirably clear and strong, the diction singularly concise and telling, and the stirring events are so managed as not to degenerate into sensationalism. Few better novels of adventure than this have ever been written."—OUTLOOK, NEW YORK.

"A wonderfully brilliant and thrilling romance. . . . Mr. Weyman has a positive talent for concise dramatic narration. Every phrase tells, and the characters stand out with life-like distinctness. Some of the most fascinating epochs in French history have been splendidly illuminated by his novels, which are to be reckoned among the notable successes of later nineteenth-century fiction. This story of 'Under the Red Robe' is in its way one of the very best things he has done. It is illustrated with vigor and appropriateness from twelve full-page designs by R. Caton Woodville."
—BOSTON BEACON.

"It is a skillfully drawn picture of the times, drawn in simple and transparent English, and quivering with tense human feeling from the first word to the last. It is not a book that can be laid down at the middle of it. The reader once caught in its whirl can no more escape from it than a ship from the maelstrom."
—PICAYUNE, NEW ORLEANS.

"The 'red robe' refers to Cardinal Richelieu, in whose day the story is laid. The descriptions of his court, his judicial machinations and ministrations, his partial defeat, stand out from the book as vivid as flame against a background of snow. For the rest, the book is clever and interesting, and overflowing with heroic incident. Stanley Weyman is an author who has apparently come to stay."—CHICAGO POST.

"In this story Mr. Weyman returns to the scene of his 'Gentleman of France,' although his new heroes are of different mould. The book is full of adventure and characterized by a deeper study of character than its predecessor."
—WASHINGTON POST.

"Mr. Weyman has quite topped his first success. . . . The author artfully pursues the line on which his happy initial venture was laid. We have in Berault, the hero, a more impressive Marsac; an accomplished duelist, telling the tale of his own adventures, he first repels and finally attracts us. He is at once the tool of Richelieu, and a man of honor. Here is a noteworthy romance, full of thrilling incident set down by a master-hand."—PHILADELPHIA PRESS.

LONGMANS, GREEN, & CO., 15 EAST 16th STREET, NEW YORK.

A GENTLEMAN OF FRANCE.

Being the Memoirs of Gaston de Bonne,
Sieur de Marsac.

By STANLEY J. WEYMAN.

AUTHOR OF "THE HOUSE OF THE WOLF," ETC.

With Frontispiece and Vignette by H. J. Ford.
12mo, Cloth, Ornamental, $1.25.

"One of the best novels since 'Lorna Doone.' It will be read and then re-read for the mere pleasure its reading gives. The subtle charm of it is not in merely transporting the nineteenth-century reader to the sixteenth, that he may see life as it was then, but in transforming him into a sixteenth-century man, thinking its thoughts, and living its life in perfect touch and sympathy . . . it carries the reader out of his present life, giving him a new and totally different existence that rests and refreshes him."—N. Y. WORLD.

" No novelist outside of France has displayed a more definite comprehension of the very essence of mediæval French life, and no one, certainly, has been able to set forth a depiction of it in colors so vivid and so entirely in consonance with the truth. . . . The characters in the tale are admirably drawn, and the narrative is nothing less than fascinating in its fine flavor of adventure."—BEACON, BOSTON.

"We hardly know whether to call this latest work of Stanley J. Weyman a historical romance or a story of adventure. It has all the interesting, fascinating and thrilling characteristics of both. The scene is in France, and the time is that fateful eventful one which culminated in Henry of Navarre becoming king. Naturally it is a story of plots and intrigue, of danger and of the grand passion, abounding in intense dramatic scenes and most interesting situations. It is a romance which will rank among the masterpieces of historic fiction."
—ADVERTISER, BOSTON.

" A romance after the style of Dumas the elder, and well worthy of being read by those who can enjoy stirring adventures told in true romantic fashion. . . . The great personages of the time—Henry III. of Valois, Henry IV., Rosny, Rambouillet, Turenne—are brought in skillfully, and the tragic and varied history of the time forms a splendid frame in which to set the history of Marsac's love and courage . . . the troublous days are well described and the interest is genuine and lasting, for up to the very end the author manages effects which impel the reader to go on with renewed curiosity."—THE NATION.

"A genuine and admirable piece of work. . . . The reader will not turn many pages before he finds himself in the grasp of a writer who holds his attention to the very last moment of the story. The spirit of adventure pervades the whole from beginning to end. . . .
It may be said that the narration is a delightful love story. The interest of the reader is constantly excited by the development of unexpected turns in the relation of the principal lovers. The romance lies against a background of history truly painted. . . . The descriptions of the court life of the period and of the factional strifes, divisions, hatreds of the age, are fine. . . . This story of those times is worthy of a very high place among historical novels of recent years."—PUBLIC OPINION.

" Bold, strong, dashing, it is one of the best we have read for many years. We sat down for a cursory perusal, and ended by reading it delightedly through. . . . Mr. Weyman has much of the vigor and rush of incident of Dr. Conan Doyle, and this book ranks worthily beside ' The White Company.' . . . We very cordially recommend this book to the jaded novel reader who cares for manly actions more than for morbid introspection."
—THE CHURCHMAN.

"The book is not only good literature, it is a 'rattling good story,' instinct with the spirit of true adventure and stirring emotion. Of love and peril, intrigue and fighting, there is plenty, and many scenes could not have been bettered. In all his adventures, and they are many, Marsac acts as befits his epoch and his own modest yet gallant personality. Well-known historical figures emerge in telling fashion under Mr. Weyman's discriminating and fascinating touch."—ATHENÆUM.

"I cannot fancy any reader, old or young, not sharing with doughty Crillon his admiration for M. de Marsac, who, though no swashbuckler, has a sword that leaps from its scabbard at the breath of insult. . . . There are several historical personages in the novel; there is, of course, a heroine, of great beauty and enterprise; but that true 'Gentleman of France,' M. de Marsac, with his perseverance and valor, dominates them all."
—Mr. JAMES PAYN in the ILLUSTRATED LONDON NEWS.

LONGMANS, GREEN, & CO., 15 EAST 16th STREET, NEW YORK.

DOREEN.

THE STORY OF A SINGER.

By EDNA LYALL,

AUTHOR OF "WE TWO," "DONOVAN," "THE AUTOBIOGRAPHY OF A SLANDER, "IN THE GOLDEN DAYS," ETC., ETC.

Crown 8vo, Buckram Cloth, Ornamental, $1.50.

"Edna Lyall has evidently made a close study of the Irish question, and she sees its varying aspects and problems with a desire to do justice to all, while she stands firmly on her own principles. . . . There is much to recommend in Edna Lyall's books, and her admirers are many. The book will be read with interest. . . . It is yet well written and comprehensive, treating of universal principles in a broad way and presenting characters in whom one becomes interested for their own sake."
—LITERARY WORLD, Boston.

"A plot which has original life and vigor. . . . Altogether a good novel, and if the author has written nothing else she could safely rest her literary reputation on 'Doreen.'"—PUBLIC OPINION, N. Y.

"Edna Lyall's . . . new story . . . is one of her best. It has, naturally, enough of tragedy to make it intensely interesting without being sensational in any offensive sense. The heroine, Doreen, is a delightful character, sturdy, strong, lovable, womanly, and genuinely Irish. Miss Bayly is a conscientious writer, imbued with deep feeling, a high purpose, and her style is attractive and pure."
—BOSTON DAILY ADVERTISER.

"The heroine is a most winsome Irish maiden with an exquisite voice, and she comes bravely out of the involved dramatic situation in which she is placed by an early vow."—PRESS, Philadelphia.

"It is a very clever story indeed, and skillfully written. The heroine is a bright and beautiful Irish girl, and a musician."—NEW ORLEANS PICAYUNE.

"A very interesting story and is full of interesting and exciting incidents, and its characters are well drawn and sustained throughout the book. It is tastefully bound, and will doubtless prove popular with this writer's many admirers."
—PORTLAND ADVERTISER.

"Doreen, the heroine of this latest novel of Edna Lyall, is an Irish girl, gentle, kind, and modest, but brave, resolute, and unflinching when there is a question of those whom she loves, of right or wrong, or of the welfare of the country which she holds dearest of all. . . . The book is thoroughly wholesome, good, and interesting. Miss Lyall writes of Ireland, of Irish ways and feelings, as well as of Catholic beliefs and customs, with knowledge and sympathy. . . . The volume is tastefully bound . . . well printed and convenient to handle and to read."
—THE SACRED HEART REVIEW, Boston.

"The heroine, clever, patriotic, self-denying, is worthy of the name, and the hero is equally excellent. . . . An interesting novel, a good picture of a bright, pure minded, high-hearted heroine."—BOSTON PILOT.

"This is perhaps one of the best of Edna Lyall's clever stories. Doreen is a young Irish girl, who loves her native land, and who is a credit to her race. . . . Interwoven with the story of her experience and of her love for a young Englishman is an interesting account of the rise and progress of the Home Rule movement. Miss Lyall's book is a charming tale, and will not fail to delight every one who reads it. The girl Doreen is a beautiful character."—CATHOLIC NEWS.

"The time is the present, the scene is laid in Ireland and England, and Doreen, the heroine, is a charming Irish girl, devoted to her country and her oppressed countrymen. . . . The story is attractively told and a very impartial view of the Irish question is taken. . . . Doreen is a most attractive character, refreshingly simple and natural, and yet with a decided personality of her own. . . . A wholesome, well-written story, and free from any touch of atheism."—CHICAGO INTER-OCEAN

LONGMANS, GREEN, & CO., 15 EAST 16th STREET, NEW YORK.

THE MATCHMAKER.

A NOVEL.

By MRS. L. B. WALFORD.

Crown 8vo, Cloth, Ornamental, $1.50.

"A new novel by the author of 'The Baby's Grandmother' and 'Mr. Smith' is always eagerly anticipated by those who enjoy a love story told with a charming freshness of style, with a satirical yet good-natured treatment of human foibles, and with a vivid, witty, and animating use of that sentiment which 'makes the world go round.' . . . 'The Match-maker' gives a piquant hint of the plot. It will be found one of the most delightful of its author's works, and comes in good time to amuse people worn by summer weather."
—New York Tribune.

"We are sure that anything from the pen of L. B. Walford will be interesting and original. There is always enough romance about these novels to keep them from any sign of dullness, and they always include some very uncommon types well worth studying. The Carnoustie family in the present instance is one to keep the reader constantly on the *qui vive* . . . a well-told, entertaining story of interesting people."
—Detroit Free Press.

"Sure to find a large circle of refined and intelligent readers. The story is constantly lighted up with touches of humor, and the picture of simple family life and the feminine occupations it affords is natural and entertaining."—Beacon, Boston.

" . . . A fresh and interesting picture of life in a Scottish castle, and introduces many characters notable for the faithfulness to nature with which they are drawn. The incidents are interesting enough to fix the attention of the reader and to hold it until the closing chapter."—The Advertiser, Portland.

"Tells what befell a gay London girl during her six months' sojourn in the Scotch castle of some old fashioned relatives. . . . The story is a good one, much the best of it being the delineation of the stiff-necked Carnoustie family, and its magisterial dowager and its pathetic and comical old maids."—Boston Traveller.

NOVELS BY MRS. L. B. WALFORD.

In Uniform Binding. Crown 8vo, Cloth, each Volume, $1.00.

COUSINS.

THE BABY'S GRAND-
MOTHER.

PAULINE.

NAN.

THE HISTORY OF A WEEK.

TROUBLESOME DAUGH-
TERS.

MR. SMITH.

DICK NETHERBY.

A STIFF-NECKED GEN-
ERATION.

THE MISCHIEF OF MONICA

LONGMANS, GREEN, & CO., 15 EAST 16th STREET, NEW YORK.

THE PEOPLE OF THE MIST.

By H. RIDER HAGGARD,

AUTHOR OF " SHE," " ALLAN QUATERMAIN," " MONTEZUMA'S DAUGHTER," ETC., ETC.

With 16 full-page Illustrations by Arthur Layard. Crown 8vo, cloth, ornamental, $1.25.

" Out of Africa, as all men know, the thing that is new is ever forthcoming. The old style is true with regard to Mr. Haggard's romances, and everybody concerned is to be congratulated upon the romancer's return to the magical country where lies the land of Kôr. Africa is Mr. Haggard's heaven of invention. Let him be as prodigal as he may, thence flows an exhaustless stream of romance, rich in wonders new and astonishing. ' The People of the Mist ' belongs to the sphere of ' She ' in its imaginative scope, and, as an example of the story-teller's art, must be reckoned of the excellent company of ' King Solomon's Mines ' and its brethren. We read it at one spell, as it were, hardly resisting that effect of fascination which invites you, at the critical moments of the story, to plunge ahead at a venture to know what is coming, and be resolved as to some harrowing doubt of dilemma. There is no better test of the power of a story than this. . . ."—SATURDAY REVIEW.

" The lawyer, the physician, the business man, the teacher, find in these novels, teeming with life and incident, precisely the medicine to rest tired brains and ' to take them out of themselves.' There is, perhaps, no writer of this present time whose works are read more generally and with keener pleasure. The mincing words, the tedious conversations, the prolonged agony of didactic discussion, characteristic of the ordinary novel of the time, find no place in the crisp, bright, vigorous pages of Mr. Haggard's books. . . . ' The People of the Mist' is what we expect and desire from the pen of this writer . . . a deeply interesting novel, a fitting companion to ' Allan Quatermain.' "—PUBLIC OPINION.

" The story of the combat between the dwarf Otter and the huge ' snake,' a crocodile of antediluvian proportions, and the following account of the escape of the Outram party, is one of the best pieces of dramatic fiction which Mr. Haggard has ever written."—BOSTON ADVERTISER.

" One of his most ingenious fabrications of marvellous adventure, and so skilfully is it done that the reader loses sight of the improbability in the keen interest of the tale. Two loving and beautiful women figure in the narrative, and in his management of the heroine and her rival the author shows his originality as well as in the sensational element which is his peculiar province."—BOSTON BEACON.

" ' The People of the Mist ' is the best novel he has written since ' She,' and it runs that famous romance very close indeed. The dwarf Otter is fully up to the mark of Rider Haggard's best character, and his fight with the snake god is as powerful as anything the author has written. The novel abounds in striking scenes and incidents, and the reader's interest is never allowed to flag. The attack on the slave kraal and the rescue of Juanna are in Mr. Haggard's best vein."—CHARLESTON NEWS.

" It has all the dash and go of Haggard's other tales of adventure, and few readers will be troubled over the impossible things in the story as they follow the exciting exploits of the hero and his redoubtable dwarf Otter. . . . Otter is a character worthy to be classed with Umslopogus, the great Zulu warrior. Haggard has never imagined anything more terror-inspiring than the adventures of Leonard and his party in the awful palace of the Children of Mist, nor has he ever described a more thrilling combat than that between the dwarf and the huge water snake in the sacred pool."—SAN FRANCISCO CHRONICLE.

" It displays all of this popular author's imagery, power to evoke and combine miraculous incidents, and skill in analyzing human motives and emotions In the most striking manner. He is not surpassed by any modern writer of fiction for vividness of description or keenness of perception and boldness of characterization. The reader will find here the same qualities in full measure that stamped ' King Solomon's Mines,' ' Jess,' ' She,' and his other earlier romances with their singular power. The narrative is a series of scenes and pictures ; the events are strange to the verge of ghoulishness ; the action of the story is tireless, and the reader is held as with a grip not to be shaken off."—BOSTON COURIER.

" Sometimes we are reminded of ' King Solomon's Mines ' and sometimes of ' She,' but the mixture has the same elements of interest, dwells in the same strange land of mystery and adventure, and appeals to the same public that buys and reads Mr. Haggard's works for the sake of the rapid adventure, the strong handling of improbable incident, and the fascination of the supernatural."—BALTIMORE SUN.

LONGMANS, GREEN, & CO., 15 EAST 16th STREET, NEW YORK.

MONTEZUMA'S DAUGHTER.

By H. RIDER HAGGARD,

AUTHOR OF "SHE," "ALLAN QUATERMAIN," "NADA THE LILY," ETC.

With 24 full-page Illustrations and Vignette by Maurice Greiffenhagen. Crown 8vo, Cloth, $1.00.

"Adventures that stir the reader's blood and, like magic spells, hold his attention with power so strong that only the completion of the novel can satisfy his interest. . . . In this novel the motive of revenge is treated with a subtle power . . . this latest production of Mr. Haggard blends with the instruction of the historical novel the charm of a splendid romance."—PUBLIC OPINION.

"Mr. Haggard has done nothing better . . . it may well be doubted if he has ever done anything half so good. The tale is one of the good, old-fashioned sort, filled with the elements of romance and adventure, and it moves on from one thrilling situation to another with a celerity and verisimilitude that positively fascinate the reader. . . . The story is told with astonishing variety of detail, and in its main lines keeps close to historical truth. The author has evidently written with enthusiasm and entire love of his theme, and the result is a really splendid piece of romantic literature. The illustrations, by Maurice Greiffenhagen, are admirable in spirit and technique."—BOSTON BEACON.

"Has a good deal of the quality that lent such interest to 'King Solomon's Mines' and 'Allan Quatermain.' . . . England, Spain, and the country which is now Mexico afford the field of the story, and a great number of most romantic and blood-stirring activities occur in each . . . a successful story well constructed, full of devious and exciting action, and we believe that it will find a multitude of appreciative readers."—SUN, N. Y.

'It is a tale of adventure and romance, with a fine historical setting and with a vivid reproduction of the manners and people of the age. The plot is handled with dexterity and skill, and the reader's interest is always seen. There is, it should also be noted, nothing like vulgar sensationalism in the treatment, and the literary quality is sound throughout. Among the very best stories of love, war, and romance that have been written."
—THE OUTLOOK.

"Is the latest and best of that popular writer's works of fiction. It enters a new field not before touched by previous tales from the same author. In its splendor of description, weirdness of imagery, and wealth of startling incidents it rivals 'King Solomon's Mines' and other earlier stories, but shows superior strength in many respects, and presents novelty of scene that must win new and more enduring fame for its talented creator. . . . The analysis of human motives and emotions is more subtle in this work than in any previous production by Mr. Haggard. The story will generally be accorded highest literary rank among the author's works, and will prove of fascinating interest to a host of readers."
—MINNEAPOLIS SPECTATOR.

"Is full of the magnificence of the Aztec reign, and is quite as romantic and unbelievable as the most fantastic of his earlier creations."—BOOK BUYER.

"We should be disposed to rank this volume next to 'King Solomon's Mines' in order of interest and merit among the author's works."—LITERARY WORLD, BOSTON.

"It is decidedly the most powerful and enjoyable book that Mr. Rider Haggard has written, with the single exception of 'Jess.'"—ACADEMY.

"Mr. Haggard has rarely done anything better than this romantic and interesting narrative. Throughout the story we are hurried from one thrilling experience to another, and the whole book is written at a level of sustained passion, which gives it a very absorbing hold on our imagination. A special word of praise ought to be given to the excellent illustrations."
—DAILY TELEGRAPH.

"Perhaps the best of all the author's stories. The great distinguishing quality of Rider Haggard is this magic power of seizing and holding his readers so that they become absorbed and abstracted from all earthly things while their eyes devour the page. . . . A romance must have 'grip.' . . . This romance possesses the quality of 'grip' in an eminent degree."—WALTER BESANT in the AUTHOR.

"The story is both graphic and exciting, . . . and tells of the invasion of Cortes; but there are antecedent passages in England and Spain, for the hero is an English adventurer who finds his way through Spain to Mexico on a vengeful quest. The vengeance is certainly satisfactory, but it is not reached until the hero has had as surprising a series of perils and escapes as even the fertile imagination of the author ever devised."—DIAL, CHICAGO.

LONGMANS, GREEN, & CO., 15 EAST 16th STREET, NEW YORK.

"CAN THIS BE LOVE?"

A NOVEL.

By Mrs. PARR,

AUTHOR OF "DOROTHY FOX," "ADAM AND EVE," ETC.

With Frontispiece and Vignette by Charles Kerr.
12mo, Cloth, Ornamental, $1.25.

"A wholesome tale. . . . . It is a pleasant story, delightfully told, and with a whole some English atmosphere."—BOOK BUYER, N. Y.

"This is a story that will repay the time spent over it. Mrs. Parr is a strong and interesting writer. Her characters are live characters, and the incidents through which they move are natural and realistic. Her present story is throughout an exceptionally interesting one, and the reader will find his interest in it kept up to the end. It is handsomely printed on good paper."—CHRISTIAN AT WORK, N. Y.

"The touches of humor . . . are pleasant; the descriptions of scenery are charming; the plot is well and artistically planned and executed; but, best of all, the whole tone of the book is pure and free from morbidness, and one can read it from cover to cover without finding the taint of vulgarity and super-emotionalism (to call it by the most polite name) which degrades so much of modern fiction."—LITERARY WORLD, Boston.

"It is a love story of more than usual interest and is well worth reading. . . . The three principal persons in the book are fine character studies, and the story is strong and interesting."—ADVERTISER, Portland, Me.

"Mrs. Parr has given us an altogether charming book."—TRAVELLER, Boston.

"One of the daintiest, most homelike and natural stories of the week . . . the girl is a downright, genuine, substantial girl, like the girls we know in the world and love."
—COMMERCIAL GAZETTE, Cincinnati.

THE HOUSE OF THE WOLF.

A ROMANCE.

By STANLEY J. WEYMAN,

AUTHOR OF "A GENTLEMAN OF FRANCE," ETC.

With Frontispiece and Vignette by Charles Kerr.
12mo, Cloth, Ornamental, $1.25.

"A delightful volume . . . one of the brightest, briskest tales I have met with for a long time. Dealing with the Eve of St. Bartholomew it portrays that night of horror from a point entirely new, and, we may add, relieves the gloom by many a flash and gleam of sunshine. Best of all is the conception of the Vidâme. His character alone would make the book live."—CRITIC, N. Y.

"Recounted as by an eye witness in a forceful way with a rapid and graphic style that commands interest and admiration.

Of the half dozen stories of St. Bartholomew's Eve which we have read this ranks first in vividness, delicacy of perception, reserve power, and high principle."
—CHRISTIAN UNION, N. Y.

"A romance which, although short, deserves a place in literature along side of Charles Reade's 'Cloister and the Hearth.' . . . We have given Mr. Weyman's book not only a thorough reading with great interest, but also a more than usual amount of space because we consider it one of the best examples in recent fiction of how thrilling and even bloody adventures and scenes may be described in a style that is graphic and true to detail, and yet delicate, quaint, and free from all coarseness and brutality."
—COMMERCIAL ADVERTISER, N. Y.

LONGMANS, GREEN, & CO., 15 EAST 16th STREET, NEW YORK.

THE ONE GOOD GUEST.

A NOVEL.

By L. B. WALFORD,

AUTHOR OF "MR. SMITH," "THE BABY'S GRANDMOTHER," ETC., ETC.

12mo, Cloth, Ornamental, $1.00.

"It is a delightful picture of life at an English estate, which is presided over by a young 'Squire' and his young sister. Their experiences are cleverly told, and the complications which arise are amusing and interesting. There are many humorous touches, too, which add no slight strength to the story."—BOSTON TIMES.

"A charming little social comedy, permeated with a refinement of spontaneous humor and brilliant with touches of shrewd and searching satire."—BOSTON BEACON.

"The story is bright, amusing, full of interest and incident, and the characters are admirably drawn. Every reader will recognize a friend or acquaintance in some of the people here portrayed. Every one will wish he could have been a guest at Duckhill Manor, and will hope that the author has more stories to tell."—PUBLIC OPINION.

"A natural, amusing, kindly tale, told with great skill. The characters are delightfully human, the individuality well caught and preserved, the quaint humor lightens every page, and a simple delicacy and tenderness complete an excellent specimen of story telling."
—PROVIDENCE JOURNAL.

"For neat little excursions into English social life, and that of the best, commend us to the writer of 'The One Good Guest.'"—N. Y. TIMES.

"The story is bright, amusing, full of interest and incident, and the characters are admirably drawn. Every reader will recognize a friend or acquaintance in some of the people here portrayed. Every one will wish he could have been a guest at Duckhill Manor, and will hope that the author has more stories to tell."—PORTLAND OREGONIAN.

BEGGARS ALL.

A NOVEL.

By MISS L. DOUGALL.

Sixth Edition. 12mo, Cloth, Ornamental, $1.00.

"This is one of the strongest as well as most original romances of the year. . . . The plot is extraordinary. . . . The close of the story is powerful and natural. . . . A masterpiece of restrained and legitimate dramatic fiction."—LITERARY WORLD.

"To say that 'Beggars All' is a remarkable novel is to put the case mildly indeed, for it is one of the most original, discerning, and thoroughly philosophical presentations of character that has appeared in English for many a day. . . . Emphatically a novel that thoughtful people ought to read . . . the perusal of it will by many be reckoned among the intellectual experiences that are not easily forgotten."—BOSTON BEACON.

"A story of thrilling interest."—HOME JOURNAL.

"A very unusual quality of novel. It is written with ability; it tells a strong story with elaborate analysis of character and motive . . . it is of decided interest and worth reading."—COMMERCIAL ADVERTISER, N. Y.

"It is more than a story for mere summer reading, but deserves a permanent place among the best works of modern fiction. The author has struck a vein of originality purely her own. . . . It is tragic, pathetic, humorous by turns. . . . Miss Dougall has, in fact, scored a great success. Her book is artistic, realistic, intensely dramatic—in fact, one of the novels of the year."—BOSTON TRAVELLER.

"'Beggars All' is a noble work of art, but is also something more and something better. It is a book with a soul in it, and in a sense, therefore, it may be described as an inspired work. The inspiration of genius may or may not be lacking to it, but the inspiration of a pure and beautiful spirituality pervades it completely . . . the characters are truthfully and powerfully drawn, the situations finely imagined, and the story profoundly interesting."—CHICAGO TRIBUNE.

LONGMANS, GREEN, & CO., 15 EAST 16th STREET, NEW YORK.

KEITH DERAMORE.

A NOVEL.

By the Author of "Miss Molly."

Crown 8vo, Cloth, $1.00.

"One of the strongest novels for the year. . . . A book of absorbing and sustained interest, full of those touches of pathos, gusts of passion, and quick glimpses into the very hearts of men and women which are a necessary equipment of any great writer of fiction." —STAR.

"A story with originality of plot and a number of interesting and skillfully drawn characters. . . . Well worthy of a careful perusal."—BOSTON BEACON.

"The few important characters introduced are very clearly and well drawn ; one is a quite unusual type and reveals a good deal of power in the author. It is a live story of more than ordinary interest."—REVIEW OF REVIEWS.

"A novel of quiet but distinct force and of marked refinement in manner. The few characters in 'Keith Deramore' are clearly and delicately drawn, and the slight plot is well sustained."—CHRISTIAN UNION.

"The author of 'Miss Molly' shall have her reward in the reception of 'Keith Deramore.' If it is not popular there is no value in prophecy."—SPRINGFIELD REPUBLICAN.

"The story is strong and interesting, worthy of a high place in fiction." —PUBLIC OPINION.

"Its development can be followed with great interest. It is well written and entertaining throughout."—THE CRITIC.

"An exceptionally interesting novel. It is an admirable addition to an admirable series." —BOSTON TRAVELLER.

"It contains character-drawing which places it much above the average love story, and makes the reading of it worth while. It is a fine study of a normally-selfish man. There is humor in it, and sustained interest.' —BUFFALO EXPRESS.

A MORAL DILEMMA.

BY ANNIE M. THOMPSON.

Crown 8vo, Cloth, $1.00.

"We have in this most delightful volume . . . a new novel by a new author. The title is happily chosen, the plot is thrillingly interesting, its development is unusually artistic, the style is exceptionally pure, the descriptions are graphic. In short we have one of the best of recent novels, and the author gives great promise."—BOSTON TRAVELLER.

"A novel of rare beauty and absorbing interest. Its plot, which is constructed with great skill, is decidedly unconventional in its development, and its denouement, although unanticipated until near its climax, really comes as an agreeable surprise. . . . As a literary work, 'A Moral Dilemma' will take high rank."—BOSTON HOME JOURNAL.

"The story is well written and gives promise of the development of a writer who will take place among the ranks of those of her sex who are supplying what is much needed at this time—entertaining, wholesome literature."—YALE COURANT.

"The author writes with vigor and earnestness, and the book is one of interest and power."—PUBLIC OPINION.

"The story is strongly told."— INDEPENDENT.

"A strong story which leaves the reader better for the perusal. A touchlight, at Barrie's carries one through the successive scenes, which are fraught with deep interest." —PUBLIC LEDGER.

LONGMANS, GREEN, & CO., 15 EAST 16th STREET, NEW YORK.

H. RIDER HAGGARD'S
Popular Novels.

THE PEOPLE OF THE MIST. Illustrated. 12mo, cloth, $1.25.

MONTEZUMA'S DAUGHTER. Illustrated. 12mo, cloth, $1.00.

NADA THE LILY. Illustrated. 12mo, cloth, $1.00 ; paper cover, 50 cents.

ALLAN QUATERMAIN. Illustrated. Half cloth, 75 cents ; paper cover, 25 cents.

MAIWA'S REVENGE. Illustrated. Half cloth, 75 cents ; paper cover, 25 cents.

COLONEL QUARITCH. Half cloth, 75 cents ; paper cover, 25 cents.

CLEOPATRA. Illustrated. Half cloth, 75 cents ; paper cover, 25 cents.

BEATRICE. Illustrated. Half cloth, 75 cents ; paper cover, 25 cents.

ERIC BRIGHTEYES. Half cloth, 75 cents ; paper cover, 25 cents.

ALLAN'S WIFE, and Other Tales. Illustrated. Half cloth, 75 cents ; paper cover, 25 cents.

THE WITCH'S HEAD. Half cloth, 75 cents.

MR. MEESON'S WILL. Half cloth, 75 cents ; paper cover, 25 cents.

DAWN. Illustrated. Half cloth, 75 cents.

THE WORLD'S DESIRE. By H. RIDER HAGGARD and ANDREW LANG. Half cloth, 75 cents ; paper cover, 25 cents.

KING SOLOMON'S MINES. Half cloth, 75 cents ; paper cover, 25 cents.

SHE. Illustrated. Half cloth, 75 cents ; paper cover, 25 cents.

JESS. Half cloth, 75 cents ; paper cover, 25 cents.

LONGMANS, GREEN, & CO., 15 EAST 16th STREET, NEW YORK.

WHAT NECESSITY KNOWS.

A Novel of Canadian Life and Character.

BY MISS L. DOUGALL,

AUTHOR OF "BEGGARS ALL."

Crown 8vo, Cloth, $1.00.

"A very remarkable novel, and not a book that can be lightly classified or ranged with other modern works of fiction. . . . It is a distinct creation . . . a structure of noble and original design and of grand and dignified conception. . . . The book bristles with epigrammatic sayings which one would like to remember. . . . It will appeal strongly by force of its originality and depth of insight and for the eloquence and dignity of style in the descriptive passages."—MANCHESTER GUARDIAN, LONDON.

"We think we are well within the mark in saying that this novel is one of the three or four best novels of the year. The social atmosphere as well as the external conditions of Canadian life are reproduced faithfully. The author is eminently thoughtful, yet the story is not distinctively one of moral purpose. The play of character and the clash of purpose are finely wrought out. . . . What gives the book its highest value is really the author's deep knowledge of motive and character. The reader continually comes across keen observations and subtle expressions that not infrequently recall George Eliot. The novel is one that is worth reading a second time."—OUTLOOK, NEW YORK.

"Keen analysis, deep spiritual insight, and a quick sense of beauty in nature and human nature are combined to put before us a drama of human life . . . the book is not only interesting but stimulating, not only strong but suggestive, and we may say of the writer, in Sidney Lanier's words, 'She shows man what he may be in terms of what he is.'"
—LITERARY WORLD, BOSTON.

NADA THE LILY:

BY H. RIDER HAGGARD,

AUTHOR OF "SHE," "ALLAN QUATERMAIN," ETC.

With 23 full-page Illustrations, by C. H. M. Kerr.
12mo, Cloth, Ornamental (Copyright), $1.00.

"A thrilling book full . . . of almost incredible instances of personal daring and of wonderful revenge. . . . The many vigorous illustrations add much to the interest of a book that may safely be denominated as Mr. Haggard's most successful venture in the writing of fiction."—BOSTON BEACON.

"The story of 'Nada the Lily' is full of action and adventure; the plot is cleverly wrought and the fighting and adventure are described with spirit. Once begun it is, indeed, a story to be finished."—N. Y. TRIBUNE.

"The story is a magnificent effort of the imagination and quite the best of all that Mr. Haggard has done. There is no example of manufactured miracle in this story, for the story of the Ghost mountain, the Stone Witch, and the Wolves is nothing but the folk-lore of the African tribes, and in no respect similar to the wonders which the author introduced into the stories in which Allan Quatermain figures."—SPRINGFIELD REPUBLICAN.

"To my mind the realization of savage existence and the spirit of it have never been so honestly and accurately set forth. The Indians of Chateaubriand, and even of Cooper, are conventional compared with these blood-thirsty, loyal, and fatalistic Zulus. . . . The whole legend seems to me to be a curiously veracious reproduction of Zulu life and character."
—Mr. ANDREW LANG in the New Review.

"Rider Haggard's latest story . . . has a more permanent value than anything this prolific author has previously given to the public. He has preserved in this latest romance many of the curious tales, traditions, superstitions, the wonderful folk-lore of a nation now extinct, a people rapidly melting away before an advancing tide of civilization. The romance into which Mr. Haggard has woven valuable material is in his own inimitable style, and will delight those who love the weirdly improbable."—BOSTON TRAVELLER.

LONGMANS, GREEN, & CO., 15 EAST 16th STREET, NEW YORK.

HEART OF THE WORLD.

A STORY OF MEXICAN ADVENTURE.

By H. RIDER HAGGARD,

AUTHOR OF "SHE," "MONTEZUMA'S DAUGHTER," "THE PEOPLE OF THE MIST," ETC.

With 13 full-page Illustrations by Amy Sawyer.

12mo, Cloth, Ornamental, $1.25.

"Here are strange adventures and wonderful heroisms. The scene is laid in Mexico. The story rehearses the adventures of an athletic Englishman who loves and weds an Indian princess. There are marvelous descriptions of the 'City of the Heart,' a mysterious town hemmed in by swamps and unknown mountains."
—COMMERCIAL ADVERTISER, NEW YORK.

"Has a rare fascination, and in using that theme Mr. Haggard has not only hit upon a story of peculiar charm, but he has also wrought out a story original and delightful to even the most jaded reader of the novel of incident."
—ADVERTISER, BOSTON.

"It is a fascinating tale, and the reader will not want to put the book down till he has read the last word."—PICAYUNE, NEW ORLEANS.

"The lovers of Rider Haggard's glowing works have no reason to complain of his latest book. . . . The story is, all in all, one of the most entertaining of the author's whole list."—TRAVELLER, BOSTON.

"In its splendor of description, weirdness of imagery, its astonishing variety of detail, and the love story which blends with history and fantasy, the book without doubt is a creation distinct from previous tales. Maya, the Lady of the Heart, is an ideal character. . . . Interest is sustained throughout."—POST, CHICAGO.

COLONEL NORTON.

A NOVEL.

By FLORENCE MONTGOMERY,

AUTHOR OF "MISUNDERSTOOD," "THROWN TOGETHER," ETC., ETC.

Crown 8vo, Buckram, $1.50.

"It is a history of the finding of a soul, which is only found through the passion of a great love or an overwhelming sorrow. But the story is more than this; it is an analysis of a character that had been repressed. Ruth Ashley is a delightful creature. It also shows the power of love to change and transform the nature of a man self-centered, cold, critical—in short, it is a story which conveys its moral without seeming to do so. It has nothing of the melodramatic in it, but is bright and interesting from beginning to end, and healthful in its every page."—ADVERTISER, BOSTON.

"The incidents are numerous and the story is interesting."—TIMES, NEW YORK.

"A book to quietly enjoy and consider. It is not one to be hastily scanned and then thrown aside, for it is full of discussions of every-day interest, which set one to thinking—in fact, it is this discussive element of the book, rather than the plot or characters, which elicits the bulk of the interest. . . . You will find it a pleasant diversion for a few summer hours. . . . "—TIMES, BOSTON.

"It is a very good tale. . . . There is some very strong writing in the book, one passage in particular, where Captain Hardy rescues Maud from his sinking ship."
—PICAYUNE, NEW ORLEANS.

LONGMANS, GREEN, & CO., 15 EAST 16th STREET, NEW YORK.

THE JEWEL OF YNYS GALON:

BEING A HITHERTO UNPRINTED CHAPTER IN THE HISTORY OF THE SEA ROVERS.

By OWEN RHOSCOMYL.

With 12 Illustrations by Lancelot Speed.
Crown 8vo, Cloth, Ornamental, $1.25.

"The tale is exceptionally well told; the descriptive passages are strong and vivid without being over-elaborated; and the recital of fights and adventures on sea and land is thrilling, without leading to any excess of horrors. The characters in the book are not all villians, but the progress of the narrative is lighted up by the ideals and strivings of brave and honorable men. The book is certainly a most attractive addition to fiction of adventure, for it shows a fine degree of imagination on the part of the author. A glance at the illustrations by Lancelot Speed will alone be enough to incite a reading of the story from beginning to end."—THE BEACON, BOSTON.

"It is a work of genius—of the romantic-realistic school. The story is one of pirates and buried treasure in an island off the coast of Wales, and so well is it done that it fascinates the reader, putting him under an hypnotic spell, lasting long after the book has been laid aside. It is dedicated to 'every one whose blood rouses at a tale of tall fights and reckless adventure,' to men and boys alike, yet there will be keener appreciation by the boys of larger growth, whose dreams 'of buried treasure and of one day discovering some hoard whereby to become rich beyond imagination' have become dim and blurred in the 'toil and struggle for subsistence.' 'The Jewel of Ynys Galon' is one of the great books of 1895 and will live long."—THE WORLD, NEW YORK.

"It is a splendid story of the sea, of battle and hidden treasure. This picture of the times of the sea rovers is most skillfully drawn in transparent and simple English, and it holds from cover to cover the absorbed interest of the reader."
—PRESS, PHILADELPHIA.

"It is a story after the heart of both man and boy. There are no dull moments in it, and we find ourselves impatient to get on, so anxious are we to see what the next turn in the events is to bring forth; and when we come to the end we exclaim in sorrow, "Is that all?" and begin to turn back the leaves and re-read some of the most exciting incidents.

Owen Rhoscomyl has just the talents for writing books of this kind, and they are worth a dozen of some of the books of to-day where life flows sluggishly on in a drawing-room. When the author writes another we want to know of it."—TIMES, BOSTON.

"The style of this thrilling story is intensely vivid and dramatic, but there is nothing in it of the cheap sensational order. It is worthy a place among the classics for boys."—ADVERTISER, BOSTON.

"The present school of romantic adventure has produced no more strikingly imaginative story than this weird tale of Welsh pirates in the eighteenth century. . . . A most enthralling tale, . . . told with great artistic finish and with intense spirit. It may be recommended without reserve to every lover of this class of fiction."
—TIMES, PHILADELPHIA.

"It is one of the best things of its kind that have appeared in a long time. . . . We do not know how far this tale may be taken to be historical, and, to be frank, we don't care. If these things did not happen, they might have happened, and ought to have happened, and that is enough for us. If you like 'Treasure Island' and 'Kidnapped' and the 'White Company' and 'Francis Cludde' and 'Lorna Doone,' get 'The Jewel of Ynys Galon' and read it. You will not be disappointed."
—GAZETTE, COLORADO SPRINGS, COL.

"Our own interest in the book led us to read it at a sitting that went far into the night. The old Berserker spirit is considerably abroad in these pages, and the blood coursed the faster as stirring incident followed desperate situation and daring enterprise."—LITERARY WORLD, LONDON.

LONGMANS, GREEN, & CO., 15 EAST 16th STREET, NEW YORK.

MICAH CLARKE.

His statement as made to his three Grandchildren, Joseph, Gervas, and Reuben, during the hard Winter of 1734.

By A. CONAN DOYLE,

AUTHOR OF "THE CAPTAIN OF THE POLE-STAR," "THE REFUGEES," ETC.

Author's Edition. Cloth, Ornamental, $1.25.

"The language has the quaintness of old times, and the descriptions are so vivid and home-like as to make us feel that we are listening to them ourselves ; indeed, the story stands very high among historical novels, and will be of great interest to any one who has followed the more critical setting forth of the troubles preceding the Restoration found in the regular histories. The author has succeeded in giving us the genuine flavor of former days."
—PUBLIC OPINION.

" . . . There is a great deal of vivid, thrilling description."—THE NATION.

"Wonderfully vivid and realistic, full of the color of the time, and characterized by remarkable power, . . . there are so many pieces of excellent workmanship in 'Micah Clarke' that it would take too long to name them."—N. Y. TRIBUNE.

"We make bold to say that . . . this story of Mr. Doyle's is easily the best example of the class of fiction to which it belongs of the year. Two descriptions of battles in this story are, it seems to us, among the most brilliant and spirited bits of writing we have lately had. But it is not merely two or three striking incidents, but the maintained interest of the entire tale, that leads us to give it such praise as we have risked above. We shall look with interest for a second story from Mr. Doyle's pen."—CHRISTIAN UNION.

"It is due to the dramatic power of the author that this story becomes so absorbing. There is quickness and vivacity in it, and the story of the soldier of fortune of that day, Saxon, who has acquired this military art in Germany, is capitally told. . . . Mr. Doyle never pauses, and so the reader can go at full gallop through the story."—N. Y. TIMES.

THE CAPTAIN OF THE POLE-STAR:
And Other Tales.

By A. CONAN DOYLE.

Crown 8vo, cloth, $1.25.

"Lovers of wild adventure, of brilliant satire, of quiet pathos, will all find wherewith to be content in the little book, which, in its variety of subject and treatment, reads more like a volume of stories from Maga than a collection of tales from one of the same pen."
—ATHENÆUM, London.

"This volume of short stories proves Mr. Doyle to be an expert of the most delightful and skillfull kind in tales of mystery, imagination, and fancy. . . . The book forms a most delightful addition to the too poor literature of good short stories."
—SCOTSMAN ATHENÆUM.

"All the stories will repay careful reading, as in addition to the interest of the plots the style is singularly varied and reveals as many devices of the literary artist as that of Robert Louis Stevenson."—SAN FRANCISCO CHRONICLE.

LONGMANS, GREEN, & CO., 15 EAST 16th STREET, NEW YORK.

www.ingramcontent.com/pod-product-compliance
Lightning Source LLC
Chambersburg PA
CBHW032309280326

41932CB00009B/757